Innovations in Management Science

Innovations in Management Science

By

Dr. Prasant Sarangi

Dr. Durga Madhab Mahapatra

Saroj Kumar Dash

GLOBAL RESEARCH PUBLICATIONS

NEW DELHI (INDIA)

First Published – 2010

ISBN: 978-81-89630-07-2

Published by

GLOBAL RESEARCH PUBLICATIONS
4830/24, 1st Floor, Ansari Road
Darya Ganj, New Delhi-110002 (India)
Phone : 23245225. Fax : 91-11-23272135
E-mail: globalresearchpublications@gmail.com, grpindia@vsnl.net

CONTENTS

PART – II
Innovations in Human Resource Management

PART – III
Innovations in Banking and Finance

PART – IV
Innovations in Production and Operations Management

PREFACE

Creativity and Innovation in management fills a crucial gap in management science between the theory and practice of organizing imagination and innovation. It gives managers insights into introducing innovation within their organizations and accelerating the development of creative performance in their operations.

Innovative activities in the business sector have shown some significant increases during the post-reform process. The concept attracted considerable attention among analysts of all hues and shapes particularly after the global financial crisis. One of the issues that is highlighted in the discussions is the emergence and rise of a number of knowledge-intensive manufacturing and service industries and these industries together now account for a growing share of the country's gross domestic product (GDP). India has now become a growing destination for the innovative activities by the multinational companies (MNCs) and this manifest itself in the form of a growing process of foreign research and development (R&D) centres in the country. Again foreign direct investment (FDI) from India has been steadily increasing and over the years 2007 and 2008, there were a number of high profile takeovers of Western-technology based companies by Indian corporates. All these indicators and more have prompted analysts to think that India has become more innovative since 1991 and recent attempts at measuring the contribution of technology to economic growth essentially through measures such as total factor productivity (TFP) appear to indicate that Indian industries, both manufacturing and service sectors, have become active from the innovation point of view.

This edition 'Innovations in Management Science' is an attempt to inquire the innovative activities that are on the rise in India through the contribution of management intellectuals. The various innovative ideas that are gathered from the researchers in different fields of management are structured into five different sections. Section-I narrates the innovations that are emerged in the area of Marketing Management. Section-II of the book analyses various ideas contributed in Human Resource Management. Ideas on Banking and Finance are the subject matter of section-III of the book where as various innovations found in Production and Operations Management is described in part-IV of the book. Part-V deals with the Innovations in Information Technology.

All the firms belonging to one industry do not behave in a similar pattern. In an industry consisting of a variety of firms with significant differences in their size, ownership, knowledge and access to technology, the liberalisation process would result in gainers and losers but there will be a productivity gap among firms in an industry. The study,

"Productivity Growth of Manufacturing Sector in India: An Inter-State Analysis" tries to measure the productivity of the manufacturing sector of nine major industrially developed states vis-a-vis the industrially undeveloped state of Orissa, and also to examine the impact of policy of liberalization on the technological progress and industrial growth of these states. Total factor productivity as the measure of productivity is taken as the base in this analysis.

The product innovation and technological upgradation in these traditional industries are astounding with multidimensional economic ramifications. Most of the studies on food industries focused its attention at macro level analysis. But in recent times spectacular diversification is found in the fast food segment. Thus the study "Diversification Patterns and Consumer Satisfaction in Masala Products" not only analyses the dynamic behaviour of firms under conditions of change but also examines the growth performance and its associated variables in greater depth.

The paper titled "Users' Preference of Motor Pumps in Rural Areas with Reference to Coimbatore District" is an empirical analysis done by the researchers to find out the impact of the use of motor pumps on the socio-economic development of the agriculturalist, particularly in the Coimbatore districts. It is observed that due to the use of motor pumps in agriculture, this sector has increased the socio- economic condition of the agriculturists in the area.

One cannot think of innovations in marketing management without analyzing the innovations in brand. Branding efforts create a feeling of involvement, a sense of higher quality, and an aura of intangible qualities that surround the brand name, mark or symbol. A good brand not only helps the company spread market share but also allows charging premium price for their products or services. Brand image is vital for fast track business in the complex corporate environment. In this regard the paper "Comprehend Brand Architecture in FMCG Sector in India" is the study by a group of well experienced authors designed to understand the concept and phenomenon call–comprehend brand architecture in FMCG sector in India. Efforts to understand the brand preference for five categories viz., Tooth paste, Bath soap, Detergent powder, Shampoo and Chocolate (Confectioneries) have been alalysed.

Based on an empirical nature of study the article "An Analytical Study of Marketing Executives' Response to Innovation" highlights that radical product innovation is a key issue for marketing executives in Pharmaceutical and Consumer Durable industries and very much related to innovation of positioning, innovation of processes, innovation of company culture, innovation of overall marketing logistics and/or innovation of business model.

Pilgrim places not only contribute to the concerned economy but also provide an employment opportunity to local people. Therefore, it needs a careful marketing strategy to overcome different constraints that hamper in its growth. In the study "Pilgrimage Satisfaction: An Appraisal of Services Provided at Jwalaji", an attempthas been made by the researchers to measure satisfaction level of pilgrims regarding different services made available to them at Jwalaji. As the demand and popularity of any destination rely heavily on the satisfaction level of pilgrims or tourist in terms of infrastructural facilities, availability of goods and services in and around the pilgrimage destination, focus on the customer environmental sensitivity, and relative competition in the pilgrimage tourism market. The present study focused and concentrated to all the above issues for identifying a better initiative in the area of pilgrim satisfaction.

Multi-channel retailing as being on the cusp of a new era in which firms start demanding more from their investments, with particular emphasis being given to financial performance in light of the current economic crisis. This presents a great opportunity both to firms that are looking to gain a competitive advantage through multi-channel retailing and to researchers who are interested in helping them make more informed decisions. In the paper "Shaping Retailing through Multi-channel Integrated Strategies" the author has provided a broad discussion of these issues like synthesizes of current knowledge, and suggests directions for future research.

There is a myth that celebrity endorsement is used to give a brand advantage over its competitors. The research titled "Demographic Dynamics of Attitude Towards Celebrity Endorsed TV Commercials: An Indian Context" suggests tentatively that the use of celebrity endorsers in TV commercials could be effective in influencing attitudes and purchase intentions. But the success of the use of celebrity endorsers varies across different products.

The other contribution is also related to retailing. The current debate on allowing foreign direct investment (FDI) in India's retail trade primarily focuses on two issues – employment and consumer welfare. Though, FDI in retail is forbidden today for fear of large unemployment, but on the other hand, it can be said that it is more required for the Indian retail industries to grow competitively in the long run. The paper titled "Should Indian Retail Market Welcome FDI? A Review" highlights on the different aspects of FDI and its probables impacts on Indian retail market as well as the population in large.

The paper titled "Influence of Goal Orientation of Salespeople on their Performance– An Empirical Study" deals with individual goal orientation of salespeople. Here the author has conceptualized goal orientation in the three-dimensional manner, focusing on learning orientation, performance-prove orientation and performance-avoid orientation. The author tries to analyse the influence of these three orientations of salespeople on their performance. Two dimensions of performance viz., behavioural performance and output performance are considered in the analysis. The sample selected are from pharmaceutical salespeople and automobile salespeople, and the sample size is 314.

Given that some forms of motivation were not significantly related to co-worker ratings, it seems unlikely that co-worker ratings were inflated by the rater liking a person who is highly motivated. The study "Innovations in Work Motivation: A Study of Employees in Software Development" suggests that proactive motivation (RBSE and, to a lesser extent, role orientation) is productive of proactive behaviour. Since previous researcher has shown that RBSE can be enhanced through training, involvement in extra-role tasks (improvement groups), and by granting job control. It is suggested that through the same means, proactive behaviour can be promoted.

Human capital management is new business paradigm that considers people to represent a capital asset, rather than a set of costs. Today HR roles of talent management is a new business science that integrates workforce planning acquisition, development, mobility and measurement into a strategic discipline that optimizes talent throughout the employee lifecycle. In this regard the paper "Changing HR Roles in Achieving Global Talent Management in Current Business Scenario" conceptualizes some issues related to talent management.

The article titled "Support System to Women Entrepreneurship in India-An Overview" is a review on the existing policies that have been implemented by the Government of India from time to time in support of development of women entrepreneurship.

Self Help Groups have an association started among the poorest women for mutual help. In order to create awareness among the women and to give a detailed analytical performance of micro-finance, the researchers have attempted to analyze the impact of microinance in Coimbatore District. This district has a large agricultural community and the women folk are involved in various SHGs. The study "Regression Model for the Improvement of Economic Status of Self Help Groups" has been undertaken to study the impact of micro finance and the role of SHGs in the development of women empowerment.

The paper titled "A Liquidity-Profitability Trade-Off Model for Working Capital Management" proposes a goal programming model for working capital management. Goal programming is necessary for motivating the working capital decision, as a balance has to be achieved between the conflicting objectives of liquidity and profitability. The results of the analysis suggest that working capital, and inventory in particular, should be streamlined to profitability. The results also show that, excess liquidity in the firm can be used to increase production capacity, ultimately increasing the profit, as determined by the turnover ratios.

Entrepreneurship is a process of creating something new with value by devoting the necessary time and effort, assuming the accompanying financial, psychic and social risks and satisfaction and independence. International entrepreneurship envisages the undertaking of business activities by entrepreneurs across national boundaries. The paper "Global Recession and International Entrepreneurship: An Assessment" analyses strategically issues related to women entrepreneurship.

Innovation of Financial Instrument focuses on the Design, analysis and construction of financial contracts to meet the needs of Financial Sector i.e., the corporate as well as investors. This is a process that seeks to adopt existing financial instruments and development of new instruments to enable financial market participants to cope more effectively with changing scenario. The paper "Choice of Financial Instruments for Indian Corporate in Financial Market" aims to highlight the concept and scope of financial instruments and some recent innovative financial instruments in Financial Sector.

The main objective of the development of the small-scale industries is the self-employment ventures with small amount of investment, production of consumer goods on a larger scale, mobilization of local skills and capital, and dispersal of units in the semi-urban and the rural areas. However, several constraints like high cost of raw materials, inadequate and delayed supply of raw materials, inefficient distribution, power cut, workers' unrest and lack of marketing facilities affect the growth of these industries in the recent years. By observing these phenomena, the researchers of the titled "Problems of the Small Scale Industries in Coimbatore District" felt that it is appropriate to study the above aspects of the small-scale industries in Coimbatore District. Moreover, it is hoped that with the help of the study remedies can be suggested to improve the working of the small-scale industries.

The paper titled "Throughput Accounting – Inventory, Cost Management and Control Analysis" aims at understanding the importance of throughput accounting and throughput costing as a measure to evaluate the inventory in such a manner to reduce cost in times when cost cutting is taken as the main agenda of all the organizations. Throughput costing focuses only on direct material cost thereby resulting into variation in contribution margins of the company in comparison to other established methods of costing like absorption costing and marginal costing. Throughput costing can be effectively utilized by the companies facing recessionary phases in the economy.

IFRS are International Financial Reporting Standards, which are issued by the International Accounting Standards Board (IASB). Nearly 100 countries use or coordinate with IFRS. IFRS are standards and interpretations adopted by the International Accounting Standards Board (IASB). Through the paper "What is IFRS and Why are Global Economics Looking at One Accounting Standard?" the author has analysed the need and scope of such standard in management innovation.

Through the paper titled "Innovation as a Tool for Improving Supply Chain Coordination and Demand Management- A Case Study on CPFR Model" an attempt has been made by the author to understand as to how the concept of supply chain management has undergone a change through a series of innovations, which has its roots in the 1960s concept of logistics management – a planning tool that seeks to develop a system-wide, integrated view of the firm. Subsequently, supply chain management extends the concept of logistics management to external integration of the firm.

"Supply Chain Management: A Global Perspective" is the use of IT for SCM purposes was studied by dividing the use of IT into three categories, 1) transaction processing, 2) supply chain planning and collaboration, and 3) order tracking and delivery coordination. Further, the drivers behind these different IT use types were examined. Based on the empirical data collected for this study, the three IT uses categories proposed represents the roles that IT plays in SCM.

The urban people are becoming very much dependent on the services provided by the street vendors. But it is very unfortunate to mention that the service takers not to talk about the other people are now and then criticized the existence of this vital sector of the economy. The study "Need of Promoting Street Vendors for Inclusive Growth: A Case Study in Assam" is a humble attempt to investigate into the problems being faced by the street vendors in running their business in Sibsagar Town and to find out an amicable solution

The paper titled "Electrical Load Forecasting Using Artificial Neural Networks and Genetic Algorithm Techniques" explores the new approaches in the area of forecasting. The authors have focused their research on electrical load forecasting which has been a major area of interest for researchers now a day as the accurate future predictions not only helps the organizations to take appropriate decision but also saves resources. The use of soft computing tools such as artificial neural network and genetic algorithm has made the article interesting and useful.

The paper "Management of E-Garbage: A Case Study of Suri and Karidhya" explores the problem related to e-garbage and to put forward some suggestions for solving this problem i.e., e-pollution. This paper has focused on the future of e-garbage of Suri town, the headquarters of the Birbhum district of west Bengal and Karidhya, a village just adjacent of Suri town. This paper purports to venture some suggestions for the control and fruitful recycling of the e-garbage, which, it is hoped, may be helpful to those who, in various parts of the world, are striving to create a more pollution-free environment.

We acknowledge for gratitude and support that we got from the contributors, well wishers and the management team of Global Research Publications, New Delhi who have supported us in their fuller length for complication of the book.

Dr. Prasant Sarangi
Dr. Durga Madhab Mahapatra
Saroj Kumar Dash

LIST OF CONTRIBUTORS

Dr. Bijay Kumar Panda (born, 1955) earned his M.A., M.Phil., and Ph.D degrees from Berhampur University, Berhampur (Orissa). He has consistently brilliant academic career. He started his career as a lecturer in the PG Department of Economics, Berhampur University. Currently he is the Professor of the same Department. Dr. Panda published more than 50 articles in various journal of national and international repute like International Journal of Environment and Development, International Journal of Financial Services and Management, Asian-African Journal of Economics and Econometrics, Finance India, Journal of Consumer Behaviour, Productivity, Journal of Rural Development, The Economic Analyst, Journal of Managerial Economics etc. He has guided a number of Ph.D. and M.Phil. scholars on topics in the areas of Micro Economics, Development Economics, Agriculture Economics and Econometrics. He is author of three books titled Economic Reforms and Emerging pattern of Employment; Consumption, Poverty and Inequality and Applied Demand Analysis

Dr. S.Ganesan is presently working as Assistant Professor, Department of Economics, Bharathidasan University, Tiruchirappalli, Tamil Nadu.

R. Rajanbabu is the Research Scholar, Department of Economics, Bharathidasan University, Tiruchirappalli, Tamil Nadu.

Dr. R. Ganapathi, earned his qualification in M.Com., MBA., (Finance) MBA., (HR) M.Phil., Ph.D., PGDCA., with eleven years of Post Graduate teaching experience. Presently he is working as Assistant Professor in Commerce, Directorate of Distance Education, Alagappa University, Karaikudi. The author is specializing in Finance, Human Resources and Marketing. He has so far presented 124 papers in both national and international conferences. He has produced 4 Ph.D., scholars, 75 M.Phil., scholars, presently guiding 39 M.Phil., scholars and 25 Ph.D. researchers apart from his regular MBA project guidance. He has published eighty three research papers/articles to his credit in the national/ international level journals and magazines. He is also a visiting faculty of various universities.

S. Anbumalar is M.Com., MBA., M.Phil., PGDCA., with specialization in finance and marketing. She is NET qualified and has ten years of teaching experience. She is presently working as Assistant Professor in the Department of Commerce, Sri Krishna Arts and Science College, Coimbatore. She is handling undergraduate and postgraduate classes and is currently pursuing her Ph.D. in the area of marketing from Alagappa University,

Karaikudi. She has presented more than 30 papers in national and international level seminars. She has published ten research papers/articles to her credit in the national level journals and magazines. She is also a visiting faculty to various universities.

M. Sivamani is M.A., M.Phil., with specialization in Indian economy and rural marketing. She is NET qualified and has fifteen years of teaching experience. She is presently working as Assistant Professor in the Department of Economics, Park's College (Autonomous), Tirupur. She is handling undergraduate and postgraduate classes. She is currently pursuing her Ph.D. in the area of marketing at Madurai Kamaraj University, Madurai. She has presented more than 15 papers in national and international level seminars. She has published five research papers / articles to her credit in the national level journals and magazines. She is also a visiting faculty to various universities.

Dr. Savanam Chandra Sekhar is presently working as an Associate Professor in Department of Business Administration, St. Ann's College of Engineering & Technology, Chirala, Andhra Pradesh. He has five years of industrial experience and twelve years of teaching experience including three years international teaching under University of Cambridge educational curriculum. He has published one article in an international journal and seven articles in various national journals, magazines and news letters in addition to three papers published in national seminars during the year 2009 to his credit. His areas of research interest includes Services Marketing, Rural Marketing of FMCG goods and Marketing of Cottonseed Products.

Dr. B.V.H. Kameswara Sastry is presently working as Faculty in the Department of Management Studies, TJPSCollege (PG Courses), Guntur, Andhra Pradesh. He has a total of fifteen years of experience with him. He possessed Six years of industrial experience dealing with FMCG and engineering products. He also had nine years of teaching experience to MBA, M.Com and MHRM Students. He authored two books and published twenty five papers in both international and national journals of repute. His areas of teaching include Marketing and Human resources.

Dr. L.P. Singh is presently working as Professor & Course Co-ordinator, Department of Commerce & Business Administration, Lalit Narayan Mithila University, Darbhanga, Bihar. He has a total of Twenty Five years of teaching experience. He has authored many books and published fifty papers in both international and national journals. His areas of teaching include Marketing and Human resources.

Dr. R. Ganapathi, is Presently working as Assistant Professor in Commerce, Directorate of Distance Education, Alagappa University, Karaikudi....

S. Anbumalar is presently working as Assistant Professor in the Department of Commerce, Sri Krishna Arts and Science College, Coimbatore....

G. Ramesh Pandi is M.Com., M.Phil., with specialization in marketing and human resources. He is NET qualified and has five years of teaching experience. He is presently working as Assistant Professor in Commerce, Ayya Nadar Janaki Ammal College (Autonomous), Sivakasi. He is handling undergraduate and postgraduate classes. He is currently pursuing his Ph.D. in the area of marketing at Dravidian University, Kuppam Andhra Pradesh. He has presented more than 10 papers in national and international level seminars. He has published seven research papers/ articles to his credit in the national level journals and magazines. He is also a visiting faculty of various universities.

Dr. Chimun Kumar Nath is presently working as lecturer in Department of Commerce, Dibrugarh University, Dibrugarh-786004, Assam.

Vikas Sharma is the research scholar in Shri Mata Vaishno Devi University, Katra, Jammu and Kashmir (J&K).

Dr. Meenakshi Gupta is presently working as faculty in the department of Shri Mata Vaishno Devi University, Katra, Jammu and Kashmir (J&K)

Indrani Majumder is a Lecturer of Barrackpore Rastraguru Surendranath College, Barrackpore, West Bengal in the Department of Commerce in M.Com, Marketing Specialization. She is MBA with specialization in Marketing and MA in Economics. The author is pursing her Ph.D. in the Department of Business Administration, University of Kalyani, Kalyani, Nadia, West Bengal. She is also the coordinator of M. Com in Marketing Management of the Department of Commerce of Barrackpore Rastraguru Surendranath College, Barrackpore, West Bengal and is the editor of the Journal of Business and Economic Issues, of the Department of Commerce, Barrackpore, W.B.

Dr D.V. Chandra Shekar is Assistant Professor, Department of Computer Science, T.J.P.S College, Guntur possessing more than 11 years of Teaching, Research in the field of computer science. His areas of expertise include Knowledge Management, Design and Analysis of Algorithms, Microprocessor and Interfacing, Real-Time Systems, Embedded Systems, Management Information System and various computer subjects. He has presented several research papers in national, international and IEEE conferences, published research papers in national and international journals. Dr. Shekar so far authored 3 books namely Management Information System, Information Technology in Business and Computer Algorithms.

Jhilam Rudra De is the lecturer at NSHM College of Management and Technology, NSHM knowledge campus Kolkata, West Bengal.

Suddhasanta De is the professor at Magnus School of Business, Kolkata, West Bengal.

Dr. Binu Markose is the faculty member at Dept. of Mechanical Engineering, Mar Athanasius College of Engineering, Kothamangalam, Kerala

Dr. Amirul Hasan Ansari is Associate Professor in OB & HRM area, serving with Centre for Management Studies, Jamia Millia Islamia (a Central University), New Delhi. He holds Masters, M.Phil, & Ph.D. from Aligarh Muslim University, Aligarh, in Psychology specialising in Organisational Behaviour, P.G. Diploma in Training & Development from Indian Society for Training & Development, Delhi. He entered into academics with national and international corporate experience. Apart from India, he has a stint of working in the United Kingdom as Training & Education Manager. His major commitment is in teaching organizational behaviour and international human resource management. He has attended and presented research papers in various national and international seminars and conferences in India and abroad. To his credit there is a good number of publications in the journals of repute. He has provided consultancy to national and international corporate in the concerned area. Issues related to strategy and leadership, minority owned businesses, investigations of factors that influence the quality of work life are the current research interest.

Vimal Babu is faculty-in-Management at senior scale in HRM & OB area and Head (Entrepreneurship-Cell) with Accurate Institute of Management and Technology, Greater

Noida. He has been teaching for more than five years. He holds Masters (HRM), MPhil (Management). At present, he is pursuing Ph.D. in Management from Centre for Management Studies, Jamia Millia Islamia, New Delhi. He has presented papers in international conferences and seminars including one at Indian Institute of Management-Kozhikode. He has published several research papers and articles in refereed journals and magazines. He has coordinated and also organised various seminars, workshops and management development programmes in the area of Human Resource Management, Organisational Behaviour and Entrepreneurship Development. Apart from academic activities, he is also a Corporate Trainer in employability skills

Vinita Sinha is Asst. Prof. in Symbiosis Center for Management and Human Resource Development, Pune. She is Ph.D in Psychology. She is a Master in Psychology from Purvanchal University, U.P. and P.G. Diploma in Health Psychology & Behavior Modification from Amity Institute of Behavioral Health & Allied Sciences, New Delhi. She also holds PGDHRM in distance learning from IMT, Ghaziabad. She has worked with Great Lakes Institute of Management, Chennai, BIMTECH, Greater Noida and EMPI Business School, New Delhi & her areas of interest in teaching and research include Psychology, O.B, Industrial Psychology, POM & HRM.

Dr. K.S. Sarala is presently working as Selection Grade Lecturer at the Department of Commerce, Sahyadri Arts and Commerce College, Shimoga, Karnataka.

Dr. R. Ganapathi is presently working as Assistant Professor in Commerce, Directorate of Distance Education, Alagappa University, Karaikudi

Dr. J. Murugesan is M.Com., M.Phil., PGDCA., Ph.D. with specialization in finance and marketing. Presently he is working as Head of the Department, Department of Commerce, Vidyasagar College of Arts & Science, Udumalpet. He has presented more than 45 papers in National and International level seminars. He has guided number of M.Phil., scholars and presently 5 Ph.D., scholars are doing research under his guidance. He has published twenty research papers / articles to his credit in the national level journals and magazines. He is also a visiting faculty of various universities.

Dr. T. Ramasamy is M.Com., MBA., M.Phil., Ph.D. with specialization in finance, human resources and marketing. He is NET qualified and has twenty years of teaching experience. He is presently working as Associate Professor in the Department of Commerce, Government Arts College, Paramkudi. He has presented more than 180 papers in national and international level seminars. He has guided 57 M.Phil., scholars and presently 8 Ph.D. scholars are doing research under his guidance. He has published 120 research papers/articles to his credit in the national/international level journals and magazines. He is also a visiting faculty of various universities.

Prof. Mihir Dash is a specialist in mathematical and statistical modeling. He is actively involved in teaching a variety of courses, including Business Mathematics, Business Statistics, Operations Research, Econometrics and Mathematical Economics, and Operations Management, and in research activities and projects. He is currently working at Alliance Business School, Bangalore.

Rani Hanuman is a research associate at Alliance Business School, Bangalore. She has completed her MBA with specialization in finance. Her research interests are in areas in financial management, including financial forecasting and planning, working capital management, and capital budgeting.

Dr. Durga Madhab Mahapatra is Head and Asst. Professor in Management institute at Greater Noida Institute of Technology (MBA Institute) Greater Noida UP. He is a young academician and researcher with experience of 08 years and regularly presented papers in National seminars and conferences.

Dr. Ashok Kumar Mohanty is currently working as Professor of the Department of Commerce and Financial Studies, Berhampur University, Orissa. Dr. Mohanty is having an excellent reputation in commerce and management field. He is associated with number of academic bodies. He has supervised a number of Ph.D scholars and M. Phil scholars and participated in various national and international seminars. He is also having the credit of authoring 6 books in the areas of banking and finance.

Ankur Srivastava is currently working as Assistant Professor – Accounting & Finance in Greater Noida Institute of Technology (MBA Institute), Greater Noida. He is a science graduate, a post graduate in commerce and has done his PGDBM in Finance and Merchant Banking from Institute of Management & Technology, Ghaziabad. He also has certification from National Stock Exchange (NSE) in Securities Market (Basic) Module and Derivatives Market (Dealers) Module. He has a total working experience of 10 years – 4 years in industry and 6 years in academia.

Shashank Dublish is currently working as Assistant Professor – Accounting & Finance in RKGIT – CMS, Ghaziabad. He is a commerce graduate, a post graduate in commerce and has done his Masters in Financial Administration from IMS, Indore. He also has certification from National Stock Exchange (NSE) in Securities Market (Basic) Module and Derivatives Market (Dealers) Module. He has a total working experience of 09 years – 8 years in industry and 1 year in academia.

Atul Shiva is working as Assistant Professor in the Department of Commerce and Management at Sri Aurobindo College of Commerce and Management, Ludhiana, Punjab. He did his M.Com from DAV College, Chandigarh under Panjab University, Chandigarh. His area of specialization is Cost Accounting and Financial Management. Ms. Monica Sethi is working as Assistant Professor in the Department of Commerce and Management at Sri Aurobindo College of Commerce and Management, Ludhiana, Punjab. She did her M.Com from SCD Government College, Ludhiana under Panjab University, Chandigarh. Her area of specialization is Corporate Accounting and Corporate Laws. She has work experience of eleven years and many research papers publications to her credit.

Dr. Atul Bansal is M.Com. with Ist Division (3rd position1993) LL.B., Personnel Management & Industrial Relations with Ist Division, M.B.A.(Financial Management) with Ist Division from IGNOU and Ph.D.(Accounting Practices in Corporate Sectors). He has more than 15 years experience in teaching and research in Financial Accounting and Financial Management. He had worked with "Institute of Business Management" (Agra University), "College of Professional Education"(C.C.S. University Meerut) and Banarsidas Chandiwala Institute of Hotel Management and Catering Technology (Indraprastha University, Delhi) . Presently he is working as Principal at C.Z. Patel College of Business and Management of S.P. University, Vallabh Vidya Nagar, Gujarat. He attended number of national and international level management development Programmes, seminars, workshops and has published several research papers at prestigious publications of national and international repute such as The Indian Journal of Commerce, 'Assest' Research journal, The Accounting World (ICFAI), International Journal of Management

Prudence", Journal of International Management and Research and 'Artha Vikas' etc. Recently he has written a book entitled as "Legal Aspects for hospitality and Tourism Industry" with S.R. Publication.

Dr. Anil Kumar Chojar is currently working as Director, Disha School of Management(DSM), Raipur(C.G.) He was formerly Director, Disha Institute of Management and Technology(DIMAT), Raipur, and Director-SJS International Institute of Management, Panipat Distt, Haryana. He had earlier worked with Apeejay Institute of Technology, School of Management, Gr. Noida as Professor (Supply Chains, and Operations management). In his earlier career with the industry totaling nearly 23 years, he had worked as General Manager (Procurement, Supply Chains, and Marketing) with Sami Labs Limited- a Phyto-Pharma company based in Bangalore and in the U.S. Besides, he had also worked as Agricultural Economist with U.S. Department for Agriculture at its New Delhi office, and worked with a Dutch agri-business firm Cebeco International Projects, B.V. as a Senior Business Development Manager at its India office in New Delhi.

Dr. Kumud Chandra Goswami has completed M. Com from Gauhati University in the year 1989 and served DHSK Commerce College, Dibrugarh, Assam from 1991 to 2004 as lecturer and then as Sr. lecturer. In the year 1999, he obtained Ph.D. degree from Dibrugarh University in the area of university finance. Dr. Goswami joined as Reader, Department of Commerce, Dibrugarh University on 1st April, 2004 and is still continuing their. He is also completed one minor research project financed by UGC in the year 1999. Till date, for his credit more then 30 research papers in the area of finance, entrepreneurship etc. which are published in reputed referred journals. He is guiding five Ph.D scholars who are on the verge of their submission. In the mean time, two scholars have got their M.Phil degree under my supervision. Presently I am working as Editor, Vanijya, A Dibrugarh University journal of commerce and business studies, Department of Commerce.

N. Venkateswaran is working as Asst. Professor in Department of Management Studies at Panimalar Engineering College, Chennai. He is having 14 years of experience in teaching and 2 years in industry. Being an Engineering graduate in the field of Electronics and Communication, Mr. Venkateswaran is also having MBA degree from Madras University with Marketing & Systems as specialization. He is currently pursuing his Doctoral program from Sathyabama University, Chennai and is so far authored two books on International Business Management, Enterprise Resource Planning for MBA courses of Anna University Curriculum. His areas of interest are Management Information Systems, ERP and Research Methodology. He is so far guided more than 250 MBA projects for IGNOU, TNOU and Madras University. He has attended various national and international conference and presented paper publications. He also published research papers in reputed national and international journals.

Pradeepta Kumar Sarangi is having his M.Tech, MCA and of 10 year teaching experience working as Sr. Lecturer in Apeejay Institute of Technology, School of Computer Science, Greater Noida, U.P, India. Mr. Sarangi has attended more than a half dozen of seminar/workshop/short term courses. Mr. Sarangi has published more than 5 research papers using ANN and Genetic Algorithm and two other research papers have been accepted for publication in various national and international journals.

Nanhay Singh, M.Tech in Computer Science & Engineering, (Ph.D pursing in Computer Science & Engineering) having 11 Year teaching experience. He is working as Lecturer in H.B.T.I, Kanpur in the Dept.of Computer Sc. & Engg. Mr. Singh has attended more than eight seminar /workshop/short term courses. Mr.Singh has published more than four research papers and two other research papers have been accepted for publication in various national and international journals.

Dr. Raghuraj Singh is Ph.D in Computer Science & Engineering (2006) having more than 18 years of experience and is working as Professor, Computer Science & Engineering Department, Harcourt Butler Technological Institute, Kanpur, India. Dr. Singh has attended more than 25 conferences and workshops and has published more than 14 research papers in national/international journals and has presented more than 8 papers in various national/international conferences. He has been the reviewer of the "Journal of Mathematics and Systems Sciences" published by the Kurukshetra University, Kurukshetra, Haryana. He is a Life Member of the Indian Society for Technical Education (ISTE), Member of the Institution of Engineers (India), Fellow Member of the Institution of Electronics and Telecommunication Engineers (IETE), Member of the Board of Studies of Computer Science & Engineering and MCA programmes of the U. P. Technical University, Lucknow. He is the supervisor of four Ph.D thesis and two M.Tech Thesis.

Dr. R. K. Chauhan, (Ph.D in Advance Database, Data Mining & Warehousing, Mobile Computing, Ad-hoc Networks, and Software Engineering) having more than 20 years of experience is working as Professor & Chairman, Department of Computer Science & Applications, Kurukshetra University (India). Dr.Singh has published 18 research papers in national journals, 19 research papers in international journals and 10 papers in conferences. Dr. Singh has also 10 research guidance (Ph.D students) to his credit

Dr. Goutam Chatterjee has been teaching as a full time teacher in K.C. College, Hetampur, Birbhum, W. B. He has a good academic repute and has a number of outstanding publications in different fields covering environments, commerce and other related fields. He attended different seminars and symposia related with commerce in different parts of the country.

Innovations in Marketing Management

Part A

Innovations in Marketing Management

1

PRODUCTIVITY GROWTH OF MANUFACTURING SECTOR IN INDIA: AN INTER-STATE ANALYSIS

Bijaya Kumar Panda

INTRODUCTION

There are increasing number of studies on factor produc-tivity growth in both developed and developing countries. It was Abramovitz (1956) who first observed the growth of output occurring due to factors other than an increase in inputs. Solow (1957) measured total factor productivity (TFP) as a shift in the production function. Since then there has been increasing number of studies on TFP. Productivity growth is a crucial factor in determining the growth of an economy. The study of productivity becomes imperative in view of the limited availability of factors of production, particularly capital. Productivity is the marginal contribution of a factor to the output growth of a product. The proportion of factors of inputs will be different in different industries. In the labour-intensive industries, the emphasis is on the capital productivity. On the other hand, for the capital-intensive industries, the concern is to increase labour productivity. If productivity is increasing in an economy it means that its factors of production and commodity inputs are manifesting an increase in their output efficiency. The productivity improvements along with the in-crease in the quantities of factors will also be contributing as an additional source of output increase (Brahmananda 1982).

Productivity growth is necessary not only to increase output, but also to enhance the competitiveness of an industry both in the domestic and international markets. Besides, productivity growth enhances the export competitiveness of a country. The estimation of factor productivity will be very useful to evaluate the variations in the performance of an industry over a period of time. The prosperity of newly developed countries has been attributed mainly to the sustained growth of their total factor productivity (Prescott, 1997).

The process of liberalization can be linked to the manufacturing productivity. The Indian government started to implement a wide range of economic reforms on various fronts to make domestic industries more efficient and internationally competitive. Indian firms were expected to respond positively to these measures. The liberalization process was to expose firms to international competition and force them to introduce new methods of pro-duction, import quality inputs, capital equipment or technology and compel them to improve their efficiency.

Indian firms experienced the reform process since 1991 and we now have enough data to estimate the impact of globalization and liberalization policies on Indian industry. There are mixed results revealed by earlier studies. Majumdar (1996) and Sharma (1999) estimated positive impact of liberalization policies on the factor productivity. But Balakrishnan et al. (2000) and Das (2004) found that trade liberalization did not yield to the productivity growth in the Indian manufacturing sector. The earlier studies on productivity growth were based on the aggregates of an industry with an assumption that all the firms in an industry behave alike and therefore industry level characteristics could be attributed to all the firms operating in that industry. But Siddharthan (2004) argues that during the period of liberalisation, new firms with more advanced technologies are likely to enter into industry and the existing firms are expected to develop a strategy to meet the challenges from the new entrants, in particular multinational enterprises (MNEs). Under such a situation, the assumption of homogeneity becomes invalid.

It is found from the earlier studies that all the firms belonging to one industry do not behave in a similar pattern. In an industry consisting of a variety of firms with significant differences in their size, ownership, knowledge and access to technology, the liberalisation process would result in gainers and losers but there will be a productivity gap among firms in an industry.

The study is organised into six sections. Section-1 is the introduction. Section-2 deals with a brief review of recent studies and the methodological controversies in the measure of TFPG. Section-3 deals with the specific objectives of the study. Section-4 presents the overall methodology adopted in the study along with the specification of the translog production function, its estimation procedure, the test criterion, the measurement of variables and the data source of the study. The empirical analysis on the trend and pattern of total factor productivity growth rate in the manufacturing sector in some major states of the country is presented in Section-5. Finally, section-6 is the summary and concluding remakes of the study.

PAST RESULTS AND PRODUCTIVITY CONTROVERSIES

In a seminal study, Tsao (1982) found that Total Factor Productivity Growth (TFPG) for the Singapore manufacturing industry had been negligible for the period 1970-79 despite high output growth. He found output growth to be mainly due to growth of factor inputs. He also found that industries with high output growth tend to have a lower TFPG rate. In a comparative study of Singapore and Hongkong, Young (1992) found similar conclusions for the total economy. While both Singapore and Hongkong have experienced high factor accumulation rates, Young found that, TFPG has contributed substantially to Hongkong's economic growth, but almost zero for Singapore. Using growth accounting, Young (1995) showed that input accumulation was the sole reason behind the high output growth of Asian Newly Industrializing Economies.

Using the framework developed in Jorgenson et al. (1987) for analysing sectoral TFP estimates, Wong and Gan (1994) found that improvement in TFPG arising from structural changes through the allocation of resources was a more important component of TFPG than the productivity changes within various individual industries. They also found that industry with larger share of the manufacturing output tends to experience higher TFPG than industries with smaller shares. This differs from Tsao's (1992) observation. Soo-Wei Koh et al. (2002) arrived at a markedly different conclusion from those in Tsao (1982 & 1985) and Young (1995). They showed that the conventional index number measure of TFPG for Singapore manufacturing is 2.7 per cent per annum for the period 1975-98 and exhibits a cyclical pattern over time.

Aschaur (1989) studied the contribution of public capital as a productive input to the private sector production function in the United States. Based on his results, new growth models began to take account of public spending as a factor for self-sustaining productivity gains and long-term growth. The positive contribution of public capital on private sector productivity was confirmed by Mohanty (1992) on the basis of time series evidence for United States. Lynde and Richmond (1993) reached a similar result for the United Kingdom estimating a translog cost function for the entire manufacturing industry.

Studies made by Bhutan (1967), Bhatia (1987), Balakrishna and Pusphangadan (1994), Shrivastava (1996), Rao (1996), Pradhan and Barik (1998) for Indian manufacturing merit attention. These studies are unanimous in not finding an increase in TFPG. Shrivastava found a declining productivity in the 1980s. Rao found a statistically significant deceleration in TFPG for manufacturing in the 1980s. Pradhan and Barik found negative growth during 1982-92 and their findings were based on both aggregate manufacturing and for the individual industries. All these results strengthened the earlier result of Balakrishna and Pusphangadan only in a refined form. On the contrary, Mitra, Varoudakis and Varoudakis (2002) found mixed results for Indian manufacturing industries across the states. They found that Indian heavy industry exhibits a higher growth potential in terms of TFP than did light industry. Light industries generally record low to negative growth rates in both labour productivity and TFP.

Thus, the empirical results on TFPG are not without controversies. The present study does not contribute to the resolution of the controversy. Instead, the study attempts to measure the productivity of the manufacturing sector of nine major industrially developed states vis-a-vis the industrially undeveloped state of Orissa, and also to examine the impact of policy of liberalization on the technological progress and industrial growth of these states.

OBJECTIVES OF THE STUDY

Though Orissa's industrial and economic performances have been brought out by some researchers while analyzing the state-wise regional growth and disparity in India in the pre-reform and post-reform decades, there is hardly any attempt to ascertain the sources for the improved performance of overall industrial sector in Orissa in the period of liberalization. This study assumes significance in this context. It is in this context, the specific objectives of this study are:

(i) To estimate the total factor productivity growth of the manufacturing industries of different states of India using the translog production function which is the generalized form of the production function with two inputs labour(L), Capital (K) and time(T) representing technical progress.

(ii) To know the structure and growth of registered manufacturing factory sector undergone changes over a period of time, particularly in the liberalization period compared to the earlier period in terms of enterprises, employment, investment, gross value added and value of output.

(iii) To examine the extent of employment concentration in Orissa's manufacturing industries relative to all India.

(iv) To explore the sources of output growth in manufacturing industries i.e. whether the output growth of manufacturing industries is input-driven or total factor productivity growth-driven.

METHODOLOGY

In the present study, we have taken total factor productivity as the measure of productivity. Total factor productivity growth is defined as the difference between the rate of growth of output and rate of growth of combined inputs (appropriately weighed). Partial productivity is defined as the real output per unit of any particular input like labour or capital partial productivity is easy to compute. But it has certain limitations. Output is produced by a combination of factor input. Hence the partial productivity indices give us a partial view of productivity. On the other hand, total factor productivity indices use the idea of combined contribution of factor inputs to the production process and hence the total factor productivity index in considered to be better than partial productivity indices as a measure of productivity.

Specification of the Model

In the estimation of total factor productivity there are two widely used approaches. They are (i) growth accounting approach and (ii) production function approach. The growth accounting process of estimation of total productivity rests on two restrictive assumptions, namely, existence of perfect competition in the factor market and the operation of constant returns to scale in the production. These two assumptions do not hold good for a developing country like India because of market imperfections. The production function estimation approach that does not make any restrictive assumption like constant return to scale and exhibits non-unitary elasticity of substitution is chosen for this purpose. In this study, the total factor productivity growth of the manufacturing industries in some major states vis-a-vis in Orissa has been estimated using a more generalized form of Translog Production Function (TPF) with two inputs-labour(L), Capital (K) and time(T) representing technical progress. The specification of this production function is as follows:

$$\ln Y = \alpha + \beta_L \ln L + \beta_K \ln K + \beta_T T + 1/2\, \beta_{LL} (\ln L)^2 + 1/2\, \beta_{KK} (\ln K)^2 + 1/2\, \beta_{TT} T^2 + \beta_{LK} (\ln L)(\ln K) + \beta_{LT} (\ln L)\, T + \beta_{KT} (\ln K)\, T \quad (1)$$

where Y denotes output (value added), L and K are labour and capital inputs respectively and T denotes time (in years). It is a flexible form imposing relatively few 'a priori' restrictions on the properties of the underlying production technology. It allows variable elasticity of substitution and non-neutral technological change. It also allows variable scale elasticity and elasticity of substitution. The symmetry condition requires,

$$\beta_{LK} = \beta_{KL};\ _{LT} = \beta_{TL}\ \ \&\ \ \beta_{KT} = \beta_{TK} \tag{2}$$

The assumption of linear homogeneity (i.e. constant returns to scale) of the production function requires:

$$\beta_L + \beta_K = 1;\ \ \beta_{LL} + \beta_{LK} = 0;\ \ \beta_{KK} + \beta_{LK} = 0\ \ \&\ \ \beta_{LT} + \beta_{KT} = 0 \tag{3}$$

The Translog Production Function reduces to a Cobb-Douglas Production Function (CDPF) if the following condition is satisfied.

$$\beta_{LK} = \beta_{KL} = \beta_{LT} = \beta_{TL} = \beta_{KT} = \beta_{TK} = 0 \tag{4}$$

The technical change/progress (TC) or Total Factor Productivity Growth (TFPG) is then derived as follows:

$$TC = \partial(\ln\ Y)/\partial T = \beta_T + \beta_{KT}\ (\ln\ K) + \beta_{LT}(\ln\ L) + \beta_{TT}\ \ T \tag{5}$$

Technological change is Hicks neutral if $\beta_{KT} = \beta_{LT} = 0$. Total factor productivity growth can also be derived using the Translog Index, the details of which are given below.

From the Translog Production Function (1), the output elasticity of labour (E_L) and the output elasticity of capital (E_K) which may be termed as share equations are given by

$$\begin{aligned} E_L &= \partial(\ln\ Y)/\partial(\ln L) = \beta_L + \beta_{LL}(\ln\ L) + \beta_{LK}(\ln\ K) + \beta_{LT}T \\ &= \beta_L + \beta_{LK}\ln\ (K/L) + \beta_{LT}T \end{aligned} \tag{6}$$

$$\begin{aligned} E_K &= \partial(\ln\ Y)/\partial(\ln K) = \beta_K + \beta_{KK}(\ln\ K) + \beta_{LK}(\ln\ L) + \beta_{KT}T \\ &= \beta_K + \beta_{KK}\ln\ (K/L) + \beta_{KT}T \end{aligned} \tag{7}$$

It is evident from equation (6) that the inter-temporal changes in output elasticity of labour depends on the change in the capital-labour ratio and the bias in the technological change is represented by β_{LT}. Similarly, the inter-temporal changes in output elasticity of capital depends on the change in the capital-labour ratio and the bias in the technological change is represented by β_{KT}.

The Translog Index of Total Factor Productivity (TFP) is a discrete approximation to the Divisia Index of technical change. It has the advantage that it does not make rigid assumptions about elasticity of substitution between factors of production (as for instance done by the Solow Index). It allows for variable elasticity of substitution. Another advantage of the Translog Index is that it does not require technological progress to be Hicks-neutral. The Translog Index provides an estimate of the shift of the production function even if technological change is non-neutral.

For the two input case, taking value added as output; labour and capital as inputs, the Translog Index (TI) of Total Factor Productivity growth is given by the following equation:

$$TI = \Delta \ \ln \ TFP(t) \ = \Delta \ \ln \ Y(t) \ - \left[\frac{S_L(t) \ + S_L(t-1)}{2} \times \Delta \ \ln L \ (t)\right]$$

$$- \left[\frac{S_K(t) + S_K(t-1)}{2} \times \Delta \ln \ K(t)\right] \quad (8)$$

In the above equation, Y is output; L and K are Labour and capital input. S_L denotes income share of labour; S_K denotes income share of capital and S_L *and* S_K add up to unity. In equation (8), Δ In *TFP* is the rate of technological change or the rate of growth of TFP, Δ In Y(t) = In Y(t) – In Y (t-1); Δ In L(t) = In L(t) – In L(t-1), and Δ In K(t) = In K(t) – In K (t-1).

Estimation Procedure and the Test Criteria

After adding an error term to the TPF (in equaion-1), its parameters can be estimated by ordinary least squares technique. However, more efficient estimates of the parameters would be obtained by estimating the production function jointly with share equations Little, Majumdar and Page (1987). Using the estimates of the parameters, these restrictions can be tested. Starting with Translog production function, we shall follow the backward elimination process to arrive at the best fitted production function for all the states taken up for the study. The samé procedure will also be followed for estimating the production function with all India figures.

We have applied three criteria to choose the best fitted production function. The tests are: (i) The best fitted production function should contain all the variables namely capital input, labour input and time as argument in any form (ii) the best fitted production function should be observationally robust in the sense that all the coefficients should be significant and its estimated values will not change significantly event when one or two observations either from the beginning or from the end of the sample set are excluded from the model or included in the same. (iii) The chosen form should have the desired property that the contribution of the inputs to the estimated output is positive. The principal interest of our analysis is the growth of total factor productivity which is calculated by differentiating the best fitted production function with respect to time.

We have also tested whether the excluded coefficients are jointly insignificant. We ignore the results that fail the F-test. The F-test is given by

$$F_{q.n-k} = \left\{ \left(R_g^2 - R_c^2\right) / \left(1 - R_g^2\right) \right\} . \left(n - k\right) / q$$

where n, k and q, are respectively the number of observation, the number of coefficients in the general form of the production function and the number of independent linear restriction, that is, the number of coefficients assumed zero in the present case. We have estimated the average annual TFPG. We have also calculated the coefficient of variation using the formula:

$$C.V. = \sigma / X.100$$

where 'σ ' is the standard deviation of the TFPG. $\overline{X}$ is the average annual TFPG coefficient of variations are used in the present context to verify whether the TFPG is consistent. We have ranked the states according to the average annual TFPG during 1970s, 1980s & 1990s to have a picture of the relative performance of the manufacturing sector of the states chosen for our study during the three decades mentioned above.

Measurement of Variables

In our study, we have taken gross value added as the index of output. Gross output is not taken directly as the index of output, in order to avoid the possibility of double counting. However, it may appear that net value added might have been a better measure of output index, but since the depreciation figures are not reliable as the entrepreneurs often provide us with inflated figures to avoid tax-laws, we have preferred gross value added as a measure of output to net value added.

In the empirical analysis, we have used two estimates of output namely (1) Single deflated gross value added and (2) Double deflated gross value added. In case of singe deflated gross value added we have deflated gross value added by the manufacturing price index. But in case of, double deflated gross value added by the manufacturing price index and the material inputs by the weighted index of the material input prices. Then we deducted deflated material inputs from deflated gross value added to have the double deflated gross value added. We have denoted single deflated gross value added by Y and double deflated gross value added by Z. Data regarding gross value added are collected from various issues of Annual Survey of Industries and the data regarding the price level are collected form National Accounts Statistics published by CSO.

With respect to the index of labour input, we have made an uncomfortable assumption that efficiency differences among different classes of labour are largely reflected in their remuneration. The assumption is, however, not particularly valid for a country like India where remuneration does not vary often to level of efficiency, because of huge surplus labour in the country side. However, the non-conformity of remuneration with the efficiency or productivity is more evident in the unorganized sector than in the organized manufacturing sector. Therefore, remuneration received by the workers may be considered as a good proxy for the and at least better than the unweighted sum of different categories of labour. Workers and other employees (including supervisors, techniques, managers etc.) are two groups of labour for which data are consistently available for the period under study. Labour index is formed by a weighted sum of the number of heads in these two groups, weights being the relevant group remuneration.

Source of Data

Relevant data is obtained from various issues of (i) *Summary Results for Factory Sector*, Annual Survey of Industries (ASI), Central Statistical Organisation, Government of India, New Delhi; (ii)Annual Survey of Industries: A Data Base of the Industrial Sector of India, EPW Research Foundation, Mumbai (iii) *Economic Survey*, Ministry of Finance, Government of India, New Delhi (various issues); (iv) *Report on Currency and Finance*, Reserve Bank of India, Mumbai (various issues); (v) *Annual Report*, Reserve Bank of India, Mumbai (various issues); (vi) *Reserve Bank of India Bulletin*, Reserve Bank of India, Mumbai (various issues); (vii) *National Accounts Statistics*, Central Statistical Organisation, Government of India (various issues); and, (viii) *Handbook of Statistics on Indian Economy*, 1999, Reserve Bank of India, Mumbai. With respect to capital, we have taken the real value of gross fixed capital at 1992-93 prices as its measure. Deflator for gross fixed capital is obtained from data on gross fixed capital formation (G.F.C.F) at current and constant prices of different years. Data for above purpose are obtained from various issues on Annual Survey of Industries and National Accounts Statistics published by CSO.

EMPIRICAL ANALYSIS OF TFPG

We have estimated the best fit production function using time-series data (1970-71 to 1999-00) of the manufacturing sector of ten major states chosen for our study. We have taken into account two indices of output denoted by variable Y (single deflated gross value added) and variable Z (double deflated gross value added) as dependent variable; weighted sum workers and other employees, net Fixed Capital Stock, and time(T) representing technical progress as independent variables in the translog production function. The regression results of the best fitted production function are presented in *Table-1* and *Table-2*. It is observed from above tables that the values of R^2 are very high and more than 0.9 in most of the cases. Most of the t-ratios are found to be significant. The values of DW statistic indicate absence of autocorrelation in the disturbance terms. We have also estimated the TFPG both for the variables Y and Z denoted these two growth rates as TFPG(Y) and TFPG(Z) respectively. The estimates of TFP growth rate in percentages separately for TFPG(Y) and TFPG(Z) for ten states as well as for all-India are presented in *Table-3* and *Table-4*.

Table 3
Total Factor Productivity Growth (in Percentages)
(Variable-Y)

Period	*A.P.*	*Bihar*	*Guj.*	*Kar.*	*M.P.*	*Maha.*	*T.N.*	*U.P.*	*W.B.*	*Orissa*	*All*
1970-71	10.4	5.7	9.2	0.2	14.0	-5.4	4.4	0.1	0.2	0.3	5.0
1971-72	11.3	5.7	9.0	0.8	13.9	-5.0	4.3	0.7	0.3	0.1	5.0
1972-73	10.3	5.7	7.7	1.4	14.0	-4.4	5.7	1.1	0.4	0.1	5.0
1973-74	9.2	5.7	7.8	2.2	14.0	-3.8	4.2	1.7	0.6	0.2	5.0
1974-75	7.4	5.8	7.5	4.3	13.7	-4.7	4.1	3.1	0.7	0.3	5.0
1975-76	6.6	5.8	6.8	4.0	13.8	-4.6	3.7	7.2	0.9	0.2	5.0
1976-77	7.0	5.9	6.9	4.0	14.1	-3.6	3.3	7.1	1.0	0.2	5.0
1977-78	7.5	5.9	6.8	4.1	14.2	-4.2	3.3	5.2	1.2	0.3	5.0
1978-79	7.3	5.9	5.0	3.4	14.3	-1.9	2.4	6.0	1.3	0.2	5.1
1979-80	7.5	5.9	4.5	5.1	14.3	-1.2	1.8	6.8	1.5	0.2	5.1
1980-81	7.1	6.0	4.4	5.8	14.5	-1.5	1.9	7.7	1.6	0.3	5.1
1981-82	5.8	5.9	5.2	7.1	14.6	-1.9	1.5	8.6	1.8	1.3	5.1
1982-83	5.7	5.9	3.5	7.5	14.7	-2.3	1.6	8.7	1.9	1.5	5.1
1983-84	6.0	5.9	3.2	7.7	14.9	-2.3	1.7	8.7	2.1	1.4	5.1
1984-85	5.4	5.9	5.3	8.6	15.1	-2.3	1.2	9.2	2.2	1.7	5.2
1985-86	5.0	5.9	5.8	9.5	15.0	-2.7	1.3	9.8	2.4	2.4	5.2
1986-87	4.8	5.9	5.8	10.0	15.1	-2.3	1.6	9.8	2.5	2.3	5.2
1987-88	4.2	5.9	5.9	9.7	15.2	-2.2	1.2	10.6	2.7	2.4	5.2
1988-89	5.1	5.9	5.8	9.7	14.6	-1.6	0.8	11.0	2.8	2.6	5.2
1989-90	5.3	5.9	5.0	10.8	15.2	-1.2	0.6	11.4	3.0	2.7	5.2
1990-91	9.8	5.9	6.0	10.8	15.3	-0.3	-0.4	11.6	3.1	2.8	5.3
1991-92	8.7	5.9	5.2	13.0	15.1	-1.0	-0.3	11.4	3.3	2.7	5.3
1992-93	8.4	5.8	5.8	11.6	15.5	0.4	-0.6	11.8	3.4	2.9	5.4
1993-94	8.2	5.8	5.4	12.1	15.5	1.1	-0.4	12.1	3.6	3.1	5.4
1994-95	7.7	5.9	5.4	10.8	15.8	1.5	0.6	11.9	3.7	3.4	5.4
1995-96	6.3	5.9	2.8	10.5	15.9	4.4	0.5	12.8	3.8	3.6	5.5
1996-97	5.1	5.9	3.8	9.0	15.8	3.9	0.2	12.7	4.0	3.6	5.5
1997-98	4.6	5.8	3.3	6.7	15.6	4.2	0.4	12.8	4.1	3.9	5.5
1998-99	5.2	5.9	3.7	7.2	15.8	4.5	0.8	13.3	4.4	4.2	5.7
1999-00	5.1	6.1	3.8	7.8	16.1	4.8	1.2	13.8	4.7	4.5	5.7

Note: Estimated from the Variable- Y (Single deflated gross value added)

Table 4
Total Factor Productivity Growth (in Percentages)
(Variable-Z)

Period	*A.P.*	*Bihar*	*Guj.*	*Kar.*	*M.P.*	*Maha.*	*T.N.*	*U.P.*	*W.B.*	*Orissa*	*All*
1970-71	8.1	5.5	9.5	0.2	8.2	3.9	0.6	0.3	1.9	1.1	1.2
1971-72	7.9	5.5	9.4	0.4	8.2	3.9	0.7	0.7	2.0	1.1	1.2
1972-73	7.4	5.5	7.3	0.6	8.2	4.0	0.9	1.0	2.0	1.2	1.4
1973-74	6.9	5.4	7.3	0.8	8.3	4.0	1.2	1.4	2.0	1.2	1.7
1974-75	6.0	5.3	6.8	1.0	8.3	4.3	2.1	1.7	2.0	1.1	2.7
1975-76	5.6	5.7	5.7	1.2	8.4	4.4	2.1	2.0	2.0	1.3	-1.4
1976-77	5.3	5.7	6.0	1.4	8.3	4.3	1.8	2.4	2.0	1.2	-1.8
1977-78	6.0	5.8	5.7	1.6	8.4	4.3	1.2	2.7	2.0	1.1	-1.7
1978-79	5.6	5.9	2.9	1.8	8.4	4.5	1.2	3.1	2.0	1.3	1.2
1979-80	6.0	5.9	2.1	2.0	8.5	4.3	1.2	3.4	2.0	1.1	2.1
1980-81	6.6	5.8	2.0	2.2	8.5	4.6	1.2	3.7	2.0	1.2	3.3
1981-82	5.6	5.8	3.3	2.4	8.5	4.4	0.8	4.1	2.0	1.1	2.9
1982-83	6.3	5.8	2.5	2.6	8.6	4.8	0.9	4.4	2.0	1.4	2.6
1983-84	6.9	5.8	2.5	2.8	8.5	4.6	0.5	4.8	2.0	1.2	2.9
1984-85	7.6	5.8	3.4	3.0	8.6	4.6	0.6	5.1	1.9	1.3	3.2
1985-86	7.8	5.8	4.2	3.2	8.5	4.4	0.6	5.4	1.9	1.3	6.0
1986-87	8.0	5.8	4.2	3.4	8.5	4.4	0.9	5.8	1.9	1.2	8.6
1987-88	7.8	5.8	4.3	3.6	8.5	4.5	1.3	6.1	1.9	1.2	7.4
1988-89	8.7	5.7	4.2	3.8	8.5	4.5	1.7	6.5	1.9	1.1	8.5
1989-90	8.8	5.7	3.0	4.0	8.6	4.6	1.4	6.8	1.9	1.1	8.7
1990-91	12.3	5.7	4.5	4.2	8.6	4.5	-2.1	7.1	1.9	1.2	9.8
1991-92	11.7	5.7	3.2	4.4	8.6	4.6	-2.1	7.5	1.9	1.1	11.5
1992-93	11.9	5.7	4.2	4.6	8.6	4.6	-2.5	7.8	1.9	1.9	11.4
1993-94	12.6	5.8	3.5	4.8	8.6	5.1	-3.3	8.2	1.9	1.9	13.5
1994-95	11.6	5.9	3.5	5.0	8.7	5.1	-4.3	8.5	1.9	2.2	11.2
1995-96	10.7	5.9	1.7	5.2	8.8	6.2	-4.3	8.8	1.9	2.1	11.4
1996-97	11.9	5.9	1.1	5.4	8.7	5.4	-4.3	9.2	1.9	2.5	11.2
1997-98	10.7	5.8	1.3	5.6	8.7	5.8	-4.6	9.5	2.2	2.8	11.5
1998-99	11.4	6.6	2.9	5.7	8.8	5.9	-3.4	10.2	2.7	3.1	11.8
1999-00	11.8	6.9	3.1	6.2	9.2	5.8	1.3	11.8	3.1	3.8	12.4

Note: Estimated from the Variable- Z (Double deflated gross value added)

It is observed from *Table-3* and *Table-4* that the productivity growth rates of both TFPG(Y) and TFPG(Z) in AP had shown a downward trend during the pre-reform as well as in the post-reform period. There was a sudden rise of the two growth rates in the initial part of the post-reform period as compared to the later part of the pre-reform period in the state. But both the TFPG(Y) and TFPG(Z) figures in Bihar were almost stable and varies in narrow interval of 5.5 to 5.9 over the years during in the pre-reform and post-reform period indicating that the structural reforms had no significant impact on TFPG rate in the state. In Gujarat, both the TFPG(Y) and TFPG(Z) rates during the pre-reform period was much higher than the post-reform period which reflects negative impact of reforms in the manufacturing sector of the state. It is also noticed that the TFPG(Y) rates are little higher than TFPG(Z) rates in the state. There was significant improvement in both TFPG(Y) and TFPG(Z) figures in Karnataka during the post-reform period as compared to the pre-reform period. It was further observed that that the TFPG(Y) rates are much higher than TFPG(Z) rates in the state. MP had the highest and stable growth rates both during the pre-reform and post-reform period as compared to other states. The TFPG(Y) rates vary in a narrow range of 14.0 to 15.6 while the TFPG(Z) rates are much lower than TFPG(Y) and vary in a narrow range of 8.2 to 8.7. On the other hand,

Maharastra had negative TFPG(Y) rates during the pre-reform and positive TFPG(Y) rate during post-reform period indicating significant improvement in the growth rate of the manufacturing sector during post-reform period in the state. But the TFPG(Z) rates are positive and stable which vary in a small margin of 3.9 to 4.1.The situation in Tamil Nadu was quite different. The TFPG(Y) rates were positive and small with a declining trend during pre-reform period but negative growth rate during the post-reform period. The negative value of TFPG(Z) rates were much higher than TFPG(Y) rates during the post-reform period. The situation in UP was little different, there was drastic improvement of both TFPG(Y) and TFPG(Z) rate with an increasing trend over the years both during the pre-reform and post-reform period. But there was wide gap between the two growth rates. The TFPG rate was the second highest among the states considered in the study. In Orissa and West Bengal, both the TFPG(Y) and TFPG(Z) rates were relatively very low during the pre-reform period and these figures significantly improved during the post-reform period with an overall increasing trend in both the states. The TFPG(Z) rates were lower than TFPG(Y) and almost stable which varies within a very narrow margin of 1.9 to 2.0 in West Bengal. The all-India TFPG(Y) figures were almost stable during both the pre-reform and post-reform period. It varies in a smaller interval of 5.0 to 5.5. On the other hand, TFPG(Z) figures were significantly improving over the years. When we compare the TFPG(Y) figures with the TFPG(Z) figures, the growth rates of the former were found to be lower than the later. Further, both the TFPG(Y) and TFPG(Z) rates in the states like AP, MP, UP and Bihar were found to be higher than the all-India figures and these two growth rates were below the all-India rates in all other states both during both the pre-reform and post-reform period.

Table 5
Annual Average TFPG and Co-efficient of Variation (Variable-Y)

	Time period					
	1970-71 to 79-80		*1980-81 to 89-90*		*1990-91 to 99-00*	
States	*Annual Average TFPG (%)*	*Coefficient of Variation*	*Annual Average TFPG (%)*	*Coefficient of Variation*	*Annual Average TFPG (%)*	*Coefficient of Variation*
Andhra Pradesh	8.45	19.98	5.44	14.43	6.91	26.97
Bihar	5.8	1.63	5.91	0.54	5.89	1.49
Gujarat	7.12	21.15	4.99	19.71	4.52	25.54
Karnataka	2.95	56.86	8.64	18.15	9.95	21.72
Madhya Pradesh	14.03	1.43	14.89	1.8	15.64	1.91
Maharashtra	-3.88	-34.7	-2.03	-22.88	2.35	95.14
Orissa	0.21	35.14	1.86	40.65	3.47	17.51
Tamil Nadu	3.72	29.55	1.34	30.3	0.2	98.92
Uttar Pradesh	3.9	73.35	9.55	12.41	12.42	6.3
West Bengal	0.81	54.73	2.3	19.98	3.81	13.12
All India	5.02	0.84	5.16	1.00	5.47	2.59

Note: Estimated from Table-4

The annual average TFPG(Y) and TFPG(Y) rates of different states during the last three decades are presented in *Table-5* and *Table-6* respectively. From *Table-5*, it is found that the annual average total factor productivity growth TFPG(Y) rate in Karnataka, Tamil Nadu, Maharashtra, Uttar Pradesh, West Bengal and Orissa were relatively low and also below the all India annual average rate during 1970s. The annual average TFPG(Y) rate of Maharashtra was negative. But the annual average TFPG(Y) rate of Andhra Pradesh, Gujarat and Madhya Pradesh are relatively high and much more than the all India figure. The annual average TFPG(Y) of Bihar is moderate and just above the all India figure during 1970s. During 1980s Karnataka, Madhya Pradesh, Orissa, West Bengal, Bihar and Uttar Pradesh witnessed an increase in TFPG(Y) rate. But the TFPG(Y) rate of Gujarat, Tamil Nadu and Andhra Pradesh has decreased. The TFPG(Y) rate of Bihar remained almost stable and that of Maharashtra is still negative. During 1990s, we observe annual average TFPG(Y) of Andhra Pradesh, Madhya Pradesh, Maharashtra, Orissa, West Bengal and Uttar Pradesh has increased. At the same time TFPG(Y) rate of Tamil Nadu and Gujarat has significantly declined and that of Bihar has remained stable with marginal decline. It is to be noted that though annual average TFPG (Y) of Maharashtra in 1970s and 1980s was negative, during 1990s it turned out to be positive (*Table-5*).

The annual average TFPG(Z) rate of different states during the last three decades are presented in *Table-6*. It was found that the TFPG(Z) rate of six states such as Karnataka, Orissa, West Bengal, Tamil Nadu, Maharashtra and Uttar Pradesh was low during the last three decades. During 1980s, TEPG(Z) of Andhra Pradesh, Karnataka and Uttar Pradesh have increased. The TFPG (Z) remained almost unchanged in case of Bihar, Madhya Pradesh, Orissa and West Bengal. On the other hand TFPG (Z) of Gujarat and Tamil Nadu has declined. During 1990s, the annual average TFPG(Z) rate has increased in all the states except Gujarat and Tamil Nadu. The TEPG (Z) rates of West Bengal and Madhya Pradesh remained almost unchanged. But it is negative in Tamil Nadu during 1990s.

Table 6
Annual Average TFPG and Co-efficient of Variation
(Variable-Z)

	Time period					
	1970-71 to 79-80		*1980-81 to 89-90*		*1990-91 to 99-00*	
States	*Annual Average TFPG (%)*	*Coefficient of Variation*	*Annual Average TFPG (%)*	*Coefficient of Variation*	*Annual Average TFPG (%)*	*Coefficient of Variation*
Andhra Pradesh	6.48	15.68	7.41	14.02	11.66	5.23
Bihar	5.62	3.73	5.78	0.73	5.99	6.93
Gujarat	6.27	38.37	3.36	25.22	2.9	40.38
Karnataka	1.1	55.05	3.1	19.53	5.11	12.32
Madhya Pradesh	8.32	1.24	8.53	0.57	8.73	2.09
Maharashtra	4.19	5.21	4.54	2.79	5.3	11.56
Orissa	1.17	7.04	1.21	8.22	2.26	36.68
Tamil Nadu	1.3	41.19	0.99	40.1	-2.96	-59.83
Uttar Pradesh	1.87	55.46	5.27	19.68	8.86	15.79
West Bengal	1.99	1.59	1.94	2.66	2.13	20.05
All India	1.64	29.20	5.41	49.56	11.57	8.12

Note: Estimated from Table-4

For comparative analysis, we have ranked the states on the basis of their annual average TFPG(Y) and TFPG (Z) rates during 1970s, 1980s and 1990s and these ranks are presented in *Table-7*. From the table, it was found that Madhya Pradesh was ahead of other states with first rank in average TFPG(Y) in all the three decades and it had also

Table 7
Ranking of States on the Basis of Average Annual TFPG

	Variable-Y			*Variable-Z*		
State	*1970-71 to 1979-80*	*1980-81 to 1989-90*	*1990-91 to 1999-00*	*1970-71 to 1979-80*	*1980-81 to 1989-90*	*1990-91 to 1999-00*
Andhra Pradesh	2	5	4	2	2	1
Bihar	4	4	5	4	3	4
Gujarat	3	6	6	3	6	7
Karnataka	7	3	3	10	7	6
Madhya Pradesh	1	1	1	1	1	3
Maharashtra	10	10	9	5	5	5
Orissa	9	8	8	9	9	8
Tamil Nadu	6	9	10	8	10	10
Uttar Pradesh	5	2	2	7	4	2
West Bengal	8	7	7	6	8	9

Note: Computed from Table-5 and Table-6.

retained the first rank in average TFPG(Z) during 1970s and 1980s but its rank deteriorated to third during 1990s. Andhra Pradesh had occupied the second rank in TFPG(Y) during 1970s but its rank deteriorated to fifth in 1980s and improved to fourth position in 1990s The state had also occupied second rank in average TFPG(Z) during 1970s and 1980s, it had improved to the first position in 1990s. Gujarat's rank in average TFPG(Y) was third in 1970s but its rank deteriorated to sixth during 1980s and 1990s. If we consider TFPG (Z), its rank was third in 1970s but its rank deteriorated to sixth in 1980s and further deteriorated to seventh and 1990s. West Bengal was in eighth rank in average TFPG(Y) during 1970s but its rank was improved to seven during the 1980s and 1990s. As regards to TFPG(Z), the state was in sixth rank in 1970s but its rank was deteriorated to eighth in 1980s and further deteriorated to ninth in 1990s. The rank in both the productivity growth rates of Orissa was very close to West Bengal. Orissa occupied ninth rank in average TFPG(Y) during 1970s but its rank was improved to eighth during the 1980s and 1990s. As regards to TFPG(Z), the state was in ninth rank in 1970s and 1980s and slightly improved to eighth rank in 1990s.The relative positions of Maharashtra, U.P., and Karnataka had improved in both the productivity growth rates i.e. TFPG(Y) and TFPG(Z) but the position of Tamil Nadu in term of both the productivity growth rates had been deteriorated over the decades.

CONCLUSION

Increase in productivity is imperative to raise the standard of living of the people and also to make the exports of the country globally competitive. This is particularly true for public sector undertakings. The private sector is allowed to enter many areas of manufacturing industry in the recent years and this accompanied by market related pricing which has resulted in an increase in productivity.

From the above analysis, it evident that there is wide differences in the figures of TFPG(Y) and TFPG(Z) for most the states and also at all-India level. Hence, it would not be too much to say that TFPG estimates depends significantly on the measurement of output. The total factor productivity of at least three states like Karnataka, Uttar Pradesh and Madhya Pradesh have significantly increased during 1990s in both the measures of output taken up for the present study. This clearly indicates that the positive impact of the recent policy changes on the manufacturing sector in the states vis-a-vis in the country.

The above analysis also indicates that manufacturing industries of Orissa did not achieve significant improvement in total factor productivity growth during the post-reforms period despite policymakers offering of the much needed flexibility in their operations. Though liberalization of technology imports encouraged them to achieve technological innovation significantly, the technical efficiency growth suffered considerably as a result of which TFPG was relatively small in post-reforms period. This implies that in the process of industrial growth in the post-reforms period, manufacturing sector of Orissa has not attained any significant industrial efficiency and the growth was primarily due to growth in demand. Given this, it is imperative for the policymakers at the regional level to look at an appropriate competitiveness enhancement strategy for the sustenance of long-term growth of manufacturing industry in the state.

All these results indicate clearly that higher industrial growth need not be accompanied with higher industrial efficiency, if this is so, sustenance of Orissa's industrial growth even with reference to the domestic market in the long run would be difficult. If Orissa has to achieve 'competitive industrialization', it is imperative that conscious policy efforts at the regional level must be made for competitiveness enhancement through efficient infrastructure building, rational technology imports and disseminating better adaptation methods of imported technologies across industries, among others.

REFERENCES

Aschauer, D.A. (1989), "Is Public Expenditure Productive", *Journal of Monetary Economics*, Vol. 23, pp.25-34.

Balakrishnan, P. and K. Pushpangadan (1994), "Total Factor Productivity Growth in Manufacturing Industry: A Fresh Look", *Economic and Political Weekly*, Vol. 29, pp.2028-35.

Balakrishnan, P. and K. Pushpangadan (1998), "What do We Know about Productivity Growth in Indian Industry?", *Economic and Political Weekly*, Vol. 33, pp.2241-46.

Bhatia, D.P.(1987), "Estimates of Value Added at Constant Prices in the Manufacturing Sector: An Erroneous Methodology", *Economic and Political Weekly*, Vol. 16, pp. 721-28.

Bruton, H. J., (1967), "Productivity Growth in Latin America", *American Economic Review*, December, 1967.

Dutt-Majumdar, D. (1967), "Productivity of Labour and Capital in Indian Manufacturing during 1951-61", *Arthaniti*, Vol. 21, January-July.

Jorgenson, D.W. and Z. Griliches (1967), "The Explanation of Productivity Change", *Review of Economic Studies*, Vol. XXXIV, pp. 249-83.

Koh Soo-Wei, Rehman S. and Tan, G.K.R. (2002), "Growth and Productivity Singapore Manufacturing Industries during 1975-1998", *Asian Economic Journal*, Vol.16, No. 3.

Mitra, A., Varoudakis, A. and Varoudakis, M.V. (2002), "Productivity and Technical Efficiencey in Indian Manufacturing Industries: The Role of Infrastructure, Economic Development and Cultural Change.

Mohanty, D. (1992), "Growth and Productivity in The Indian Economy", *Reserve Bank of India Occasional Papers*, Vol. 13, No.2, pp. 55-80.

Pradhan, G. and Barik, K. (1999), "Total Factor Productivity Growth in Developing Economies: A Study of Selected Industries in India", *Economic and Political Weekly*, Vol. 34, pp M-92-105.

Rao, J. M., (1996), "Manufacturing Productivity Growth: Method and Measurement", *Economic and Political Weekly*, Vol. 31, pp. 2927-36.

Shrivastava, V. (1996), "Liberalisation, Productivity and Competition: A Panel Study of Indian Manufacturing", Oxford University Press, Delhi.

Tsao, Y. (1985), "Growth without Productivity: Singapore Manufacturing Industries during 1980s", *Journal of Development Economics*, Vol. 19.

Wong, F.C. and Gan, W.B. (1994), "Total Factor Productivity Growth in Singapore Manufacturing Industries during 1980s", *Journal of Asian Economic Review*, Vol. 5.

Young, A. (1995), "The Tyranny of Numbers Confronting the Statistical Realities of the East Asian Growth Experience, *Quarterly Journal of Economics*, Vol. 110.

Table 1

Parameter Estimates of Translog Production Function for Ten Major States and all-India

(VARIABLE-Y)

Explanatory Variable	*Parameters*	*W.B.*	*M.P.*	*Guja.*	*Kar.*	*U.P*	*Bihar*	*A.P.*	*T.N.*	*Maha.*	*Orissa*	*All India*
INTERCEPT	α	-4.422(-2.78)	11.144(3.42)	6.981(7.42)	9.782(2.34)	9.864(4.46)	4.568(1.89)	7.526(2.97)	-6.324(-5.62)	-3.892(-3.65)	-5.746(-3.72)	14.234(7.86)
LOG L	β_L	-2.745(-2.87)	2.585(3.86)	-1.462(-1.98)	-3.472(-2.28)	0.872(7.63)	0.241(3.79)	2.235(5.02)	-1.245(-3.11)	0.523(1.52)	1.238(3.24)	0.892(8.72)
LOG K	β_K	3.142(2.57)	3.564(3.25)	-3.197(-8.64)	-1.364(-2.87)	1.898(3.98)	1.628(4.52)	2.841(3.58)	-0.452(-1.47)	-3.241(-1.48)	2.436 (4.12)	0.486(8.76)
T	β_T	0.241(1.54)	1.222(1.85)	1.862(4.44)	1.034(1.76)	-0.125(-2.36)	-0.004(-1.58)	-0.146(-2.21)	0.825(6.84)	-2.012(-5.88)	-1.454(-3.86)	-0.587(-1.81)
$(LOGL)^2$	β_{LL}	0.258(2.46)	-0.089(-1.76)	4.148(1.92)	-3.122(-2.41)	0.156(1.52)	0.075(4.27)	-0.485(-2.34)	0.338(6.93)	0.221(4.32)	1.362(4.84)	0.345(5.24)
$(LOGK)^2$	β_{KK}	0.133(1.51)	-0.165(-3.07)	0.144(11.58)	-1.574(-2.09)	0.169(1.52)	-0.245(-4.45)	-0.462(-2.27)	0.344(7.52)	0.012(4.35)	-0.521(-3.86)	0.423(4.04)
T^2	β_{TT}	0.001(4.98)	0.034(1.56)	0.002(2.04)	0.004(2.32)	0.003(2.25)	0.104(3.46)	0.004(1.66)	-0.001(-3.03)	-0.005(-1.42)	0.040(2.85)	0.045(3.21)
738	β_{LK}	-0.514(-2.12)	0.246(7.89)	1.122(3.16)	1.141(2.47)	-0.313(-2.56)	-0.138(-6.05)	0.742(3.44)	-0.616(-5.22)	0.074(8.15)	-1.345(-2.59)	1.424(5.23)
LOGL*T	β_{LT}	0.014(2.87)	-0.024(-3.56)	-0.138(-4.38)	0.003(1.34)	-0.038(-1.72)	0.006(11.27)	0.008(4.16)	-0.047(-8.74)	0.186(5.21)	-0.732(-1.58)	-0.117(-2.13)
076	β_{KT}	0.012(1.25)	0.017(3.44)	0.114(1.11)	-0.095(-1.79)	-0.038(-1.58)	0.042(2.10)	0.076(2.56)	0.112(1.65)	0.005(2.16)	-1.341(-3.18)	0.039(5.25)
D.W.	-	1.92	2.05	1.84	1.98	2.12	1.98	1.68	1.85	1.72	2.03	2.11
R^2	-	0.89	0.93	0.92	.094	0.97	0.94	0.93	0.96	0.96	0.94	0.84

Note: Figures in parentheses are values of t-ratios. We denote single deflated gross value added by lYm

Table 2

Parameter Estimates of Translog Production Function for Ten Major States and all-India

(VARIABLE-Z)

Explanatory Variable	*Parameters*	*W.B.*	*M.P.*	*Guja.*	*Kar.*	*U.P*	*Bihar*	*A.P.*	*T.N.*	*Maha.*	*Orissa*	*All India*
INTERCEPT	α	-6.515(-4.12)	12.142(7.24)	3.835(4.34)	10.124(2.59)	5.627(3.68)	8.261(6.62)	7.3412.32	-3.798(-1.54)	5.632(9.58)	8.124(5.21)	21.427(2.91)
LOG L	β_L	-0.194(-2.45)	-0.612(-1.79)	-0.012(-9.43)	-2.146(-2.49)	0.847(4.68)	0.924(12.47;	-0.782(-1.89)	1.531(6.18)	0.865(3.46)	0.624(3.08)	0.767(4.18)
LOG K.	β_K	0.812(3.76)	0.272(1.72)	1.625(8.24)	0.655(5.02)	0.289(3.54)	-1.112(-1.86)	2.456(4.58)	-0.854(-2.05)	1.474(14.89)	1.248(6.52)	-1.352(-2.89)
T	β_T	-0.115(-3.24)	-0.004(-2.75)	2.934(5.26)	1.021(5.04)	-1.852(-7.24)	0.004(4.26)	2.762(1.82)	0.005(2.96)	-1.522(-2.04)	-1.341(-6.72)	2.314(2.79)
$(LOGL)^2$	β_{LL}	0.249(2.46)	0.224(4.85)	0.048(1.45)	0.078(3.58)	0.047(7.63)	-0.123(-3.42)	0.062(1.06)	0.008(2.05)	0.124(8.21)	-1.088(-2.45)	0.047(3.02)
$(LOGK)^2$	β_{KK}	0.131(1.50)	0.128(9.14)	0.089(1.13)	-0.942(-2.43)	-0.117(-1.89)	0.316(6.27)	-0.312(-2.06)	0.069(6.49)	-0.047(-5.54)	1.081(5.15)	-1.67(-2.63)
T^2	β_{TT}	0.001(5.94)	0.085(2.56)	0.002(2.99)	0.001(2.97)	0.002(4.22)	-0.124(-1.21)	0.025(4.23)	-0.002(-3.46)	0.004(1.19)	-0.129(-7.16)	0.011(2.11)
LOGL.LOGK	β_{LK}	2.154(3.79)	1.428(2.01)	2.521(7.57)	1.824(2.44)	0.784(3.82)	0.211(2.26)	0.532(2.02)	0.118(4.19)	0.520(2.46)	2.232(1.78)	1.857(2.89)
LOGL.T	β_{LT}	-0.004(-1.21)	0.728(4.25)	-0.214(-5.13)	-0.211(-1.81)	0.002(1.46)	0.057(3.32)	0.047(2.44)	0.005(3.55)	0.003(5.36)	-0.128(-2.02)	-0.824(-2.77)
LOGK.T	β_{KT}	0.001(1.06)	0.017(6.96)	0.004(2.79)	0.142(3.79)	-0.018(-5.32)	0.006(8.07)	0.547(2.76)	0.058(6.32)	-0.032(-1.14)	1.141(2.29)	0.213(3.78)
D.W.	-	1.94	1.67	1.82	1.47	1.62	1.45	1.86	2.17	1.82	2.12	2.16
R^2	-	0.94	0.92	0.91	0.94	0.93	0.89	0.92	0.87	0.95	.96	0.95

Note: Figures in parentheses are values of t-ratios. We denote double deflated gross value added by lZm

2

DIVERSIFICATION PATTERNS AND CONSUMER SATISFACTION IN MASALA PRODUCTS

S. Ganesan, R. Rajanbabu

INTRODUCTION

India is known as "The home of spices". No Indian meal is considered complete without the tangy and delectable flavour of Indian spices, locally known as 'Masala'. Indian spices famous the world over for their gastronic value is known to possess high medicinal values. There is no other country in the world that produces as many kinds of spices as India. Some of the most widely consumed spices in the country inter *alia* include: chilli, cinnamon, cumin, curry leaf, fennel, asafetida, basil, bay leaves, cardamom small, cardamom-large, ginger, mustard, bishops weed, cassia, celery, clove, coriander, fenugreek, garlic, kokam, mint, onion, parsley, pomegranate, turmeric, tamarind, pepper, poppy, rosemary and vanilla. The climate of the country is found suitable for growing almost all spices.

India is one of the largest producer, consumer and exporter of spices. India is reported to grow over 50 spices in different parts of the country. USA is the largest market for Indian spices. In the year 2006 India emerged as the largest exporter of spices in the world and had registered a phenomenal growth of 66.55 percent (Rs.2,200 crore).

According to the data released by the Spices Board, India's exports of spices in 2007-08 registered a growth of 24.04 percent when the same reached a level of Rs.4,435 crore. USA continues to be the largest market for Indian spices. In 2007-08, the country registered a growth of 12.19 percent when the exports to this market reached a level of Rs.867 crore.

INDIAN SPICES SECTOR

India produces 25 lakhs tonne to 30 lakhs tonne of spices annually. India produces spices of different categories worth around Rs.14,000 crore. In terms of volume and value, India accounted for 46 percent and 23 percent in value of global spice trade. India accounts for

25-30 percent of world's pepper production, 35 percent of ginger and about 90 percent of turmeric production. Among the Indian Federal states, Kerala tops in pepper (96 percent), Cardamom (53 percent), Ginger (25 percent) production in the country. Andhra Pradesh leads in Chilli and Turmeric production in the country with 49 percent and 57 percent respectively. In corriander, cumin and fengugreek production in the country, Rajasthan emerges as the largest producer with 63 percent, 56 percent and 87 percent. The world spice trade is estimated at Rs.7,050 crore to Rs.9,400 crore in terms of value and 5,00,000 tonne in terms of quantity.

According to UNCTAD-International Trade Centre estimate, in terms of volume, pepper contributes 34 percent of total global spices trade followed by chillies 22 percent, seed spices 17 percent, tree spices 14 percent, turmeric 5 percent, ginger 4 percent, cardamom 3 percent and vanilla 1 percent. In last five years (1997-98 to 2001-02) India's spice exports increased marginally by 1.20 percent in terms of volume but export earnings in rupee terms registered an impressive growth of 45.72 percent reflecting marked value addition. In terms of export earnings pepper accounts for 45 percent of India's total spice exports. In terms of quantity, the position is just the reverse with chilli taking the largest share (28.10 percent) in India's spice export basket compared with pepper (20.16 percent). Spice oil and Oleoresins, value added items, together accounts for 15.33 percent of total export earnings from Indian spices. The present paper attempts to analyse the diversification patterns and consumers satisfaction in masala products.

NEED FOR THE STUDY

It may be observed that most of the existing studies on food industries focused its attention on the economics of food products manufacturing viz: productivity, profitability, capital intensity, capacity utilization etc., at macro level. But in recent times spectacular diversification is found in the fast food segment. The product innovation and technological upgradation in these traditional industries are astounding with multidimensional economic ramifications. But no study focused its attention on this aspect.

The existing industries studies have not only inadequately dealt with the dynamic behaviour of firms under conditions of change but have also not examined the growth performance and its associated variables in greater depth. Most of the industry studies that exist have also tended to be historical-cum-descriptive. The few studies available were primary directed towards examining industrial concentration.

PROBLEM FORMULATION

In this moving world, people have very less time to do a lot of work in their day-to-day life. In order to complete their works quickly, make use of ready-made masala products, pickles, etc., that save them a lot of time in doing a work, since it is less time consuming, saving energy, etc.

Since the potential for market expansion of the masala products are vast, mushrooming of masala units in and around Madurai and the competition among them is very acute. One such concern is Eagle Food Products Company, which produces masala products, pickles, etc on large-scale under the brand name of Eagle. Across four p's viz: Product, Place, Price and Promotion available to tackle the competition, Madurai masala units preferred product and strategied to fight it out through diversification (Product Innovation). The product diversification patterns are phenomenal, horizontally and vertically with multi-dimensional economic ramifications.

Questions Rose

1. What is the concept of diversification?
2. What is the pattern of diversification and what is the time-log involved across each diversification?
3. What are the products that are preferred in Eagle Food Products by the consumers?
4. How frequently do they purchase the products?
5. What is the degree of satisfaction derived by the consumers?

HYPOTHESES FORMULATED

The null hypothesis has been farmed to test the relationship between the level of satisfaction and factors influencing satisfaction.

OBJECTIVES OF THE STUDY

1. To trace the diversification patterns in masala products.
2. To find out the factors considered by consumers while purchasing Eagle Food Products.
3. To analyze the factors which are influencing the consumer satisfaction.

METHODOLOGY

Scope

This study covers diversification patterns towards the product of Eagle Food Products Madurai and it also deals with the consumer satisfaction. The reasons behind selection of masala industry are:

1. Masala units dominate the small food industry.
2. The diversification rate is higher and faster.
3. Time-lag across each diversification is low rendering the predication difficult and
4. The diversification pattern is fascinating. Period of analysis is 36 years from 1972 to 2008.

Data Collection

The study is mainly based on primary data. Convenient sampling method is adopted for selecting samples. A sample of 200 women respondents has been selected for the study. Care has been taken to include both urban and rural consumers and hence respondents have been selected from different parts of Madurai. A structured questionnaire was used for collection of data. Necessary secondary data have also been collected from sources like books, magazines and internet.

Data Analysis

For the purpose of detailed analysis, the following statistical tools have been used in the study:

The satisfaction index is used to estimates the consumers level of satisfaction in masala products.

1. Percentage analysis is employed for analyzing the socio-economic characteristics of the respondents and product related factors.
2. Chi-square test has been applied to establish the relationship between the level of product satisfaction and factors influencing consumer satisfaction.

REVIEW OF LITERATURE

The following earlier studies reviewed the various aspects on the food industry: Subramanian and Mohanan Pillai (1986), Jairus Banaji (1997), Sukhpal Singh (1997), Carol M. Michael (1999), Sarin K.P (1999), Michalis M. Efstratiadis (2000), Omesh Saigal (2001), Takahashi Kazuhito (2003), Cates, S.C & Carter-Young, H., (2004), Nandagopal R and Chinnaiyan P (2004), Ferdaus Hossain & Ruchi (2005), Robert W.Ivester (2008), Spyridon Mamalis (2009). Some of the studies devoted on product diversification and satisfaction: Rumelt (1982), Cynthia A. Montgomery (1985), Barbara W Keats (1990), Mythili (1996), Michael A. Hitt, et.al (1997), Anbumani (1999), Gongming Qian (2002), and Prema (2005).

Thus it is evident that the number of studies analyzed the food industries, diversification and product satisfaction. But the studies related to consumer satisfaction level in masala product company is very few and scanty. So the present study makes an attempt to overcome this shortcoming by focusing on diversification patterns and consumer satisfaction.

DIVERSIFICATION PATTERNS

Quick food styles are catching up fast because of more number of working couples, domestic fuel crisis, non-availability of reliable domestic servants and breaking up of joint family system. Neither time nor patience to prepare the ingredients and wholesome food in the house itself, the high price of ingredients and ready mix are also a significant factor responsible for the spectacular increase in the demand for masala products. Hence this paper discusses the diversification pattern in masala products.

CLASSIFICATIONS

The masala products of Eagle Food Products that are being sold in the market can be classified as follows: (1) Ground Spices (2) Masala Powder (3) Instant Mixes (a) Powder (b) Pastes (c) Chutney. It is analyzed the process of diversification in each of these items and they involved for the emergence of new products through a flow chart and network diagram.

Ground Spices

The Eagle Food Products (EFP) started to produce ground spices in 1972. Initially it produced concurrently two variant of powder namely (1) Chilly Powder (2) Turmeric Powder. New variant viz: coriander powder, cumin powder and pepper powder were added in 1975 i.e. after 3 years. In other words, the EFP firm waited for 3 years to introduce these new variants in the ground spices category. It is to be noted that once the idea of diversification started, the firm in trying to add more variants.

Point of divergence: The diagram-1 represents the network of diversification process in spices and condiments. It indicates the point of divergence beyond which the firm continues to produce all variants. It is interesting to note that we have not come across the instance of any variant becoming absolute thus dying out of the market. This phenomenon is in direct contrast to the engineering industry where a particular product dies out of the market because of obsolescence at the end of its life cycle. In other words, we find that the life of the food product is not a cycle but parallel lines: traditional items going strong with new variants.

Diversification Pattern and Time-lag in Ground Spices: From the Table-1, it is noted that once diversification started, then the process is quicker with lesser time interval. Any scientific discovery invention follows the same pattern. Inventing the basic theory takes a longer time frame but subsequent applications are quicker and faster. The emerging conclusion is that higher degree of diversification is possible if the product is a food item. In other words more diversification will be forthcoming in food item.

Table 1
Diversification Pattern and Time-lag in Ground Spices

Name of theProduct	*Year*	*TimeInterval*
Chilly Powder	1972	0
Turmeric Powder	1972	0
Coriander Powder	1975	3
Cumin Powder	1975	3
Pepper Powder	1975	3

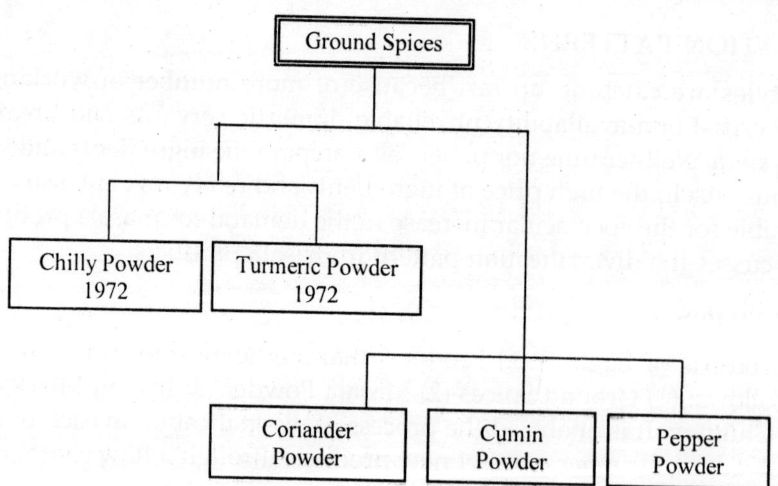

Chart 1: Diversification Pattern under Ground Spices

Masala Powder

In 1973, the Eagle Food Products produced the sambar powder only under this category. In first three variants namely; chicken masala, garam masala and curry masala were introduced in 1974 after a time gap of one year. In second, two variants namely; mutton masala and fish masala were introduced in 1975. The process of diversification in this category is represented as follows. It is noted that in masala category the EFP introduced new variants concurrently as in the case of ground spices. Further the EFP remains dynamic through out the period of analysis by continuing the process of diversification.

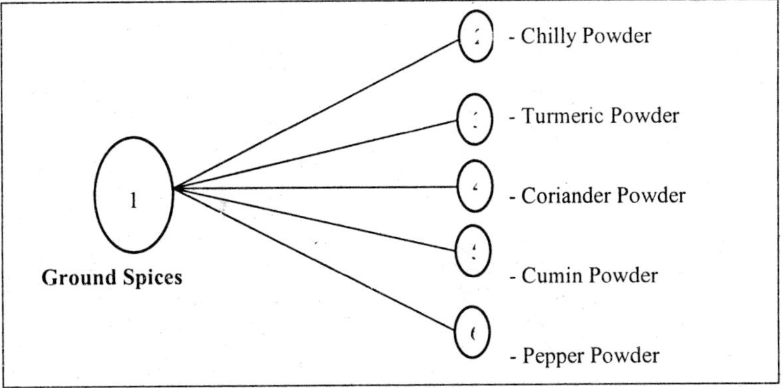

Diagram 1: Network of Diversification Pattern under Ground Spices

Diversification Pattern and Time-lag in Masala Powder: The Table-2 indicates the time frame of diversification for masala powder. It is evident that diversification was quicker in non-vegetarian categories, which reflects that majority consumers (77 percent) of the masala powder are non-vegetarian. The inference is that Eagle Food Products tries to shed the opinion that it is varianting to the non-vegetarian segment of the population only.

Table 2
Diversification Pattern and Time-lag in Masala Powder

Name of theProduct	*Year*	*TimeInterval*
Sambar Powder	1973	0
Chicken Masala	1974	1
Garam Masala	1974	1
Curry Masala	1974	1
Mutton Masala	1975	2
Fish Masala	1975	2

Flow chart shows diversification in masala powder items and time-lag.

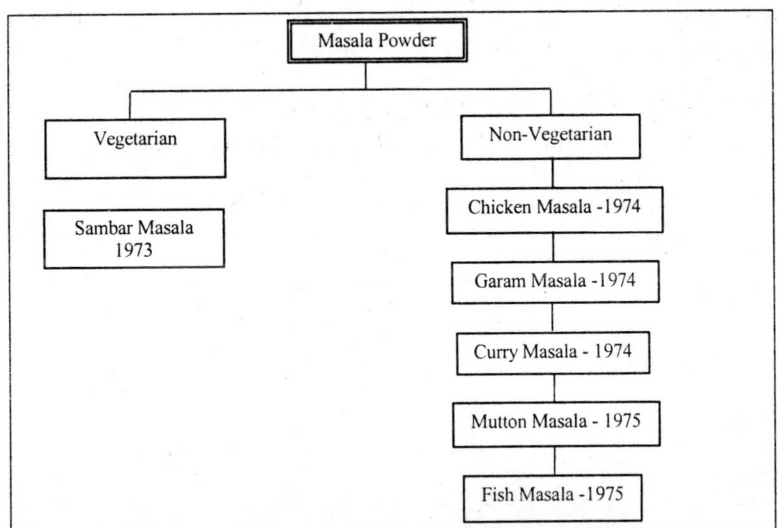

Chart 2: Diversification Pattern Under Masala Powder

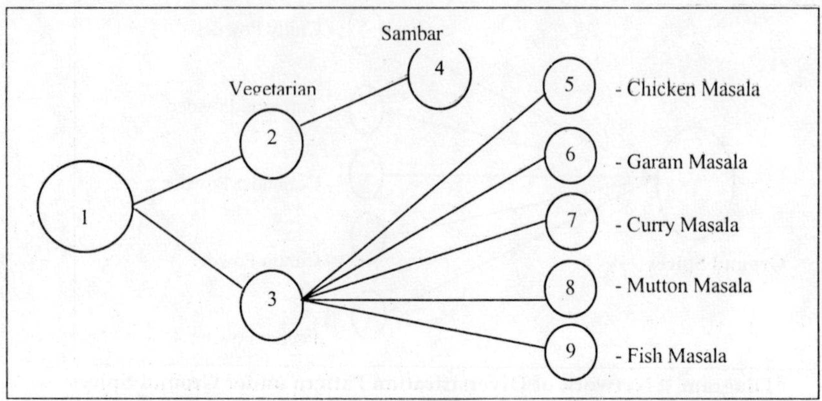

Diagram 2: Network of Diversification Pattern Under Masala Powder

Instant Mixes

Introduction of instant mix was due to time saving and busy working time schedule. Even though it took nearly 18 years for diversification in this product line, there is a considerable momentum and hence the future prospects will be bright. This is the area where diversification has taken a longer time to enter into. This is latest area where masala industry is concentrating on. In fact the first diversification started only in 2003 and subsequently variants are introduced as the following flow chart shows.

A new variant viz., bajji mix was added in 2003 i.e. after 18 years. Rice briyani mix was introduced in 2005, after a time gap of two years. In 1996, EFP introduced the paste item concurrently namely; (1) vathal kuzhambu paste (2) puliyodharai paste. A new special variant i.e. garlic coriander chutney was introduced in the year 1997. It is to be noted that once diversification started, the time gap is shrinking for each addition.

Diversification Pattern and Time-lag in Instant Mixes: The Table-3 indicates the time pattern of diversification under instant mixes segment. The initial introduction took longer time frame subsequent addition were quick implying faster development. The discussion with the R&D using of the firm reveals that the firm is very particular in diversifying into instant mixes segment.

Table 3
Diversification Pattern and Time-lag in Instant Mixes

Name of the Product			*Year*	*Time Interval*
Powder	*Pastes*	*Chutney*		
Briyani Mix			1978	0
Puliyodharai Mix			1978	0
Lemon Mix			1978	0
Tomato Mix			1978	0
Paruppu Mix Idly			1978	0
Idly Milagai Powder			1978	0
Vathal Kuzhambu Paste			1996	18
Puliyodharai Paste			1996	18
Garlic Coriander Chutney			1997	19
Bajji Mix			2003	25
Rice Briyani Mix			2005	27

The detailed analysis of diversification patterns under different categories suggest that product diversification is taking place in all segments, of course with varying time frames. The Eagle Food Products could increase the value of production considerably through the introduction of new variants and hence diversification has a direct bearing on the product satisfaction. Further analysis indicates the changing consumption pattern of the population and the varieties prefer by the young age group.

Measurement of Satisfaction level in Masala Products: To measure the consumer satisfaction in EFP products, nine aspects of products, viz., Smell, Taste, Quality, Cost, Availability, Packing, Hygienic preparation, Durability and Variety of products are considered.

Flow chart showing diversification in instant mixes items and time-lag.

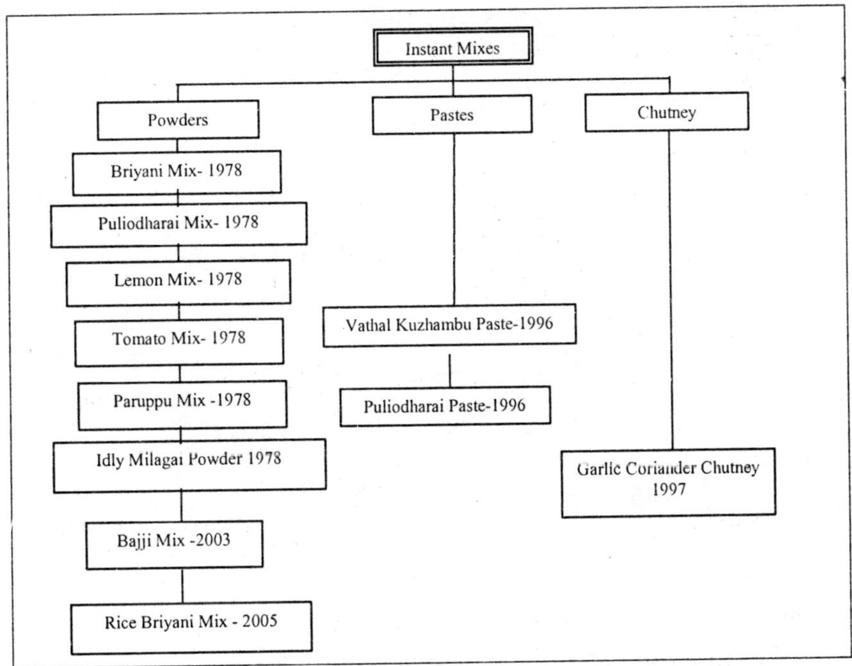

Chart 3: Diversification Pattern Under Instant Mixes

The consumer responses for these aspects are measured by adopting Likert 3 point scale viz., highly satisfied, satisfied and dissatisfied. These responses are assigned scores respectively 3, 2, and 1. The sum of the scores obtained by each respondent for all responses represents her satisfaction score. From the sum of scores, satisfaction index for each respondent has been calculated as follows:

$$Satisfaction\ Index = \frac{Sum\ of\ scores\ obtained\ by\ each\ respondent}{Maximum\ Score} \times 100$$

Based on Satisfaction Index, the respondents are classified as highly satisfied, satisfied and dissatisfied as follows:

Mean Score + Standard deviation = Highly Satisfied

Between (Mean Score - Standard deviation) and (Mean Score + Standard deviation) = Satisfied

Mean Score - Standard deviation = Dissatisfied

Mean score is 61.35 and the Standard deviation is 5.78.

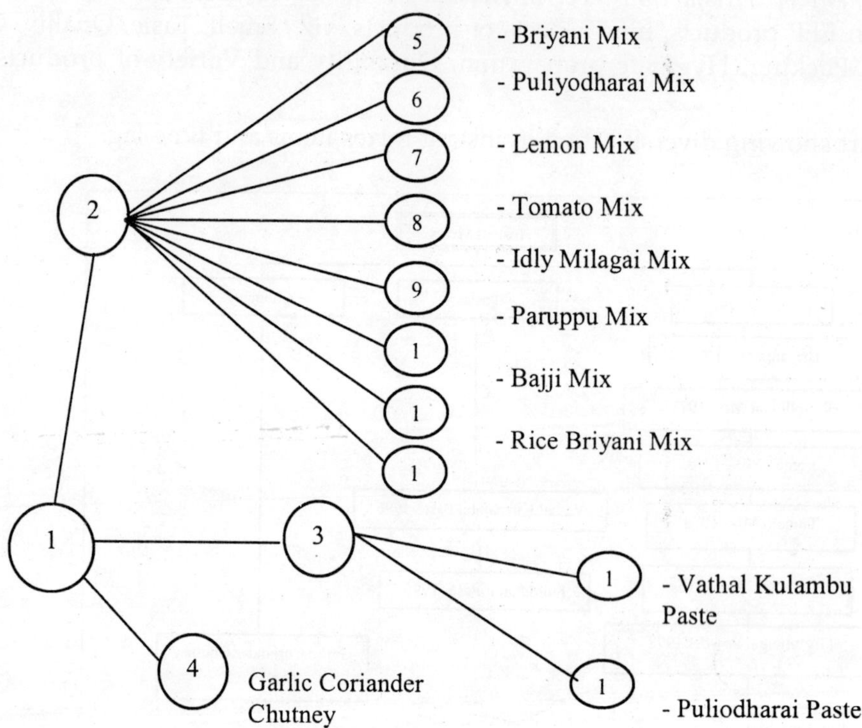

Level of Satisfaction of Respondents

Satisfaction level of the respondents is envisaged in Table-4.

Table 4
Level of Satisfaction of the Respondents

Level of Satisfaction	*No. of Respondents*	*Percentage*
Highly Satisfied	68	34
Satisfied	103	52
Dissatisfied	29	14
Total	200	100

The above table shows that 68 respondents (34 percent) have obtained higher satisfaction by using eagle masala products and 103 respondents (52 percent) are satisfied and the remaining 14 percent of the respondents are not getting any satisfaction, but merely they have used this brand. It is evident that majority of the respondents (86 percent) are having positive approach towards this brand.

Satisfaction and Factors Influencing Level of Satisfaction

The satisfaction level of individual is influenced by many independent factors such as: (1) Age (2) Formal education (3) Occupation (4) Family status (5) Monthly income (6) Residential status (7) Size of the family (8) Food habits (9) Period of usage (10) Frequency of purchase (11) Awareness about ingredients (12) Awareness about expiry date.

Age and Level of Satisfaction

The age of respondents range from 20 to 62 years. On the basis of age, respondents are classified into three categories; young those who up to 30 years, those who between 30 and 40 years of age as middle aged and old those who above 40 years. The classification of respondents based on age and their satisfaction index are presented in the following table.

Table 5
Age and Level of Satisfaction

	Level of Satisfaction			
Age Group	*Highly Satisfied*	*Satisfied*	*Dissatisfied*	*Total*
Young	30 (32%)	54 (57%)	10 (11%)	94 (100%)
Middle aged	16 (24%)	44 (66%)	7 (10%)	67 (100%)
Old	11 (28%)	23 (59%)	5 (13%)	39 (100%)
Total	57 (28%)	121 (61%)	22 (11%)	200

Degrees of Freedom = 4; Calculated value of χ^2 = 1.49; Table value at 5% level = 9.49

Table-5 envisages that the percentage of highly satisfied respondents is highest among young aged (32 percent) followed by other two groups. In case of satisfied respondents the percentage of satisfaction is higher for middle-aged group (66 percent). Further the percentage of dissatisfied respondents is found to be high among the old age group (13 percent). Hence no relationship is observed between age and level of satisfaction. The result of Chi-square test also proves that there is no significant relationship between the age group and level of satisfaction. The hypothesis is accepted because the calculated value of χ^2 is less than the table value.

Education Level and Level of Satisfaction

The education level of the respondents is another factor, which influences the satisfaction. The respondents range from illiterate to degree holders. On the basis of formal education, the respondents are classified as illiterate, school, under graduate and post graduate educated. The classification of respondents is based on their education level and satisfaction is presented in the following table.

Table 6
Education Level and Level of Satisfaction

	Level of Satisfaction			
Education level	*Highly Satisfied*	*Satisfied*	*Dissatisfied*	*Total*
Illiterate	10 (25%)	22 (55%)	8 (20%)	40 (100%)
School	21 (26%)	52 (63%)	9 (11%)	82 (100%)
UG	19 (32%)	36 (60%)	5 (8%)	60 (100%)
PG	6 (33%)	10 (56%)	2 (11%)	18 (100%)
Total	56 (28%)	120 (60%)	24 (12%)	200

Degrees of Freedom = 6; Calculated value of χ^2 = 4.04;Table value at 5% level = 12.59

According to Table-6, majority of the satisfied respondents (63 percent) are up to school level. The percentage of highly satisfied respondents is at high in both post graduate educated (33 percent) and under graduate educated (32 percent). Incase of dissatisfied respondents, illiterate are at high level (20 percent). Hence it is concluded that there is no significant relationship between education level and level of satisfaction expressed by the respondents. The result of the Chi-square test also in support of the findings as the hypothesis is accepted because the calculated value is less than the table value.

Occupation and Level of Satisfaction

The factors of job content may at times have an impact on the level of satisfaction. Occupation is classified into five groups namely agriculturists, housewives, professional, business and employed. The distribution of the respondents based on occupation and satisfaction index is presented in the following table.

Table 7
Occupation and Level of Satisfaction

Occupational Category	*Level of Satisfaction*			*Total*
	Highly Satisfied	*Satisfied*	*Dissatisfied*	
Agriculturists	6 (21%)	18 (62%)	5 (17%)	29 (100%)
Housewives	21 (26%)	47 (57%)	14 (17%)	82 (100%)
Professional	4 (18%)	17 (77%)	1 (5%)	22 (100%)
Business	6 (30%)	13 (65%)	1 (5%)	20 (100%)
Employment	18 (38%)	25 (53%)	4 (9%)	47 (100%)
Total	55 (27%)	120 (60%)	25 (13%)	200

Degrees of Freedom = 8; Calculated value of χ^2 = 9.49;Table value at 5% level = 15.51

Table-7 shows that the highest number of people i.e., professionals (77 percent) are satisfied when compared to the other categories while incase of highly satisfied respondents, the percentage is higher in employed category (38 percent) followed by business (30 percent) and housewives (26 percent). Among the percentage of dissatisfied respondents the housewives and agriculturists categories are more. Since the calculated value of the chi-square test is less than the table value, the hypothesis is accepted. Hence it is inferred that there is no significant relationship between occupation and level of satisfaction.

Type of Family and Level of Satisfaction

The development of individual proceeds under the influences of many socializing force and agencies from joint to nuclear families. The respondents are classified into two groups namely; nuclear and joint family. The classification of respondents based on family status and satisfaction index is presented below.

Table 8
Type of Family and Level of Satisfaction

Type of Family	*Level of Satisfaction*			*Total*
	Highly Satisfied	*Satisfied*	*Dissatisfied*	
Nuclear	43 (26%)	105 (64%)	15 (19%)	163 (100%)
Joint	10 (27%)	19 (51%)	18 (22%)	37 (100%)
Total	53 (26%)	124 (62%)	23 (12%)	200

Degrees of Freedom = 2; Calculated value of χ^2 = 4.88; Table value at 5% level = 5.99

As per the above table, a majority of the satisfied respondents (64 percent) belongs to the nuclear family type, while a higher percentage of the highly satisfied respondents (27 percent) and dissatisfied respondents (22 percent) belongs joint family. The hypothesis is accepted, since the calculated value is less than table value. Hence it is confirmed that there is no significant relationship between type of family and level of satisfaction.

Income and Level of Satisfaction

Wants and desires are based on income. Based on income, the respondents are classified into three categories, like low-income group (below Rs.10,000), moderate-income group (Rs.10,000 - Rs.20,000) and high income group (above Rs.20,000). The distribution of respondents based on income and satisfaction index is presented in the below table.

Table 9
Income and Level of Satisfaction

	Level of Satisfaction			
IncomeLevel	*Highly Satisfied*	*Satisfied*	*Dissatisfied*	*Total*
Low	24 (21%)	70 (60%)	23 (19%)	117 (100%)
Moderate	25 (37%)	36 (53%)	7 (10%)	68 (100%)
High	3 (20%)	11 (73%)	1 (7%)	15 (100%)
Total	52 (26%)	117 (59%)	31 (15%)	200

Degrees of Freedom = 4; Calculated value of χ^2= 54.81; Table value at 5% level = 9.49

Table-9 indicates that most of the satisfied respondents (73 percent) come under the category of the high-income group followed by low-income group (60 percent), while the highest percentage of the middle income group (37 percent) is expressed high satisfaction when compared to others. The high percentage of dissatisfied respondents (19 percent) belongs to the low-income group. Hence the level of satisfaction is influenced by the income level. Since the calculated value is higher than the table value, the hypothesis is rejected. Hence it is evident that there is a significant relationship between the income and satisfaction levels of the respondents.

Residential Status and Level of Satisfaction

Generally the expectations of the people residing in rural and urban differ with effect of product features, which in turn would affect the level of satisfaction. The respondents belong to urban and rural areas. The classification of respondents based on residential status and satisfaction index is presented in the table below.

Table 10
Residential Status and Level of Satisfaction

	Level of Satisfaction			
Place of Residence	*Highly Satisfied*	*Satisfied*	*Dissatisfied*	*Total*
Rural	17 (24%)	43 (62%)	10 (14%)	70 (100%)
Urban	39 (30%)	76 (58%)	15 (12%)	130 (100%)
Total	56 (28%)	119 (59%)	25 (13%)	200

Degrees of Freedom = 2; Calculated value of χ^2= 0.87; Table value at 5% level = 5.99

According to Table-10, majority of the highly satisfied respondents (30 percent) are residing in urban areas but high percentage (62 percent) in satisfied category is occupied by rural respondents. More percentage (14 percent) of the dissatisfied respondents belongs to rural area. The result of the chi-square test proves that there is no relationship between the residential status and the level of satisfaction.

Size of the Family and Level of Satisfaction

Depending upon the size of the family, the respondents are classified into three groups, small (upto 3 members), medium (4 and 5 members) and large families (6 and above). The distribution of respondents based on size of the family and satisfaction index is shown by the following table.

Table 11
Size of the Family and Level of Satisfaction

Size of the Family	*Level of Satisfaction* Highly Satisfied	Satisfied	Dissatisfied	*Total*
Small	17 (31%)	28 (52%)	9 (17%)	54 (100%)
Medium	28 (25%)	67 (59%)	18 (16%)	113 (100%)
Large	8 (25%)	60 (48%)	9 (27%)	33 (100%)
Total	53 (27%)	111 (55%)	36 (18%)	200

Degrees of Freedom = 4; Calculated value of $\chi^2 = 3.31$; Table value at 5% level = 9.49

Table-11 envisages that majority (59 percent) of the satisfied respondents belongs to the medium size family followed by the small size family respondents (52 percent) and the large family (48 percent). In the case of the more dissatisfied respondents (27 percent) comes under large size family. It is a strong support for diversification patterns because medium and small size families are interesting to enjoy with different variants of food products. Since the calculated value of the chi-square test is less than the table value, the hypothesis is accepted. Hence it is confirmed that there is no significant relationship between the size of family and satisfaction level of the respondents.

Food Habits and Level of Satisfaction

The food habit of the respondents is yet another factor which influences the satisfaction. On the basis of food habits, the respondents are classified as vegetarian and non-vegetarian. The distribution of respondents based on food habits and satisfaction index is presented in the table below.

Table 12
Food Habits and Level of Satisfaction

Food Habit	*Level of Satisfaction* Highly Satisfied	Satisfied	Dissatisfied	*Total*
Vegetarian	11 (24%)	27 (60%)	7 (16%)	45 (100%)
Non-Vegetarian	44 (28%)	90 (58%)	21 (14%)	155 (100%)
Total	58 (28%)	117 (58%)	28 (14%)	200

Degrees of Freedom = 2; Calculated value of $\chi^2 = 0.32$; Table value at 5% level = 5.99

It is evident from Table-12 that the percentage of the non-vegetarian category is higher than the vegetarian category regarding the highly satisfied. In general most of the respondents of both groups are satisfied with the eagle branded masala products. But it is concluded that there is no significant relationship between the food habits and level of satisfaction obtained by the respondents. The hypothesis is accepted because the calculated value is less than the table value.

Period of Usage and Level of Satisfaction

The period of usage of a product may at times have an impact on the level of satisfaction. The period of usage range from 1 year to 25 years. On the basis of period of usage, respondents are classified into three categories viz., upto 5 years is classified as short-period, 5-10 years as medium and more than 10 years as long-period. The classification of respondents based on the period of usage and satisfaction index is shown in the following table.

Table 13
Period of Usage and Level of Satisfaction

	Level of Satisfaction			
Period of Usage	*Highly Satisfied*	*Satisfied*	*Dissatisfied*	*Total*
Short Period	16 (28%)	34 (60%)	7 (12%)	57 (100%)
Medium Period	17 (28%)	35 (56%)	10 (16%)	62 (100%)
Long Period	22 (27%)	46 (57%)	13 (16%)	81 (100%)
Total	55 (28%)	115 (57%)	30 (15%)	200 (100%)

Degrees of Freedom = 4; Calculated value of χ^2 = 0.47; Table value at 5% level = 9.49

It is evident from Table-13 the higher percentage (60 percent) of the satisfied respondents comes under short-period usage. Both short and medium period's usage of respondents under highly satisfied are recorded same percentage of 28 and followed by long period usage (27 percent). It is evident that the diversification pattern in masala products of eagle brand attracts more and more new consumers. The hypothesis is accepted, since the calculated value of chi-square is less than the table value. Hence it is confirmed that there is no significant relationship between the period of usage and satisfaction level of the respondents.

Frequency of Purchase and Level of Satisfaction

The frequency of purchase is also an important factor to determine the level of satisfaction. Frequency of purchase is classified as weekly, monthly and as and when required. The distribution of respondents based on the frequency of purchase and satisfaction index is shown in the table below.

Table 14
Frequency of Purchase and Level of Satisfaction

	Level of Satisfaction			
Frequency of Purchase	*Highly Satisfied*	*Satisfied*	*Dissatisfied*	*Total*
Monthly	14 (30%)	23 (50%)	9 (20%)	46 (100%)
Weekly	18 (26%)	43 (61%)	9 (13%)	70 (100%)
As andwhen required	24 (29%)	49 (58%)	11 (13%)	84 (100%)
Total	56 (28%)	115 (58%)	29 (14%)	200

Degrees of Freedom = 4; Calculated value of χ^2 = 1.94 Table value at 5% level = 9.49

Table-14 shows that the percentage of highly satisfied respondents with monthly purchase is higher (30 percent) and followed by those (29 percent) who purchase the product as and when required. While the maximum (61 percent) of satisfied respondents (43) come under weekly purchase. Further a higher percentage of dissatisfied respondents (20 percent) fall under monthly category. Hence satisfaction level is not influenced by frequency of purchase. It is also proved by the result of chi-square analysis. The calculated value is less than the table value and hence the null hypothesis is accepted. A conclusion is so derived that there is no significant relationship between frequency of purchase and the level of satisfaction of the respondents.

Awareness about Ingredients and Level of Satisfaction

The awareness about ingredients of these products is another main factor, which influences the level of satisfaction. The respondents are classified into two groups according to their awareness on ingredients or contents of these products, such as those who are aware and those who are not aware.

Table 15
Awareness about Ingredients and Level of Satisfaction

Awareness about Ingredients	*Level of Satisfaction*			
	Highly Satisfied	*Satisfied*	*Dissatisfied*	*Total*
Aware	40 (32%)	70 (56%)	16 (12%)	126 (100%)
Not Aware	16 (22%)	46 (62%)	12 (16%)	74 (100%)
Total	56 (28%)	116 (58%)	28 (14%)	200

Degrees of Freedom = 2; Calculated value of χ^2 = 45.37; Table value at 5% level = 5.99

It is evident from Table-15, majority (88 percent) of highly satisfied and satisfied respondents are aware about the contents or ingredients of masala products whereas respondents who are not aware of the ingredients of these products are less satisfied and more dissatisfied (16 percent) than the awareness group. Since the calculated value of chi-square is higher than the table value the null hypothesis is rejected and it is concluded that there is a significant relationship between awareness about ingredients and level of satisfaction.

Awareness about Expiry Date and Level of Satisfaction

The awareness about expiry date is also one of the important factors, which influences the level of satisfaction. The respondents are classified into two groups according to the awareness about expiry date of masala products, such as those who are aware and not aware. The distribution of respondents based on their awareness about expiry date and satisfaction index is shown in the below table.

Table 16
Expiry Date and Level of Satisfaction

Awareness about Expiry Date	*Level of Satisfaction*			
	Highly Satisfied	*Satisfied*	*Dissatisfied*	*Total*
Aware	37 (33%)	58 (52%)	17 (15%)	112 (100%)
Not Aware	19 (22%)	45 (51%)	24 (27%)	88 (100%)
Total	56 (28%)	103 (51%)	41 (21%)	200

Degrees of Freedom = 2; Calculated value of χ^2 = 6.01; Table value at 5% level = 5.99

From Table-16 it is observed that the percentage of awareness in both satisfied (52 percent) and highly satisfied (33 percent) level respondents is higher than those who are not having any awareness about expiry date. It is evident that the unaware respondents are more dissatisfied (27 percent) than awareness respondents. The null hypothesis is rejected, since the calculated value is higher than the table value. Hence it is confirmed that there is certainly a significant relationship between awareness about expiry date and satisfaction level of the respondents.

CONCLUSION

From the analysis it is evident that out of 200 respondents, 34 percent are highly satisfied, 52 percent are satisfied and only 14 percent are dissatisfied with the Eagle brand masala products. However the overall analysis of the study indicates that majority of the respondents is satisfied with the Eagle brand masala products which have different variants of diversification pattern.

Further the research from analysis shows that there is a significant relationship between level of satisfaction and following factors: (1) Income (2) Awareness about ingredients and (3) Expiry date. However no significant relationship is proved between level of satisfaction and following factors: (1) Age (2) Education (3) Occupation (4) Family type (5) Residential status (6) Size of the family (7) Food habits (8) Period of usage and (9) Frequency of purchase.

SUGGESTIONS

The followings are the suggestions made on the findings of the analysis and informations are collected from respondents.

- The Eagle Food Products Company may introduce some variants of masala products in vegetarian category.
- People like to buy small size pouch packs for the every day purpose. This kind of pouch packs will reach people easily.
- The present advertisement covered by Eagle Food Products is inadequate. Television advertisement is effective one. So that company may consider this to promote the market size in rural areas.
- Some of respondents feel to change the brand because of non-availability of eagle products in all shops.
- High price of masala products is the major problem faced by the respondents. So it may be reduced to catch more consumers.
- The company may consider to avoid the artificial colour in some products.

REFERENCES

Anbumani. V. (1999), "A Study of Growth and Diversification Pattern in Small-Scale Bakery Industry", ICSSR-MRP, Bharathiar University, Coimbatore.

Barbara W Keats (1990), "Diversification and Business Economic Performance Revisited: Issues of Measurement and Causality", *Journal of Management*, Vol.16, No.1, pp.61-72.

Carol M. Michael (1999), "Opportunities for the Advancement of Home Economists in the Food Manufacturing Industry", *Family and Consumer Sciences Research Journal*, Vol.27, No.3, pp.293-319.

Cates, S.C. & Carter-Young, H. (2004), "Consumer Attitudes Towards and Preferences for Food Standards of Identify", *Journal of Food Products Marketing*, Vol.No.10 (1), pp.67-84.

Cynthia A. Montgomery (1985), "Product-Market Diversification and Market Power", *The Academy of Management Journal*, Vol.28, No.4, December, pp.789-798.

Ferdaus Hossain & Ruchi (2005), "Financial Structure, Production, and Productivity: Evidence from the U.S. Food Manufacturing Industry", Agricultural Economics, Vol.33, pp.399-410.

Gongming Qian (2002), "Multinationality, Product Diversification and Profitability of Emerging US Small and Medium-sized Enterprises", The Chinese University of Hong Kong, Vol.17, pp.611-633.

Jairus Banaji (1997), "Globalization and Restructuring in the Indian Food Industry", *The Journal of Peasant Studies*, Vol.24, No.1, pp.191-210.

Michael A. Hitt, Robert E. Hoskisson and Hicheon Kim (1997), "International Diversification: Effects on Innovation and Firm Performance in Product-Diversified Firms", *The Academy of Management Journal*, Vol.40, No.4, August, pp.767-798.

Michalis M. Efstratiadis (2000), "Implementation of ISO 9000 to the Food Industry: An Overview", *International Journal of Food Sciences and Nutrition*, Vol.51, pp. 459-473.

Mythili.G (1996), "Diversification of Enterprises: The Measurement Problem", Productivity, Vol.37, No.3, October-December.

Nandagopal, R. and Chinnaiyan, P (2004), "Small Scale Food Processing Industries: A Case Analysis", *Small Enterprises Development Management and Extension (SEDME) Journal*, Vol.31, No.2.

Omesh Saigal (2001), "Food Processing Industry: Current Scene and Prospectus", *Yojana*, Vol.45, No.1.

Phillp Kottler (1995), "Principles of Marketing", Prentice-Hall of India Pvt., New Delhi, p.553.

Prema.M. (2005), "Brand Loyalty and Product Satisfaction–A Case Study in Sakthi Trading Company (STC)", Unpublished M.Phil. Dissertation, Vellalar College for Woman, Erode.

Robert W. Ivester (2008), "Comprehensive Reviews in Food Science and Food Safety", *Comprehensive Reviews in Food Science and Food Safety*, Vol.7, pp.182-191.

Rumelt (1982), "Diversification Strategy and Performance", *Strategic Management Journal*, Vol.26 No.10, pp.967-985.

Sarin K.P. (1999), "Food Processing: An Introspection for the Next Millennium", *Processed Food Industry*, Vol.45, No.9.

Spyridon Mamalis (2009), "Critical Success Factors of the Food Service Industry", *Journal of International Food & Agribusiness Marketing*, Vol.21, pp.191-206.

Subramanian, K.K. and P. Mohanan, Pillai (1986), "Kerala's Industrial Backwardness: Exploration of Alternative Hypotheses", *Economic and Political Weekly*, Vol. XXI, No.14, pp.577-592.

Sukhpal Singh (1997), "Aspect of Entrepreneurship in Primary Food-Processing Industries in Punjab", *The Journal of Entrepreneurship*, Vol.6, No.2, pp.223-231.

Takahashi Kazuhito (2003), "Solutions for the Food Manufacturing Industry", *Fuji Electric Journal*, Vol.76, No.5, pp.271-276.

3

USERS' PREFERENCE FOR MOTOR PUMPS IN RURAL AREAS WITH REFERENCE TO COIMBATORE DISTRICT

R. Ganapathi, S. Anbumalar, M. Sivamani

INTRODUCTION

Agriculture plays a major role in India and continues to be central to all strategies of planned socio-economic development of the country. It contributes 27% to gross domestic product, sustains about 64% of livelihood, employs about 29% of the total work force, contributes 12% to the export and is a major source of income of the agrarian folk. Apart from this the major Indian industries like textile, sugar, jute etc., depend on the agriculture for their raw materials. In simple words, it is the life line of the Indian economy.

The growth of agriculture depends mainly on the various inputs like factors of production and others and their effective utilization in the process of the agriculture activities. The factors of production include land, labour, capital and organization and other inputs are in the form of seeds, fertilizers, manures, pesticides, water, power, machinery and cattle.

Among these inputs, water is the most important prerequisite for agricultural development. Water for agriculture is met by rain and rivers, canals and wells made available by means of bore wells and motor pumps. In India, agriculture continues to be a gamble with the monsoon. Vast areas in the country continue to be at the mercy of the monsoon. In certain areas where rains are not adequate or completely nil, there is a need for the construction of irrigation projects. So more importance is given by the government to the construction of major and minor irrigation projects during the plan periods because these irrigation projects help to utilize 40% of the utilizable water for the required irrigation.

Now-a-days due to failure of monsoon the possibility of normal flow into irrigation canals has been almost exhausted. Thus, there is a necessity for a shift in the areas where there is no flow of irrigation to construction of minor irrigated works such as tanks and wells and installation of water lifting devices. The technology of lifting water is not new in our country. In olden days people used different devices to take water from the ground level. It includes buckets and pots, then they used horses and buffaloes and slowly moved to the use of pumps and motors, an invention of new technology. The invention of pumps is a great advantage in a country like India which is not a water served country particularly, in Tamilnadu, where the western and southern parts are mostly affected by this problem.

ROLE OF AGRICULTURE

In India, agriculture is the largest and most important industry. It promotes the economic development of the country. Most of the industrialized nations of the present day world like UK, USA, Japan were once agricultural oriented. The increased agricultural production and productivity leads to increase in the income of the farmers. The increased income of the farmers will lead to more savings which can be used either for further development of the agriculture or the establishment and development of non-agricultural operations as well as industry. So the first and foremost role of agriculture is the promotion of economic progress in the country by enlarging the savings of the rural sector and making them available for the development of industries. Thus, the economic developments in general and industrial development in particular depend on agricultural development.

STATEMENT OF THE PROBLEM

Water is one of the indispensable inputs to agricultural production. In areas where rainfall is plentiful and well-distributed over the year, there is no problem of water. But rainfall in certain areas is very scanty as well as uncertain. Such areas constitute 40% of the cultivated area. In these areas provision of canal irrigation will support agriculture activities in an effective manner. These irrigation systems are jointly managed by the government and farmers. The responsibility of water distribution upto the outlet is in the hands of the government agency and the beneficiaries take over the responsibility after the outlet. Agriculturists also depend on pump set irrigation to a large extent in areas where there is no possibility of canal irrigation or in areas where water cannot be brought through canals because of the distance or other reasons. The pump set irrigation is widely concentrated in 5 States of the country viz., Andhra Pradesh, Karnataka, Tamil Nadu, Kerala and Maharashtra. The pump set irrigation in these 5 States cover 60% of the irrigated area in the country. If the farmers can get suitable pump sets to face the problems like drawing water from depth, to withstanding power instability etc., it would enable them to make use of the available water table efficiently and thereby increase the production, adding to the economic growth of the country. Thus, the researchers are taking up a study to understand the preference of agriculturists towards the type of motor pumps.

OBJECTIVES OF THE STUDY

The following are the specific objectives of the study.

1. To examine the awareness of the user towards the availability of various motor pumps.
2. To identify the brand preference of users of motor pumps.
3. To examine the factors influencing the user choice of particular motor pumps.
4. To study the problems faced by the users of motor pumps.

5. To find out the level of satisfaction towards the usage of motor pumps and
6. To offer suggestions to manufacturers to improve the quality and service of motor pumps.

SCOPE OF THE STUDY

The need for increasing agricultural production demands on increase in the cultivated area regardless of the water resources available for irrigation. Moreover efficient irrigation calls for getting more than one yield in a year. This necessitates the continued use of water by the agricultural sector. So there is a growing competition for water between the agricultural and non-agricultural sectors which has also increased the concern for the sustainability of the irrigated system. Water has thus become a limiting factor in many of the irrigation projects. The agriculturists have to depend on the technology developments in the form of motor pumps to minimize their water problems. So the use of pump sets to draw water continuously has become inevitable. The use of motor pumps for agricultural purpose has increased the socio- economic condition of the agriculturists in the area. Moreover, the decrease in the ground water level and untimely rain necessitates the use of different pumps sets to draw water efficiently. So the researchers have chosen the Coimbatore District to study the preference of motor pumps by the agriculturalists.

METHODOLOGY

As far as this research work is concerned, descriptive study is considered to be the most appropriate to understand the preference towards motor pumps. Hence, the present study is based on primary data and secondary data which would make the research work more analytical. For the purpose, an interview schedule relevant to the requirements of the study has been prepared. The suggestions of the study emerge from the inferences drawn from the sample survey towards the selected people. The primary data is gathered through the random sampling survey method. The structured interview schedule was administered to collect the respondent's preference towards motor pumps. The schedule is designed to gather data relating to the users personal data, their preferences and level of satisfaction in using the motor pumps and also the factors influencing the choice of a particular motor pump. The study also depends on secondary data from the text books of related topics, journals, magazines, news papers, websites, etc.

SAMPLING

For the purpose of the present study, the researchers have selected the ten villages situated in Coimbatore district. Coimbatore District is a multifaced one having industrial and commercial activities apart from agriculture. Even though commercial activities are largely taken up in Coimbatore, agricultural also form a major part of the activity of the people. Out of the total geographical area of 3,42,949 hectares, nearly 1,99,279 acres are used for different agricultural purpose. The major crops in the area are coconut, sugarcane, paddy, cotton and groundnut.

The Coimbatore district comes under Siruvani and Pillur belt. The villages located in Coimbatore district including many villages are getting water from the rivers and canals using motor pumps to their areas and from the wells. For the purpose of drawing water, the agriculturists make use of different motor pumps based on the length from which water is brought from canals, the available ground water etc. This requirement for different types of motor pumps used by the agriculturists in the area inclined the researchers to take up a study on the preference of the motor pumps by the user in the area. As the study involves the use of motor pumps by the agriculturist, a sample of 300 agriculturists who use motor pumps to draw water for agriculture purposes was selected. The study covers a period from June 2009 to November 2009. The collected data were classified according to their personal profile with the help of frequency table. Statistical tools such as Descriptive analysis. Chi -square analysis, Average rank analysis and Average score analysis were used to analyze the data.

LIMITATIONS OF THE STUDY

Utmost care and effort have been taken by the researchers to avoid faults and short coming in the process of data collection. In spite of such care and effort, the study is prone to some limitations which are mentioned below:

1. The findings of the study depend purely on the responses given by the sample respondents.
2. The tools used in this study have its own limitations and
3. Generalization cannot be made.

ANALYSIS AND INTERPRETATION OF DATA

The results of the analysis of the collected data are presented under different heads.

Profile of the Sample Respondents

The Table 1 describes the gender-wise classification of the sample respondents in the selected study area.

Table 1
Gender-wise Classification of the Respondents

Gender	*Number of Respondents*	*Percentage*
Male	253	84.33
Female	47	15.67
Total	300	100.00

Source: Primary Data

It is clear from the table above that out of the 300 respondents 84.33 are males and the rest are female. It means that the male members are deciding the type of pumps required for irrigation. Female members are not worry about the pumps than male members. Moreover, male members are visiting the shops where pumps are available and make enquiry about the pumps.

Table 2
Age Group of the Respondents

Age Group	*Number of Respondents*	*Percentage*
Below 20 years	19	6.33
20 - 40 years	125	41.67
Above 40 years	156	52.00
Total	300	100.00

Source: Primary Data

It is clear from the table that, 52% of the respondents come under the age group of 40 years and above. It means that young generation is ready accept the views of elders with regard to buying of motor pumps for irrigation. In other words, lower age groups of respondents are deputing their parents to buy motor pumps. Hence, majority of the respondents are having the age of above 40 years.

Table 3
Educational Qualification of the Respondents

Education	*Number of Respondents*	*Percentage*
Illiterate	96	32.00
School Level	106	35.33
Graduate	59	19.67
Post Graduate	30	10.00
Others	9	3.00
Total	300	100.00

Source: Primary Data

It is clear from the above table that 35.33% of the respondents have school level education. It means that majority of the respondents are doing cultivation soon after their completion of school education. If anybody enters higher education, they do not prefer the cultivation at the maximum. Moreover, less educated people find difficulty to search any other job than cultivation.

Table 4
Annual Income of the Respondents

Annual Income	*Number of Respondents*	*Percentage*
Below Rs.1,00,000	72	24.00
Rs.1,00,000 – Rs.2,00,000	137	45.67
Rs.2,00,000 – Rs.3,00,000	56	18.67
Above Rs.3,00,000	35	11.66
Total	300	100.00

Source: Primary Data

The above table shows that, out of the total respondents 45.67% of the respondents belong to the income level of Rs.1,00,000 to Rs.2,00,000. It shows that agriculture does not give more return to farmers. Hence, majority of the respondents are earning upto Rs.2,00,000 per annum. Moreover, the farmers are unable to fix the price for their produce. Hence, it is very difficult to earn more as businessmen.

Table 5
Area of Land Possessed by the Respondents

Area of Land Possessed	*Number of Respondents*	*Percentage*
Below 5 acre	112	37.33
5 - 10 acre	130	43.33
10 acres & above	58	19.34
Total	300	100.00

Source: Primary Data

Table 6
Brands of Motor Pumps Used by the Respondents

Type of brand of motor pumps	*Number of respondents*	*Percentage*
CRI Pumps	42	14.00
TEXMO Pumps	110	36.67
Sharp Pumps	35	11.67
Suguna Pumps	57	19.00
Aqua Pumps	47	15.66
Others (specify)	9	3.00
Total	300	100.00

Source: Primary Data

The above table shows that 36.67% of the respondents are using Texmo Pumps. It means that Texmo pumps are available in every area. This company gave more number of dealership than other companies. Hence, the farmers did not find any difficulty to buy the Texmo pumps. Therefore, it is inferred that Texmo pumps is preferred by many respondents when compared with other pumps.

HYPOTHESIS-1

The personal factors of the respondents have no significant influence on the type of motor pumps purchased.

Table 7
Personal Factors and Types of Motor Pump Purchased

Personal Factors	*Chi square Value*	*Table Value*	*Significant/Not significant*
Sex	2.963	7.81	Not significant
Age Group	6.386	12.59	Not significant
Educational Status	65.123	21.03	Significant
Annual Income	98.942	16.92	Significant

Source: Primary Data

It is evident from the table that the null hypothesis is rejected (significant) in two cases "Educational status and annual income" and in other two cases "sex and age" the null hypothesis is accepted (Not significant). It is concluded that Educational Status and Annual Income are having significant influence on the type of Motor Pumps purchased. Both male and female respondents are equally preferring all brands of motor pumps. Likewise, all levels of age group of respondents are liking all brands of motor pumps. But, the levels of education of respondents change the preference of motor pumps. Likewise, the annual income of the respondents is also playing a vital role in deciding the type of motor pumps.

HYPOTHESIS-2

The personal factors of the respondents have no significant influence on the factors considered in purchasing the motor pumps.

It is evident from the table that the null hypothesis is rejected in three cases viz., Age, Educational Status, and Annual Income and in the case sex the null hypothesis is accepted. Personal factors of respondents i.e. age, educational status and annual income have significant relationship with factors of purchase of motor pumps. It is concluded that

Table 8
Personal Factors and the Factors for the Purchase

Personal Factors	*Chi square Value*	*Table Value*	*Significant / Not significant*
Sex	2.463	7.81	Not significant
Age	17.319	15.51	Significant
Educational Status	65.175	26.3	Significant
Annual Income	38.379	21.03	Significant

Source: Primary Data

Age, Educational Status and Annual Income have significant influence on the factors considered for the purchase of the motor pumps. Both male and female respondents are equally influenced by all the factors of purchase of motor pumps.

HYPOTHESIS-3

The personal factors of the respondents have no significant influence on the source of knowledge.

Table 9
Personal Factors and Sources of Knowledge

Personal Factors	*Chi square Value*	*Table Value*	*Significant / Not significant*
Sex	1.0452	7.81	Not significant
Age	4.516	12.59	Not Significant
Educational Status	45.664	21.03	Significant
Annual Income	11.748	16.92	Not Significant

Source: Primary Data

It is clear from the table that the personal factors Sex, Age and Annual Income have no significant influence over the source of knowledge and so the null hypothesis is accepted. It means that both male and female respondents, all the age group and annual income group of the respondents are getting information about motor pumps in all the channels. Educational status shows that there is the significant influence over the source of awareness and so the null hypothesis is rejected. It means that level of education of the respondents is forcing to select the channels to collect the information.

HYPOTHESIS-4

Personal factors of the respondents have no significant influence on the choice of capacity of the Motor Pumps.

Table 10
Personal Factors and Capacity of the Motor Pumps

Personal Factors	*Chi square Value*	*Table Value*	*Significant / Not significant*
Sex	5.706	7.81	Not significant
Age	5.757	12.59	Not Significant
Educational Status	17.032	21.03	Not Significant
Annual Income	40.539	16.92	Significant

Source: Primary Data

It is evident from the table that null the hypothesis is rejected (Significant) in the case of annual income and the null hypothesis is accepted (Not significant) in other three cases viz., sex, age and educational status it is rejected. It means that all capacity motor pumps are preferred by both male and female respondents, all level of age group and educational status of the respondents. But, annual incomes of the respondents significantly influence the choice of capacity of the motor pumps. It means that high income group of respondents are preferring high capacity of the motor pumps and vice versa.

Table 11
Brand of Motor Pumps Possessed and Level of Satisfaction

Brand or Motor pumps	*Highly satisfied*	*Satisfied*	*Average*	*Dissatisfied*	*Highly Dissatisfied*	*Total*	*Average score*
CRI Pumps	5	14	10	6	7	42	3.095
Texmo Pumps	12	70	20	4	4	110	3.781
Sharp Pumps	10	10	4	2	9	35	3.285
Suguna Pumps	5	18	12	9	13	57	2.877
Aqua Pumps	3	24	6	9	5	47	3.234
Others (specify)	-	7	1	-	1	9	3.555
Total	35	143	53	30	39	300	-

Source: Primary Data

It is hereby understood from the above table that the respondents have high level of opinion regarding Texmo pumps and it is followed by Suguna pumps, other category, sharp pumps, aqua pumps and CRI, pumps. It is concluded that the respondents selected for the study have high level of opinion towards Texmo pumps and it is mostly preferred by them.

Table 12
Average Rank - Factors of Pump

Factors	*Average Rank*	*Final Rank*
Compactness	2.713	2
Price	2.806	3
Quality	1.856	1
After Sales Service	3.880	5
Durability	3.410	4

Source: Primary Data

It is evident from the table that the respondents of the study have given first rank for quality, second rank for compactness, third for price and so on. It is concluded that the respondents have given top priority for quality than the other factors of pumps in the purchase of motor pumps.

SUGGESTIONS

1. The pump manufactures should take research activities to reduce the cost of pumps thereby ensuring its availability at a cheaper rate.
2. They have to undertake periodic survey to know the need of the agriculturist in terms of design, capacity etc.

3. The pump manufactures have to use effective advertisement media to reach the agriculturists.
4. Steps should also be taken by the pump manufacturers to rectify the complaints reported in an effective way and
5. The manufactures may take initiatives to make available their own people in their areas where their products are being used to ensure immediate and effective service facilities required by the users of pumps.

CONCLUSION

Both the Central government and State governments are giving great impetus to the green revolution by way of rural electrification, development of ground water resources for irrigation, credit facilities to the farmers for purchase of pumps and so on. They give a broad impression to the pump manufacturers that the demand for varieties of pumps continues to increase. So the pump manufactures are under compulsion to understand as to what is the need of the agriculturists based on the nature of land, crop, and level of ground level water. Hence, they have to take initiatives to fulfill the requirements of the agricultural sector thereby improving the standard of agriculture, themselves and the economy of the country.

REFERENCES

Arya I. C, "*Production Function Estimates for Pump Set Units in Coimbatore*", Indian Journal of Industrial Relations, No. 20, July 1, p. 83.

Eresh. K. (1980), "*Problems of Small-Scale Industries*" Economic and Political Weekly, No. 18 (40), June 1, p. 21.

Khark and Ali (1982), "*Development of Small Scale and Cottage Industries*", Southern Economist, No. 30 (10), August 15, p. 47.

Michael Cartillier (1975), "*Role of Small-Scale Industry in Economic Development: Irrigation Pump Set Industry in Coimbatore*" Economic and Political Weekly, No. 44 & 45, November 1, p. 1734 .

Prema G.R. (1985), "*Financial Analysis in Pump Sets and Motor Manufacturing Industries*", Economic and Political Weekly, No. 20 (41), October 12, pp. 2011-2015.

Reddy (1982), "*Financing Pump Sets in Farm Economy Its Impact on Profitability*", Southern Economist, No. 21 (2), May 15.

Tarun T.N.S (1986), "*Small-Scale Industries and India's Economic Development*", Ashish Publishing House, New Delhi, pp. 37-40.

4

COMPREHEND BRAND ARCHITECTURE IN FMCG SECTOR IN INDIA

Savanam Chandra Sekhar, B.V.H. Kameswara Sastry, L.P. Singh

INTRODUCTION

A successful brand is the most valuable resource to a company and incorporates aesthetic product attributes such as years of advertising, goodwill, quality evaluation, product experience. Apposite use of branding can make the launch of a new product or service, and accelerate the growth of a mature product. Branding plays a pivotal role in a firm's growth. Strong brands help in establishing the firm's identify in the market place and develop a solid customer franchise (Aaker, 1996; Kapferer, 1997; Keller, 1998). A strong brand name can also provide the basis for brand extensions, which further strengthen the firm's position in the marketplace as well as potentially enhance the brand's value (Aaker and Keller, 1990). Brands generally fail because: they become stale as customer needs or preferences change over time; they become clouded by haphazard product extensions; or their marketing fails to resonate with the targeted customer group. Correctly defining your brand essence and supporting it with clear brand architecture is critical to long-lasting success. While brand architecture must evolve and product lines should expand (or contract) over time as the market changes, brand essence must remain constant as the core value for which the particular product or service is sought out.

As consumers' lives become more complicated, rushed, and time-served, the ability of a brand to simplify decision making and reduce risk is invaluable. Brands communicate the reasons why a customer should purchase a specific item. They make claims and set expectations their products have to fulfill. Brands can be a powerful source of competitive advantage. Harley-Davidson, Apple Computers, Nike, and Coca-Cola have built superior success with brands that enjoy loyal–at times fiercely loyal–customers. Many brands, however, fail to achieve or maximize/maintain brand loyalty and recognition. Marketing of such a brand may have failed to resonate with customers. Keeping current with market trends and staying competitive in the face of new market entrants may have proven challenging for the brand. Attempts at brand extension may have been unsuccessful due to the haphazard nature of the brand's approach to expansion. The brand's identity may be ill-defined, with a myriad of marketing messages, product introductions, and customer experiences having joined together over time to create perceptions of the brand and its key competitors. While there are a number of possible reasons for a brand's limited success, a common root cause lies at the heart of these brand issues – the failure of management to construct a brand hierarchy that will foster brand equity with customers. Management fails to thoughtfully establish the brand's essence and to support the brand's essence with brand and product line architecture and brand marketing. In order for managers to construct a brand hierarchy successfully, they must understand the needs of and purchasing decisions employed by their customers and segment their customers accordingly. Conducting a systematic, disciplined examination of the effectiveness of perceptions of the brand and its product structures is fundamental to achieving this understanding and segmentation. Three interrelated tasks are at the center of this process: understanding customer needs; reviewing the brand hierarchy; and, examining the current and future product line architecture. The following is a detailed discussion of these tasks and the competitive advantage that can be achieved with an effective brand hierarchy.

Stanley Moss has defined in the Global Brand Trends that – How an organization structures and names brands within its portfolio. There are three main types of brand architecture systems: monolithic, where the corporate name is used on all products and services offered by the company; endorsed, where all sub-brands are linked to the corporate brand by means of either a verbal or visual endorsement; and freestanding, where the corporate brand operates mainly as a holding company, and each product or service is individually branded for its target market.

CONSTITUENTS OF BRAND ARCHITECTURE

David Aaker, in his book Brand Leadership accentuated the aspect with – "Brand Architecture is an organizing structure of the brand portfolio that specifies the brand roles and the relationships among brands and different product market brand context. Brand architecture is defined by five dimensions – the brand portfolio, portfolio roles, product market context roles, the portfolio structures and portfolio graphics".

Apart from brand portfolio, Aaker added that decentralized groups those have little feel or care about total brand portfolio may damage it by adding brands too promiscuously. The portfolio decisions are crucial and require contemplation on the part of brand champions or product managers. Both addition in the portfolio or pruning may determine the destiny of the company. Aaker also described the concern for portfolio roles viz. Strategic Brands, Linchpin brands, Silver Bullets and Cash Cow Brands. Further, the Product-Market Context Roles have undeniable vitality in Brand architecture of the organization. Product-Market Context roles broadly involves the decisions pertaining to the Endorser and sub-brands roles, benefit brands, Co-Brands and Driver role of Brands.

Brand Architecture is a powerful tool that can help companies better organize various brands within their business portfolios and focus on strategic goals for individual brands. Doing so has enabled more effective and consistent brand management and helped put an increased focus on strategies to meet specific growth, sales, and profit goals for individual brands. Brand Portfolio structure is also an important constituent for Brand Architecture which involves the concerns for Brand Groupings, Brand Hierarchy Trees and Brand Range Logos and Visual presentations have unique contributions in Brand architecture and eventually brand building. Companies are cautious about their portfolio graphics and choosy about colour schemes. Coca-Cola, Kodak, UPS, Fuji, Unilever, Wipro and Pepsi are few among the corporate, believe colour scheme is vital component in their brand building exercise and they benefited because of their logo and portfolio graphics. Effective and wise use of the five constituents of Brand architecture may result in powerful brands; help the company in optimal allocation of brand building resources. The poise brand architecture components also facilitate the company in synergy creating by good visibility, proper association building and efficiency. In addition, a proper brand architecture deliberate clarity of offerings from the company side and give little room to bewildering situations from the customer perspective. Proper Brand Architecture facilitates the leveraging brand assets and also provides the platform to the company for its future growth.

BRAND ARCHITECTURE –CORPORATE CONCERN

Today, most brand architecture efforts focus on either the past-rectifying problems caused by a lack of defined brand roles and inconsistent brand-building or acquisition strategies- or the present-organizing brands to best meet short-term objectives. Further, brand architecture is primarily treated as an internal exercise aimed at defining brand "territories," where brands are viewed as separate and distinct and are managed independently rather than collectively. The customer perspective is rarely included in the process. Finally, most brand architecture decisions still tend to be highly subjective and driven more by emotional sentiment and baggage than by rational, data-based judgment. Truly effective brand architecture focuses on managing brands collectively and unearthing inherent synergies to increase the collective value of the brand portfolio. When approached in this manner, brand architecture goes from being a simple yet valuable organization tool to becoming a forward-looking strategic weapon. This requires a few key elements:

- Viewing brand architectures not as hierarchical and static, but as dynamic and evolving.
- Identifying and understanding the customer-based inter-relationships of various brands within the portfolio.
- Fundamentally shifting the role and objectives of brand management away from individual brands and toward the collective value of the portfolio.

BRAND ARCHITECTURE – GLOBALIZATION IMPACT

Globalization causes the firms operating in different sectors finding new benchmarks in the same journey. A firm's brand architecture is continually evolving (Susan Douglas and C. Samuel Craig, April 2002). As it enters in new countries or markets, acquired brands are integrated into the architecture, new brand extensions or product lines are added, and positioning may be modified or radically changed. Proliferation of media, increasing promotional cost due to fragmentations of markets and the trend towards globalization cause brand architecture subject to pressures at both the corporate and product level to become more cost effective and better integrated across country markets. As a result, increasingly complex brand structures are beginning to emerge, characterized by corporate endorsement of product brands in order to consolidate branding structure and by extension of strong brands across countries and product businesses so as to achieve cost economies.

BRAND ARCHITECTURE -CUSTOMER CONCERN

Customer is the key concern for the corporate brand architecture. For understanding the same, lets cut the long story in to short; one fine day customer X was choosing the product from the shelves for his/her monthly grocery; the customer visualized a new variant of reputed food brand but didn't pick up the brand. At the same time, she found a new Sauce brand launched by the regional company and she picked the brand. The crux of the story is we cannot understand this behavior of the customer and that is why it is very important to understand the customer. The reality is that customers – who are the ultimate arbiters of a brand's success or failure – don't experience brands in the neat, organized way they are typically portrayed on an organizational chart. Instead, they experience brands inter-dependently and differently over time. Effective brand architecture doesn't just take the customer brand experience into account; they are based upon it. For knowing the same thing in this paper, the researcher tried to understand the brand architecture constituents with some of the FMCG products in the Indian context.

OBJECTIVE OF THE STUDY

The main objective of the study is to understand the phenomenon call – comprehend brand architecture in FMCG sector in India. Plethora of variants from different marketers is available in the market so far as the FMCG sector is concerned. Some of the companies face problem due to promiscuous brand portfolio and some others are perplexed because of umbrella or master brand. The only way to rid from the situation is proper understanding of the one's own brand architecture vis-à-vis competitor and painstaking exercise in context of, brand portfolio. Again, tremendous transformation has been witnessed by Indian economy in the last decade and the consumers-choices become contemporary. In the same line researcher effort to understand the brand preference for five categories viz. Tooth paste, Bath soap, Detergent powder, Shampoo and Chocolate (Confectioneries) is not in vain.

METHODOLOGY

Here under exploratory design extensive literature review is performed by the researcher and in the light of this study, objectives have been developed. The researchers feel that for appropriate justification to the title, it is necessary to conduct primary survey of youngsters, housewives and males performing buying activities Interviewing both the groups from Vijayawada city and surrounding areas has collected cross section data. Due to time constraint, the survey is limited to Vijayawada city and by non-probability–convenience-sampling method. Total 256 respondents have been surveyed. The questionnaire was printed in English and it is an interviewers-administered questionnaire. It included open ended as well as close-ended questions. For the sake of ensuring validity and reliability cronbach-á has been calculated for the scale.

RATIONAL FOR SELECTING THE CATEGORIES AND COMPANIES IN THE RESEARCH

In India, there is fierce competition between the players who operate in Tooth paste, Bath soap, Detergent powder, Shampoo and Chocolate (Confectioneries) categories and at the same thing is true for their global operations also. Effective implementation of brand architecture becomes possible when companies understand and devise their strategies in line with competitors. In Indian scenario, HUL, P&G, Nestle, Cadbury, Colgate-Palmolive, Godrej, Dabur, Wipro, Cavin Kare, Nirma, Paras Pharmaceuticals are major players who constantly fight for increasing their pie in terms of market share. All these players have multiple product-line and brands in their Indian operation. The researchers tried to understand the brand preference for five categories of FMCG products and retrieved the responses from the respondents in a manner; which throw light on the brand architecture of the particular companies.

BRANDS USED BY CUSTOMERS FOR TOOTH PASTE AND RELEVANT FACTS

Respondents were asked about the brand of Tooth Paste they are using and recalling other brands and the name of the companies which manufacture and market them. The outcome was eye-opening. The question was asked to the respondents with deliberation of knowing the usage, awareness and recall of the brands available in tooth paste category.

Table 1 reveals the fact about tooth-paste used by respondents and 1.2 divulges facts about brand recall and correct company name recall by the respondents respectively. Colgate is used by 45.34%, Pepsodent is used by 21.46%, Close-up is used by 10.98% of respondents, Anchor is used by 7.03% and Dabur is used by 3.52% of respondents. Glister of Amway is used by 1.23% of respondents, Cibaca is used by .91% of respondents and 7.75% of respondents do not use tooth-paste and did not respond. Again table 1.2 indicates the respondents who recalled the brands in tooth-paste category and the companies which manufacture them and the situation is astonishing. One brand was recalled by 6.98% of the respondents, two by 16.52%, three by 26.88%, four by 25.32% and five brands were recalled by 24.30% of respondents. The average recall in tooth paste category is 3.340 brands which indicate the mind space available from the respondent's side for the tooth-paste category. At the outset, the situation is worst in recalling the name of the company. One company name was correctly recalled by 19.82%, two companies' names were correctly recalled by 13.97% of respondents, three companies' names were correctly recalled by only 5.63% of respondents, five companies' name were correctly recalled by 0.57% of respondents and none of the respondents were recalled four companies' correct name. Apart from average company recall in tooth-paste category, .69companies divulge the fact about lack of awareness of respondents in context of manufacturing and marketing companies. Again if we consider the companies then Colgate's at least one brand is recalled in 93.78% of cases, HUL's at least one brand is recalled in 82.84% instances while Dabur's at least one brand is recalled in 45.34% of instances. Now these facts are evident Colgate's good brand architecture followed by HUL and to certain extent Dabur which has been supported by its acquisition of Balsara Group. But still there is lot of room for improvement in HUL and Dabur's brand architecture for its tooth-paste category. Colgate has its variants with Colgate-Gel and its rejuvenation of Cibaca and Colgate has done co-branding with highlight of Colgate-Cibaca. In upper price, Colgate perfectly suits while with lower-price of Colgate-Cibaca, it has perfect architecture (200gm Colgate-Rs.52, Colgate-Cibaca

Rs.27). Pepsodent have variants like Pepsodent Whitening, Pepsodent Complete, Pepsodent Fresh and Pepsodent Germi-Check. In case of HUL, it does not have any low-price variant in tooth-paste category. The company may suffer due to this in future because bottom of pyramid may have definite space in India. Again, it becomes evident that respondents know little about the companies and they heavily rely on individual brands.

Table 1
Brands Used by Respondents

Tooth-paste Brand	*Used by Respondents in %*
Colgate	45.34
Pepsodent	21.46
Close-up	10.98
Anchor	7.03
Meswak	1.78
Cibaca	.91
Glister	1.23
Dabur	3.52
Do not use Tooth Paste	7.75

Source: Computed from Primary Data

Table 2
Effective Brand and Company Recall

Brand Recall		*Company Recall (Correct Name)*	
No. of Brands Recalled by Respondents	*% of Respondents*	*No. of Companies Recalled by Respondents*	*% of Respondents*
6.98	1	19.82	
16.52	2	13.97	
26.88	3	5.63	
25.32	4	0	
24.30	5	.57	
No brand recall	0	No company recall	60.01

Source: From Primary Data

BRANDS USED BY CUSTOMERS FOR BATH SOAP AND RELEVANT FACTS

Respondents were asked about the brand of Bath Soap which they used and recalled the other soap brands and the name of the companies which manufacture and market them. The following responses have been obtained:

Table 3
Bath Soap Brand and User Esponse

Bath Soap Brand	*Used by Respondents in %*
Lux	28.95
Lifebuoy	8.31
Santoor	2.62
Rexona	6.28
Pears	3.82
Dove	3.98
Dyna	2.26

Contd.

Bath Soap Brand	*Used by Respondents in %*
Fairglow	2.28
No.1	0.83
Breeze	0.81
Hamam	1.48
Liril	1.49
Dettol	7.89
Cinthol	7.43
Person	0.81
Nirma	3.34
Jo	0.76
Aloevera	0.77
Chandan	0.84
Savlon	0.75
Margo	1.65
Mysore Sandal	1.44
Not responded	11.21

Source: Computed from Primary Data

It is apparent from the Table 3 that HUL brands have considerable proliferation in bath soap market, while Godrej, Wipro and Anchor require some meticulous work in bath soap category. Lifebuoy occupies second place so far as individual brand usage of bath soap is concerned, as if most of rural consumers are price conscious. All HUL bath soap brand usage accounts for 48.57%, which indicate the strong position of HUL in this category. At the same time, it is indicative that Lux has commendable 28.58% of share in brand usage while other 8 HUL brands carry 19.53% market share only. So here, HUL requires scrupulous work on power branding and eventually brand architecture. We can find that there is lot of brands which accounts for less than 1% in terms of brand usage. There is tremendous clutter in bath soap categories so marketers need to undertake painstaking exercise for sustainable growth. The following table reveals the fact about brand and company recall for bath soap category in India.

Table 4
Compant and Brand Recall

Bath Soap Brand Recall		*Company Recall (Correct Name)*	
No. of Brands Recalled by Respondents	*% of Respondents*	*No. of Companies Recalled by Respondents*	*% of Respondents*
1	1.49	1	25.41
2	13.34	2	13.93
3	17.25	3	3.22
4	28.01	4	3.79
5	38.20	5	2.64
6	1.23	6	0
No brand recall	.48	No company recall	51.01

Source: Computed from Primary Data

The situation is obvious again, respondents were comfortably recalled brands but company recall was again emerging as a problematic area. Bath soap category is flooded with lot of regional and national brands, so 38.20% of respondents can recall five brands, while 28.01% can recall four brands, 17.25% can recall three brands and 13.34% can recall two brands. Again, in bath-soap, respondents have substantial choices and according to seasons they use bath soap and do not mind experimentation. Average brand recall for bath-soap category is 3.967 (approx 4 brands) which clearly shows the respondents awareness and preference. Yet, it is quite possible that the new entrant can occupy mind space of the customer. Again, for company recall the fact is daunting, only .895 (approx 1 company name) can recall bath-soap company. Thus, further it becomes apparent that stand alone strong brand can make mark in the market and may enjoy substantial sales.

BRANDS USED BY CUSTOMERS FOR DETERGENT POWDER AND RELEVANT FACTS

Respondents were asked about the brand of Detergent Powder which they use and recall the other detergent powder brands and the name of the companies which manufacture and market them are as follows:

Table 5
Detergent Powder Brand and Respondents Response

Detergent Powder Brand	*Used by Respondents in %*
Wheel	18.81
Surf (Variants)	13.97
Rin	4.01
Nirma	31.96
Tide	7.26
Ariel	3.92
Ghadi Detergent	1.63
S & A	0.69
Not Responded	17.75

Research reveals the fact that 31.96% of respondents use Nirma in detergent powder category followed by Wheel with 18.81% usage, Surf with 13.97%, Tide with 7.26%, Ariel with 3.92%, Rin with 4.01% and Ghadi detergent with 1.63% brand usage. Nirma has strong brand image so apparently it rules the category. P&G aggressively focused on the category when they have launched Tide in India and in 2005, the detergent powder was at culmination. HUL suffers because of aggressive marketing by P&G supported by its good brand architecture. But if we observe consolidated figures of HUL brands then, 36.79% of respondents are using Wheel, Surf and Rin brands. P&G brands are used by 11.18% respondents in detergent powder category which comprise Tide and Ariel brands. P&G is rapidly emerging with Tide brands and it has beaten HUL's brand in several places and categories. Nirma's brand share will also suffer because of fierce competition between HUL and P&G. Ghadi detergent from Kanpur is also emerging rapidly and becoming the National Brand with considerable market share. Hipolin detergent almost lost its image among customers and its market share.

It is apparent from the Table 6 that respondents can recall 3, 4 and 5 brands and their percentage proportion almost resembles with 24.03% can recall 3, 24.98% can recall 4 and 23.56% can recall 5 brands. The average brand recall in detergent powder category is 3.382 brands which are quite near to other personal care items. Company name recall is again the concern due to the fact that only .608 companies recalled by the respondents. So it is apparent that the respondents even could not recall one company. In case of P&G, they have to promote their brands as product brand while HUL due to its name and logo change faces problem in corporate identity issues. One company is recalled by 34.97% of respondents, two by only 7.93%, three companies recalled by 2.45% and four by .79%, while 53.86% could not recall a single company. In detergent powder, promoting product brand makes sense for the marketer and if the company uses its power brand for the category, it can get extra edge in the market.

Table 6

Detergent Powder Brand Recall		*Company Recall (Correct Name)*	
No. of Brands Recalled by Respondents	*% of Respondents*	*No. of Companies Recalled by Respondents*	*% of Respondents*
1	4.74	1	34.97
2	19.96	2	7.93
3	24.03	3	2.45
4	24.98	4	0.79
5	23.56	5	0
No brand recall	2.73	No company recall	53.86

BRANDS USED BY CUSTOMERS FOR SHAMPOO (HAIR CARE CATEGORY) AND RELEVANT FACTS

Respondents were asked about the brand of Shampoo which they use and recall the other shampoo brands and the name of the companies which manufacture and market them. The following responses have been obtained:

Table 7

Shampoo Brands	*Used by Respondents in %*
Clinic Plus	16.01
Clinic All Clear	5.03
Sunsilk	9.72
Chik	3.86
Rejoice	0
Head & Shoulders	7.01
Pantene	1.48
Clinic 2 in 1	0.69
Dove	0.84
Garnier	1.52
Nyle	0.74
Asharam's Ashram's brand	0.76
Not Mentioned	52.34

It is really astonishing that half of the respondents did not respond to the question or were reluctant to say anything about the usage of their shampoo brands. The HUL brands rule the shampoo category; say for the sake Clinic Plus is used by 16.01% of respondents followed by Sunsilk used by 9.72%, Clinic All Clear is used by 5.03%. From the total responses obtained (47.66%), HUL brands of shampoo command 31.85% of market share. P&G brands have 8.78% of market share. Head & Shoulder became very popular and acceptable, while Pantene and Rejoice are gaining the ground. Cavin Kare's brands have 4.83% of brand usage, among which Chik is heading the ground. L'oreal's Garnier brand is becoming popular in the upper segment. The following table divulges the facts about brand and company recall in shampoo category by the respondents.

Table 8

Shampoo Brand Recall		*Company Recall (Correct Name)*	
No. of Brands Recalled by Respondents	*% of Respondents*	*No. of Companies Recalled by Respondents*	*% of Respondents*
1	11.68	1	11.05
2	17.95	2	6.95
3	20.38	3	4.02
4	27.43	4	0.65
5	18.04	5	0.68
No brand recall	4.52	No company recall	76.65

The situation is apparent in shampoo category. Respondents were recalled the brands with average 3.153 brands in which one brand is recalled by 11.68% of respondents, two by 17.95%, three by 20.38%, four by 27.43% and five brands were recalled by 18.04%of respondents. While in the same category, company recall is pathetic, on an average, respondents were recalled .448 companies. So again, it is indicative in shampoo category that strong positioning of product brands may win the battle, exactly what is happening in the case of P&G with its three brands H&S, Pantene and Rejoice, HUL may suffer erosion in its market share due to its Hybrid Brand Architecture Strategy.

Respondents were asked about the brand of confectionery (Chocolates and Mints) which they use and recall the other confectionery brands and the name of the companies which manufacture and market them. The following responses have been obtained:

Table 9

Confectionery Brands (Chocolates and Mints)	*Used by Respondents in %*	*Confectionery Brands (Chocolates and Mints)*	*Used by Respondents in %*
Dairy Milk	35.05	Melody	3.20
5 Star	2.21	Perk	4.72
Munch	3.25	Amul	0.74
Alpenlibe	1.62	Parle	2.43
Kit-Kat	2.44	Cofee-Bite	0.62
Eclairs	4.03	Cloro-mint	0.64
Kismi	0.79	Coca	0.68
		Not Responded	37.58

It is apparent from the Table 9 that Cadbury brands have commendable market share due to its meaningful and innovative advertising and brand building exercises. Dairy Milk is used and preferred by 35.05% of respondents while, 5 Star is preferred by 2.21% of respondents and Eclairs by 4.03% respondents. But the astonishing fact is that 5 Star is lagging behind the Cadbury brand, because Cadbury Dairy Milk followed the co-branding strategy in India and made the brand for every occasion. Nestlé's brand Munch and Kit-Kat also possess good command but not as substantial as Cadbury's brand. Perk of Cadbury, possesses 4.72% of brand usage share, which is second highest after Dairy Milk brand. In total, Cadbury's brand possesses the market share of 45.73%, which is commendable. Parle's brands also have significant presence with Melody having 3.20% of share, Kismi with .79% and Parle with 2.43% of brand usage share. Perfetti-Van Melle's brands have noticeable presence with Alpenlibe and Chloro-mint brand. The fact about brand and company recall in confectionery category is divulged by the following table:

Table 10

Confectionery (Chocolate and Mint) Brand Recall Company Recall (Correct Name)

No. of brand Recalled by Respondents	*% of Respondents*	*No. of companies Recalled by Respondents*	*% of Respondents*
1	4.73	1	20.87
2	15.01	2	12.03
3	33.42	3	7.65
4	18.63	4	2.42
5	24.88	5	0.76
No Brand Recall	3.33	No Company Recall	56.27

Respondents recalled 3 to 4 brands in confectioneries (Chocolate and Mint) while the recall value for the companies which manufacture and market them became a cause of concern again. On an average, 3.369 brands are recalled by the respondents while they could recall only .818 companies, which is even less than one. So in this category also, product brands need support of the corporate identity like Cadbury Dairy Milk.

BRANDS USED BY CUSTOMERS FOR THE FAIRNESS CREAM AND RELEVANT FACTS

When respondents were asked about fairness cream, their answers baffled the researchers. The mind-set of Indian and especially Andhra Pradesh respondents was such that it became a cause of concern again. They divulge little about fairness creams. Research reveals the fact that 44.62% of respondents use the fairness cream. Out of the respondents who mention the brands they are using, Fair & Lovely occupies first place with 64.62% brand mention in terms of usage, followed by Nivea, Ponds, Fairever, Vicco etc. Respondents, even find it difficult to recall the brand and company name in case of fairness cream. Average brand recall in fairness cream category is 1.951 and company recall is .453 brands.

OVERVIEW OF BRAND AND CORPORATE IDENTITY OF SOME FOOD BRANDS IN INDIA

The researchers tried to unveil the facts about some of the popular food brands operating at national level and they encompass Nestle's Maggi which is also recognized as mother brand for the company, HUL's Quality Walls ice-cream (Quality is popular endorser for HUL), Kurkure and Lays from Fritolay division of Pepsico India Holdings Pvt. Ltd and Sun-feast Pasta from ITC. The responses again divulge the fact that the product brands rule the market and respondents know little about the companies which own the brands. Out of the respondents who replied, 89.03% are aware about Maggi brand while 11.28% are unaware about the brand, surprisingly only 6.72% are aware about Nestle, the parent company of Maggi brand. Again the fact is that Nestle's brand tree consists of 10 world wide brands, such as Nestle, Carnation and Buitoni, 45 worldwide strategic product brands such as KitKat, Polo and After Eight (these are always endorsed by a corporate level brand); 25 regional corporate brands; 100 regional product brands, such as Contadina and Stouffer; 700 local strategic brands, and approximately 7,000 local brands (Parsons 1996). The awareness of Quality Walls ice-cream is 51.86% which is low compared to other regional ice-cream brands in Gujarat. The astonishing fact is that only 2.69% respondents are aware about the fact that Quality Walls ice-cream is the brand of HUL. Kurkure, the packaged snack brand is known by 87.78% of the respondents which is considerable but only .79% respondents know the fact that it is the brand of Pepsico India Holdings Pvt. Ltd. Again Lays, the packaged snack brand enjoy 69.07% of awareness. That Pepsico India Holdings Pvt. Ltd is the parent brand of Lays is known by 1.71% of respondents. It is apparent from the research that Kurkure enjoys good brand status and loose parent brand association while Lays enjoys moderate brand awareness but relatively good parent company association. In fact, Pepsico with its Fritolay division achieved remarkable success in packaged snacks business. ITC's Sun-feast Pasta is known to 55.97% of respondents, in spite of Pasta being relatively little known food product and limited to premium segment in India at this juncture. Sun-feast is a strong brand of ITC and apart from biscuits; ITC stretched it to some other food categories like Pasta. ITC is successful compared to other FMCG brands in context of parent company relation, 6.05% of respondents know Sun-feast Pasta is brand of ITC which is considerable. Succinctly, product brands carry strong awareness in India and parent company is overlooked or ignored by the people in many of the instances. But only those companies are successful in India which have good brand status across the world and are smartly managing their product brands. It is very difficult for the FMCG players to manage the portfolio at national level because of diversity in income, culture and reference groups.

BRAND PERSONALITY SCALE: MEASUREMENT ON TOOTH PASTE CATEGORY

Researcher measured the Brand Personality Scale with 40 parameters on different FMCG companies like HUL, Colgate, Wipro, Reckitt-Benckiser, Cadbury, Anchor and Nestle's leading brands. For qualifying the parameters as perfect association to the brand, parameters need to score more than 35% of responses in favour of that parameter. In tooth paste category, the companies like Colgate, HUL and Anchor's brands have been taken with their strong brands like Colgate, Pepsodent and Anchor. Colgate has its association with the brand personality character, like Original, Honest, Genuine, Friendly, Unique, Reliable, Secure, Efficient, Trustworthy, Careful, Leader, Confident, Smooth and Gentle. The best three associations as per the score are, Original (67.65%), Honest (66.02%) and Genuine (53.45%). When it comes to Pepsodent, then again honest, original, secure and trustworthy are the parameters which people associated with it. Anchor did not qualify in the single parameter of the test and respondents did not associate any brand personality characteristics to the brand Anchor. It's very apparent from the research that Colgate occupies substantial space in the mind-set of people of India and stands for originality over the years. Anchor needs to position itself with specific identity except low cost brand in tooth paste category. (Cronbach á for Colgate's parameters; Honest, Original, Genuine and Reliable = .72, Cronbach á for Pepsodent tooth paste parameters; Honest, Original, Reliable, Secure and Trustworthy = .79, Cronbach á for Anchor's parameters; Honest, Original and Reliable = .75).

BRAND PERSONALITY SCALE: MEASURMENT ON BATH SOAP CATEGORY

In bath-soap category, the researcher measured the scale with Lux (HUL), Dettol (Reckit-Benckiser) and Santoor (Wipro) brands which are actively involved in the brand building exercise and know for their good advertisement campaign. Again, these three brand possess different characteristics so far as their categories are concerned, one is positioned as beauty soap (Lux), other is possessing medicinal properties (Dettol) and third one is nearer to Ayurvedic properties (Santoor). Lux has association with Honest, Original, Genuine, Cheerful, Friendly and Reliable brand characteristics. Top three associations are Original (45.03%), Reliable (42.39%) and Honest (41.54%) for Lux beauty soap. Dettol is associated with Honest, Original, Genuine, Reliable, Secure, Trustworthy and Careful brand characteristics. Here, the top three associations for Dettol are Honest (57.62%), Original (55.11%), Secure (43%) and Genuine (44.03%). It is astonishing that Dettol as a brand carries more reliability and trustworthiness than Lux brand soap, but though people prefer Lux brand as their bath soap. Santoor needs scrupulous working for associating personality characteristics and eventually strong brand preference. (Cronbach á for Lux parameters; Honest, Original, Genuine, Sentimental and Warm = .86, Cronbach á for Dettol soap parameters; Honest, Original, Genuine, Reliable, Secure, Careful and Trustworthy= .83, Cronbach á for Santoor parameters; Honest and Original = .73).

BRAND PERSONALITY SCALE: MEASUREMENT ON CONFECTIONERY (CHOCOLATE) CATEGORY

In Chocolate category, leading brand of Cadbury, Dairy Milk and Nestlé's KitKat were taken for brand personality measurement. Dairy Milk is associated with the brand personality characteristics like Honest, Original, Genuine, Ageless, Cheerful, Friendly, Happy, Young, Fun and Smooth. It is apparent from these personality associations that Dairy Milk is very popular, Young and associated with Fun. Top three associations for Dairy Milk are Happy (56.5%), Original (54.5%) and Honest (48.5%). Nestle's KitKat brand does not qualify for even single brand personality characteristic. That is why Nestle's is lagging behind in chocolate category than Cadbury. Cadbury has very strong brand value in India and its corporate endorsement has given edge to all its brands. Its leading brands are Dairy Milk, Eclairs, Perk and 5 Star. (Cornbach á for Dairy Milk parameters; Honest, Original, Genuine, Ageless, Checful, Friendly, Daring, Cool, Young, Fun and Reliable = .82, Cronbach á for KitKat chocolate parameters; Honest, Original, Genuine, Secure, Cheerful, Friendly and Happy = .79).

PICUTRE (LOGO) IDENTIFICATION BY THE RESPONDENTS

The research unveiled the facts about the logos of Hindustan Unilever Ltd, Nestle, Cadbury, Procter & Gamble and Wipro by and large. The new name and logo of HUL had been approved in 74th AGM on May 18, 2007. In fact, this transformation is systematic movement of Unilever towards enforcing the corporate identity of the company in India to its various products. The new logo is symbolic of the company's mission 'Adding Vitality to Life'. All the 25 different icons representing the organization, its brands and the idea of vitality are represented in the logo. Basically, the new logo has borrowed the 'U' symbol (loaded with 25 different vitality icons) from the Unilever basket and gelled it with the 'Hindustan Unilever Ltd' brand identity. Each of those apparently represented the company's new mission: adding vitality to life. The 25 different icons which stands for- 'Our brands, our peoples, our values' are Bowl, Spice and Flavors, Fish, Sparkle, Bird, Recycling, Lips, Ice-cream, Tea, Particles, Frozen, Wave, Liquid, Container, Clothes, Heart, Sun, DNA, Bee, Hand, Flower, Hair, Palm tree, Sauces or spreads and spoon. The logo is blue and 'U' shape but this transformation is tough and Indian consumer found it difficult to digest. The logo seems to be the creation of intellectual minds, and difficult to digest by layman. Research divulges the fact that 29.77% respondents recognized the picture as the log of HUL. HUL needs to show the transformation of logo through television commercial, print medium and hoardings. In fact, in television commercials, they should play some jungle when they expose the logo behind every product advertisements, so they can attract the attention of viewers. In fact in India, HUL needs some concrete actions in terms of establishing the corporate identity. And the change in name and log added difficulties to HUL, because the green HLL logo was popular from last several decades. Tough time for HUL can be visualized in context of corporate identity and brand portfolio management. Some of the respondents identified the logo as "Swaminarayan Sampraday" logo.

Cadbury's logo was identified by 32.86% of respondents, which is again a daunting fact for such popular and strong brand. Some of the respondents perceive the picture as the logo of Amul because it shows two milk glasses.

Nestle's logo was identified by 61.69% of the respondents, which is highest among the all five company logos. The simplicity of the picture and years of operation in India and across world's operation make this true for company. Nestle's hybrid branding strategy and simple communication "Good food. Good life" given the company's remarkable success in majority of their product lines.

Procter & Gamble's earlier logo was recognized as satanic logo and lot of controversy happened in the USA for that. Today, P&G is the logo for Procter & Gamble. Research reveals the fact that 32.5% respondents correctly identified the picture as logo of Procter & Gamble. Some of the respondents perceived the logo as logo of Parle-G.

Wipro's logo has been correctly identified by only 20.99% of respondents. In fact, the company designed the logo and punch line "Applying Thoughts" with some specific deliberation. Logo contains rainbow flower which stands for Youthful & Energetic, Multifaceted, Innovative, Large-diversified and Vibrant. The punch line "Applying Thoughts" stands for Powerful, Intellectual, Futuristic-visionary, Maturity and Commitment to Innovation. Because of Wipro's diversification and limited range in FMCG products, it carries lower visibility. The company requires some meticulous work for brand management and corporate identity creation.In the entire exercise, Nestle emerged as a clear winner in Brand Portfolio Management and identity creation, followed by Cadbury, P&G, HUL and Wipro.

SUGGESTED LEVERAGE FOR SOME EMINENT COMPANIES IN INDIA

HUL	*Existing Strategy*	*Suggested for India.*
Nestle	Hybrid Branding	Need to move towards endorse branding in some of the categories. Can use power branding in some products.
P&G	Product Branding	Successful in India (e.g. Shampoo Brands). Needs to promote bath-soap and detergent category and tooth paste to much extent.
Cadbury	Endorse Branding	Successful in India. Can extend the successful brands to some other product categories.
Nirma	Umbrella Branding	Having Brand Trap in India. Needs to transform identity to launch other FMCG products.

SCOPE FOR FURTHER RESEARCH: BRAND RELATIONSHIP MAPPING

Brands today play a number of important roles that improve consumers' lives and enhance the financial value of firms. Brand relationship mapping goes for beyond the traditional approach of simply inventorying, classifying, and grouping the existing brands within a given portfolio. Instead, it defines the relevance and credibility of brands, from the customer perspective, across various need states and product/service sets; perceived limitations and extendibility of brands; areas of inter-relationship and overlap between the brands; and gaps within the portfolio. All these issues are vital to explore some meaningful information in context of Brand Architecture.

CONCLUSION

Succinctly, HUL is in transformation phase of identity to enforce the corporate identity as its hybrid branding strategy across the world. But in the entire exercise of promoting 30 National and 10 regional brands, they give substantial room to regional brands and other National brands. At the same time, the power brands of HUL, Lux and Fair & Lovely could not achieve stretching successfully. Now they again co-branded Surf-Rin but its success is again the big question. Bath soap, fairness cream, cosmetics, detergent cake are the categories where HUL rules but at the same time, in Shampoo category, P&G gives it a tough fight. At present, the research indicates that in shampoo category also, HUL brands are ruling. In tooth paste category, Colgate rules with the strong brand image and preference, while Pepsodent and Close-up of HUL follow Colgate. Pepsodent has baffled the customers by so many variants. In detergent powder category, Nirma rules the market as per the research, followed by Wheel and Surf (the strong National brands of HUL in category), Tide of P&G which got commendable success in short period of time. In fairness cream category, Fair & Lovely, the power brand of HUL rules the market. Other HUL brands have also considerable share in the category. HUL should stretch Fair & Lovely by up-scaling, and again it should reduce the variants of Fair & Lovely. In confectionery category, Cadbury rules the market for chocolate as it follows corporate endorse branding. Cadbury Dairy Milk is the undisputable leader in chocolate category, while other brands–Eclairs, Perk, and 5 Star have also considerable market share. Nestle is still struggling with its strong brand Kit-Kat and Munch in chocolate category. Parle's Melody and Kismi have stagnant position in the category. It is vital to note where there is no recall in more than 60% of cases.

REFERENCES

Aaker David A., Building Strong Brand, The Free Press.

Aaker David A and Joachimsthaler Erich., Brand Leadership, Published by The Free Press, pp. 134-136.

Aaker. David & Erich Joachimsthaler (1999), The Lure of Global Branding, *Harvard Business Review*, 77 (November/December): 137-144.

Aaker. David & Kevin Keller (1990), Consumer Evaluations of Brand Extensions, *Journal of Marketing*, 54(1): 27-33.

Bartlett, Christopher A. & Sumantra Ghoshal (1989), *Managing Across Borders*, Boston, MA: Harvard Business School Press.

Barwise, Patrick and Thomas Rebertson (1992), Brand Portfolios, *European Management Journal*, 10(3), 277-285.

Chernatony Leslie de, From Brand Vision to Brand Evaluation, Published by Butterworth Heinemann.

Court, David C., Anthony Freeling, Mark C. Lerter & Andrew J. Parsons (1997), If Nike Can 'Just Do It' Why Can't We? *McKinsey Quarterly*, 3: 25-34.

DeMooij, Marieke (1997), *Global Marketing and Advertising, Understanding Cultural Paradoxes,* Thousand Oaks, CA: Sage Publications.

Douglas, Susan P. & C. Samuel Craig and Edwin J. Nijssen (2001), Executive Insights: Integrating Branding Strategy Across Markets: Building International Brand Architecture, *Journal of International Marketing*, 9(2): 97-114.

Echikson, William & Dean Foust (2000), For Coke, Local Is It, *BusinessWeek,* (July 3): 122.

Kapferer, Jean-Noel, *Strategic Brand Management,* 2nd edition, London: Kogan Page, 1997.

Keller, Kevin (1998), *Strategic Brand Management,* New Jersey: Prentice Hall.

Khermouch, Gerry, Stanley Holmes & Moon Ihlwan (2001), The Best Global Brands, *BusinessWeek,* (August 6): 50-57.

Laforet, Sylvie & John Saunders (1994), Managing Brand Portfolios: How the Leaders Do It. *Journal of Advertising Research,* (September/October): 64-76.

Melewar, T.C. & John Saunders (1999), International Corporate Visual Identity: Standardization and Localization, *Journal of International Business Studies.*

Olins, W. (1989), *Corporate Identity,* London: Thames and Hudson.

Parsons Andrew (1996), Nestle: The Visions of Local Managers, *McKinsey Quarterly,* 2: 5-29.

Quelch, John (1999), Global Brands: Taking Stock, *Business Strategy Review,* 10(1): 1-14.

Roth, Marvin S. (1995), Effects of Global Market Conditions on Brand Image Customization and Brand Performance, *Journal of Marketing Research,* 32 (May): 163-175.

Schmitt, Bernd H. and Alex Simenson (1997), *Marketing Aesthetics: The Strategic Management of Brands, Identity and Image,* New York: The Free Press.

5

CUSTOMER RELATIONSHIP MANAGEMENT IN PRIVATE HOSPITALS – A STUDY

R. Ganapathi, S. Anbumalar, G. Ramesh Pandi

INTRODUCTION

The new millennium is in the midst of explosive change witnessing rapidly changing market conditions, volatile equity markets, reconstructed value chains and new global competitors. And customers themselves are changing – natural customer loyalty is a thing of the past. Little wonder then, the concept of Customer Relationship Management (CRM) has taken center stage in the business world for sustainable business advantages. Long-term success requires a great Customer Relationship Management strategy. A technology enabled CRM strategy to meet Customer-focused objectives involves the vast majority of any organization's activity. Today customers are looking for service on channels and regardless of media; this is possible because of new technologies. Customers have experienced new techniques like online, self-help, mail, chat, phone, e-mail, which are making them interact with the company more easily. Some of the major benefits for customer management include the use of latest technologies like universal agent's desktops, CTI, customer data repositories and product knowledge bases. With the latest technologies, other areas like e-commerce, logistics and distribution, marketing services and inbound sales are also coming into the picture and companies have already started implementing the same.

The CRM segment has significantly contributed to the recent IT growth. Less growth in the CRM segment from small and medium sized companies showed that these groups of companies either have fewer resources or they do not have the required skills to generate positive results from CRM investments. In the new economy only a few organizations are providing their customers high quality products and service experience. They are reaching, interacting and transacting with customers through multiple channels and providing them ultimate satisfaction. Customers do not have the same value similarly all organizations cannot adopt a full-fledged CRM model. In some cases, the cost of developing a CRM infrastructure may prove to be greater than the returns involved. The world economy is becoming an increasingly volatile system. Any enterprise that can make volatility its "Friend" by adapting quickly to changes in the external environment will be rewarded with success and growth.

Success at harnessing the full value, of the customer is increasingly dependent on the effectiveness of your relationships not only with customers themselves, but also with suppliers and partners. Adaptive companies are those that are not only integrated internally, but which are also connected to the outside world. The competition for the most profitable customer relationship is fierce. To win the battle, companies have to provide customers with a consistently high-quality experience and be able to manage this over time, and across a multitude of touch-points. "You've got to know who your customers are – their habits, their preference, their experiences with you, and their ultimate value to you – if you want to thrive in today's relationship economy."

At the same time, the congestion for customers, along with abundant customer's choices, has pushed customer expectations to new heights. Who has the patience for a provider that doesn't deliver on time with quality – and with a burning desire to satisfy their needs? Who wants to be bombarded with the same promotion after saying "yes" the first time? Adding to the challenge, a company is providing more across points than ever before to reach and interacts with customers. Not only the companies have more channels to manage and integrate, channels like the Internet have made it easier for customers to shop for the best service and deals, creating even more competition for the same customer base. Customers are demanding that you are accessible and easy to do business with.

Well, does CRM have any role in improving business performance? While the paths to winning the hearts and wallets of your customers are as varied as your customers themselves, the first step is to define the stages of the customer experience from the customer's point of view. Then you must determine how to invest in each stage to generate the greatest customer and business impact. Global companies are beginning to implement CRM strategies, tools and infrastructure to acquire new and leverage existing relationships.

Indeed, a third of the sales, marketing and customer services executives' recently surveyed view of almost CRM are demonstrated by the finding that 65% of the companies surveyed expect an increase in the IT budget for CRM during 2008. Overall CRM efforts are transitioning from point or departmental solutions to more enterprise-wide initiatives. The true value of CRM in building profitable relationships is dependent on understanding that is an enterprise-level strategy that presents a unified organization and experience to the customer.

STATEMENT OF THE PROBLEM

The new millennium is in the midst of explosive change witnessing rapidly changing market conditions, volatile equity markets, reconstructed value chains and new global competitors. And Customers themselves are changing–natural customer loyalty is a thing of the past. Little wonder then, the concept of customer relationship management (CRM) has taken center stage in the business world for sustainable business advantages. Long-term success requires a great Customer Relationship Management strategy. A technology-enabled CRM strategy to meet Customer-focused objectives involves the vast majority of any organization's activity. No doubt about that Customer Relationship Management (CRM) has become a top priority for companies seeking to gain competitive advantage in today's stormy economy. However, confusion reigns about exactly what CRM is, how to best implement it, or even what role it should play in enhancing customer interaction. Against this background, it will be worth, undertaking a study to evaluate the consumer retention of selected hospital.

OBJECTIVES OF THE STUDY

The following are the specific objectives of the study.

1. To examine the present system of customer care in Hospital.
2. To analyze the factors influencing the customers to select the hospital.
3. To study the competitive strategies of hospitals in Coimbatore city and
4. To suggest better ways and means to retain the customers.

RESEARCH METHODOLOGY

The validity of any research is based on the systematic method of data collection and analysis. Both primary and secondary data were used for the present study. The primary data has been collected from 200 sample respondents in Coimbatore city. For this purpose stratified random sampling method was used to select the samples. The researcher has approached the managers of various hospitals in Coimbatore city to collect the list of customers in the hospitals. Due to time, money and inconvenience, the researcher has selected only top ten hospitals in the Coimbatore city. The questionnaires were collected from 200 respondents from 10 reputed hospitals. The ten hospitals selected for this study were K.G. Hospital, PSG Hospital, Ramakrishna Hospital, Abirami Hospital, Ganga Hospital, Kongu Nadu Hospital, Aravind Eye Hospital, G.K.N.M. Hospital, Lotus Hospital and Aswini Hospital. The present study highlights the extent of utilization of the hospital services by the selected sample respondents. It also shed light on the common problems faced by the respondents. The major features of the service sectors especially on hospital performance is projected in order to utilize the services as per the expectation of the patients (customer).

For this study data have been collected from both primary and secondary source. An exclusive field study and interview have been conducted. It included rural semi-urban areas, business, employed and self-employed from both genders are identified and the sampling unit is finalized. Interview schedule was the main tool used to collect the pertinent data from the selected sample respondents. Secondary data have also been collected for the study from books, leading journals, newspapers, magazines and textbooks related to study and from the internet sources. The collected data were analyzed through percentage, average, range, standard deviation and weighted average. In connection with this two way tables were prepared and chi-square test were also employed to find the associationship. Likert's scaling technique is used to identify the customer preference and satisfaction on hospital services. Henry Garrets ranking method is also used to judge the ranking especially on the hospital services. The study is confined to a period of 6 months since June 2009 to November 2009.

ANALYSIS AND INTERPRETATION OF DATA

Customer relationship is the crucial element in the marketing function, which decides the goodwill of any concern. An attempt is made to analyze the various factors influencing the customer relation level of the selected sample respondents. The variables are classified into two important strata viz. Dependent variables and Independent variables. The level of relationship of customer is taken as the dependent variables. The independent variables used in the study are age, gender, category, marital status, monthly income, occupation and educational qualification.

AGE AND LEVEL OF SATISFACTION ON CRM

Age is an important factor in customer relationship management. Hence, the respondents have been grouped under three categories viz. Below 25 years, 26-30 years and above 30 years. The sample consisted of 88 respondents (44%) below 25 years, 74 respondents belong to (37%) 26 to 30 years and 38 (19%) respondents belong to above 30 years. The distribution of respondents according to age is observed from the following table. It could be observed from Table 1 that level of satisfaction on customer relationship management among the respondents of below 25 years category ranged between 35 and 51 with an average of 43.83. Level of satisfaction on customer relationship management between 26-30 years category of respondents ranged between 36 and 53 with an average of 45.84. On the other hand, the respondent's level of satisfaction on customer relationship management among the above 30 years category ranged between 45 and 56 with an average of 50.00. Thus, it may be concluded from the analysis that respondents of the age above 30 years are having maximum level of satisfaction. Using chi-square test the age and level of satisfaction on CRM has been tested. For this purpose, the age and level of satisfaction on CRM are given in the following table.

Table 1
Age and Level of Satisfaction

	Level of Satisfaction					*Range*		
Age Group	*Low*	*Medium*	*High*	*Total*	*Average*	*Min*	*Max*	*S.D*
Below 25 years	21(14.96)	35(26.40)	32(46.64)	88	43.83	35	51	5.08
26-30 years	13(12.58)	16(22.20)	45(39.22)	74	45.84	36	53	5.43
Above 30 years	0 (6.46)	9(11.40)	29(20.14)	38	50.00	45	56	3.98
Total	34	60	106	200				

Source: Survey Data
Note: Figures given in the brackets represent the Expected Frequency

Null hypothesis: The association between the age of the respondents and their level of satisfaction on CRM is not statistically significant.

The percentage of high level of satisfaction is the highest (42.5) among the 26-30 years age group and the lowest (27.4) among the above 30 years age group. The percentage of medium level of satisfaction is the highest (58.3) among the aged below 25 years respondents and the lowest (15) among the above 30 years aged respondents. On the other hand, the percentage of low level of satisfaction is the highest (61.8) among the respondents aged below 25 years and the lowest (38.2) among the 26-30 years aged respondents. As the calculated chi-square value (23.295) is greater than the table value (9.488) at 5% level of significance for 4 degrees of freedom, the null hypothesis is rejected and it could be concluded that the association between the age of the respondents and their level of satisfaction on CRM is statistically significant.

GENDER AND LEVEL OF SATISFACTION ON CRM

Today there is no discrimination to study the level of satisfaction on customer's relationship in any kind of product and services among the male and female group. Today women are equally competing with men in all the fields, including business, military organization and space research centers. In this study, most of the business activities are supported by women (especially financial support). For the purpose of the study, gender classification is observed. The sample consists of 134 (67%) male respondents and 66 (33%) female respondents. The distribution of respondents according to sex and level of satisfaction on customer's relationship is shown in the Table 2. The maximum level of satisfaction on customer's relationship among the female respondents ranged between 37 and 54 with an average of 46.38. Whereas, male respondents level of satisfaction on customer's relationship ranged between 35 and 56 with an average of 45.43. Thus the table reveals that the maximum level of satisfaction on customer's relationship is among the female respondents. Using chi-square test the gender and level of satisfaction on CRM has been tested. For this purpose, the gender and level of satisfaction on CRM are given in the following table.

Table 2
Gender and Level of Satisfaction on CRM

	Level of Satisfaction					*Range*		
Gender	*Low*	*Medium*	*High*	*Total*	*Average*	*Min*	*Max*	*S.D*
Male	26(22.78)	38(40.20)	70(71.02)	134	45.43	35	56	5.55
Female	8(11.22)	22(19.8)	36(34.98)	66	46.38	37	54	5.35
Total	34	60	106	200				

Source: Survey Data Note: Figures given in the brackets represent the Expected Frequency

Null hypothesis: The association between the gender of the respondents and their level of satisfaction on CRM is not statistically significant.

The percentage of high level of satisfaction on customer's relationship is the highest (66.0) among the male respondents and the lowest (34.0) among the female respondents. The percentage of medium level of satisfaction on customer's relationship is the highest (63.3) among the male respondents and the lowest (36.7) among the female respondents. On the other hand, the percentage of level of satisfaction on customer's relationship is the highest (76.5) among the male respondents and the lowest (23.5) among the female respondents. As the calculated chi-square value (1.788) is less than the table value (5.991) at 5% level of significance for 2 degrees of freedom, the null hypothesis is accepted and it could be concluded that the association between the gender of the respondents and their level of satisfaction on CRM is not statistically significant.

CATEGORY AND LEVEL OF SATISFACTION

The level of satisfaction may be varying according to the types of customers. For the purpose of the study, category sample consists of 40 (20%) in-patient respondents, 78 (39%) out-patient respondents and 82 (42%) attenders respondents. The distribution of respondents according to category and level of satisfaction on customer's relationship is shown in the following Table 3. The maximum level of satisfaction on customer's relationship among the in-patient respondents ranged between 39 and 54 with an average of 47.15. On the other hand the respondents' level of satisfaction on customer's relationship among the Out-patient respondents ranged between 41 and 52 with an average of 47.05, whereas attenders level of satisfaction on customer's relationship ranged between 35 and 56 with an average of 43.82. Using chi-square test the category of customers and level of satisfaction on CRM has been tested. For this purpose, the category of customers and level of satisfaction on CRM are given in the following table.

Table 3
Category of Customers and Level of Satisfaction on CRM

	Level of Satisfaction					*Range*		
Category	*Low*	*Medium*	*High*	*Total*	*Average*	*Min*	*Max*	*S.D*
In-patient	4(6.8)	12(12.0)	24(21.20)	40	47.15	39	54	4.22
Out-patient	0 (13.26)	27(23.40)	51(41.34)	78	47.05	41	52	3.54
Attenders	30(13.94)	21(24.60)	31(43.46)	82	43.82	35	56	6.86
Total	34	60	106	200				

Source: Survey Data Note: Figures given in the brackets represent the Expected Frequency

Null hypothesis: The association between the category of the respondents and their level of satisfaction on CRM is not statistically significant.

The percentage of high level of satisfaction on customer's relationship is the highest (48.1) among the Out-patient respondents and the lowest (22.6) among the In-patient respondents. The percentage of medium level of satisfaction on customer's relationship is the highest (45.0) among the Out-patient respondents and the lowest (20.0) among the In-patient respondents. On the other hand, the percentage of low level of satisfaction on customer's relationship is the highest (88.2) among the attenders' respondents and the lowest (0.0) among the Out-patient respondents. As the calculated chi-square value (50.560) is greater than the table value (9.488) at 5% level of significance for 4 degrees of freedom, the null hypothesis is rejected and it could be concluded that the association between the category of the respondents and their level of satisfaction on CRM is statistically significant.

MARITAL STATUS AND LEVEL OF SATISFACTION

Marital status is an important factor to find the level of satisfaction. For the purpose of this study marital status has been studied under three heads viz., Single, Married and widow. The study sample consists of 93 (46.5%) single category respondents, 104 (52%) married category respondents and 3 (1.5%) widow category respondents. The distribution of respondents according to category and level of satisfaction on customer's relationship is shown in the Table 4. The maximum level of satisfaction on customer's relationship among the married category respondents ranged between 36 and 56 with an average of

47.12. On the other hand the respondents' level of satisfaction on customer's relationship among the single category respondents ranged between 35 and 51 with an average of 44.20, whereas widow category level of satisfaction on customer's relationship ranged at 46 with an average of 46. The study reveals that the maximum level of satisfaction on customer's relationship is among the married category respondents in the study area. Using chi-square test the marital status and level of satisfaction on CRM has been tested. For this purpose, the marital status and level of satisfaction on CRM are given in the following table.

Table 4
Marital Status and Level of Satisfaction on CRM

Marital Status	*Level of Satisfaction* Low	Medium	High	Total	Average	*Range* Min	Max	S.D
Single	21(15.81)	35(27.9)	37(49.29)	93	44.20	35	51	5.12
Married	13(17.68)	25(31.20)	66(55.12)	104	47.12	36	56	5.55
Widow	0 (0.51)	0 (0.9)	3(1.59)	3	46.00	46	46	0.00
Total	34	60	106	200				

Source: Survey Data Note: Figures given in the brackets represent the Expected Frequency

Null hypothesis: The association between the marital status of the respondents and their level of satisfaction on CRM is not statistically significant.

It is found that the percentage of high level of satisfaction on customer relationship is highest (62.3) among married respondents and the lowest (2.8) among widow category respondents. The normal level of satisfaction on customer relationship is highest (61.8) among the single category respondents and lowest is widow category which has no respondent. On the other hand, the percentage of low level of customer relationship is the highest (61.8) among single category respondents and lowest is widow which has no respondent. As the calculated chi-square value (13.752) is greater than the table value (9.488) at 5% level of significance for 4 degrees of freedom, the null hypothesis is rejected and it could be concluded that the association between the marital status of the respondents and their level of satisfaction on CRM is statistically significant.

MONTHLY INCOME AND LEVEL OF SATISFACTION

Patients make the choice of the hospital or doctor based on their income for normal treatments. Hence, the researcher has given utmost importance to the monthly earning of respondents. For the purpose of the study income has been studied under three heads viz. namely below Rs.5000, Rs.5001 to Rs.8000 and Rs.8001 and above. The sample consists of 66 (33%) respondents from below Rs.5000 category, 64 (32%) respondents from Rs.5001 to Rs.8000 category and 70 (35%) from Rs.8001 and above category. The distribution of respondents according to the income and level of satisfaction on customer's relationship is shown in the following table. It is observed from the Table 5 that maximum level of satisfaction on Customer Relationship is among the Rs.5001 to Rs.8000 income group which has ranged between 41 and 54 with an average of 48.70. The level of satisfaction of Customer Relationship among the Rs.8001 and above income group ranged between 36 and 56 with an average of 45.26. On the other hand the below Rs.5000 income group with a range of 35 and 51 has an average of 43.39. Thus it may be concluded that the level of satisfaction on Customer Relationship is maximum among Rs.5001 to Rs.8000 income group of respondents. Using chi-square test the monthly income and level of satisfaction on CRM has been tested. For this purpose, the monthly income and level of satisfaction on CRM are given in the following table.

Table 5
Monthly Income and Level of Satisfaction on CRM

Monthly Income	*Level of Satisfaction* Low	Medium	High	Total	Average	*Range* Min	Max	S.D
Below Rs.5000	21(11.22)	19(19.8)	26(34.98)	66	43.39	35	51	5.24
Rs.5001 to Rs 8000	0 (10.88)	17(19.2)	47(33.92)	64	48.70	41	54	3.93
Rs.8001 & above	13(11.90)	24(21.0)	33(37.10)	70	45.26	36	56	5.77
Total	34	60	106	200				

Source: Survey Data Note: Figures given in the brackets represent the Expected Frequency

Null hypothesis: The association between the monthly income of the respondents and their level of satisfaction on CRM is not statistically significant.

It is found that the percentage of high level of satisfaction on Customer Relationship is highest (44.3) among Rs.5001 to Rs.8000 income group of respondents and the lowest (24.5) among the below Rs.5000 income group of people. The medium level of satisfaction of Customer Relationship is the highest (40) among the Rs.8001 and above category and lowest (28.3) among the Rs.5001 to Rs.8000 income group. The low level of satisfaction on Customer Relationship is highest (61.8) among below Rs.5000 income respondents and lowest is Rs.5001 to Rs.8000 category, which has no respondent. As the calculated chi-square value (28.022) is greater than the table value (9.488) at 5% level of significance for 4 degrees of freedom, the null hypothesis is rejected and it could be concluded that the association between the monthly income of the respondents and their level of satisfaction on CRM is statistically significant.

OCCUPATION AND LEVEL OF SATISFACTION

Occupation is an important factor in determining the level of satisfaction on Customer Relationship. For the purpose of this study occupation has been studied under six heads viz. government employees, private company employees, business men, farmers, housewives and others. The sample consists of 8 (4) respondents from Government employee, 24 (12) respondents are working in the private companies, 21 (10.5) respondents are running their own business, 37 (18.5) are farmers, 16 (8) are house wives and 94 (47) respondents belong to others category. The distribution of respondents according to occupation and level of satisfaction in utilizing the services of hospital is shown in the following Table 6. The maximum level of satisfaction on Customer Relationship is among the housewives, which has ranged between 45 to 54 with an average of 51.5. The level of satisfaction of CRM among the farmers ranged between 41 and 54 with an average of 48.30. The level of satisfaction of CRM among the others category respondents has ranged between 35 and 53 with an average of 44.61. The level of satisfaction of CRM among the private employees have ranged between 36 and 51 with an average of 44.50. The level of satisfaction of CRM among the businessmen has ranged between 37 and 56 with an average of 44.43. On the other hand, the level of satisfaction of CRM among the government employees has ranged at 43 with an average of 43.00. Thus, it is concluded that the level of satisfaction on customer relationship is maximum among the housewives. Using chi-square test the occupation and level of satisfaction on CRM has been tested. For this purpose, the occupation and level of satisfaction on CRM are given in the following table.

Table 6
Occupation and Level of Satisfaction on CRM

Occupation	*Level of Satisfaction*			Total	Average	*Range*		S.D
	Low	Medium	High			Min	Max	
Government Employees	0 (1.36)	8(2.4)	0 (4.24)	8	43.00	43	43	0.00
Private Company Employees	9(4.08)	0 (7.2)	15(12.72)	24	44.50	36	51	6.53
Businessmen	8(3.57)	5(6.3)	8(11.13)	21	44.43	37	56	7.27
Farmers	0 (6.29)	8(11.1)	29(19.61)	37	48.30	41	54	3.85
Housewives	0 (2.72)	3(4.8)	13(8.48)	16	51.50	45	54	3.31
Others	17(15.98)	36(28.2)	41(49.82)	94	44.61	35	53	4.90
Total	34	60	106	200				

Scurce: Survey Datanote: Figures given in the brackets represent the Expected Frequency

Null hypothesis: The association between the occupation of the respondents and their level of satisfaction on CRM is not statistically significant.

The percentage of high level of satisfaction in utilizing hospital services is the highest (38.7) among the other groups. The percentage of high level of satisfaction in utilizing hospital services is the highest (15) among others group and the same is the lowest (9) among the Private Company Employees. The percentage of medium level of satisfaction in utilizing hospital services is the highest (8) among the others group and the same is the lowest (0) among the Government Employee. As the calculated chi-square value (60.094) is greater than the table value (18.307) at 5% level of significance for 10 degrees of freedom, the null hypothesis is rejected and it could be concluded that the association between the occupation of the respondents and their level of satisfaction on CRM is statistically significant.

EDUCATIONAL QUALIFICATION AND LEVEL OF SATISFACTION

Education of the respondents is one of the most important influencing factors of the study. It is acquiring or imparting skills, values and knowledge. Education also means preparing people to develop new ideas and to adjust to the changing environment. For this purpose the respondents have been classified according to their educational level viz. illiterate, higher secondary, under graduation and post graduation level. Out of 200 respondents, 7 (3.5%) respondents are Illiterate, 37 (18.5%) respondents are higher secondary 122 (61.0%) respondents are under graduates and 34 (17.0%) respondents are post graduates. The distribution of respondents according to education and level of satisfaction on CRM is shown in the following Table 7. The level of satisfaction on CRM based on educational qualification in utilizing hospital services ranged between 39 and 46 with an average of 42 among Illiterate. The level of satisfaction among people with Higher Secondary qualification ranged between 45 and 54 with an average of 50. The range of Under Graduates and Post Graduates level of satisfaction in utilizing hospital services is between 35 and 53 and between 36 and 56 with an average of 45.14 and 44.06 respectively. From the analysis it is inferred that the maximum level of satisfaction is found among Higher

Secondary qualified customers. A two way table is prepared and is shown below. Using chi-square test the educational qualification and level of satisfaction on CRM has been tested. For this purpose, the education and level of satisfaction on CRM are given in the following Table-7.

Table 7
Educational Qualification and Level of Satisfaction on CRM

	Level of Satisfaction					*Range*		
Educational Qualification	*Low*	*Medium*	*High*	*Total*	*Average*	*Min*	*Max*	*S.D*
Illiterate	4(1.19)	0 (2.1)	3(3.71)	7	42.00	39	46	3.74
HSC	0 (6.29)	5(11.1)	32(19.61)	37	50.00	45	54	3.35
Under Graduation	21(20.74)	42(36.6)	59(64.66)	122	45.14	35	53	5.21
Post Graduation	9(5.78)	13(10.2)	12(18.02)	34	44.06	36	56	6.32
Total	34	60	106	200				

Source: Survey Data: Note-Figures given in the brackets represent the Expected Frequency

Null hypothesis: The association between the educational qualification of the respondents and their level of satisfaction on CRM is not statistically significant.

The percentage of high level of satisfaction in utilizing hospital services is the highest (55.7) among the under graduate category and same is the lowest (2.8) among the Illiterate. The percentage of medium level of satisfaction in utilizing hospital services is the highest (70) under among graduates and the same is the lowest (0) among the illiterate. The percentage of low level of satisfaction in utilizing hospital services is the highest (61.8) among the under graduates and the same is the lowest (0) among the respondents with HSC qualification. As the calculated chi-square value (32.211) is greater than the table value (12.592) at 5% level of significance for 6 degrees of freedom, the null hypothesis is rejected and it could be concluded that the association between the educational qualification of the respondents and their level of satisfaction on CRM is statistically significant.

EXISTING FACILITIES IN THE HOSPITALS – HENRY GARRETT RANKING

An attempt is made to analyze the reasons for selecting the hospital. Various factors such as doctor's treatment, room cleanliness, lab service, pharmacy service, emergency service, canteen service, fees, nursing, reception service, ambulance service, dietician and insurance are selected for the purpose of the study. The respondents are asked to rank their preferences based on the factors that motivated them most. Table-8 shows the details of various factors that influenced the respondents.

Table 8
Existing Facilities in the Hospitals

Various Facilities	*Total Score*	*Mean Score*	*Rank*
Doctors Treatment	15082	75.4	I
Room Cleanliness	13056	65.3	II
Lab Service	10078	50.4	V
Pharmacy Service	9482	47.4	VII
Emergency Service	10725	53.6	IV

Contd.

Various Facilities	Total Score	Mean Score	Rank
Canteen Service	8051	40.3	XI
Fees	7561	37.8	XII
Nursing	11559	57.8	III
Reception Service	8900	44.5	VIII
Ambulance Service	9898	49.5	VI
Dietician	8083	40.4	X
Insurance	8239	41.2	IX

Table-8 indicates that the 'Doctors Treatment' 'Cleanliness' and 'Nursing are the main motivating factors that influenced them to select the hospital which is ranked first, second and third with the score of 15082, 13056 and 11559 points respectively. The factors like Emergency Service, Lab Service, and Ambulance Service are ranked to fourth, fifth and sixth position with the score of 10725, 10078 and 9898 respectively. Pharmacy Service, Reception Service, Insurance and Dietician are ranked in the seventh, eighth, ninth and tenth positions with Garret scores of 9482, 8900, 8239 and 8083 points respectively. The last two positions are occupied by canteen and fees are ranked in the eleventh and twelfth place with a score of 8051 and 7561 points respectively. From the analysis it is concluded that the 'Doctors Treatment' 'Cleanliness' and 'Nursing were the main factors in choosing the hospitals.

PERFORMANCE OF THE HOSPITAL IN RESPECT OF TREATMENT

Success of any service depends upon competitive factors that differentiate the services with competitive advantages over traditional services. A selected hospital holds some competitive advantage over other traditional hospitals. The Table-9 shows the competitive gains of hospitals.

Table 9
Performance of the Hospital in respect of Treatment

Types of Treatment	Total Score	Mean Score	Rank
Cardiology	11216	62.60	II
Gastroenterology	9368	46.84	VI
Neurology	10734	53.67	IV
Gynecology	11099	55.50	III
Ortho	9841	49.21	V
Urology	8078	40.39	IX
ENT	9014	45.07	VII
Physiotherapist	8552	42.76	VIII
Pediatrics	12520	56.08	I

It is noted from the above table that Pediatrics is ranked first among all the services with 12520 Garret points which distinguishes the hospital from other traditional hospitals. The second rank is given to Cardiology with Garret score of 11216. Gynecology, Neurology and Ortho are secured third, fourth and fifth with score of 55.50, 53.67 and 49.21 respectively. The Gastroenterology, ENT and Physiotherapist were secured sixth, seventh and eighth rank with score of 9368, 9014 and 8552 respectively. The last preference is given for Urology with 40.39 points. From the analysis it is found that Pediatrics is the major competitive advantage gained by the hospital when compared to other traditional hospitals.

SUGGESTIONS

1. From the analysis it is observed that advertisement does not play a major role. The management should create awareness about their services in local television channels (Polimer, MCN, KARAN) and tamil news papers (Dinakaran, Dinamalar, Dinathanthi) to attract the beneficiaries.
2. Doctor's treatment is the prime factor to select the hospital for their treatment. Hence, it is suggested that the management puts more efforts to sustain the doctor's quality and recruit talented doctors if necessary.
3. Management should concentrate on free camps, mobile services and plying free transport services to the hospital to turn-up the new customers.
4. Management should slowly change its services from traditional to technology based services by acquiring new technology i.e. implementing effective CRM system.
5. Recruitment and training of staff should be standardized.
6. Hospital Management should increase the physician referral centers and
7. Implementing feedback, complaint handling and service recovery systems should be strengthened to enhance effectiveness of services.

CONCLUSION

In the health care business, technology is really important in managing the customer and employee relationship to guarantee the best service, and most important of all prevent errors. That is because in the area of healthcare, a small mistake might lead to a permanent error or even death. This is made possible by using special application healthcare software. Nowadays, many healthcare centers use special application software in order to run their services. Many companies develop software compete to provide the market with the best software, which guarantees high performance, and thus more benefits for employees, and of course for the patients.

Technology is healthcare not only support patients, but also helps employees such as doctors and nurses, and managers in order to take the right decisions. Healthcare software helps in managing the duties of each employee, and givens the bottom line for important decisions on how to deal with different situations. In an industry such as medical health care, the main keys are speed and accuracy. That is because, as we mentioned earlier, the industry affects patients' lives directly. So technology is a major element in this industry in order to guarantee the best treatment for the patients, and the best coordination of employees. For example, a CRM system can transform a patient's medical record into an analytical tool for optimizing the care of each patient individually. Not only do organizations use CRM systems or detecting, reporting, and correcting the sources of fraudulent activities, but also helps them to proactively evaluate the quality of patient care and how the workers are performing their daily tasks.

REFERENCES

Basu (2003), *"Healthcare: India's Nest Tourism Booster"*, United Press International, August 19.

Gupta S.P. (2000), *"Statistical Methods"* Sultan Chand & Sons Publications, New Delhi.

James F. Engel, Roger D. Blackwell, David T. Kollat, *"Consumer Behaviour"* The Dryden Press, New Delhi.

Kothari. C.R. (1990), *"Research Methodology Methods & Techniques"*, Wishwa Prakashan, New Delhi.

Philip Kotler (2000), *"Marketing Management"* The Millennium Edition, Prentice – Hall of India Private Limited, New Delhi.

Pillai R.S.N., and Bagavathi (2009), *"Modern Marketing Principles and Practices"*, Second Revised and Enlarged Editions. S. Chand and Company Limited, New Delhi.

Rajan Nair N. (2009), *"Marketing Management"*, Seventh Edition, Sultan Chand and Sons Publications, New Delhi.

Revathy L.N. (2003), *"Health Care Spending May Cross Rs.2,00,000 Crore – Mark"*, The Hindu Business Line, May 12.

Rohit Saran (2004), *"Too Many Crooks"*, India Today, June 14.

Shela Raza Hasan (2003), *"India bids for Healthcare Tourism"*, Asia Times Online, July 19.

William J. Stanton (2009), *"Fundamentals of Marketing"*, International Edition, McGraw–Hill Publishing Company, New Delhi, pp.597-598.

6

AN ANALYTICAL STUDY OF MARKETING EXECUTIVES' RESPONSE TO INNOVATION

Chimun Kumar Nath

INTRODUCTION

A general proposition in the literature on strategy, marketing and innovation management is that the members of a firm's top management team exert a major influence on the success and the magnitude of product innovation, whether incremental or radical, Davenport, Leibold, & Voelpel, (2006); Fiol, (1996); Sanchez & Heene, (2004); to name a few. This influence comes from the fact that it is the top management team who make the decisions regarding the desired organisational form, resource allocation and capability development, so that the firm is able to come up with a successful balance between exploitation and exploration - implicitly between incremental and radical product innovation, Atuahene-Gima, (2005). In the literature it is also noted that those top managers most likely to realise radical product innovation are the ones who communicate a clear vision for innovation, who inspire and create a climate for creativity and who act as a promoter for knowledge creation processes on various organisational levels Armistead & Meakins, (2002); Yadav, Prabhu, & Chandy, (2007).

Although the propositions mentioned above are supported by an increasing amount of conceptual and empirical research in the field of upper echelons research; Yadav et al., (2007), and innovation management, Adams, Bessant, & Phelps, (2006), it is evident that more research is needed in order to develop framework to assist top managers in marketing and in other functions in enacting their role for firm's renewal and innovation capability. In order to develop such frameworks, the stance taken here is that a first and needed step is to gain more insight about the meaning of product innovation among top managers representing different functions, decision levels or fields of perspectives and competencies within companies. This stance has also been put forward by others. As for example do

Yadav et al. (2007, p. 85) conclude the following: 'The extant studies tend to ignore the processes by which top mangers influence innovation, focusing instead on demographic characteristics of CEOs and top management teams'. Another prevalent stance, or proposition, in the literature on strategy and management is that the mental models, or mindsets, of top managers is one relevant object of study when the aim is to gain further understanding about management and leadership for a firm's learning and innovation behaviour, Bettis & Wong, (2003); Day & Schoemaker, (2004); Jacobs & Heracleous, (2005)

A mental model, or mindsets, is a recognised concept in the literature and so is the notion that mental models may consists of a picture of future customer needs; an understanding of a business model; a set of relationships showing some causality or consequences in the market place; a diagram of critical interdependencies in the value chain; or a mental motion picture of chain of events in a strategic plan. Karp, (2005, p. 89)

The mental model concept has given rise to many theoretical discussions and definitions; Doyle & Ford, (1998, 1999). However, there is a recurrent theme in these definitions, namely that: 'mental models affect experience (active) and are affected by experience (passive)', Chermack, (2003). Thus, mental models are described as 'tools that managers employ to understand the complex environment by giving meaning to a plethora of signals received from the environment'; Adamides, Stamboulis, & Kanellopoulos, (2003), and as a management approach for linking companies to an external environment through a sense making process. According to Weick (1977, p. 279), the latter view makes us aware that: 'an enacted environment is the residue of a sense making episode that is stored in the retention processes of past wisdom'. Dougherty, Borrelli, Munir and O'Sullivan (2000, p. 322) describe the sense making concept in relation to product innovation as follows: 'For product innovation, people would construct a market opportunity, relevant technology, and product concept, bracket the knowledge they will attend to, and make this knowledge meaningful by interpreting its role in the ongoing accomplishment of the new product'.

According to the literature, a mental model is a tool 'to categorize an event, assess its consequences, and consider appropriate actions (including doing nothing), and to do so rapidly and efficiently', Prahalad & Bettis, (2004). Due to the latter, there is a possibility mental models may act as a blinder for the organisation in the sense that they direct top managers' attention on certain knowledge, and on certain suggestions regarding how to increase the innovativeness of their company, among other things. In the marketing and strategy literature, this phenomenon and the mental model concept is noticed, but empirical analysis is lacking behind, Day, (2002); Yadav et al., (2007). Thus, little is know about how top managers in marketing perceive or define their involvement for the firm's renewal and innovation capability. In an attempt to ratify this situation, the following overall research question was formed to provide the basis for an explorative analysis: What is product innovation all about in marketing executives' mental models of marketing management?

Companies from the pharmaceutical and the consumer durable industry were chosen as cases in dealing with the research question. The reason to this choice of industries relates to an apparent and general difference as well as similarity in innovation and marketing strategy. In the pharmaceutical industry, radical product innovation has always been regarded as the basis for success, and as noted by Harms, Rohman, Heinrich, Druener and Trommsdorff (2002), pharmaceutical companies have continuously increased their expenses for research and development. And because the large pharmaceutical companies are still expanding their R&D budgets it appears as if R&D is still viewed as 'the ivory tower'; Becker & Lillemark, (2006). However, although the latter still holds in many pharmaceutical companies, it also appears that marketing is getting more resources and influence in pharmaceutical companies. Indicators of this are that pharmaceutical companies are increasingly adopting marketing and brand management principles from the consumer durable industry, and expanding their marketing budgets, Schuiling & Moss, (2004). A recurrent theme in analysis of the consumer durable industry is the opposite as regards to innovation history. That is, an industry that prefers to re-develop old products and that shows up a low intensity of R&D; Alfranca, Rama, & von Tunzelmann, (2004). However, it has been found that some consumer durable items are increasingly implementing new scientific approaches and technological opportunities; as modern technology and new product concepts and packaging technologies, Bröring, Cloutier, & Leker, (2006).

Against these developments, difference and similarity between the two industries' innovation experiences the following sub-questions were formulated: Do the mental models of marketing executives in the pharmaceutical industry, differ from their equivalents in the Consumer durable industry, due to the fact that the former ones are working within a business context wherein investments in radical product innovation traditionally have been high? Or is it so, that top managers in marketing are guided by a common mental model, a kind of dominant logic for marketing management and product innovation, due to some general environmental forces and values in business life and/or because marketing executives will come to follow 'what everyone' appears to perceive as representing the logic of an innovative and successful company?

A broad selection of companies within the consumer durable and the pharmaceutical industry was asked for, in order to secure that the situation of marketing executives would be considered as some central features of companies' internal and external business environment. Thus a quality of the study aimed for was that a majority of the marketing executives in the two industries would be able to recognise and relate to one of the mental models being identified, if they were to be confronted with the findings of the study. The article contains a presentation of the worked out framework for capturing managers' mental models is provided together with a description of the cases and of the methodology. Main findings are presented in a section, followed by conclusions, and managerial implications.

METHOD TO CAPTURE MANAGERS' MINDSETS

Semi-structured in-depth interviews with marketing executives in 22 companies or regional business units represent the main empirical base (14 consumer durable companies and 8 pharmaceutical companies). The companies differ considerably as regards to company age, and number of employees, as shown in Table 1. In addition to this, the represented Consumer Durable and pharmaceutical companies also differ as to market and product segments.

The total number of represented Consumer Durables (CD) companies is 14. In addition to marketing executives, the present researcher also interviewed other members of the middle management team. The reason for carrying out these interviews was to get additional insight about the decision situation of marketing executives in the CD industry,

Table 1.
Profile of the Sampled Companies

Years since establishment	*Less than 10*	*11-25 years*	*26-50 years*	*51-100 years*
CD	6	6	2	0
PHARMA	1	3	2	2
Number of employees	100 or less	101-250	251-500	501-1000
CD	2	4	4	3
PHARMA	3	3	2	0

and implicitly to secure credibility in the interpretation of 'the company agenda'. In the methodological literature such an approach is called 'data triangulation'; Denzin, (1978); Janesick, (1994); Yin, (1994); Hall & Rist, (1999). In the pharmaceutical (PHARMA) industry, the present researcher interviewed 08 marketing executives who all worked in companies holding a dominating market position within a particular therapeutic field for prescription-only medicine, and/or health care over-the-counter products. At the time of the interviews, four of the interviewed managers had a strategic responsibility for the marketing of prescription-only medicine, whereas rest four were primarily engaged with health care over-the-counter products. Half of the represented companies are subsidiaries within a multinational American, German, Dutch or British company. A common feature of this group of managers is that their strategic responsibility encompasses the North Eastern India market and that they have experiences of managing innovation projects.

All interviews followed the same guide (Appendix 1), lasted for about one-and-a-half to two hours and were documented. The structure of the interview guide reflects the framework, and the core motive to work with interview methods was to be able to focus on the 'actual details of one aspect of social life'. In relation to this it should be noted that the managers were encouraged to prolong their talk around a certain aspect or to further develop their talk around a process or a field of knowledge by describing a decision or project.

A three-stage process was followed when analysing the data, as suggested in the literature on conducting qualitative research and on analysing sense making processes; Thomas et al., (2001). Accordingly, the analysing process started with a reconstruction of the interviews to texts and to abstracts. Thus, each interview was fully transcribed and resulted in an empirical material. Thereafter, in the process of working out the abstracts, the data from each interview were arranged, as far as possible, into sections (issues, tasks and knowledge) and sub-sections. In the second stage, this was oriented to identify major trends in the data. In each individual abstract terms and statements were identified and marked out as a basis for creating codes (labels of the data) and categories subsequently. The aim was to break down the data into discrete ideas and beliefs relating to the three sections: 'issues', 'tasks' and 'knowledge'. Thereafter the present researcher looked for relationships between codes within and between sections for each interview. The output from this stage was one condensed version of the data in the form of terms and statements, and one abstracted version in the form of concepts and tentative categories. It can be noted, that all of the interviewed managers used a lot of established marketing concepts as well as popular terms stemming from the management literature, as is shown in the *Tables-1 to Table-4.*

When a first comparative analysis of mental models within and between companies had been made, some overall trends and themes emerged, and so did four overall and preliminary categories of mental models. One overall feature of managers' mindsets was a preoccupation with issues relating to radical product and/or brand innovation processes. And as regards to 'knowledge', the following two overall themes were identified: 'Market Actors and Market Phenomenon' and 'Company Culture and/or Brand Identity'. Furthermore, it then appeared as if managers' field of attention could be captured in a four-field matrix with the following dimensions: emphasis on market actors (high vs low) and emphasis on company culture (high vs low). And, that an attention to knowledge about new or evolving packaging technologies was a recurrent feature of all of the four preliminary categories, that is, in all of the four fields. The expansion of the data resulted in one additional theme ('Product and Process Technology') and two additional categories. In order to check and further verify this finding, a second coding process and comparison of all identified mental models in the CD industry was carried out. The result of this process did not change the number or the principal meaning of the categories. Thus, the identified categories in the CD industry were considered as saturated. However, during the second coding process it became evident that technology and then not only packaging technology has a central position in many marketing executives' mindsets. Another important result was that it became possible to give each one of the categories a name expressing a central feature of each one of the categories of mental models. The Same process has been followed for Pharmaceutical industry.

FINDINGS

New product innovation is a key corporate issue and that this also means being involved with innovation of positioning, innovation of processes, innovation of company culture, innovation of overall marketing logic and/or of business model. Accordingly, the findings show that 'marketing knowledge' at a corporate management level is about knowledge for developing new products above all, and not knowledge for making minor variations on existing products through: '(1) changing basic technologies, (2) adding features, or (3) "me-too" entrants that closely resemble existing (competitors) products'. In relation to this, it shall be noted that some marketing executives are captured by their previous experiences. That is, their mental models reflect a strategy that they are aiming to defuse, that is, a preoccupation with making minor variations of existing products. Henceforth, the term 'product innovation' or 'new product development' is used to denote radical product innovation.

Innovation is a key word for us. We need to continuously come up with new products. To realise this, we have to think differently in our production. There has to be room to make new products that we have no experience with. (CME in the CD industry)

If asked to put one word on what our strategy is then it is innovation, product development and innovation in the way of communicating the product. We focus very much on innovations. However, to come up with innovative ideas is not so hard, but to get them docked in the existing operation demands a lot. It's sometimes about a mental shift. (CME in the pharma industry)

Figure 1 shows that nine mindsets, or mental models, were identified and these were found as being 'in-use' at the time of the interviews. The remark being 'in-use' and the line around the Political Market Model (the PMM model) is made to highlight the dynamic character of mental models. The placement of the models in relation to the four overall themes in the data (the four boxes) illustrates similarities between mental models. Accordingly, due to an emphasis on internal structures and processes by three of the identified models in the CD industry, they have been labelled: 'Organisation Oriented Models'. A preoccupation with 'political and societal issues and processes' was only identified in the pharmaceutical industry. The study also revealed similarities between the two industries. Thus, three 'Market Oriented Models' were identified in both industries. The presentation of findings is structured around the above mentioned three broad categories of mental models. The presentation of the three categories is partly made by direct quotations and additionally by a listing of terms and sentences stemming from individual interviews *(See Tables 2- 4)*.

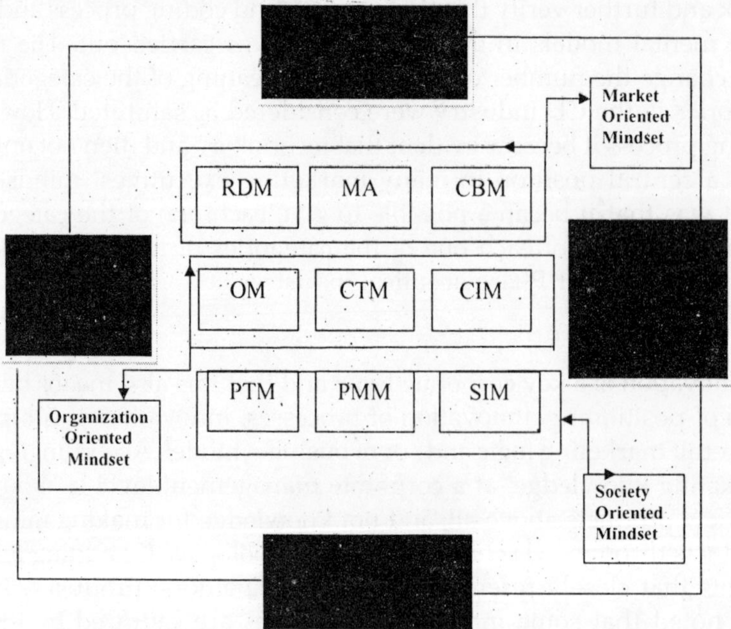

Figure 1: Four Themes and Three Overall Categories of Mindsets

MARKET ORIENTED MINDSETS

According to the Research & Development Model (RDM), product innovation means, above all, being concerned about linking knowledge about product and process technology with knowledge about key customers' values and strategies. Furthermore, it means being involved in processes that aim to integrate further these two fields of knowledge. Due to the latter, knowledge about how to manage projects and teams is regarded as central. The RDM also stresses the importance to secure that knowledge about product and process technology is kept up-to-date, and then not only in R&D but also in the marketing department. As expressed and as shown in Table 2, a key task is to nurture relationships with research organisations and with governmental organisations. Furthermore, the perception is that the knowledge emerging from these relationships has to be supplemented with a deep insight about the technologies, strategies and values of key customers.

The core issue for us is to build up trust. We are very much dependent upon journalists and doctors and a large part of my job concerns working together with different institutions for the sake of getting some documentation on our products. (CME in the health care sector/RDM)

The Market Actors Model (MAM) is focused on the generation and dissemination of explicit knowledge about end-users', resellers' or hospitals' decision processes, and of the positioning strategies and immediate actions of competitors. A key managerial task is to develop further a market oriented business culture through the bringing in of market facts and of a marketing vocabulary, and to identify new ways to combat an ever-increasing competition. As regards to product innovation, key tasks concern managing projects dealing with radical new packaging formats and designs and with new brand positioning strategies. In the pharmaceutical industry, a key task is also to prolong the patent period of branded cash cows through identification of radical new ways to formulate and to document brand values. Furthermore, a key task is to identify new products for licensing through continuous contacts with brokers. Table 2 highlight that important knowledge is about unambiguous market measurements and about key client customers' attitudes and competitors actions.

In the market for cough and cold and multivitamins you got to differentiate and you got to satisfy the trade. You have to offer a unique presentation form. Key account management is becoming very important. (The health care sector/MAM)

It is getting harder and harder to create new products, we have to think a long way ahead and we have to be extremely good at finding out how our competitive situation looks like when we are ready to launch. (The prescription medicine sector/MAM)

One aspect that sets the Customer Brand Model (CBM) apart from the other two 'Market Oriented Models' is that the co-operation between marketing and product development is perceived as being close, continuous and productive. The motive to be engaged with organisational structure issues is to ensure that one's ideas and practices reflect the values and the various use situations of end-users. In relation to this, it shall be noted that the model also expresses an eagerness to emancipate oneself from a marketing logic that has impressed knowledge creation and innovation for a long time. However, although the CBM shows up a self-critical stance regarding the existing stock of 'marketing knowledge', the model also shows up an inclination to constrain its interpretations. The latter has to do with some clear-cut policies and programmes for the identities and the positioning strategies of brands. A second aspect that set the CBM apart is shown in Table 2 and in the two quotations below. Thus, a recurrent theme in these interviews was the vision to decrease the communication gap with end-users, through making use of new and evolving forms of communication technology (in the market and inside the company).

The demands for us to work with innovation and consumer knowledge are strong. We have been trapped, by tactical activities, and by line extensions. We have spent entirely too little time thinking about the fundamentals, about what consumers want. That is good health, clear conscience and pleasure and the things that add value. (CME in the consumer Durable industry/CBM)

Previously we tended to be very focused on professional customers. We were naive in not dealing with consumers. The trend is that consumers want to get more involved in health care. We have to make sure that we meet their needs and communicate properly. (CME in the prescription medicine sector/CBM).

Table 2
Market Oriented Mindsets

CD & PHARMA	*Research/Development Model (RDM)*	*Market Actors Model (MAM)*	*Consumer Brand Model (CBM)*
OTC = over-the-counter.			
Product segments:	Ingredients to the CD industry, prescription medicine and health care OTC products	Technology Oriented, prescription medicine and health care OTC products	Half and fully technological products, prescription medicine and health care OTC products
Issues:			
Company	Market position, category growth, true innovation and differentiation	An ageing product portfolio, innovation, brand loyalty and brand positioning	End-user driven, genuine innovation, company growth, brand growth
Marketing	Product innovation and security, knowledge creation, relationships	Competition, availability, trying out new ways, thinking differently, in production, company culture	The fundamentals, consumers' health, conscience and pleasure, marketing creativity
Tasks:			
Marketing	Product documentation, category management, relationship building, the bringing in of new knowledge, integration	Establish a market vocabulary, competitor intelligence, life-cycle mgt, b-to-b marketing	Understanding consumer needs and situations, new concept development, new modes of communication
Key processes:	Knowledge creation, key account management, corporate management of radical innovation	Branding, packaging design, market research, market planning, key-account management and distribution	Marketing as a bridge, consumer communication, and incremental and radical product development
Knowledge: CD & Pharma	Managing projects, how to implement a market view, product technology, clients' technology and strategy	Fact-based marketing, buying behaviour, competitor intelligence, brand image, category knowledge	Consumer values, situations and problems, needs related to a meal, doctor-patient interactions, brand values

The agenda for product innovation is according to MAM set by other parties (the retailing trade, the packaging industry, the manufacturing plant and/or the department for research and development). However, as shown by Table 2, this is a situation that marketing executives are eager to change through the bringing in of explicit market knowledge in the corporate process for market planning or for product development. Following RDM and CBM, product innovation presupposes a radical new way of organising product development and/or marketing. The RDM also stresses the development of a new process to manage knowledge about customers. A total reorientation as regards to 'marketing knowledge' is another antecedent to product innovation according to CBM.

ORGANISATION ORIENTED MINDSETS

According to the Operations Management Model (OMM), product innovation is carried out in close co-operation between marketing and manufacturing and as 'a probe and learn process'. Furthermore, the OMM expresses the idea that radical product innovation comes very much from combining existing knowledge about food technology in new ways, or from combining existing electronic technology with a new packaging technology. Being customer oriented means according to OMM to 'listen to' the big retailing organisations' claims, above all. As implied above, another important source for new product ideas is the packaging industry; an industry to which one has a number of close learning relationships with. A creation of the latter with the big retailing organisations is an issue that stands at the top of the OMM agenda.

A key feature of the Culture Technology Model (CTM) is the notion that product innovation rests on having established 'a passion for technology culture', and then not only in the department for marketing and for product development. The creation of such culture, or more correctly attitude towards electronics technology, presupposes according to CTM an identification of key values that everyone can understand and relate to. Furthermore, it necessitates the running of educational programmes about technologies to all categories of employees. The middle position of the CTM in Figure 1 is also due to its emphasis on 'product security' and on systems for checking quality. The reason for naming the third model Corporate Identity Model (CIM) has to do with its focus on the actual versus the desired identities of brands. According to the CIM, new product development rests on having some common and basic ideas and beliefs about 'what characterises a good and an excellent bread?' The approach to get an answer to this question is not market analysis, but instead internal discussions to reach an agreement on the meaning of 'excellence' with regard to the look, texture, durability, nutritional content, etc. (other terms that were mentioned besides good and excellence were uniqueness and character). One field of knowledge stemming from external sources that is regarded as important concerns new technologies. In addition, knowledge about the aesthetic dimension of electronic goods packaging design is regarded as an emergent and important field. This goes also for knowledge about general cultural trends in the society.

We have to acquire more competencies within the convenience sector, to be able to develop that sector. We also have to listen more to the market, what they really want. We are all in agreement on that. At the moment we have a 24 hours logistic project running together with our big customers, our wholesalers. (CME in the CD industry/OMM)

We have created five values: teamwork; craftsmanship; diving for pearls; balance in life; magic thinking. We have worked with them on all levels during the last two years. They are in place. They back us up. Craftsmanship means different things. It's something you cannot talk about. (CME in the CD industry/CTM)

In the marketing department, we say 'we want products with character'. It is about being unique, being a bit special. It is about standing out, being different. That is a claim we should be able to make all the time, all the way through. The thing is that it has to be something that exists inside the company. The thing is, however, what we do not do today. (CME in the CD industry/CIM)

Although the three 'Organisation Oriented Models' show up a common focus on knowledge about internal structures and processes - a difference exists between them. The first one of the three quotations above expresses an eagerness to expand the present knowledge domain with some specific and explicit knowledge about the processing and the distribution of food. Thus, the OMM is a model that approaches product innovation through developing the upper part of the value chain (see Table 3). In the second quotation,

Table 3
Organisation Oriented Mindsets

Consumer Durable industry	*Operations Management Model (OMM)*	*Culture Technology Model (CTM)*	*Corporate Identity Model (CIM)*
Issues:			
Company	Increased foreign competition, low price trend, new trends in food technology	The creation of a food culture, product and brand restoration, total quality management (TQM), a culinary competence	What values should be our key values? Decreasing brand loyalty, deteriorating performance
Marketing	The big retailing chains' brand strategies and claims, the low-price trend	A house of strong but old brands, product security, decreasing brand loyalty and first trials	The consumers want to know more, live up to promises, consistency and continuity
Tasks:			
Marketing	Listen to what the key customers really want, manage new product development (PD) projects, branding	Think outside the box, networking, establish a common language, consumer insight	Brand management, to find out the right things to stand for, create new product and brand concepts
Key processes:	Product and process development, logistics, key account management, branding	supply chain management (SCM), human resource management (HRM), PD and customer relationship management (CRM) are all equally important - the critical thing is the interplay	Communication and product development: create consistency and continuity
Knowledge: Consumer Durable Industry	Key customer's claims, project management, new processing and packaging technologies	Business idea, technology, market insight, brand values, marketing tools, finance	Values that we all believe in, packaging technologies, general values and functional food

technology is also stressed. However, it is not explicit knowledge that stands at the centre in the CTM, but know-how knowledge about usage of technology. In addition to this is knowledge about the company culture regarded as important, and so is knowledge about the identities of some key sub-brands and how to develop brands. A central theme in the third quotation is also company core values. However, for the CIM this is a perception that only is resident within the marketing department.

SOCIETY ORIENTED MINDSETS

One feature that two of these models share is an emphasis on knowledge about attitudes regarding particular health care problems and their causes (as high blood pressure and cholesterol caused by food consumption, smoking, etc.) among consumers and, above all, among decision makers in the business and institutional world (insurance companies, employers' associations, public health care committees, parliament, etc.). Another common feature relates to issues that had been in focus in the past, and thus implicitly that a change has taken place. Previously, the focus was on sources for ideas to build up product and brand awareness in the market and, above all, on sources for ideas to 'bring about changes within a number of laws and decrees to open up the market a little more' (cf. CME is the health care industry/PTM). This 'abandoned' model relates to a period lasting for about 25 years when the interest of some health care innovations showed up a positive trend among end-users, but when the market was highly regulated (the products were available only on a doctor's prescription and/or were not allowed to be sold outside traditional pharmacies). The Political Market Model (PMM) was described as 'the' model until the end of 2001. At this point in time some non-prescriptive products were allowed to be sold in consumer durable retailing stores.

One of the Society Oriented Models that was identified as 'being in use' has been named the Political Technology Model (PTM) and the reason has to do with its emphasis on knowledge about 'what is happening' in R&D for prescription-only medicine. The motive for this engagement was explained by one of the interviewed managers:

In general, health care innovations start as medicine. That is, we start to sell the product profitably in the Rx sector, [the prescription medicine sector] were we have a patent and are alone. Then, eventually, it becomes generic and it is handed over to the OTC world [over-the-counter sector]. (cf. CME is the health care industry/PTM)

Thus, an early insight into the development process of new prescription medicine is perceived as important, to at all being able to influence product innovation in the health care over-the-counter sector. Due to this, knowledge about particular therapeutic fields is conceived as important, and so is knowledge about methods for infusing end-user knowledge into innovation processes. Public relation is still regarded as representing a key knowledge area. However, in contrast to the second model that is 'in-use' in the pharmaceutical industry, it is knowledge about how to influence 'the political debate' that has a priority.

According to the Society Identity Model (SIM), the overall issue is 'category growth', compared with previously 'brand growth'. For corporate level marketing, this claim has given rise to an intense search and exploration of new ideas and to the formulation of a new business model for health care over-the-counter products. The latter has to do with that the perspective on strategy has changed from micro (product lines and brands) to macro marketing (health care issues and solutions). In addition to this, the primary unit of exchange has changed (from goods to services) and so has the relationships with authorities, regulatory agencies and end-users. The mode of interaction with these constituencies has changed from 'acting to create transactions to relational exchanges and co-production'. Furthermore, another view of health care products is under formation: 'from transmitters of values to appliances in value-creation processes'. This way of clarifying the meaning of the change, as it was described by the interviewed managers, stems from Vargo and Lusch (2004).

Innovation is not just about products. It can also mean finding out that a product could be used successfully in another field of application, treating another type of condition, than what was defined and communicated previously. We have got to think broader otherwise we have a big problem. (CME in the health care industry/PTM)

We have got to find new ways to grow and to see the market from another perspective. It's about running a number of projects and starting up a good dialogue with our authorities in different parts of the world. It's all about finding a good dialogue with authorities so that we fulfil the health promotion goals that they have, that we have. (CME in the health care industry/SIM)

A recurrent theme in the 'Society Oriented Model' concerned realising a change in the dominating model for product innovation and/or for marketing. As expressed in the quotations above, a shift is aimed for in the dominating conception of what product innovation is and who represents the market (see also Table 4). The study showed in addition that these managers are also involved with developing processes to increase further the level of market intelligences in product innovation, and/or with developing new processes for communicating with constituencies in the institutional environment.

Table 4
Society Oriented Mindsets

PHARMA	*Political Technology Model (PTM)*	*Political Market Model (PMM)*	*Society Identity Model (SIM)*
Product segments:	Health care OTC products	Health care OTC products	Health care OTC products
Issues:			
Company	Price consciousness, the negative image of the industry, the long time between real innovations	Slow product growth/ market penetration due to decrees and laws that regulate the market	Industry growth, innovation, the general health consciousness - a trend to be kept alive
Marketing	The link between prescription (Rx) and over-the-counter (OTC), liberalisation in the OTC trade, the scope for product innovation	Barriers to think about and to buy health care products among consumers	A good dialogue with authorities, innovation in ways of communicating, how to do things differently, a mental shift
Tasks:			
Marketing	Influence the political debate, provide R&D with market input, link OTC to Rx, branding: the emotional bond	Create awareness and an interest among politicians and authorities about health care problems and their solutions	Initiate and push changes, manage projects together with authorities, generate innovative ideas, market communication, and trend analysis
Key processes:	Public relations, the interface between Rx and OTC and that between marketing and R&D, marketing communication	Open up the market public relations, distribution and customer relationship management (pharmacies)	Public relations, corporate management processes to push innovation, market research to secure the right consumer insight
Knowledge:	The political agenda, tools for political marketing, what we think end-users are looking for, therapeutic fields and medicine	Public relations, distribution and customer relationship management (pharmacies)	Facts about deceases and how to create health, consumer insight, a number of alternative scenarios, our brand's soul

CONCLUSIONS

Conclusion to be drawn from the study is that marketing management has different meanings among marketing executives in the same industry. Three overall themes and six categories of mental models were identified in both of the industries. Furthermore, the study also showed that realising growth through launching new products is considered a key, or more prominently, 'the' key issue among marketing executives in both industries (although minor variations on existing products are a recurrent element in the companies' marketing strategies). Accordingly, another conclusion is that product innovation is managed differently by marketing executives in the same geographical region, industry and even within the same product segment. As previously stated, the term 'product innovation' or 'new product development' is used to denote radical product innovation.

In the typology of mental models (Figure 2), there are six models that show up a focus on concepts, issues, etc. outside the traditional scope of marketing. Additionally, there are two 'Market Oriented Models' for which 'technology' and/or 'organisational values' is a central theme. Thus, another conclusion is that product innovation at a corporate marketing level is also about knowledge outside the traditional scope of marketing's periphery. On the basis of the above and with the support from Wind's (2005, p. 864) discussion of the 'need for a broader, multidisciplinary approach to marketing challenges' the following proposition is laid out: in research and education there is a need to notice that valuable marketing knowledge is not constrained to 'pure' marketing concepts. Accordingly, there is a need to notice that a 'general management' perspective may be asked for in order to work out tools for marketing executives (concepts, frameworks, etc.).

In addition to the above, it was found that managers in the pharmaceutical industry have changed their focus, or more correctly strategy, as regards to societal and political issues. Furthermore, some managers in the food industry have replaced their 'Market Actors Model' with an 'Organisation Oriented Model'. These similarities and that marketing executives in both industries also where found to be involved with other innovation areas have given rise to the following another conclusion: marketing executives in the CD and in the pharmaceutical industry use different approaches and change their approaches for product innovation over time, in order to improve the market orientation of their companies. The comprehensive study by Harris (2002) supports this conclusion and points at a research field that until now has been sparsely explored.

One central idea behind the study has been that marketing executives are engaged with product innovation, and that this engagement is governed by some more or less stable ideas and beliefs, a mental model, about marketing management. In order to capture these cognitions, an analytical framework was worked out and an interpretative research approach was followed. Finally in conclusion concerns the framework and the empirical results that it generated. On the basis of the insight that the study has provided about marketing executives mental models, it can be more correctly asserted, that the framework makes a contribution to the literature on strategic marketing.

MANAGERIAL IMPLICATIONS

A critical issue for general managers concerns recruiting the right top managers for marketing, human resource management, research and development, etc., considering the company agenda. As regards to this, the mental model concept and the study's typology not only inspire but also provide support for general managers to reflect critically on the present dominant logic for marketing management and to come to a conclusion whether or not a shift is asked for and whether or not such a shift may call for recruiting a new marketing executive. One main implication to be drawn from the study from a corporate level marketing perspective is that there exists more than one potential logic, or approach, to follow, when the vision is to increase marketing's contribution or influence on firms' innovation capability. Furthermore, that radical product innovation in some situations may presuppose an involvement with non-marketing knowledge and with non-marketing tasks. Although no single logic is pointed out as being 'the' preferable one, another important implication concerns that the typology provides a basis and a provocation for a reflective and productive dialogue within the marketing function about existing, evolving and/or potential new mindsets for product innovation.

APPENDIX- I: INTERVIEW GUIDE

Issues	What issues stand at the top of the agenda of your company? And, what issues do you regard as being core for your company in the nearest future?
	You have mentioned ... Can you please elaborate the meaning of it?
	With respect to marketing - what issues do you regard as core in the nearest future?
	What issues stand at the moment at the top of your agenda and why?
	You have mentioned ... Can you please elaborate the meaning of it?
Tasks	What is corporate marketing management all about?
	What decisions and other management activities are you involved with?
	What task or tasks do you consider as being the most important one(s)?
	You have mentioned ... Can you please elaborate the meaning of it?
	What are the key business processes for marketing to be involved with?
	You have mentioned ... Can you please elaborate the meaning of it?
Knowledge	What knowledge do you regard as being important to realise strategy? What marketing knowledge, market facts, etc. are regarded as 'alpha & omega' for your company?
	What knowledge is regarded as 'alpha & omega' for marketing?
	Is some knowledge more important and if so what is the reason?
	You have mentioned ... Can you please elaborate the meaning of it?
	What knowledge do you relate to product innovation?
	You have mentioned ... Can you please elaborate the meaning of it?

REFERENCES

Adamides, E.D., Stamboulis, Y. and Kanellopoulos, V. (2003), "Economic Integration and Strategic Change: The Role of Managers' mental models.." Strategic Change, Vol. 12 , pp. 69-82.

Adams, R., Bessant, J. and Phelps, R. (2006), "Innovation Management Measurement: A Review.." Journal of Management Reviews, Vol 8 , pp. 21-47.

Alfranca, O., Rama, R. and von Tunzelmann, N. (2004), "Innovation Spells in the Multinational Agri-food Sector.." Technovation, Vol. 24 , pp. 599-614.

Armistead, C. and Meakins, M. (2002), "A Framework for Practicing Knowledge Management.." Long Range Planning, Vol. 35, pp. 49-71.

Atuahene-Gima, K. (2005), "Resolving the Capability-rigidity Paradox in New Product Innovation.." Journal of Marketing, Vol. 69, pp. 61-83.

Becker, M.C. and Lillemark, M. (2006), "Marketing/R&D Integration in the Pharmaceutical Industry.." Research Policy, Vol. 35, pp. 105-120.

Bettis, R. and Wong (2003), Dominant Logic, Knowledge Creation, and Managerial Choice.., Edited by S. Easterby-Smith, M. and Lyles, M. A. The Blackwell handbook of organisational learning and knowledge management pp. 343-355. Blackwell Publishing , Malden, MA

Brring, S., Cloutier, M. and Leker, J. (2006), "The Front End of Innovation in an Era of Industry Convergence: Evidence from Nutraceuticals and Functional Foods" R&D Management, Vol. 36, pp. 487-498.

Chermack, T. (2003), "Mental Models in Decision Making and Implications for Human Resource Development.." Advances in Developing Human Resources, Vol 5, pp. 408-422.

Davenport, T., Leibold, M. and Voelpel, S. (2006), "Strategic Management in the Innovation Economy" Wiley , Erlangen

Day, G. (2002), "Managing the Market Learning Process.". Journal of Business & Industrial Marketing, Vol. 17, pp. 240-252.

Day, G. and Schoemaker, S. (2004), "Driving through the Fog: Managing at the Edge.." Long Range Planning, Vol. 37, pp. 127-142.

Denzin, N. K. (1978), "The Research Act: A Theoretical Introduction to Sociological Methods", McGraw-Hill, New York — (2nd ed.)

Dougherty, D., Borrelli, L., Munir, K. and O'Sullivan, A. (2000), "Systems of Organisational Sensemaking for Sustained Product Innovation..", Journal of Engineering and Technology Management, Vol. 17, pp. 321-355.

Fiol, M. (1996) "Squeezing Harder doesn't always Work: Continuing the Search for Consistency in Innovation Research.." Academy of Management Review, Vol. 21, pp. 1012-1021.

Hall, A.L. and Rist, R.C. (1999), "Integrating Multiple Qualitative Research Methods.". Psychology & Marketing, Vol. 16, pp. 291-304.

Harms, F., Rohman, S., Heinrich, M., Druener, M. and Trommsdorff, V. (2002), "Innovative Marketing.." Pharmaceutical Policy and Law, Vol. 5, pp. 135-149.

Harris, L.C. (2002) "Developing Market Orientation: An Exploration of Differences in Management Approaches.." Journal of Marketing Management, Vol. 18, pp. 603-632.

Jacobs, C.D. and Heracleous, L.T. (2005), "Answers for Questions to Come: Reflective Dialogue as an Enabler of Strategic Innovation.." Journal of Organisational Change Management, Vol. 18, pp. 338-352.

Janesick, V.J. Denzin, N.K. and Lincoln, Y.S. (1994), The Dance of Qualitative Research Design.. Edited by Janesick, V.J. Denzin, N.K. and Lincoln, Y.S. Handbook of qualitative research. Sage, London, pp. 209-219.

Karp, T. (2005), "Unpacking the Mysteries of Change: Mental Modeling.." Journal of Change Management, Vol. 5, pp. 87-96.

Sanchez, R. and Heene, A. (2004), "The New Strategic Management" Wiley , New York

Schuiling, I. and Moss, G. (2004), "How Different are Branding Strategies in the Pharmaceutical Industry and the Fast-moving Consumer Goods Sector?". Brand Management Vol. 11, pp. 366-380.

Thomas, J.B., Sussman, S.W. and Henderson, J.C. (2001), "Understanding Strategic Learning: Linking Organisational Learning, Knowledge Management, and Sensemaking.." Organisation Science, Vol. 12, pp. 331-345.

Vargo, S. and Lusch, R. (2004), "Evolving to a New Dominant Logic for Marketing.." Journal of Marketing, Vol. 68, pp. 1-17.

Weick, K.E. Staw, B. and Salancik, G. (1977), "New Directions in Organisational behaviour" St. Clair Press , Chicago, IL , pp. 209-219

Wind, J. (2005), "Marketing as an Engine of Business Growth: A Cross-functional Perspective.." Journal of Business Research, Vol. 58, pp. 863-873.

Yadav, M.S., Prabhu, J.C. and Chandy, R.K. (2007), "Managing the Future: CEO Attention and Innovation Outcomes.." Journal of Marketing, Vol. 71, pp. 84-101.

Yin, R.K. (1994) "Case Study Research", Sage , London

7

PILGRIMAGE SATISFACTION: AN APPRAISAL OF SERVICES PROVIDED AT JWALAJI

Vikas Sharma, Meenakshi Gupta

INTRODUCTION

Pilgrims are persons in motion, passing through territories not their own and seeking something we might call completion, or perhaps the word clarity will do as well a goal to which only the spirit's compass points the way (Richard, 2004). As the pilgrims of all castes, classes of different states and countries have devotion and faith in the matter of religious worship. It is believed that there is a sacred aim behind this and that aim is to fulfill the desire of obtaining "Punya" and to get rid of "Paap" apart from their personal motives. The pilgrims coming from different areas and castes stay together and all of them observe the rules and tradition of that faith of religious recitations, sacred fasts, restriction of food and diet. Travel for religious purposes has assumed an increasing significance these days. It is a well-established custom in many parts of the world. In India due to diversity of culture and emotions people give utmost importance to spiritual matters and visit holy places. India being a second largest populated country in the world generates huge revenue through its pilgrimage places (Jha, 1978). The tourism traffics both domestic and international for various purposes like ethnic, socio-cultural understanding; pleasure, environmental change, and religious purpose have been increased significantly since recent time. It is the pilgrimage or "tirath yatra" or tourism for religious purpose that has caused people to travel for regeneration of spirit, mental peace and quick cultural exchange. The pilgrimage destinations and religious centers ought to have facilities and aesthetic requirements which not only meet the pilgrim's religious and spiritual needs but also keep them generating a desire to visit the destination time and again. Being a country of the pious, India is dotted with pilgrimages which are wide spread through out the country. Pilgrimage tourism in India is extremely popular. Great religions like Hinduism, Buddhism and Sikhism have originated on the Indian soil. There are seven main sacred cities in India Varanasi, Puri (Jagannath temple), Mathura, Ayodhya, Dwarka, Haridwar and Kanchi. Many of the great spiritual teachers are associated with these sacred places. Probably the greatest concentration of pilgrims in any region in the world occurs in India's mountain regions of Jammu and Kashmir, Himachal Pradesh and Uttar Pradesh, where millions of pilgrims each year arrive the major entry point into the Pahari region. Major sites of pilgrimage (dhams) like Shri Mata Vaishno Devi, Amarnathji, Shiv Khori, Budha Amaranth and temples under Kangra valley Shrines like Jwalaji, Chitpurni, Chamunda Devi have existed in this region since the beginning of Hindu civilization, if not before. Apart from this Sri Harmandir Sahib Temple, Hemkund Sahib, most revered shrines for Sikhs and Buddhist Shrines also have several pilgrim spots in Punjab and Himachal Pradesh apart from Sarnath in Bihar. Today tourism accounts for nearly half of the domestic product of hill areas of Jammu and Kashmir, Himachal Pradesh and Uttar Pradesh. Sixty per cent of the tourists are pilgrims; almost entirely from other parts of India (Goswami et al. 2003). These pilgrim places not only contribute to the economy of the state but also provide an employment opportunity to local people and therefore need a careful marketing strategy so as to overcome different constraints that hamper its growth. In the present study an attempt is made to measure satisfaction level of pilgrims regarding different services made available to them at Jwalaji. As the demand and popularity of any destination rely heavily on the satisfaction level of pilgrims or tourist in terms of infrastructural facilities, availability of goods and services in and around the pilgrimage destination, focus on the customer environmental sensitivity, and relative competition in the pilgrimage tourism market. The present study focused and concentrated to all the above issues for identifying a better initiative in the area of pilgrim satisfaction.

OBJECTIVE

Keeping this in view, the present study was conducted with the following objectives:

- To ascertain the satisfaction level of pilgrims visiting the holy shrines as per their demographic profile.
- To measure satisfaction level of pilgrims for major Pilgrimage services available during the pilgrimage to the shrine.
- To identify various problems and suggest viable remedies to develop sustainable Pilgrimage tourism

REVIEW OF LITERATURE

A pilgrim can be in a secular state and spend a day at a sea resort during a pilgrimage and was impossible to distinguish between religious tourists and ordinary travelers (Smith, 1992). Pilgrimage tourism may be of short-term religious tourism and long-term tourism (Rinschede, 1992). Marketing of religious organization is sufficiently different from business and other non business marketing (Wrenn, 1993). His study has focused on dominance of non financial objectives. Williams 2003 focused on the importance of satisfying religious needs as a part of a tailor-made tourist product in the hospitality industry. Study pointed out that personal values and cultural orientation of various customers not only determined what attributes a customer seeks in the hospitality product but also affected its tariff. Hence, adding religious values to the attributes of the augmented hotel product was recommended to attract new customer segments. Shalini 2006 attempted to describe the prototypical pilgrim from amongst the wide array of contemporary religious and secular tourists. Firstly, the concept of pilgrimages was discussed, so to distinguish it from the tourism concept secondly, the geographical notion of genus loci was employed to exemplify the fundamental quest. Pamela 2007 examined the relationship between two sets of variables that were used in evaluating a travel destination. Five variables divided into two parts were used to evaluate travel destination. Tim Wintera 2007 witnessed a seemingly relentless surge in the movement of tourists of Asian origin. It was observed that tourism in Asia had received little attention to date. . Fang Mengs et al. 2008 examined the relationship between destination attribute importance and performance, travel motivation, and satisfaction in South-East Virginia. Factor analysis was employed to identify the dimensions of the destination attributes on importance and performance and composite delineated factors were used as indicators to measure the overall tourist satisfaction in the regression analysis. Study Revealed that quality services and lodging performance was significant factors in determining the overall satisfaction, food and location was of significant importance in the satisfaction evaluation. Raghuraman and Madhvan 2000 studied the pilgrim's inflow at holy shrines of Tirupati Balaji, Shiridi, and Sabrimala. The study was based on personal observation, questionnaire, and primary data. The study suggested for the improvement in quality of services at shrines, waiting time, queue management and increase in darshan time and making availability of accommodation facility through computerized system. Goswami and Raveendran 2003 evaluated the overall scenario of pilgrim tourism in India and found shortcomings in different facilities offered to the pilgrims. He suggested the improvement in infrastructure in pilgrimage places, betterment of basic facilities like adequate accommodation facility, satisfactory street lightning, good roads, drinking water facility and public conveniences. He also suggested the development of tourist circuits to group smaller destinations with popular destinations. Sushma, 2001 studied the pilgrim tourism at Shri Mata Vaishno Devi. Factor analysis was applied to the transport services and multiple regression was used to work out the strength of association between marketing mix variables. Study focused on betterment of transport, accommodation and food facilities so as to develop sustainable marketing strategy for pilgrim tourism.

HYPOTHESES OF THE STUDY

1. There is no significant variation in satisfaction level among the pilgrims as per their domicile.
2. There is no significant variation in the satisfaction level derived by different income groups visiting the shrines.

RESEARCH METHODOLOGY

The study is based mainly on the primary data collected from pilgrims visiting the shrine with the help of a well drafted pre tested structured questionnaire. Data were collected from the sample respondents on the pre-structured and pre-tested questionnaire and personal interview method for the period 2007-08. The total sample consisted of 120 respondents. These respondents were selected randomly from Kangra the District Head Quarter and Jwalamukhi the base camp for Jwalaji. Further the population was divided into local and non local pilgrims.

Tool used for Analysis of Data

Discriminant analysis was carried out to study the pilgrim's demographic and traveling profile. Mean scores were used to rank the respondents satisfaction level towards the fifty three attributes accessing the satisfaction level of pilgrims from different services. Before applying the factor analysis Kaiser-Meyer-Olkin (KMO) measure of sampling adequacy and Bartlett's test of sphericity was used to test correlation matrix. Principal component method of factor analysis with varimax rotation was employed to reduce the fifty three attributes into a few, correlated and meaningful dimensions. Only items with factor loading of (0.50) or above and Eigen values greater than (1) were extracted.

Multiple regression analysis was used to examine the relative importance of the overall satisfaction about a particular service (dependent variable) and different marketing mix variables (independent variables). Coefficient of determination (R^2) was used to work out the strength of association between these dependent and independent variables.

T-test was used to test the statistical significance of the variations in satisfaction level among the pilgrims as per their domicile and to check the significance variation in the satisfaction level derived by different income groups one way ANOVA was used.

RESULTS AND DISCUSSIONS

Satisfaction Level of Pilgrims Visiting the Holy Shrine as per their Demographic Profile

The result revealed that the largest majority of the sample respondents (75%) were male and 76% were married. Based on their domicile, local and non local pilgrims were 24% and 76% respectively The majority of the pilgrims at Shri Mata Vaishno Devi were in the age group of 30-45years (42%) which was followed in 45-60 years (30%), 17-30 years (26%) and above 60 years (2 %) The above figures indicated that majority of the pilgrims were in middle age group who lead the group, had sufficient experience and knowledge of

Table 1
Demographic Profile of the Pilgrims Visiting the Holy Shrines

Category	*Respondents*		*Category*	*Respondents*	
	No.	*%age*		*No.*	*%age*
Gender			*Education*		
Male	90	75%	Under Graduate	55	45%
Female	30	25%	Graduation	47	40%
			Post graduation	18	15%
			Income(in Rs)		
Marital Status			Up to 5000	11	9%
Married	89	76%	5000- 10000	75	62%
Unmarried	31	24%	10000- 15000	27	23%
			15000 & above	7	6%
Domicile			*Occupation*		
Local	31	24%	Agriculturist	22	18%
Non- Local	89	76%	Professional	37	31%
			Business	26	22%
			Service	28	23%
			Others	7	6%
Age (in Years)					
17- 30	31	26%			
30- 45	51	42%			
45- 60	36	30%			
Above 60	2	2%			

traveling to these sacred places. Education- wise it was discernible that the largest majority of the pilgrims were undergraduates (45%) followed by graduates (40%) and post graduates (15%). It was discernible that 9% pilgrims had income up to 5000, 62% had income between 5000- 10000, 23% had income between 10000- 15000. However, 6% pilgrims had income of 15000 & above It was discernible based on visitors profile that 18% pilgrims were agriculturist, 31% were professional, 22% were businessman, 23% pilgrims were from service class and 6% were from other class.

Majority of the sample respondents (66%) were satisfied and 34% were dissatisfied in respect to their overall satisfaction level with the shrine

Table 2
Overall Satisfaction Level of the Pilgrims

	Respondents	
Satisfaction Level	*No.*	*%age*
Satisfied	80	66%
Dissatisfied	40	34%

To analyze the role of demographic variables in predicting satisfaction level of pilgrims visiting the holy shrines, discriminant analysis was used. The dependent variable is satisfaction level and the independent variables are gender, marital status, age, education, occupation and income. Among the independent variables, it can be inferred that the best predictor for satisfaction level was age with a higher coefficient of (0.705) followed by martial status (0.381), education (0.349), annual income (0.345), gender (0.286), and occupation (0.118).

Table 3
Better Predictor Among Demographic Variables in Predicting Satisfaction Level of Pilgrims

Variable	*Coefficient*
Age	0.705
Gender	0.286
Marital Status	0.381
Education	0.349
Income	0.345
Occupation	0.118

Table 4
Independent Samples Test for Statistical Significance of the Variations in Satisfaction Level Among the Pilgrims as per their Domicile

	Levene's Test for Equality of Variances		*t-test for Equality of Means*						
	F	*Sig.*	*t*	*df*	*Sig. (2-tailed)*	*Mean Difference*	*Std. Error Difference*	*95% Confidence Interval of the Difference*	
								Lower	*Upper*
Equal variances assumed	1.598	.209	-.586	118	.559	-.05799	.09900	-.254	.13805
Equal variances not assumed			-.597	54.16	.553	-.05799	.09720	-.253	.13686

T-test was used to test the statistical significance of the variations in satisfaction level among the pilgrims as per their domicile. The significance value for the t test was .559 which indicated that no significant difference existed between the two group means. In other words it can be said that our null hypothesis was accepted and it can be concluded that there is no significant variation in satisfaction level among the pilgrims as per their domicile.

One-way ANOVA was used to test the statistical significance of the variations in satisfaction level among the pilgrims as per their income. In one-way ANOVA, the total variation is partitioned into two components; Between Groups represents variation of the group means around the overall mean. Within Groups represents variation of the individual scores around their respective group means. Sig. indicates the significance level of the F-test. Small significance values (<.05) indicate group differences. The significance level is.158 which is more than the level of .05 we had set, so the null hypothesis is accepted and it is concluded that there is no significant variation in satisfaction level among the pilgrims as per their income.

Table 5
ONE WAY ANOVA for Statistical Significance of the Variations in Satisfaction Level Among the Pilgrims as per their Income

Source of variation	*Sum of Squares*	*d f*	*Mean Square*	*F*	*Sig.*
Between Groups	1.164	3	.388	1.765	.158
Within Groups	25.502	116	.220		
Total	26.667	119			

Satisfaction Level of Pilgrims for Major Pilgrimage Services

To access the satisfaction level of pilgrims visiting shrine of Jwalaji from different services fifty three attributes were identified and a model was developed with satisfaction level as dependent variable and these fifty three attributes as independent variables i.e.

$$P(S) = f(x_1, x_2, x_{3,\dots\dots,} x_{53})$$

Where $x_1, x_2, x_{3,\dots,} x_{53}$ are various attributes accessing the satisfaction level of pilgrims from the different types of services and these are explained in Table 6.

Table 6
Satisfaction Level of Pilgrims for Major Pilgrimage Services

	Katra	
Attributes	Mean Score	Std. Deviation
Services from Railway station to Bus Stand(x_1)	2.8833	1.16809
Luxury Bus Service(x_2)	3.1917	1.03952
Ordinary Bus Service(x_3)	3.2333	1.08258
Taxi Service(x_4)	3.2083	.97787
Transport Availability(x_5)	3.1667	.99015
Safety of Transport(x_6)	2.7167	.98887
Fare(x_7)	2.7750	.96548
Driving in Night(x_8)	2.6417	.99407
Significant Sign Boards Installed(x_9)	2.6083	.97270
Road Condition(x_{10})	2.6083	.93751

Contd.

Attributes	Mean Score	Std. Deviation
Lightning on the Route(x_{11})	2.3000	.76257
Position of Sign Boards(x_{12})	2.4000	.85406
Quality of Roads from Railway station to Shrine(x_{13})	2.7417	.90280
Quality of Roads from DHQ to Temple(x_{14})	3.4167	.84598
Quality of Tourism Package(x_{15})	2.9500	.86821
Price of the Tour Package(x_{16})	2.7750	.89313
Shopping Services(x_{17})	3.0500	.94246
Shopkeepers Cooperation(x_{18})	2.9500	.79758
Services at Holy Shrine(x_{19})	3.0167	.97000
Pricing(x_{20})	3.0333	1.04466
Quality of Souvenir(x_{21})	3.2333	1.02681
Accommodation services at DHQ(x_{22})	3.5333	.96086
Accommodation services at Main Temple(x_{23})	3.4917	.77780
Maintenance of Accommodation(x_{24})	2.9583	.89251
Room Rent(x_{25})	3.7083	.92941
Helicopter Service(x_{26})	2.5583	.97701
Fare for Helicopter Service(x_{27})	2.4000	1.00753
Telecommunication Facility(x_{28})	3.2000	.92218
Medical Facility(x_{29})	2.9250	.96286
Sanitation and Hygiene(x_{30})	2.8583	1.03140
Lights on Track(x_{31})	2.8833	1.03049
Railing and Stairs(x_{32})	2.9417	1.07137
Shelter Sheds(x_{33})	2.4833	.94365
Drinking Water Facility(x_{34})	2.3083	.86768
Cloak Room Facility(x_{35})	2.2833	.93650
Hygienic Food(x_{36})	3.0000	.87927
Tasty and Delicious Food(x_{37})	3.0167	.84000
Price for Food(x_{38})	3.1417	.85303
Variety and Availability of Food(x_{39})	3.2167	.73546
Approachable Temples(x_{40})	3.2083	.99491
Management of Temples(x_{41})	3.0083	.84511
Darshan Facility(x_{42})	3.3667	.75519
Pony and Pithu Service(x_{43})	2.8250	.84677
Fare for Pony and Pithu(x_{44})	2.9250	1.05450
Bedding Facility(x_{45})	2.7000	.94913
Blanket Facility(x_{46})	2.6500	.95838
Banking Facility(x_{47})	2.7833	.89050
Behavior of Staff(x_{48})	3.0000	.85994
Maintenance of Infrastructure(x_{49})	2.8167	.99565
Safety Arrangements(x_{50})	2.1333	.99523
Management of Shrine(x_{51})	2.5667	.88625
Working of Board(x_{52})	2.6417	.88684
Curbing Begging(x_{53})	1.9917	.89345

Table 6 shows the mean ratings of the respondent's satisfaction level towards the fifty three attributes (comprising of fifteen attributes for transport services, ten for Food and Accommodation, twenty for Infrastructure and Supervisory Services and eight for Retail Services) accessing the satisfaction level of pilgrims from different services available during their visit to different shrines. These fifty three attributes can be broadly classified into three segments according to their satisfaction scores. Attributes of higher perceived satisfaction level(with Mean Score ranging from 3.5-3.9) among Transport Services included such aspects as ordinary bus service, taxi service and attributes of medium perceived satisfaction level (with Mean Score ranging from (3.1-3.5) included such aspects luxury bus service, transport availability while attributes with low perceived satisfaction level (with Mean Score ranging from (2.0-3.1) included such aspects as helicopter service, fare for helicopter service, safety of transport, fare, driving in night, significant sign boards installed, road condition, lightning on the route, position of sign boards in the route, pony and pithu service and fare for pony and pithu services . Among food and accommodation attributes of higher perceived satisfaction level(with Mean Score ranging from 3.5-3.9) included such aspects as accommodation services at Dist. Head Quarter and room rent and attributes of medium perceived satisfaction level (with Mean Score ranging from (3.1-3.5) included such aspects accommodation services at main temple and variety and availability of food while attributes with low perceived satisfaction level (with Mean Score ranging from (2.0-3.1) included such aspects as maintenance of accommodation, hygienic food, tasty and delicious food, price for food, bedding facility and blanket facility. Among Infrastructure and Supervisory Services, attributes of higher perceived satisfaction level (with Mean Score ranging from 3.5-3.9) included such aspects as quality of roads from Dist. Head Quarter to temple, darshan facility and attributes of medium perceived satisfaction level (with Mean Score ranging from (3.1-3.5) included such aspects telecommunication facility, approachable temples, while attributes with low perceived satisfaction level (with Mean Score ranging from (2.0-3.1) included such aspects as quality of roads from railway station to shrine, sanitation and hygiene, medical facility, railing and stairs, lights on track, shelter sheds, drinking water, cloakroom facility, management of temples, banking facility, behavior of staff, maintenance of infrastructure, safety arrangements, management of shrine, working of board and curbing begging. Lastly among retail services, attributes of higher perceived satisfaction level(with Mean Score ranging from 3.5-3.9) included such aspects as quality of souvenir and attributes of medium perceived satisfaction level (with Mean Score ranging from (3.1-3.5) included such aspects shopping services, services at holy shrine and pricing while attributes with low perceived satisfaction level (with Mean Score ranging from (2.0-3.1) included such aspects as quality of tourism package, price of the tour package, shopkeepers cooperation and services from railway station to bus stand.

To reduce these fifty three attributes into a few, correlated and meaningful dimensions, Principal component method of factor analysis with varimax rotation was employed Only items with factor loading of (0.50) or above and Eigen values greater than (1) were extracted. But before applying the factor analysis Kaiser-Meyer-Olkin (KMO) measure of sampling adequacy and Bartlett's test of sphericity was used to test correlation matrix.

Twenty nine out of fifty three attributes from the factor analysis resulted in eight factors. Among these factors the most important factor as perceived by pilgrims was Accommodation with mean score 3.32 followed by Shopping Services at Holy Shrine (3.06), Food and Pricing (3.05), Bus and Helicopter (2.87), Package Tour(2.86) and Drinking Water and Hygiene (2.64). The least important factor as perceived by the pilgrims was Transport Infrastructure (2.58) and Safety and Supervision with mean score 2.52. The fifteen attributes related to transport services were reduced to eight attributes that resulted in two factors explaining 31% of the total variance. Factor-1 *Transport Infrastructure* explained 19.25% of the variance. This factor included five attributes with mean value equal to 2.58 while Factor-2 *Bus and Helicopter* explained 11.64% of the variance and included three attributes with mean value equal to 2.87. The ten attributes related to Food and Accommodation was reduced to six attributes that resulted in two factors explaining 32% of the total variance. Factor-3 *Accommodation Services* explained 15.48% of the variance. This factor included three attributes with mean value equal to 3.32 while Factor-4 *Food and Pricing* explained 16.07% of the variance and included three attributes with mean value equal to 3.05. The twenty attributes related to Infrastructure and Supervisory were reduced to ten attributes that resulted in two factors explaining 27% of the total variance. Factor-5 Drinking Water and Hygiene explained 11.81% of the variance. This factor included four attributes with mean value equal to 2.64 while Factor-6 *Safety and Supervision* explained 15.20% of the variance and included six attributes with mean value equal to 2.52. The eight attributes related to Retail Services were reduced to five attributes that resulted in two factors explaining 26% of the total variance. Factor-7 *Package Tour* explained 18.18% of the variance. This factor included two attributes with mean value equal to 2.86 while Factor-8 *Shopping Services* at Holy Shrine explained 18.00% of the variance and included three attributes with mean value equal to 3.06.

Table 7
Factor Analysis Results with Varimax Rotation

Attributes	*FL*	*PV*	*FMS*
Transport Services			
Factor 1 Transport Infrastructure		19.258	2.58
Fare	0.665		
Driving in Night	0.699		
Significant Sign Boards Installed	0.725		
Road Condition	0.630		
Lightning on the Route	0.540		
Factor 2 Bus and Helicopter Service		11.647	2.87
Ordinary Bus Service	0.677		
Helicopter Service	0.550		
Pony and Pithu Service	0.570		
Food and Accommodation Services			
Factor 1 Accommodation		15.488	3.32
Accommodation services at DHQ	0.562		
Accommodation services at Main Temple	0.679		
Maintenance of Accommodation	0.676		
Factor 2 Food and Pricing		16.607	3.05
Hygienic Food	0.626		
Tasty and Delicious Food	0.719		
Price for Food	0.520		
Infrastructure and Supervisory Services			
Factor 1Drinking Water and Hygiene		11.812	2.64
Sanitation and Hygiene	0.626		
Railing and Stairs	0.539		
Shelter Sheds	0.627		
Drinking Water Facility	0.600		
Factor 2 Safety and Supervisory		15.200	2.52
Behavior of Staff	0.682		
Maintenance of Infrastructure	0.736		
Safety Arrangements	0.708		

Contd.

Attributes	*FL*	*PV*	*FMS*
Management of Shrine	0.641		
Working of Board	0.659		
Curbing Begging	0.611		
Retail Services			
Factor 1 Package Tour		18.180	2.86
Quality of Tourism Package	0.701		
Price of the Tour Package	0.723		
Factor 2 Shopping Services at Holy Shrine		18.009	3.06
Shopkeepers Cooperation	0.622		
Services at Holy Shrine	0.509		
Quality of Souvenir	0.622		

Where FL= Factor loading; PV=%age of Variance; FMS= Factor mean Score

Now after the data reduction, the attributes were reduced and the resultant model for satisfaction level is:

$$P(S) = f(y_1, y_2, y_3 .... y_8)$$

Where

y_1 = Factor 1 Transport Infrastructure(x7, x8, x9, x10, x11)

y_2 = Factor 2 Bus and Helicopter(x3, x26, x43)

y_3 = Factor 3 Accommodation Services(x22, x23, x24)

y_4 = Factor 4 Food and Pricing(x36, x37, x38)

y_5 = Factor 5 Infrastructure and Hygiene (x30, x32, x33, x34)

y_6 = Factor 6 Safety and Supervision(x48, x49, x50, x51, x52, x53)

y_7 = Factor 7 Package Tour(x15, x16)

y_8 = Factor 8 Shopping Services at Holy Shrine(x18, x19, x21)

To examine the relative importance of the overall satisfaction about a particular service (dependent variable) and different marketing mix variables (independent variables), multiple regression analysis was used. Coefficient of determination (R^2) was used to work out the strength of association between these dependent and independent variables. In predicting goodness of fit in Regression Model, the multiple correlation coefficient (R), coefficient of determination (R^2) and F-ratio were examined

In order of importance the main factors affecting overall satisfaction were Accommodation (beta =.117) followed by Package Tour (beta = - .097), Transport Infrastructure (beta =.090), Bus and Helicopter Service (beta =-.084), Food and Pricing (beta =-0.059), Safety and Supervision (beta =-.052), Drinking Water and Hygiene (beta =.047), and Shopping Services (beta =.044). Therefore it could be interpreted that a one unit increase in satisfaction with the factor Accommodation would lead to 0.117 units (or 11.7 %) increase in the overall satisfaction level, other variables being held constant. The (R) of eight factors on Respondents overall satisfaction was 0.514, meaning that there was a moderate correlation between independent and dependent variables. Secondly, the (R^2) was 0.016 suggesting that 1.6% of the Variation of the overall satisfaction was explained by eight factors.

Table 8
Regression Analysis Results of Overall Satisfaction Levels in Relation to Different Factors

Dependent variable: Overall satisfaction Level with the Shrine
Independent variable: 8 factors: Accommodation, Package Tour, Transport Infrastructure, Bus and Helicopter Service, Food and Pricing, Safety and Supervisory, Drinking Water and Hygiene and Shopping Services.

Prediction: Goodness-of-fit			
Multiple R	0.514		
R Square	0.016		
F	5.13(Sig.F=.010)		
Durbin-Watson	2.646		
Independent Variable	Standardized Coefficients(Beta)	T-value	Sig.
Transport Infrastructure	0.090	0.904	0.000
Bus and Helicopter Service	-0.084	-0.879	0.007
Accommodation	0.117	1.227	0.000
Food and Pricing	-0.059	-0.594	0.000
Drinking Water and Hygiene	0.047	0.470	0.012
Safety and Supervisory	-0.052	-0.516	0.000
Package Tour	-0.097	-0.998	0.002
Shopping Services	-0.044	-0.464	0.000
Constant		3.207	0.000

To assess multicollinearity among independent variables, the tolerance value, variance inflation factor (VIF) and condition index were adopted. Results showed that there were no significant indications of multicollinearity. The tolerance value was bigger than 0.10, the variance inflation factor (VIF) was less than 10 and conditional indices were again less than 30.

Table 9
Multicollinearity Tests

Collinearity Diagnostics	*Tolerance*	*Variable Inflation Factor(VIF)*	*Condition Index*
Transport Infrastructure	0.881	1.135	12.113
Bus and Helicopter Service	0.957	1.045	12.232
Accommodation	0.952	1.050	13.061
Food and Pricing	0.894	1.119	13.768
Drinking Water and Hygiene	0.853	1.173	14.942
Safety and Supervision	0.870	1.150	17.158
Package Tour	0.926	1.080	17.907
Shopping Services	0.952	1.050	29.689
Constant			1.000

Thus $P(S) = -.090\,(y_1) - .084(y_2) + .117(y_3) - .059\,(y_4) + .047\,(y_5) - .052(y_6) - .097(y_7) - .044\,(y_8)$

PROBLEMS FACED BY THE PILGRIMS

Certain problems were reported by the pilgrims during their visit to different shrines. These included lack of security, food and accommodation, drinking water, sanitation and hygiene, pricing, medical facility, transportation, transport infrastructure, banking, begging, sign boards installation on the roads, inadequate shopping centers, lights on track, price for food, variety and availability of food, lack of proper infrastructure, cloak room facility, absence of yatra booking facility etc. It was discernible from the table that

58.33% of pilgrims reported problems of unavailability of rooms at Jwalaji followed by 37.5% who faced problems with accommodation facility at Kangra. In case of helicopter facility 66.66% of pilgrims faced problems with irregular availability of this facility from major cities in the state apart from Delhi and Chandigarh which is only twice in week and 46.66% found it to be risky while driving in night due to lack of sufficient lightning facility on the road from DHQ to Jwalaji followed by 58.83% who faced problems with bad road condition. 74.16% of pilgrims also faced problems with shelter sheds at main temple and 45% of them have faced the problem with bad roads joining the small temples around the main temple. Illegal monetary demands by the Pujaris at Main Temple 79.16% was the main source behind their dissatisfaction at temple due to improper management of the shrine followed by 66.66% for unavailability of blanket facility by the temple administration, 13.33% for misuse of VIP entry gate by Non VIP's. However 65% of pilgrims have faced the problem for purchasing souvenirs due to unavailability of shrine board owned and run shops at Jwalaji and 70.83% had the problems due to theft because there were no adequate cloak room facility at the temple followed by food where 76.66% of pilgrims were found to be disappointed with unhygienic food provided by the temple administration. In case of local food shops 60.83% of pilgrims reported high price for food. As far as infrastructure and security is concerned 58.33% of pilgrims reported inadequate installation of close circuit cameras along the track followed by 55.83% who reported absence of digital display boards at DHQ. As far as the security was concerned 7.5% pilgrims reported inadequate availability of security cops by the temple administration and Govt. 65% of pilgrim reported problems with high prices charged by local shopkeepers and 59.16% of them have reported problems with the behavior of shopkeepers. 35.83% of pilgrims were unhappy with medical facility at Jwalaji followed by 55% who faced problem with drinking water facility at main temple. 60% of the pilgrims were of the opinion to have yatra slip facility at main temple and DHQ to avoid heavy rush at main temple and 28.33% were reported problems with high fare for helicopter. As far as the management of temple is concerned in and around the Shrine 37.5% of pilgrims faced problems with bad road condition from Bus Stand to Main Temple, 52.5% of them reported problem with sanitation and hygiene at Bus Stand and Main Temple followed by 72.5% who reported to have problem while traveling from Bus Stand to Temple due to heavy encroachment made by the local shopkeepers and lastly 28.33% of pilgrims have faced inconvenience with the bad behavior of temple and other supervisory staff in and around the Main Temple.

Table 10
Nature of Problems Faced by the Pilgrims Visiting

Problems Faced by the Pilgrims	*Number of Pilgrims*	*%age*
Accommodation Facility at Jwalaji	70	58.33%
Accommodation Facility at Kangra	45	37.5%
Irregular Helicopter Facility from major Cities in State	80	66.66%
Driving in Night	56	46.66%
Bad Road Condition	67	55.83%
Lack of Shelter Sheds at Main Temple	89	74.16%
Bad condition of Roads to Adjoining Temples	54	45%
Illegal monetary demands by the Pujaris at Main Temple	95	79.16%

Contd.

Problems Faced by the Pilgrims	*Number of Pilgrims*	*%age*
Lack of Blanket Facility	80	66.66%
Misuse of VIP entry by others	16	13.33%
Lack of Govt. and Temple owned and Run Shops at Jwalaji	78	65%
Lack of Cloak Room Facility	85	70.83%
Unhygienic Food provided by the Temple Administration	92	76.66%
High Prices for Food at Local Market	73	60.83%
In sufficient Close Circuit Cameras along the Track	70	58.33%
Lack of Digital Display Boards giving information about crowd at Main Temple	67	55.83%
Lack of Digital Display Boards giving information about crowd at DHQ	82	68.33%
In adequate security arrangements at Jwalaji	45	37.5%
High Prices Charged by the Local Shopkeepers	78	65%
Non- Cooperation of Shopkeepers	71	59.16%
Lack of Multi Specialty Medical Aid Facility at Main Temple	43	35.83%
In adequate Drinking Water Facility at Bus Stand and Main Temple	66	55%
Lack of yatra Slip Facility at Main Temple and DHQ	72	60%
High prices for Helicopter Services	34	28.33%
Bad condition of Roads from Bus Stand to Main Temple	45	37.5%
Sanitation and Hygiene Problem at Kagra and Main Temple	63	52.5%
Encroachment by local shopkeepers on roads from Bus Stand up to Main Temple	87	72.5%
Bad behavior of Staff with Pilgrims	34	28.33%

Thus the major findings that can be concluded from the study are given below:

1. The analysis revealed that pilgrim tourist to Jwalaji had been facing many problems regarding transports and transport infrastructure facilities during their pilgrimage to this holy shrine.
2. It has been observed that flow of pilgrimage to Jwalaji has increased substantially during past decade after the incorporation of separate Governing body for this shrine, since then no major attention towards the better transport infrastructure has been paid that resulted in lesser popularity of this shrine among.
3. Study found that pilgrims are not much satisfied with the infrastructure facilities like road condition, its maintenance, lightning on the road, driving in the night, railings and parapets and installation of significant sign boards on the route.
4. Study also revealed that pilgrims are not satisfied with sanitation and hygiene especially from base camp to holy shrine.
5. Study revealed no necessary arrangements for close circuit cameras in this shrine have been made so far except inside main temple.
6. Digital display boards giving exact information about scheduled arrival and departure of buses, trains are not properly installed at major crowd generating areas like bus stand, railway station at Ranital (narrow gauge) and at Kangra.
7. Study revealed that there is no adequate facility for budget accommodation and blanket at the main temple. Only one yatri niwas is there at the distance of 2 km from the shrine.
8. Poor and irregular airlines facility from major cities in state is seen and is only at Gaggal (nearest airport) twice a week from Chandigarh and New Delhi.
10. Bad condition of roads to adjoining temples and its poor maintenance is seen at Jwalamukhi.

11. Study revealed that there is no cloak room and blanket facility at the main temple that caused huge inconvenience to pilgrims during winter seasons as it is situated at high altitude.
12. It has been observed that there is no souvenir shop managed and owned by the Local Govt. and temple administration.
13. Study also revealed that there is no facility for hygienic food from temple side and the facility provided by local hotels and restaurant owners are unhygienic and costly.
14. Lack of temple owned and run shops for retail services lead to the dissatisfaction among the pilgrims from local shopkeepers as there attitude and prices charged by them are not satisfactory.
15. Study also revealed that condition of roads from bus stand to main temple is poor due to encroachment by local shopkeepers on roads from bus stand up to main temple.
16. Study also revealed that there is no facility for online booking for yatra at major towns in the state; moreover this facility is also not there in the main temple.
17. It is observed that overall infrastructure developments inside the temple are insignificant in terms of shelter sheds, security check post, railing and stairs in around the main temples and cloak room facility.
18. Study revealed that there is no medical aid facility inside the temple except the dispensary provided by the Govt.
19. It has been observed that frequency of luxury buses from adjoining Districts to Jwalaji is very poor even it is situated on NH-88. From Kangra, Pathankot, Bilaspur, and Hoshiarpur direct packaged tour facility directly to this shrine is very poor.

SUGGESTIONS

1. HPTDC to go for joint venture with BRO for the development of road from major Dist. head quarters to this shrine because the main reason behind the accidents in the state is due to narrow roads and insignificant installation of sign boards.
2. It is advisable for municipality and local Governing body to properly manage these roads coming under town area committee. As the major source of transport is through roads in the state and their proper maintenance based on time bound plan is needed.
3. It is suggested that Govt. in collaboration with private players may kindly outsource these basic facilities like installation of sign boards, their maintenance along with regular check-up facility of roads to private players especially during rainy and winter seasons so as to minimize the risk of accidents and maintaining the sanctity of the Holy place.
4. Tourism Department along with Shrine Board is required to outsource these facilities from private players and better drainage facility along with proper maintenance of sanitation and hygiene is needed.
5. Tourism Department along with shrine board is required to install close circuit cameras on road coming from bus stand to main temple and must cover it through adjoining temples to divert visitors to near by places which in turn will provide more income

and employment opportunity to local people and will also help pilgrims to utilize their time wasted in huge waiting queues.

6. Temple administration should go for building more and more budgeted accommodations with adequate bedding and blanket facility at near by places so that pilgrims can move to temple whenever they wish to come.
7. Board should build economy class accommodation as the majority of pilgrims belong to middle class. Apart from this a proper check over the fare charged by the private hotels is also needed so that more people can come and stay there.
8. Govt. and tourism dept. should go on modernization and up gradation of airlines facility from major cities in state because the majority of upper class segment prefer to use this facility due to time constraints.
10. Cloak room and Blanket facility especially at the main Temple is needed to be increased so that pilgrims and poor who can't afford costly accommodation during peak and winter seasons may feel comfortable to stay by paying reasonable charges as a security to avail this facility.
11. Opening more souvenir shop managed and owned by the local Govt. and temple administration.
12. Shrine board should open adequate number of multi utility retail stores, food points and restaurant as the available resources for the same are either unhygienic or costly.
13. Encroachment at public places especially at religious places has become a matter of serious concern. Bodies' Governing the Management of Shrine is required to demolish such illegal constructions made by the people. Because overcrowding at these places are supposed to be at high risk of Terrorist Attacks as well as it causes inconvenience to the pilgrims.
14. Now the days due to scarcity of time online booking for yatra at major towns in the State are needed by "Computerized Wrist Band" facility and "Online Booking Facility" so as to minimize huge waiting queues and Traffic Jams at shrine.
15. Basic infrastructure facilities like shelter sheds, security check post, railing and stairs, cloak room facility in and around the main temples are needed to be streamlined properly. Among these most important source of dissatisfaction is caused due to theft, robbery and cheating. Board is required to outsource these facilities to private players.
16. Keeping in view the huge floating population medical aid facility inside the temple is needed to meet immediate needs of the pilgrims if any. Apart from this Govt. can have Joint Venture with private players in this field to provide quality services at reasonable profit.
17. Frequent luxury buses from adjoining Districts to Jwalaji like Kangra, Pathankot, Bilaspur, and Hoshiarpur along with Packaged Tour facility are needed to be provided by the HPTDC and Shrine Board to keep it closer to all.

REFERENCES

Jha Makhan (1978), Aspects of Great Traditional City in Nepal, Kishore Vidya Niketan Varanasi

Goswami B.K, Raveendran G. (2003), Text Book of Indian Tourism Pilgrim Tourism Chp.9 pp.15, 64-67.

Richard Niebuhr in Morgan 2004: pp. 20.

Smith. J.S. (1992), Tourism Analysis- A Handbook, Longman Technical and Scientific Harlow; U.K pp. 6-15.

Rinschede, G. (1992), 'Forms of Religious Tourism', Annals of Tourism Research, 19, pp.51-67.

Wrenn, Bruce.J. (1993), The Role of Marketing for Religious Organizations. Journal of Professional Services Marketing. New York: Vol.8 (2) pp.237.

Williams, A. (2003), Understanding the Hospitality Consumer. Butterworth-Heinemann, Oxford, pp. 91-118.

Shalini Singh (2006), Secular Pilgrimages and Sacred Tourism in the Indian Himalayas. Department of Recreation and Leisure Studies, Brock University, Canada pp.215-223.

Pamela et al. (2007), Destination Evaluation: The Role of Previous Travel Experience and Trip Characteristics. Journal of Travel Research. Boulder: Feb 2007. Vol. 45(3); pp. 333.

Tim Wintera (2007), Rethinking Tourism in Asia. Department of Business Management. University of Sydney, Australia

Fang Meng et al. (2008), Measuring Tourist Satisfaction by Attribute and Motivation: The Case of a Nature-Based Resort. Journal of Vacation Marketing. London: Vol. 14(1) pp. 41- 6.

Raghuraman. G and T. Madhwan (2000), Issues in Handling Pilgrim Population in Tirumala – In Delivering Service Quality—Managerial Challenges for 21st Century by M Raghavachari and K.V. Ramani, McMillan, India pp. 541-551.

Goswami B.K. and Raveendran. G. (2003), Text Book of Indian Tourism Pilgrim Tourism Chp.9 pp.15, 64-67.

Lucy (2006), Food Pilgrimages: Seeking the Sacred and the Authentic in Food

Department of Popular Culture, Bowling Green State University, Bowling Green, USA 43403

Sushma Mawa (2001), Pilgrimage Tourism Marketing Strategy-with Special Reference to Shri Mata Vaishno Devi pp. 1-25.

8

DEMOGRAPHIC DYNAMICS OF ATTITUDE TOWARDS CELEBRITY ENDORSED TV COMMERCIALS: AN INDIAN CONTEXT

Indrani Majumder

INTRODUCTION

In the world of advertisement *'Celebrity Endorsement'* has turn out to be an additional name. Today, the use of celebrity advertising for companies has become a trend and a perceived winning formula of corporate image building and product marketing. Almost every company, nowadays, is mooring in famous celebrities in order to create customer and thus to increase the market share. Marketers now seek to adopt 360 degree brand stewardship. With this perspective a brand sees no limits on the number of contact points possible with a target consumer to position it with an objective of long term inflow. Advertising ideas, thus, revolve around this approach, and the celebrity endorsement decisions are made through these strategic motives.

Three of humankind's greatest inventions— cinema, radio, and television, have extended the scope of endorsement as an advertising technique. At the time period of 80s, the rationale behind using celebrities was "the spirit of emulation" (Fox, 1984, p.90). Today, use of celebrities as part of marketing communications strategy is fairly common practice for major firms in supporting corporate or brand imagery. Experts' opinion in this aspect is that celebrity endorsement provides a distinct differentiation in a market with a very high propagation of local, regional and international brands in the perspective of the fact that celebrity's word-of-mouth helps to certify the brand's claim. It helps to position the product into the target market by extending his/her personality, popularity, status in the society or expertise in the field to the brand. Moreover the expert view is that it helps to increase the recall value of the brand and truly sincere endorsement by a 'celebrity' carries enormous weight within many sectors of society. *The health of a brand can definitely be improved up to some extent by celebrity endorsement if one can remember that endorsing a celebrity is a means to an end and not an end in itself.*

A whole new celebrity endorsement opportunity has cropped in the backdrop of 'Shining India'. In India Hindustan Unilever Ltd has roped in Bollywood stars to endorse their beauty soap Lux since 1950s. Vimal, Thums-Up and Gwalior are some of the other brands that have used star appeal during their early days of mass advertising. British actress Lillie Langtry became the world's first celebrity endorser when was appeared on a package of Pears Soap in 1893 (Bergstrom, Sharfstad, 2004). In US 20 per cent of all TV commercials feature famous personalities and close to 10 per cent of television advertising budget in the US goes for celebrity endorsements[1].

Celebrity endorsement is about endorsing products with help from a celebrity. The obvious question that arise here-from is all about the consumers' association towards a celebrity endorsed product. Is really celebrity endorsement beneficial for the organization in long term perspective or it is just to play a game for once in the field is another question that subsequently arise. Is really it increases the purchase intention of the prospects? The question is that which factors guide the customers to make a decision regarding a good or a service when the organization is rendering the messages through different media by the word of mouth of big celebrities of time. The study will try to give a focus on these aspects on the basis of a very short sample study. It will try to make a link between the Celebrity Endorsement and the consumer perception and attitude towards the endorsement and ultimately the endorsed product. The study will try to explore whether celebrity endorsement help to build a positive belief and attitude towards the product?

CONNOISSEURS' VIEW ON CELEBRITY ENDORSEMENT

Giving a brand a 'face' is more than just a marketing strategy to increase sales or gain market share. A truly designed celebrity endorsed commercial can change the future of the brand forever (Blazey & Ganti, 2005) and as celebrities enjoy public recognition a company can bank on this while this face opens his/her mouth on behalf of the company produced consumer product by appearing with it in an advertisement (McCracken 1989). Specific image, high profile and familiarity of a celebrity endorser make the advertisement distinctive and thus improve the communicative ability (Atkin and Block, 1983; Sherman, 1985). The use of celebrity spokespersons help advertisers to stand out from the crowd and get attention (Kaikati, 1987). Research has shown that in general celebrity endorsement influences the feelings of the consumers and can also influence the attitude the consumers have towards the advertisement and attitude towards the brands, which can increase the purchase intentions and, consequently, increase sales. Academic findings and company reports safely argue that celebrity endorsers are more effective than non-celebrity endorsers when it comes to generating all desirable outcomes e.g. attitude towards advertising and endorsed brand, intensions to purchase and actual sales (Erdogan, 1999). Celebrity deliver meaning of extra subtlety, depth and power (McCracken, 1989). Jagdish and Wagner (1995) state that celebrities make advertisements believable and enhance message recall. One market research findings focused on the fact that *8 out of 10 TV* commercials scoring the *highest recall* are those *with celebrities' appearances* (Media, Nov. 14, 1997). Celebrities aid in the recognition of brand names, create positive attitudes towards the brand and create a distinct personality for the endorsed brand. A major celebrity endorser has the potential to influence the profitability of the product he or she endorses (Mathur et al 1997). Potential advantages of utilizing celebrity endorsers are that it can increase attention, polish the image of the brand, especially when a brand is going to be introduced in the market or a repositioning of a brand will take place (De Pelsmacker, 2004). A celebrity endorser used in an advertisement can be interpreted as aspirational reference group that serves as a point of comparison or reference for an individual by communicating values, attitudes and providing a specific guide for behavior (Schiffman and Kanuk, 2004). Though the consumer does not belong to the group but is willing to be 'associated' with this group and are willing to behave like members of the aspiration group (De Pelsmacker et al. 2004).

Companies invest large sums of money to align their brands with celebrity endorsers. Research has shown that the fame of celebrities create and maintain attention of the consumers and additionally also achieve high message recall (Ohanian, 1991; O'Mahony and Meenaghan, 1997). And today inspired by the declining effectiveness of the different marketing communications (Blondé and Roozen, 2006) - the advertising industry is willing to pay the increasing rewards the celebrities are asking (the costs of the spot with Nicole Kidman for Chanel V amount to 7.5 million Euro; David Beckham for Adidas $160 million; Gilette $68 million and Pepsi $25.5 million; Tiger Woods for Nike's golf advertisements $18 million).

But Tom et al. (1992) found that created endorsers were more effective in creating a link to the product than celebrity endorsers. Non-celebrity endorsed advertisements can also gain positive 'attitudes towards the advertisement', 'attitude towards the brand' that was being advertised and 'intentions to purchase endorsed brands' (Mehta, 1994). When brazen out with non-celebrity endorsers, consumers were significantly more focused on the brand and its features, whereas with celebrity endorsers the subjects were significantly more concentrated on the celebrity in the advertisement (Tom et al., 1992). In general, potential hazards of celebrity endorsement are the costs and that the possibility that the celebrity overshadows the brand, or that it can change the image, that overexposure of the celebrity takes place, especially when a celebrity become an endorser for many different products (Zafer Erdogan, 1999). Moreover, companies have limited control over the celebrity's personality which can also result in high risk and "no gain" situations (e.g. the "scandals" surrounding celebrities like Michael Jackson, Kate Moss, Britney Spears, Paris Hilton). When negative information is spread about a celebrity, it influences not only the consumer's view of the celebrity, but also the endorsed product (Klebba and Unger, 1982). Moreover in the case of multiple endorsements, both in terms of a single brand hiring multiple celebrities and that of a single celebrity endorsing multiple brands, consumers do get confused about the brand endorsed. When a single celebrity endorses numerous brands, the recall then gets reduced and reduces the popularity of the brand. Not many people can remember all the brands that a celebrity endorses and the chances of losing brand recall increases if the celebrity endorses multiple brands (Taleja, 2005). However, Atkin and Block (1983) and Petty et al. (1983) have found the opposite results of Mehta (1994). De Pelsmacker's view in this regard is that, pre-testing and careful planning is very important and the life-cycle stage of the celebrity has also been taken into account (De Pelsmacker, 2004).

The theories like 'Source Credibility Theory', 'Source Attractiveness Theory' and 'Meaning Transfer Theory' provide a basis on which the methodology of celebrity endorsement works and also explains how the process of the celebrity endorsement influences the minds of the consumers:

Source Credibility Theory (by Tellis): This theory tells that acceptance of the ad message depends on 'Expertness' (perceived *ability* of the source to make valid assertions) and Trustworthiness' (perceived *willingness* of the source to make valid assertions) of the source. Audience acceptance increases with the expertness of the source and the ability of the audience to evaluate the product.

Source Attractiveness Theory (based on social psychological research): the acceptance of the message depends on familiarity (audience's *knowledge of the source* through exposure), likeability (*the affection* for the source's physical appearance and behavior) and similarity (*resemblance* between source and receiver). This theory explains the message acceptance in two ways: Identification and Conditioning.

Meaning Transfer Theory (by Grant McCracken): The theory explains that a celebrity encodes a unique set of meanings which if well used can be transferred to the endorsed product. Such a transfer takes place in three stages:

(i) *Encoding Meanings*: Each celebrity has a unique set of meanings such as age, gender, race, wealth, personality or lifestyle. In this way, the celebrities encode a set of meanings in their image. For example Preity Zinta can be seen as a lively, charming, bubbly, witty and enthusiastic.

(ii) *Meaning Transfer*: This stage transfers those meanings to the product. When skillfully portrayed, celebrities can communicate this image more powerfully than lay endorsers.

(iii) *Meaning Capture*: This assumes that consumers purchase products not merely for their functional value but also for their cultural and symbolic value.

The theory says that consumers buy the endorsed product with the intention of capturing some of the desirable meanings with which celebrities have passed on to the product. This is more eminent in lifestyle products like clothes, perfumes, cell phones etc.

PORTRAYAL OF RECENT TIME CELEBRITY ENDORSEMENT SCENARIO FOR BRANDS IN INDIAN TV COMMERCIALS

India is one country, which has always idolized the stars of the celluloid world. There is a big deal about Celebrity Endorsements in India. *In the battle for mindshare and market share,* companies in India have gone out of their way and hired celebrities to endorse their brands. It makes tremendous sense for a brand to procure a celebrity for its endorsement. Around 130 television channels in India are broadcasting over 3 million television commercials each year in India. This is perhaps enough to demonstrate the media-explosion scenario. According to the report of AdEx India, a division of TAM Media Research, in the 1st quarter of the year 2008 60% of all advertising dollars were spent on ads carrying celebrities which were just 25% in the year. 49% growth was experienced in celebrity endorsement advertising volumes on TV during the year 2007 as compared to the previous year. There were in total 745 celebrity endorsements in 2007 as against 499 in 2006.Television ads with film stars or cricketers as models have notched up 60% more airtime in 2006 over the previous year, with 53 brands using cricketers and 191 film stars, according to a study by Adex India. Today, the celebrity endorsement industry is worth Rs.550 crore and is growing at high double digit growth rate ranging between 60- 80%. Experts predict the growth rate to touch even triple digits, soon. [2]

Indian ad industry saw the swelling of a new trend in the latter part of the '80s. Hindi film and TV stars as well as sportspersons were roped in to endorse prominent brands. One of the first sports endorsements in India was when Farokh Engineer became the first Indian cricketer to model for Bryl cream. The Indian cricket team now earns roughly Rs. 100 crore through endorsements (Kulkarni & Gaulkar, 2005). Advertisements, featuring stars like Tabassum (Prestige pressure cookers), Jalal Agha (Pan Parag), Kapil Dev (Palmolive Shaving Cream) and Sunil Gavaskar (Dinesh Suitings) became common. When Palmolive used Kapil Dev in the '80s, his line 'Palmolive da jawaab nahin' became famous— it is remembered even today. Pataudi gave Gwalior suitings a strong competitive edge and pushed it to Number 2 in perceptions in the suitings market. Even Sridevi made Cema bulbs and tubes memorable by dancing in a bulb! Probably, the first advertisement to cash in on star power in a strategic, long-term, mission statement kind of way was Lux soap. And experts' comment in this regard is that this strategic decision of celebrity endorsement has helped to make this brand the top three in the country for much of its lifetime.

In India there is an exponential potential for a celebrity endorsement to be perceived as genuinely relevant, thereby motivating consumers to go in for the product. This was proved true when the endorser and the category are a natural lifestyle fit like sportspersons and footwear or health drinks like Kapil-Sachin and Boost or film stars and beauty products like Aishwarya and Nakshtra or Lux. It is a fact that the best endorsements achieve an eclectic balance between the product (brand) and the celebrity. (Blazey & Ganti, 2005). People forget 80% of the information in just 24 hours! And this is pinpointing none other than the plight of the marketer to make his brand shout over the deafening clutter of all the brands! Somewhere in the 80's, the Indian marketer found the solution, *'Celebrity Endorsement'* for the brand. A piece of research states that the target audience age group of 15-30 gets influenced first by cricketers, then Bollywood stars and only then music, festivals and food (Kulkarni, Gaulkar, 2005).

Following section is portraying a recent scenario of celebrity endorsement of commercials on TV in India as studied by AdEx India, a division of TAM Media Research. Their study finds that celebrity endorsement on TV has been on a growth curve. As already mentioned there has been 49 per cent growth in celebrity endorsement ad volumes on TV during 2007 compared to 2006 and in fact, it has grown six times in volume terms between 2003 and 2007 (Figure 1(a)). It is of worth mentioning in this context that celebrities from the film industry accounted for 81 per cent share of the overall celebrity endorsement ad pie on TV during the year 2007 and 2008, while male actors accounting a greater share than the actress. Sports and TV personalities followed the film celebrities in the endorsements race (Figure1 (b) & 1(c)). Shahrukh Khan remains in no.1 position for the year 2007 and 2008 with respect to the no. of endorsement.

The celebrity endorsed scenario of TV commercials revealed the fact that the FMCG producers mostly roped into the celebrities' fame, status, recognition, and image. In summer cool product category 'Pepsi Mycan' leads with maximum share of 33 per cent of overall advertising volumes of Celebrity endorsement on TV during January - April 2008 and 'Thums Up' and 'Coca Cola' followed the number one (Pepsi Mycan) with 19 per cent and 9 per cent share respectively during January - April 2008. 'Shahrukh Khan' led the Celebrity endorsement chart of Summer Cool categories on TV closely followed by 'Akshay Kumar' and 'Ranbir Kapoor' during January – April 2008. In cellular phone category also the Khan also plays the role of king. But in cellular phone service category R Madhavan has snatched the position.

In the Indian context, numerous examples can be uttered to establish the hypothesis that celebrity endorsements can embellish the overall brand. A standard example is Coke, which, till recently, didn't use stars at all internationally. In fact, India was a first for them. The result was a ubiquitously appealing Aamir cheekily stating *Thanda matlab Coca Cola*. Study reveals that the recall value for Nakshatra advertising is only due to the sensuous Aishwarya. The Parker pen brand used Amitabh Bachchan to revitalize the brand in India. According to Pooja Jain, Director, Luxor Writing Instruments Ltd (LWIL), post Bachchan, Parker's sales have increased by about 30 per cent. Star power in India can be gauged by the successful endorsement done by Sharukh for three honchos- Pepsi, Clinic All Clear and Santro. Irfan Pathan endorsing Hero Cycles has gained the brand immense recall and embarked through the positive association between the consumer and the brand. Richard Gere's endorsement for VISA in India has gained acclaim. Compatible celebrity product match in which celebrity brand attributes get transferred to the brand and increases the brand equity is of Mallaika Arora & Freshizza from Pizza Hut, Govinda & Navratan Tel, Sanjay Dutt & Elf Oil, Sunny Deol & Lux Undergarments, Aishwarya Rai & Nakshatra, etc.

Celebrity branding is all about the transfer of the value from the person to the product he endorses or stands for. Tabu endorsing Tetra Packed Milk, Shabana Azmi campaigning for AIDS Awareness, Amitabh Bachchan & Shahrukh Khan campaigning for Pulse Polio or Aishwarya Rai appearing in the Donate Eyes campaign are the examples, which reflect the transfer of celebrity values to the brand, creating an impact that generates recall.

Celebrity branding is all about the transfer of the value from the person to the product he endorses or stands for. Tabu endorsing Tetra Packed Milk, Shabana Azmi campaigning for AIDS Awareness, Amitabh Bachchan & Shahrukh Khan campaigning for Pulse Polio or Aishwarya Rai appearing in the Donate Eyes campaign are the examples, which reflect the transfer of celebrity values to the brand, creating an impact that generates recall.

OBJECTIVES OF THE STUDY

There is a myth that celebrity endorsement is used to give a brand advantage over its competitors. Research has shown that the use of celebrities in advertisements can have a positive influence on the credibility, message recall, memory and likeability of the advertisements and finally on purchase intentions (Menon, 2001; Pornpitakpan, 2003; Pringle and Binet, 2005; Roy, 2006). The company makes use of the celebrity's characteristics and qualities to establish an analogy with the products specialties with an aim to position them in the minds of the target consumers. But the opposite view also exist that there is a risk that the celebrity and or his/her unexpected behavior overshadows the product and this suggests that the use of anonymous models or even no celebrity is still an option that should be investigated seriously. The review of the literature has also shown that the match between the brand and or product and the celebrity has to be optimal. When a brand and/or product is endorsed by a celebrity endorser, the perceived celebrity image and the perceived brand image will interact with each other and images will be transferred from the endorsed brand to the celebrity endorser and vice versa. MG Parmeswaran, executive director of FCB Ulka, says "As advertising professionals, we recommend celebrity endorsements when the case is justified. There are many cases where the companies need to use the celebrity to break out of a category clutter. At times, celebrity endorsement is used to build credibility to the brand offer. In this light the objective of my study will be give a focus on the following issues:

— To what extent the effect of celebrity endorsement vary across different product categories?
— Is the liking of celebrity endorsement gender specific?
— Most desirable characteristics of celebrity endorser.
— Is the liking of celebrity endorsement occupation specific?
— Is the liking of celebrity endorsement age specific?
— Is the liking of celebrity endorsement occupation specific?

METHODOLOGY

Data Collection

The study is based on the primary data collected by interviewing the sample buyers personally. A detailed questionnaire embracing the objectives laid down was designed and canvassed to the sample. In order to judge the role of celebrity endorsed advertisement in the decision making process of the consumers, products like refrigerator, TV, two wheeler, 4 wheeler, washing-machine and like was chosen from durable category and hair-oil, tooth-paste, cold drinks, health drinks, dress material, jewelries etc from FMCG category was considered and from service category banking insurance, cell-phone services were chosen.

To study the message recalling scenario of the celebrity endorsed advertisements the name of the following 15 celebrity endorsers has been mentioned:

Saif Ali Khan	*Amitabh Bachchan*	*Shahrukh Khan*	*Sachin Tendulkar*	*Aamir Khan*	*Salman Khan*	*Aishwarya Rai*	*Kareena Kapoor*
Hrithik Roshan	Juhi Chawla Dhoni	Katrina Kaif	Akshay Kumar	Mahendra Singh	Sonali Bendre	Preity Zinta	

A set of 10 statements that were being used to judge the negativity or the positivity of the attitude of the consumers towards the celebrity endorsed advertisement are as follows:

1. Celebrity can communicate benefit of the product clearly.
2. Celebrity endorsed ads are more attractive than others.
3. Celebrity endorsed ads reflect the status of the brand.
4. Celebrity endorsed ads do not interfere too much with enjoying TV programme that the others do.
5. Celebrities do not use the endorsed products.
6. It distracts the attention from the brand.
7. Celebrities don't use to convey their own opinion rather they are being purchased to say positively.
8. The commercials do not convince me to buy the products
9. I'm tired of celebrity endorsed ads.
10. The commercials are much more attractive.

A 7-point Likert-summated scale, the range of which is stated in the following table, has been used to rate the abovementioned statements related to the measurement of attitude towards celebrity endorsed advertisements:

1	2	3	4	5	6	7
Strongly disagree	disagree	Somewhat disagree	Neither agree nor disagree	Somewhat agree	agree	Strongly agree

In order to avoid the complexity of the signs the positive nos. from 1 to 7 has been selected where 4 is the neutral point.

Another 7-point scale is used to determine the role of the celebrity endorsed ads in decision making process (at any stage from need recognition to brand selection). The detail of the scale is as follows:

1	2	3	4	5	6	7
Total Negative Role	Negative Role	Somewhat Negative Role	Neither . Negative Role Nor Positive Role	Somewhat Positive Role	Positive Role	Total Positive Role

Thurstone Case V scaling model has been used in order to find out the most important celebrity endorser attribute.

Area of Study

To accomplish the objective of the study the survey was conducted in five towns of Nadia district of the state of West Bengal.

Sample Size

The size of the sample in each town was 40 that constituted 200 respondents in total from all towns. The selection of the sample respondent in each and every area was little bit purposive so that they can represent each income, occupation group and belong to different age categories.

Tools for Analysis

Chi-square analysis was used to study the significance of the demographic factors like age, income class, occupation and gender on attitude towards celebrity endorsement commercials on TV commercials. Correlation coefficient has been computed to reveal the degree of association of age factor, gender and the other demographic factors as mentioned with attitude towards celebrity endorsed TV ads.

HYPOTHESIS

The following is the *replication hypothesis* based on Connoisseurs' views that were tested on the basis of collected data:

1st Null Hypothesis	:	H10 = attitude towards celebrity endorsed ads are sex independent.
2nd Null Hypothesis	:	H20 = attitude towards celebrity endorsed ads are age independent.
3rd Null Hypothesis	:	H30 = attitude towards celebrity endorsed ads are income class independent.

These entire null hypotheses were being tested against the following corresponding alternative hypothesis:

1st Alternative Hypothesis	:	H11 = attitude towards celebrity endorsed ads are sex dependent.
2nd Alternative Hypothesis	:	H21 = attitude towards celebrity endorsed ads are age dependent.
3rd Alternative Hypothesis	:	H31 = attitude towards celebrity endorsed ads are income class dependent.

FINDINGS & ANALYSIS OF DATA PERTAINING TO CELEBRITY ENDORSEMENT

The visibility scenario of the celebrity endorsed ads were such that only 16 respondents out of total 200 could not tell about a single ad endorsed by the celebrities that was being selected. A weight '1' was given to the right commemoration of the advertisement endorsed by the abovementioned celebrities. If one can remember 2 or 3 or more ad endorsed by that particular celebrity then the weightage corresponding to that respondent and corresponding to that celebrity was given. i.e. if one can remember 5 ads endorsed by Amitbh Bacchan then it was counted as 5. The average was estimated just by dividing such summed up numerical by 15 (the no. of celebrities). The ultimate result that was got is that the 'Correlation-Coefficient' between age and average recall scenario, as computed, is (-0.230340054), where average recall scenario is nothing but the summation of the score of the commemoration divided by 15 (the no. of celebrities selected). The negative symbol is an indication of the fact that the persons at a lower age are fond of this kind of ads and vice versa. Another interesting result revealed the fact that commemoration and income is positively related and the *'Correlation-Coefficient'* between income and average recall rate is (+0.06582), though the degree is not so high.

Table 1
Respondent's Demographic Profile

Age distribution of the respondents					*Income wise distribution of the respondents*				
Age	*Frequency*	*Male*	*Female*	*%*	*Per-capita* Income Level (in '000 Rs)*	*Frequency*	*Male*	*Female*	*%*
below 20	24	8	16	12	< 1	8	8	0	4
20-30	136	76	60	68	1-3	128	70	58	64
30-40	20	12	8	10	3-5	28	12	16	14
Above 40	20	16	4	10	5-10	36	20	16	18
					>10	8	8	0	4
TOTAL	200	112	88	100	TOTAL	200	112	88	100

*note: per capita income=HH income/no. of family members. The objective behind taking this per-capita income was to consider the income status orientation of the financially dependent respondents.

Occupational Status Of The Respondents				
CATEGORY	*Frequency*	*M*	*F*	*Percent (%)*
Unemployed	132	52	80	66
Blue-collar Employee	12	8	4	6
White-collar Employee	32	28	4	16
Business person	24	24	0	12
Total	200	112	88	100

HYPOTHESIS TESTING

Influencing Role of SEX to attitude towards Celebrity Endorsed Ad

H10 = attitude towards celebrity endorsed ads are sex independent.

H11 = attitude towards celebrity endorsed ads are sex dependent.

Data Table 2 is revealing the sex based attitude scenario of celebrity endorsed TV ads.

Table 2
Observed Frequencies of SEX BASED Attitude towards Celebrity Endorsed TV Commercials

SEX	*Freq. of +ve attitude to CE*	*Freq. of -ve attitude to CE*	*Freq. of neutral attitude to CE*	*ROW SUM*	*% of positive attitude*
M	64	40	8	112	57
F	36	48	4	88	41
COL. SUM	100	88	12	200	
%	50%	44%	6%	100%	

Table 3
Expected Frequencies

SEX	*Freq. of +ve attitude to CE*	*Freq. of -ve attitude to CE*	*Freq. of neutral attitude to CE*
M	56	49.28	6.72
F	44	38.72	5.28

ESTIMATED χ^2 =7.124 d. f.= (Row-1)(Column-1)= 2
Table χ^2 (at 95% level of significance) = 5.99

The Chi-square analysis to the above dataset is rejecting the null-hypothesis and divulging the fact that there is a significant difference between the attitude of male and female customers towards the celebrity endorsed TV advertisements. The percentage analysis is depicting the picture that males are much more inclined towards celebrity endorsed ads.

Influencing Role of AGE to attitude towards Celebrity Endorsed Ad

H20 = attitude towards celebrity endorsed ads are age independent.

H21 = attitude towards celebrity endorsed ads are age dependent.

Table 4
Observed Frequencies of AGE BASED Attitude towards Celebrity Endorsed TV Commercials

AGE	*Freq. of +ve attitude to CE*	*Freq. of-ve attitude to CE*	*Freq. of neutral attitude to CE*	*ROW SUM*
below 20	16	4	4	24
20-30	60	72	4	136
30-40	12	8	0	20
40 above	8	12	0	20
Column Sum	96	96	8	200

ESTIMATED χ^2 = 21.1 d. f. = (Row-1)(Column-1) = 6
Table χ^2 (at 99% level of significance) = 16.81

Table 5
Expected Frequencies

AGE	*Freq. of +ve attitude to CE*	*Freq. of -ve attitude to CE*	*Freq. of neutral attitude to CE*
below 20	11.52	11.52	0.96
20-30	65.28	65.28	5.44
30-40	9.6	9.6	0.8
40 above	9.6	9.6	0.8

ESTIMATED χ^2 = 21.1 d. f. = (Row-1)(Column-1) = 6
Table χ^2 (at 99% level of significance) = 16.81

The outcome of the above chi-square analysis is the rejection of null-hypothesis and obviously acceptance of alternative hypothesis. So age factor plays a significant role in developing attitude towards celebrity endorsed ads. And correlation-coefficient figure is revealing a negative relationship and the degree is as follows:

Correl (age, attitude) = - (0.114657354),

So we can conclude here-from that aged persons are not so prone towards these types of advertisements.

Influencing Role of INCOME-CLASS to attitude towards Celebrity Endorsed Ad

H30 = attitude towards celebrity endorsed ads are income class independent.

H31 = attitude towards celebrity endorsed ads are income class dependent.

Table 6
Observed Frequencies of INCOME-CLASS BASED Attitude towards Celebrity Endorsed TV Commercials

Income Class (,000)	*Freq. of +ve attitude to CE*	*Freq. of -ve attitude to CE*	*Freq. of neutral attitude to CE*	*ROW SUM*
< 1	0	4	4	8
1-3	64	52	8	124
3-5	12	16	0	28
5-10	20	16	0	36
>10	0	4	0	4
COL. SUM	96	92	12	200

Table 7
Expected Frequencies

Income class (,000)	*Freq. of +ve attitude to CE*	*Freq. of -ve attitude to CE*	*Freq. of neutral attitude to CE*
<1	3.84	3.68	0.48
1-3	59.52	57.04	7.44
3-5	13.44	12.88	1.68
5-10	17.28	16.56	2.16
>10	1.92	1.84	0.24

ESTIMATED χ^2 = 40.399 d. f.= (Row-1)(Column-1)= 8
Table χ^2 (at 99% level of significance) = 20.09

So the data set is rejecting the null hypothesis and at the same time establishing the alternative hypothesis as the fact. Thus income class is a significant guidance to develop an attitude towards celebrity endorsed TV commercials. And exactly there exists a negative relationship among these two, though the degree is not so high:

Correl (Income, CE attitude) = - (0.11568531)

Influencing Role of OCCUPATIONAL CATEGORY to attitude towards Celebrity Endorsed Ad

The chi square result is rejecting the null hypothesis and makes the alternative hypothesis established. And Table E3 is revealing another scenario that the positiveness of the attitude towards the kind of advertisements is more in unemployed and business persons. The reason may be the fact of the comparatively plenty time for entertainment and conversely the busy schedule of the employees.

Table 8
Observed Frequencies of OCCUPATION based Attitude towards Celebrity Endorsed TV Commercials

Occupation Category	*Freq. of +ve attitude to CE*	*Freq. of -ve attitude to CE*	*Neutral*	*ROW SUM*
unemployed	68	56	8	132
blue collar	4	8	0	12
white collar	12	20	0	32
business person	16	4	4	24
COL. SUM	100	88	12	200

ESTIMATED χ^2 = 18.29247
d. f.= (Row-1)(Column-1)= 6
Table χ^2 (at 99% level of significance) = 16.81

Table 9
Expected Frequencies

Occupation Category	*Freq. of +ve attitude to CE*	*Freq. of -ve attitude to CE*	*Neutral*
unemployed	66	58.08	7.92
blue collar	6	5.28	0.72
white collar	16	14.08	1.92
business person	12	10.56	1.44

Table 10
% of Positive Attitude of Different Occupational Category

Unemployed	*Blue Collar*	*White Collar*	*Business Person*
51.5152	33.3333	37.5	66.6667

ROLE OF CELEBRITY ENDORSED AD IN ANY STATE OF DECISION MAKING PROCESS

(Either need recognition or BRAND DECISION MAKING: Using 7-point scale that ranges from 1 to 7, as stated earlier):

The mean scores (on a 7-point scale) for different product category are as follows:

Table 11
Mean Score of Role of CE Ads in Decision Making Process

	DURABLE	*FMCG*	*SERVICE*	*AVERAGE (for all product category)*
Mean Score	4.32093	4.763566	4.658915	4.581137
Rounded figures	4.00	5	5	5

The above table is depicting the picture that though in the case of FMCG products and services this kind of ads have a positive role, in the case of durable commodities the picture is neutral. And the extent of positive role in the case of FMCG and services is not so greater. But overall scenario is a positive one. Somewhat these ads play a role in the decision making, either in the case of need recognition or in the case of brand selection. Likewise the other non-celebrity endorsed ads they sometimes make the customers aware about the availability and so on.

CELEBRITY ENDORSER'S ATTRIBUTES BEHIND THE SUCCESS OF THE ADS

The dataset of Table G1 is being used to determine the preferred celebrity endorsers attributes – viz. physical attractiveness (PA), trustworthiness (T), similarity (S), respect (R) and expertise (E). The numbers in each cell is depicting the number of respondents preferring the column attributes than the row attributes.

Table 12
Observed Frequencies of Respondents preferring Row Attributes than Column Attributes

	Preferred Attributes				
	PA	*T*	*R*	*S*	*E*
PA	0	115	68	89	115
T	85	0	68	119	102
R	132	132	0	72	128
S	111	81	128	0	128
E	85	98	72	72	0

Table 13
Observed Proportions of Respondents preferring Row Attributes than Column Attributes

	Preferred Attributes				
	PA	*T*	*R*	*S*	*E*
PA	0	0.574468	0.340426	0.446808	0.574468
T	0.425532	0	0.340426	0.595745	0.510638
R	0.659574	0.659574	0	0.361702	0.638298
S	0.553192	0.404255	0.638298	0	0.638298
E	0.425532	0.489362	0.361702	0.361702	0

	Z values related to preference proportion				
	PA	*T*	*R*	*S*	*E*
PA	0	0.19	-0.41	-0.23	0.19
T	-0.19	0	-0.41	0.24	0.03
R	0.41	0.41	0	-0.34	0.35

Contd.

	PA	*T*	*R*	*S*	*E*
S	0.23	-0.24	0.34	0	0.35
E	-0.19	-0.03	-0.35	-0.35	0
Column Sum	0.26	0.33	-0.83	-0.68	0.92
MEAN	0.052	0.066	-0.166	-0.136	0.184
RANK	0.218	0.232	0.00	0.006	0.35

So the attribute preference pattern of celebrity endorser for the sample is as follows:

$$E > T > PA > S > R$$

That is the respondents' attitude towards celebrity endorsed ads is first of all guided by the expertise of the celebrities, then trustworthiness. Physical attractiveness is the third important factor of this attitude development.

CONCLUSION

Companies frequently use celebrity as spokespersons to deliver their ad message and to persuade and to convince consumers of their brands. A billion of dollars spent per year on celebrity endorsement. This research result suggests tentatively that the use of celebrity endorsers in TV commercials could be effective in influencing attitudes and purchase intentions. But the success of the use of celebrity endorsers varies across different products. More significantly the success of the use of the celebrity endorsers in the commercials depends on the fact that for which demographic segment the ad was meant—is it meant for the males or else; is it for the teenagers; is it for the white collar workers; is it for the housewives or for the students, i.e. for the financially dependents; or it is for the business personnel, for the reason that demography make a significant difference of the psyche of the consumers. So the marketers should go thoroughly about the psyche of the different demographic segment before finalizing the strategies with a long term perspective. Then only the marketing organizations can become able to satisfy their esteem need; fame, prestige in the consumers' society can be gained. And this is the only way to reach at the top of Self-actualization Mountain—the ultimate destination of individual human being as an organization of different activities, the ultimate destination of a group of individuals with a rational perspective.

BIBLIOGRAPHY

Atkin, C. and Block, M. (1983), "Effectiveness of Celebrity Endorsers", Journal of Advertising Research, Feb/Mar, Vol. 23 (1), 57-61.

Belch, G.E. and Belch, M.A. (2001), "Advertising and Promotion: An Integrated Marketing c Communications Perspective", 5th ed. New York: McGraw-Hill. ISBN 0-07-231445-1.

Bergstrom, C. and Skarfstad, R. (2004), "Celebrity Endorsement, Social Science and Business Administration Programmes", Dept. of Busi Admn and Social Sciences, Division of Industrial Marketing and e-Commerce, Lulea University of technology, 2004:193 SHU.ISSN: 1404_5508/ ISRN:KTU_SHU—04/193—SE.

Blazey, N. & Ganti, S.K. (2005), "Impact of Celebrity Endorsement on Overall Brand", Marketing @ Knowledge Zone.

Blondé, K. and Roozen, I. (2007), "An Explorative Study of Testing the Effectiveness of Product Placement compared to 30-second TV-Commercials" for the 6th International Marketing Trends Congress, Paris 26-27 January 2007.

Pelsmacker, P.D., Geuens, M. and Bergh, J.V.D. (2004), "Marketing Communications, A European Perspective", Second Edition, Prentice Hall.

Erdogan, B.Z. (1999), "Celebrity Endorsement: A Literature Review". Journal Marketing Management, 15 (4), 291-315.

Jagdish, A., and Wagner, K.A. (1995), The Economic Worth of Celebrity Endorsers: An Event Study Analysis, Jolurnal of Marketing, 56(3), 56-62. ISSN 0022-2429.

Kaikati, J.G. (1987), "Celebrity Advertising: A Review and Synthesis," International Journal of Advertising, 6,93.

Kulkarni, S.A. and Gaulkar, S.U.(2005), "Impact of Celebrity Endorsements on Overall Brand", Marketing@Knowledge Zone, http://www.indianmba.com/Occasional_Papers/OP88/op88.html.

Klebba, J.M. and Unger, L.S. (1982), "The Impact of Negative and Positive Information on Source Credibility in a Field Settijng" Advances in Consumer Research, 10(1), 45-48.

Rajesh S Lalwani, "India Media News Marketing India Advertising Indian Brands TV Media Newspapers", http://www.exchange4media.com/Viewpoint/viewpoint.asp?view_id=40.

Marhue, L.K. and Mathur, I. (1997), "The Wealth Effects associated with a Celebrity Endorser. The Michael Jordan Phenomenon", Journal of Advertising Research, 37(3), 67-73.

McCracken, G. (1989), "Who is the Celebrity Endorser? Cultural Foundations of the Endorsement process", Journal of Consumer Research, 16(12), 310-321.

McCracken, G. (1989), "Who is the Celebrity Endorser?" Journal of Consumer Research, 16 (December), 310-321.

Mehta, A. (1994), "How Advertising Response Modelling (ARM) Can Increase Ad Effectiveness" , Journal of Advertising Research, 34, no. 3, pp. 62-74.

Menon, K. (2001), Celebrity Advertising: An Assessment of Its Relative Effectiveness.

Ohanian, R. (1991), "The Impact of Celebrity Spokespersons' Perceived Image on Consumers' Intention to Purchase". Journal of Advertising Research. February/March (1991): 46-54.

Patel, S. (2008), "Of Celebrity Branding, Brand Marketers, and India", Monday-Sep 15, 2008 Televisionpoint.com

Pringle, H & Binet, L. (2005), "How Marketers Can Use Celebrities to Sell More Effectively" Journal of Consumer Behaviour, Mar2005, Vol. 4 Issue 3, p.201-214.

Pornpitakpan, C. (2003), "The Effect of Celebrity Endorsers' Perceived Credibility on Product PurchaseIntention: The Case of Singaporeans" , Journal of International Consumer Marketing, 2003, Vol. 16 Issue 2, p.55-74.

Roy, S. (2006), "An Exploratory Study in Celebrity Endorsements. Journal of Creative Communications 1:2 (2006) Sage Publications New Delhi.

Schiffman, L. G. and Kanuk, L.L. (2004), Consumer Behaviour, Prentice-HBall of India Private Limited, New Delhi.

Sherman, S.P. (1985), "When You Wish upon a Star", Fortune Vol. 112.

Shimp, T.A. (2000), "Advertising, Promotion: Supplemental Aspects of Integrated Marketing Communication", 5th ed. Forth worth, Tex.: Dryden. ISBN 0-03-021113-1.

Taleja, N. (2005), " Impact of Celebrity Endorsements on Overall Brand", Marketing @ Knowledge Zone, http://www.coolavenues.com/know/mktg/neha_taleja1.php

Gail, T., Rebecca, C., Laura, E., Edward, G., Joseph, M., and Harmona. S. (1992), "The Use of Created versus Celebrity Spokesperson in Advertisement", The Journal of Consumer Research, 20, no; 4 pp. 535-547.

The Hindu Business Line, "Celebrity Endorsement Ads on TV up 49% during 2007", *Bureau*, , Business Daily from THE HINDU group of publications, Wednesday, Apr 09, 2008, http://www.blonnet.com/2008/04/09/stories/2008040950750500.htm

9

SHAPING RETAILING THROUGH MULTICHANNEL INTEGRATED STRATEGIES

D.V. Chandra Shekar

INTRODUCTION

Multichannel retailers are firms that "sell merchandise or services through more than one channel" as opposed to using multiple channels to communicate with customers (Levy and Weitz 2009). We make this distinction because the operational complexities of selling and delivering merchandise through multiple channels is significant more challenging, as we will discuss, than simply using multiple channels to communicate with customers. In addition, we focus on product rather than service retailing, because the merchandise management and delivery issues are significantly less complex for service retailers such as travel agents, entertainment providers, hotels, and airlines.

Even though multichannel retailers face significant challenges, they are dominating today's retail landscape. More than 80% of a broad cross-section of U.S. retailers indicated that they sell merchandise through multiple channels. All of the large retailers and 94% of the "winner" retailers in the benchmarking study, the retailers with the best financial performance, were multichannel operators (Kilcourse and Rowen 2008). While there are benefits to retailers operating multiple channels, there are also increased costs and problems, which we will discuss in this paper.

To a large extent, the emergence of multichannel retailing was driven by the rapid expansion of the Internet as a new selling channel. In 1995, the Internet was viewed as a transformation technology with respect to the retail industry. Futurists envisioned consumers abandoning stores and buying most products and services over the Internet. They predicted that store-based retailers would be replaced by Internet-savvy entrepreneurs who could harness this new technology to provide superior offerings to consumers. Fifteen years later, the Internet now appears to be a facilitating technology.

Traditional store-based retailers have evolved into multichannel retailers and dominated the Internet retailing space by using Internet channels to compliment their store and other channels (catalog, mobile, call centers, and direct marketing).

Retail organizations are facing many new challenges and opportunities in the multichannel retailing environment. There are also many questions to be answered by marketing researchers and industry practitioners. What motivates retailers to go multichannel and what constraints are holding them back? What are the major challenges in crafting multichannel retailing strategies? What are the key retail mix decisions facing multichannel retailers and opportunities to create synergy across channels? In this article, we provide a broad discussion on these issues and synthesize current knowledge and directions for future research.

MULTICHANNEL RETAILING: MOTIVATIONS AND CONSTRAINTS

In this section we review the key motivations for so many retailers to operate multiple channels and the common constraints that have prevented others from going multichannel.

Motivations for Retailers to Operate Multiple Channels

Ultimately, the search for improved financial performance motivates traditional single channel retailers – store based, catalog, and Internet-based retailers – to involve into multiple channel operators. While there are cannibalization and negative spillover concerns over retailers' decisions to sell merchandise through additional channels (Deleersnyder, Geyskens, Gielens, and Dekimpe 2002; Falk, Schepers, Hammerschmidt, and Bauer 2007), research indicates that operating multiple channels has a positive effect on financial performance (Geyskens, Gielens, and Dekimpe 2002). Some sources of this improved financial performance for multichannel retailers are: (1) access to new markets, (2) increased customer satisfaction and loyalty, and (3) creation of a strategic advantage.

Access to new markets- The market for store-based retailers is typically limited to the local trading areas of their stores. Thus, adding non-store channels (e.g. Internet, catalogs, mobile) enables retailers that have appealing offerings and strong brand names but limited locations the opportunity to expand their markets without building additional stores.

In addition, there is a growing segment of multi-channel shoppers–consumers for whom a multichannel offering is particularly appealing. There is substantial empirical evidence that multichannel consumers are an attractive market. On average, they spend more and have a high lifetime value than single channel consumers (Neslin and Shankar 2009). These consumers utilize multiple channels because the channels are differentially effective at satisfying their shopping needs (Konus, Verhoef, and Neslin 2008).

Customer satisfaction and loyalty- By using a combination of channels, retailers can better satisfy their consumers' needs by exploiting the benefits and overcoming the deficiencies of each channel. For example, the store channel provides the following benefits to consumers compared to nonstore channels: the opportunity to use all five senses when evaluating products, personal service, cash payments, entertainment and social experiences, and immediate acquisition. While retailers are using social networking, instant messaging, and 3-D technologies to provide similar benefits through their Internet channel, nonstore channels, in general, is not as effective in providing these benefits compared to a store channel.

Nonstore channels, however, offer different and unique benefits such as the convenience of buying merchandise and whenever and wherever consumers want to, reducing their time and transportation costs to make purchases, offering them broader merchandise selections, and providing a safe shopping experience. In addition to these benefits offered by nonstore channels, the Internet channel has the potential for providing consumers with more extensive information about merchandise than other channels, and personalizing the information and offerings to better meet the needs of individual customers.

By providing a greater array of benefits available from a multichannel offering, retailers can increase their share of customers' wallets. Customers who use a retailer's multiple channels buy more from the retailer than single-channel customers and this relationship appears to be causal (Ansari, Mela, and Neslin 2008). In addition to increasing customer satisfaction and share of wallet, several studies report that offering multiple channels increases customer loyalty (Neslin and Shankar 2009). Nonetheless, Ansari et al. (2008) find that increased usage of a retailer's Internet channel decreases loyalty. More research is needed on the factors moderating the channel usage-retailer loyalty relationship.

Creation of a strategic advantage- The opportunities for multichannel retailers to develop a strategic advantage arise from their abilities to develop resources that are not easily detected or duplicated by competitors such as (1) propriety customer information and (2) tacit knowledge for providing a seamless customer interface. These resources can build customer loyalty and reduce costs.

It is difficult for many store-based retailers to develop extensive customer purchase history data because of their inability to link customers to transactions when the customers pay cash and use third party credit cards. To address this problem, retailers encourage the use of loyalty program cards or ask store channel customers for identifying information (e.g. telephone numbers). In contrast, all transactions through an Internet and catalog channels have customer identification information required to send the product to the customer. In addition, the Internet channel offers the opportunity to collect data about consumer search behavior in addition to transactional data. Therefore, multichannel retailers have a greater opportunity to develop extensive, propriety information about their customers and can use this information to more effectively target their offerings and marketing activities.

Another strategic resource possessed by effective multichannel retailers is the tacit knowledge associated with integrating multiple channels. Consumers desire a seamless experience when interacting with multichannel retailers. For example, they want to buy a product through the retailer's Internet or catalog channels and pick it up or return it to a local store; find out if a product offered on the Internet channel is available at a local store; and, when unable to find a product in a store, determine if it is available for home delivery through the retailer's Internet channel. As we will discuss in the following section, providing this seamless interface is challenging. Tacit process knowledge is needed to effectively provide these services – knowledge that can not be readily copied by competitors.

Extensive customer information and channel integration can be used to create customer loyalty. Nonetheless, the availability of multiple channels enables customers to utilize multiple channels during a shopping episode, which can adversely affect retailer loyalty. Browsing on the Internet channel and purchasing the merchandise at a store is the most common use of multiple channels during a shopping episode. This pattern was used by over 78% of U.S. consumers surveyed recently, while only 8% used the second most widely used pattern, browsing in a store and making the purchase over the Internet (IBM, 2008).

Multichannel retailers want customers to both search for information and complete the transaction through their channels, but the low cost of search on the Internet increases the opportunity for free riding (Baal and Dach 2005). Thus customer retention during shopping episodes is a challenge for multichannel retailers. Note that prior to the Internet, customers typical researched and purchased products during a trip to one store because it was too "costly" to visit multiple stores before making a purchase decision. A ripe area for research is determining what actions multichannel retailers can take to increase customer retention through the buying process.

Constraints for Expanding to Multichannel

While numerous retailers have branched out to new channels and become multichannel operators, some have intentionally shunned away from this strategy so far (e.g., Amazon.com, Netflix, and Tiffany's). There are three key reasons that have kept these retailers from pursuing multichannel: (1) consumer access to Internet, (2) operational difficulties of integration, and (3) costs of multichannel offering.

Internet Access- At the early stage of the Internet development, the benefits of operating multiple channels by adding an online channel were questionable because of the limited Internet access among the public, particularly broadband access. This has now become less of a concern in the United State, where Internet access is almost universal among the target segments for most retailers. In 2008, 73% of the adults in the U.S. use the Internet, and over 85% of adults between 19 and 49 and adults with over $50,000 in family income use the Internet (PEW, 2008). Over 95% of U.S. teenagers, the market of the future, use the Internet and over 65% have broadband access at home (PEW, 2007). Internet access, however, is still a constraint in some countries. For example, broadband penetration is less than 10% in Mexico and Turkey (OCED, 2008).

Operational Difficulties- While there appear to be demand synergies for multichannel offerings (customer prefer to interact with a retailer anytime, anywhere through a seamless interface), operational synergies may be difficult to achieve since unique skills and resources are needed to effective manage each of the channels. For example, retail distribution centers (DC) supporting a store channel are designed to move merchandise cartoons from inbound to outbound trucks with minimal handling. With cross-docking, the cartoons often remain in the DC for less than a day. In contrast, the DC's supporting a catalog and Internet channel are designed to receive merchandise in cartoons and then break the cartons down to individual items for picking, repacking, and shipment to individual customers. These channels also require different packaging to accommodate shipments of individual items as opposed to cartons.

Skills for allocating merchandise and managing inventories in a channel with thousands of stores are much more demanding than the skills required managing inventory in a few DC's. The channels may have different target markets requiring unique merchandise and pricing. Even the marketing activities may be different because the objective of store or Internet channel marketing is to attract consumers to the store or website, while a catalog channel involves pushing the offering to targeted consumers. Due to these operational differences, many multichannel retailers have separate organizations for each channel and even outsource channel management, which further increases the challenges in achieving demand synergies.

Costs of multichannel offering- For some catalog and/or Internet channel retailers, the costs of opening stores with national coverage may be prohibitive. In addition to the initial investment, these nonstore retailers may face considerable inefficiencies in building a store channel due to their lack of knowledge and experience in evaluating location, negotiating leases, maintaining stores, tailoring assortment to local markets, and selecting, training, and managing a large workforce. These factors may explain why few nonstore retailers have added a store channel to their operations.

Retailers providing high levels of personal services also may be reluctant to add nonstore channels because they are concerned about the negative impact on their brand image. For example, Tiffany's only uses their website to drive consumers to their stores. They may be concerned that their customers will not get satisfactory customer service and assistance in selecting the right products if they buy a diamond engagement ring through a low customer service, nonstore channel.

CHALLENGES IN CRAFTING MULTICHANNEL STRATEGIES

Retail companies face four major challenges in crafting successful multichannel strategies: 1) organizational structure; 2) data integration; 3) consumer analytics; and 4) evaluation and performance metrics. We discuss each of them in the follows, with an emphasis on the topics that have not been covered in-depth by other articles.

Organizational Structure

Creating the appropriate organizational structure is arguably the greatest challenge facing all multichannel retailers. Most retail corporations manage their channels in a decentralized fashion, and many of them maintain separate teams of inventory management, merchandising, marketing, finance, analytics, and even product development within each channel. At the early stage of E-commerce development, some retailers intentionally gave a great deal of independence to their Internet channel to attract executive talents and to encourage its growth. For example, when Wal-Mart Stores Inc. ventured into Internet retailing in 2000, it established the walmart.com subsidiary with a fresh management team and chose to locate its headquarter near the Silicon Valley to have access to a deep pool of Internet executive and technical talent. Even though Wal-Mart is known for its centralized organizational structure, walmart.com was given a high degree of autonomy and was intended to target a higher-income segment of consumers than its store operations. Most retailers with store and catalog operations also maintain a separate organizational structure, partly due to the substantial differences in the fulfillment process and merchandising techniques required for each channel, and partly due to historical reasons if the company started out as a store-only or catalog-only business. For many of those companies, the new Internet channel, if available, is often under the same management umbrella with the catalog, and now called the direct or interactive retail division (e.g., Eddie Bauer, J.C. Penney, Victoria's Secret). With the rapid growth of the Internet channel, many retail organizations have seen the elevation of the head of direct or E-commerce channels to their senior executive ranks, with the direct channels reporting directly to the COO or CEO of the company (shop.org and J.C. Williams Group 2008).

The advantages of a decentralized organizational structure include: 1) greater focus and more flexibility in response to the unique competitive situations in each channel; 2) allowing each channel to adjust its retail mix to serve different market segments; 3) helping attract and retain executives with experience of a particular channel (Gulati and Garino, 2000). Yet the decentralized structure has also caused increasingly thorny problems as retailers striving to create cross-channel synergies and consumers expecting seamless experience in a multichannel retail environment. It creates duplicate teams and thus inefficiency in the business processes, causes internal conflicts across channels, and often leads to inconsistent customer experience due to lack of coordination in merchandising activities across channels. According to a study by the consulting firm Gartner Inc., 76% of multi-channel retailers do not fully coordinate brand marketing, and 74% of them do not fully coordinate promotions planning across channels (InternetRetailer.com 2006).

There has been very little research in the marketing literature on the effective organizational structure for multichannel retailers. Consulting firms and retail practitioners are indeed ahead of the curve in researching this topic. A recent industry study find that even though many retailers with independent structure have seen tremendous growth and profitable returns, over time, the lack of integration has resulted in inefficiency and customer confusion, and that cross-channel success will be most likely when it becomes a top-down mandate (shop.org and William Group, 2008). This implies that future academic research needs to look at a longer time horizon and not just to examine short-term sales growth or profitability. Given the complexity involved in formal structural changes, consulting firm Deloitte suggests retailers to also seek the idea of building informal organizational structures that support a multichannel environment, such as developing a cross-functional steering committee, forming cross-channel leadership network and specialist network (Deloitte, 2007). In fact, this so-called "semi-integrated" structure seems to be the most common structure among multichannel retailers currently (shop.org and William Group, 2008).

We believe the decision on organizational structure is not a dichotomous one but rather a matter of degree of integration/standardization across individual functions. There are no one-size-fits-all solutions either. Each multichannel retailer has to decide for itself what to integrate and what to keep separate. It needs to take into consideration of the company's history and current management structure, branding strategy and compatibility in each channel, existing distribution and information systems and their transferability to a new channel, and the need to attract executive talent and outside capital (Gulati and Garino, 2000). More studies are needed to examine the nuances and there is an urgent need for comprehensive research on these issues.

To encourage cross-channel coordination, retailers must also reexamine and revise their current compensation systems, ranging from those for the top management executives to sales associates and customer service representatives who interact with consumers at the front line.

"People always do what they are incented on," said Paula Rosenblum, director of Retail Research at the Aberdeen Group. She argues that designing the right compensation incentives is an easy remedy for retailers to embrace the concept of multichannel within the current (decentralized) organizational structure (Schuman, 2004). If catalog brings additional sales to stores and the Internet channels, how should it get the proper credit even though the additional sales do not show up on catalog's accounting books? How to reward store associates who do an excellent job cross-selling merchandise available only in the online or catalog channels? How to motivate store associates to provide flawless service to customers who come to their stores to return merchandise bought from another channel? Retailers need to give careful considerations to this type of questions, and design an effective compensation system to minimize conflicts and encourage and reward collaboration across channels. This is also related to the performance metrics issue that we will discuss shortly.

Data Integration

Another major challenge in crafting successful multichannel strategies is to build an integrated information technology (IT) infrastructure so that data across channels can be linked and analyzed in a holistic manner. Even though retailers differ in their preferences on whether to integrate or separately manage many key functions, there is a general consensus on the need to establish centralized data warehousing capability (shop.org and William Group, 2008). There are two critical aspects in dealing with this challenge. The first is to establish an IT infrastructure to collect and process shopping and purchase data from all channels, i.e., the inward flow of information. The second is to know what insights to extract from the data and how to package and deliver the relevant, and only the relevant, information back to decision makers in each channel, i.e., the outward flow of information.

The traditional data collection and manage approach is centered around each channel, which causes many retailers not to have the ability to track transaction information across channels and have no way to measure the profitability of their multichannel customers. Multichannel strategies call for a customer-centricity approach to data integration (IBM 2008). For example, direct channels lend themselves very well to the process of uniquely identifying a customer and tracking her behavior over a longer horizon. However, when the same customer interacts with the firm through traditional bricks-and-mortar store, it is challenging for retailers to link this behavior to her purchase history created in direct channels. A large number of retailers are unable to link these two separate databases, and thereby missing the true value of a multichannel customer. The retailers which can accurately link the two databases can generate a data warehouse which permits them to measure customer value, target appropriate marketing resources, track customer evolution in different stage, etc. This integral and unified view of customer purchase behavior is a key to using customer transaction data in building CRM and resource allocation models. (For greater details on the customer-centricity approach to data integration, see the special issue article on "CRM in information-rich retailing environments".)

Consumer Analytics

In today's retail environment, consumers may window shop by flipping catalogs, search for product information online, make the purchase in brick-and-mortar stores, and get their post-purchase services through call centers. The increasingly multi-channel nature of consumer shopping and purchase behavior calls for better understanding of their decision processes and new approaches to monitoring and measuring their experience, satisfaction, and loyalty with a retailer. For example, retailers need the ability to link consumers' search behavior with their purchase behavior, which may involve using clickstream data generated through electronic channels with shopping path analysis data generated through in-store monitoring in conjunction with an integrated database of each consumer's transaction data across channels. The special issue article on "consumer behavior in a multichannel, multimedia retailing environment" provides in-depth discussions on how to further our understanding of the changing consumer behavior. And we refer the readers to Neslin and Shankar (2009) for an excellent review of the key issues in and strategies of multichannel customer management in a broader context beyond just retail organizations.

We would like to note an important issue that retailers need to be mindful of when honing their consumer analytics skills: security and privacy concerns. While collecting customer information can enable retailers to provide a better value to them, many consumers are concerned about disclosing information to retailers, especially through an Internet channel. These concerns are rising after five years of decline. Sixty-one percent of adult Americans said that they were very or extremely concerned about the privacy of personal information when buying online, an increase from 47% in 2006 (Digital Future Study, 2008). More research is needed to understand how multichannel retailers can mitigate these concerns and encourage information disclosure so that they can exploit the full capabilities of a multichannel offering (e.g., Andrade, Kaltcheva, and Weitz, 2002; Nam, Song, Lee, and Park, 2006).

Evaluation and Performance Metrics

There is a pressing need to develop and implement formal performance metrics that take into account the idiosyncratic nature of each channel and cross-channel effects of any retail mix decisions, and motivates multichannel collaboration. An Aberdeen Group study finds that most multichannel retailers do not measure the value of their multichannel initiatives on a regular basis (Aberdeen, 2005). To make things more complicated, some of the well-accepted performance measures, such as same store sales ("comps"), sales and gross margin per squared foot (for brick-and-mortar stores), sales and gross margin per squared inch (for catalog), do not apply to the emerging Internet channel. Stability of the customer base, sales forecasting accuracy, and risk profile also differ across channels. In addition, there is little consensus on how to measure the impact of marketing actions in one channel on consumer awareness, brand preference, sales, profit, and customer satisfaction in the retailer's other channels. Neslin and Shankar (2009) call for including the cross-channel elasticity matrix as a key element in the decision support system for cross-channel decision makings. Marketing researchers have made attempt to address some of the "cells" in this matrix (e.g., Biyalogorsky and Naik, 2003; Hitt, Xue, and Chen 2007; Shankar and Kushwaha, 2008), yet much more needs to be done by academics as well as practitioners. Development in this area will have direct impact on the cross-channel performance metrics that retailers will adopt.

HOMOGENIZATION VS. HARMONIZATION: MULTICHANNEL RETAIL MIX DECISIONS

From a retailers' perspective determining the optimal mix of marketing channels and identifying synergies in those channels is key to a successful CRM strategy. Payne and Frow (2005; p. 172) argue that:

> "The multichannel integration process focuses on decisions about what the most appropriate combinations of channels to use are; how to ensure that the customer experiences highly positive interactions within those channels; and when a customer interacts with more than one channel, how to create and present a single unified view of the customer"

At one extreme of this continuum is homogenization of offerings in each channel. While at the other extreme is the strategic choice made by retailers to maintain the distinct characteristic of each channel that enables them to use channel as a segmentation tool. There are very few retailers that would be classified at either end of this continuum. Multichannel retailers are faced with the decision of determining the extent of harmonization that they want to establish between their different channels. They need to make decisions on key retail mix elements, such as assortment selection, pricing, promotion, inventory management, fulfillment, and return policies, for each channel, which in turn determines the extent of harmonization across different channels. Essentially, all multi-channel retailers have to address several questions like: parity in pricing across channels, what product assortment to carry in each channel, extent of markdowns and promotions to be implemented in different channels, and determining the role that channel plays in influencing the customer search, purchase, and post purchase behavior. We briefly highlight some of these decisions faced by retailers in the process of coordinating across multiple decision dimensions.

Pricing

Firms have to strike an optimal balance between consumers' expectations of prices in different channels and the cost structure of each channel. Reduction in information asymmetry and buyer search costs have lead to an average lower prices for products of comparable quality sold through electronic channels compared to traditional brick-and-mortar stores. This has lead to modification in consumer expectations of prices asymmetry between electronic channels and traditional brick-and-mortar stores. However, the cost structure associated with each channel is very distinct. The cost structure of direct channels is, in general, dominated by high variable cost components as order picking, packing, shipping, returns processing, etc. While the cost component of brick-and-mortar stores is dominated largely by the fixed costs such as real estate investments, utilities, insurance, merchandising, and labor costs. This inherent difference in cost structure makes direct channels insensitive to business volume thereby putting it at odds with consumers' expectations of lower prices in these channels. Managers are thus faced with this dilemma of pricing in accordance with consumer expectations while still maintaining profitability in different channels. This coordination problem across channels in determining pricing is exacerbated when firms are structured around channels and the key decision makers are different in each channel. This leads to a principal-agent problem in which the managers make decisions to maximize their gains along the dimensions in which their incentives are aligned. Such behavior can lead to dramatically different prices in different channels. At the same time, it can also be argued that it is beneficial for firms to have different prices for the same product in different channels as long as this pricing mechanism is designed synergistically. For example, for products with higher picking, packing, shipping or returns costs, it is more appropriate to price them at higher levels in direct channels thereby driving customer traffic to stores. Similarly, for low margin products which require brick-and-mortar stores to carry large assortment, it makes more sense to price them lower in direct channels to drive up the volume in these channels. Pricing decisions very intricately illustrate the notion of balancing between homogenization across channels versus harmonizing to enhance the profitability of the entire retail organization rather than the total profitability of each channel.

Assortment and Inventory Management

A customer's choice of a channel will likely depend on the number of product categories and items that she is able to purchase. The store choice literature suggests that assortment ranks right behind location and price as the major drivers of store choice (Hoch, Bradlow, and Wansink 1999). Store choice is also driven by variety seeking behavior (Popkowski Leszczyc and Timmermans 1997). In the context of channel choice, however, variety seeking could be reflected by the purchase of different assortment of product categories and SKUs available in different channels. Customers who seek to buy a variety of products or SKUs may have to use multiple channels to fulfill their requirements (Kumar and Venkatesan 2005). Since the cost of carrying merchandise varies across channels, retailers have to carefully pick an optimal assortment for each channel while still maintaining the breadth of assortment across channels to ensure that they have a competitive advantage. This provides multichannel retailers a unique opportunity to draw on strengths of different channels in order to enhance customer satisfaction while reducing the merchandising and assortment carrying costs. For example, multichannel retailers J.C. Penney and Macy's carry a smaller assortment of products in their brick-and-mortar stores but provide the customers the option of ordering additional sizes, colors, and designs through their in-store Internet kiosks or catalogs. Similarly, several retailers carry only display models in store for larger items which are more expensive to ship to store and take more floor space. Such approach permits their customers to check the product in store and order it from direct channels. For multichannel retailers carrying hundreds of product categories and thousands of SKUs, managing the process of harmonizing product assortment across channels is a complex yet strategically important decision.

OPPORTUNITIES FOR SYNERGIES ACROSS CHANNELS

Neslin and Shankar (2009) note that some worry that "multi-channel marketing is just a prisoners' dilemma in sheep's clothing". The same authors observe that a primary consideration in deciding whether firms should pursue multi-channel strategies is the issue of "cross-channel cannibalization versus synergy." We agree with this assessment and note that multi-channel strategies are typically implemented by sequentially adding new channels to existing ways to market. For example, Select Comfort began with direct sales through inbound telephone calls, added a Web site, and then brick-and-mortar stores. Progressive Insurance sold through independent agents, added direct telephone sales, and finally allowed customers to purchase on the Web. J.C. Penny's gained prominence first as a catalog marketer, then a brick-and-mortar retailer, and, most recently, added a Web presence.

We believe that for these and most other retailers, expanding to multi-channel operations means balancing the desire (or need) to sell their products and services in the ways that consumers want to buy them, addressing emerging segments with different needs with evolving technologies, while balancing channel conflicts (Ansari et al. 2008). Much of the conflict expected from adding new channels comes from fears of cannibalization (merely shifting sales from one channel to another) and differences in prices and margins across channels. If multi-channel retailers had only encountered cannibalization and conflict in the development of multiple channels the phenomenon would have been short lived. Synergies, on the other hand, represent potential increases in overall productivity and customer value that stem from the ability to employ combinations of channels. In this section, we lay out a categorization of potential synergies for multi-channel retailers. Reviewing the quickly-emerging literature on multi-channel marketing and exploratory interviews with senior executives at three Fortune 500 multi-channel marketers (retailer, furniture, and financial services) produced five categories of potential synergies:

1. *Cross-channel customer communication and promotions.* One of the most common synergies is the use of one channel to promote another. This extends beyond the potential of multiple channels to make more efficient use of advertising (e.g., television advertising can drive traffic to stores, telephone centers, or Web sites). In many categories customers may "shop" in one channel and buy in another (Framback et al. 2007 and Verhoef et al. 2007). In some cases this behavior is anticipated (e.g., automobile purchases), but in other instances customers may encounter unexpected questions and require person-to-person interactions (phone centers) or inspection (stores). Especially when conversion and up-sell rates differ among channels, retailers may desire to direct customers to another channel to complete the purchase.
2. *Leveraging cross-channel information and marketing research from one channel to improve decisions in other channels.* Routinely, multi-channel retailers may be able to gather information on customers or purchase patterns in one channel to improve sales in another. For example, online sales may yield information on the conversation rates between display and sales for various products that inform choice of products for valuable in-stores display space. Since online displays and conversions are often faster, easier, and cheaper to manipulate and monitor, the entire channel may be made more productive with information sharing of this nature.
3. *Cross-channel price comparisons.* In some cases companies have established presence in multiple channels to complement pricing strategy of the other channels. For example, showcase stores, such as those maintained by Nike, Sony, and Levi's have helped to establish reference prices for other channels. When the same companies begin to sell online, direct to consumer, the prices they charge online may help control the threat of double marginalization (Chiang et al., 2003).
4. *Digitization.* Digitization of products such as operating manuals, bills, warranty documents, registrations and using the Internet to distribute and/or process them can reduce personnel costs in all channels. In addition, the production and distribution of these products through online channels make it more convenient for customers and free up service personnel for more profitable and higher value-added customer interactions.
5. *Share of common physical assets and operations.* Spreading fixed costs across channels can create economies of scale and scope (Neslin and Shankar, 2009). For example, when Progressive Insurance developed a database that enabled quick and accurate price comparison with competitors, that capability was extended from inbound telephone channels to the Web, and then to agents. Progressive's Web site allows customers recruited by agents to check bills and add coverage. A cross-channel return policy also creates cross-selling opportunities, because retailers can encourage customers to shop in the stores when they come to return online and

catalog orders. Neslin and Shankar (2009) report that one firm experienced a 20% increase in sales from stores after using stores to accept returns from online sales. However, these increases in revenues and retention may take time to materialize and, given the costs required to support additional channels, in the short run, customer profits may decline (Hitt et al., 2007).

DYNAMICS OF MULTICHANNEL RETAILING

The ability of the multichannel marketers to discover, develop, and exploit fully the potential synergies among multiple channels may depend on the degree of commitment to the new channels and commitment is likely to depend on early results. In the beginning, companies that have had success with one channel form are likely to be skeptical or agnostic with respect to the potential of emerging channels. Experimentation or separate organizations that are designed to develop "options" to exploit new channels may not immediately yield or permit exploitation of the potential synergies discussed above. In fact, if not properly designed and positioned, such experimentation may produce conflicts and what some have termed "dissynergies" (Falk et al., 2007), which is even worse than mere cannibalization.

Furthermore, emerging research suggests that caution should be taken in evaluating the effectiveness of a multi-channel retailing program on the basis of short-term results alone. The effects of opening a new channel can be multi-faceted, and the benefits from embarking on a multi-channel strategy can take some time to develop. For example, Avery et al. (2009) examined the effects of opening a retail store on existing direct channel sales and found a complex set of interactions. They found that the retail store had an immediately detrimental effect on sales in the direct channels, with both catalog and web-based sales suffering in the short run. Yet, both of these channels benefited from the presence of the retail store in the long run, with sales increasing over time. The effects of the retail store opening on customer acquisition and retention provided additional insight to how the channel was working. Although existing customers tended to purchase less frequently in the direct channel immediately after the store opened, they also tended to come back to the direct channel over time. The story was even rosier for new customer acquisitions. The store opening did not immediately slow new customer acquisitions, and these customers arrived at a faster rate over time.

Over time, new organizational forms may emerge as the potential for new channels proven true. Certainly, the ability of a retailer to exploit synergies may well depend on how the organization is structured (e.g., ranging from separate silos for the channels to centralized operations). Bagge (2007) cites a multi-channel "maturity model" developed by Archabal and

Kalyaman that consists of the following stages:

1. Creating presence (new channel is up and running);
2. Aligning fundamentals (basic value propositions coordinated);
3. Achieving proficiency (adept at function integration of customer processes);
4. Leveraging across channels (exploiting channel-capabilities and collaboration);
5. Optimizing operating mode (optimal resource allocation and achieving repeatable cross-channel processes).

This would be an interesting model to validate for its potential to predict and structure multi-channel strategy development and the evolutions of synergies. Only the last two stages seem to promise the synergies that we have discussed in this section.

FUTURE DIRECTIONS

The past fifteen years has been a period of rapid growth in the practice of multi-channel retailing, mirroring the rise of the Internet as a nearly ubiquitous tool that firms use to interact with customers. We see multi-channel retailing as being on the cusp of a new era in which firms start demanding more from their investments, with particular emphasis being given to financial performance in light of the current economic crisis. This presents a great opportunity both to firms that are looking to gain a competitive advantage through multi-channel retailing and to researchers who are interested in helping them make more informed decisions. We conclude with highlighting some of the themes discussed in this paper that may lead to particularly interesting research topics.

One of the leading challenges in practice is to determine how to set up an organizational structure to manage multiple channels. Currently, firms tend to manage each of their channels separately, as opposed to having a common person to which all channel reports. Although channel conflict is bound to exist in any organization, a silo managerial approach would seem to heighten the problem. Research would be helpful in addressing the question of whether firms with a common reporting structure get more out of their channel assets than those with silos. Does having a CMO who coordinates pricing and promotion decisions facilitate cooperation among channels for customers? Do these firms make more consistent pricing and promotional decisions? Do customers of these companies have a more coherent experience as they migrate across channels? In turn, does this make them more loyal to the company? How should incentives be structured to facilitate the right cooperation among division mangers?

A parallel opportunity for research exists in helping firms get more out of the information that they collect about customers. Currently, customer data are rarely analyzed to understand how individual customers behave across channels. This, however, seems to be the key to understanding the intricacies of how the channels work together. Research has shown that introducing price promotions can hurt demand from existing customers, but can boost it from new ones (Anderson and Simester 2004). We might ask related questions about pricing and promotion decisions across channels. Do customers tend to visit all channels before making a purchase if prices are allowed to vary across them, thereby slowing down their decision making process? Or does price discrimination lead to greater profitability? Does inter-channel competition tend to lead to greater customer acquisition because all channels are working hard to acquire new customers or does it lead to waste? Should each channel be allowed to tailor their message to their customer base because these customers differ or is it better to provide a common experience even if it results in inefficiencies within each channel?

What makes multi-channel retailing a particularly interesting area of research is that the problems are both complex and lend themselves well to extensive field-testing. We believe that many interesting questions will be asked and answered as firms and researchers try to come to grips with them.

REFERENCES

Anderson, Eric T. and Duncan I. Simester (2004), "Long-Run Effects of Promotion Depth on New versus Established Customers: Three Field Studies," *Marketing Science*, 23 (1), 4-20.

Aberdeen (2005), "The Multi-Channel Retail Benchmark Report," Aberdeen Group, Inc., December 2005.

Andrade, Eduardo, Velichka Kaltcheva, and Barton Weitz (2002), "Self-Disclosure on the Web: The Impact of Privacy Policy, Reward, and Company Reputation," *Advances in Consumer Resarch*, 2002, 350-353.

Ansari, Asim, Carl F. Mela, and Scott A. Neslin (2008), "Customer Channel Migration," *Journal of Marketing Research*, 45 (1), 60-76.

Avery, Jill, Thomas J. Steenburgh, John Deighton, and Mary Caravella (2009), "Adding Bricks to Clicks: The Contingencies Driving Cannibalization and Complementarity in Multichannel Retailing," *SSRN working paper*, available at http:\\ssrn.com\ abstract=961567.

Bagge, Danny (2007), "Multichannel Retailing: The Route to Customer Focus," white paper, IBM Global Business Services.

Biyalogorsky, Eyal and Prasad Naik (2003), "Clicks and Mortar: The Effect of On-line Activities on Off-line Sales," *Marketing Letters*, 14 (1), 21-32.

Chiang, Wei-Yu Kevin, Dilip Chhajed, and James D. Hess (2003), "Direct Marketing, Indirect Profits: A Strategic Analysis of Dual-Channel Supply-Chain Design," *Management Science*, 49 (1), 1-20.

Deleersnyder, Barbara, Inge Geyskens, Katrijn Gielens, and Marnik G. Dekimpe (2002), "How Cannibalistic Is the Internet Channel? A Study of the Newspaper Industry in the United Kingdom and The Netherlands," *International; Journal of Research in Marketing*, 19 (December), 337-348.

Deloitte (2007), "So you think you're a multi -channel retailer, but do your employees know?" white paper, Deloitte Development LLC.

Digital Future Study (2008). *Annual Digital Future Study* . Center for the Digital Future, Annenberg School for Communication, University of Southern California.

Falk, Tomas, Jeroen Schepers, Maik Hammerschmidt, and Hans Bauer (2007),"Identifying Cross-Channel Dissynergies for Multichannel Service Providers," *Journal of Service Research*, 10 (November), 143-160.

Frambach, Ruud T., Henk C. A. Roest, and Trichy V. Krishnan (2007), "The Impact of Consumer Internet Experience on Channel Preference and Usage Intentions across the Different Stages of the Buying Process," *Journal of Interactive Marketing*, 21 (2), 26-41.

Geyskens, Inge, Katrijn Gielens, and MarnikG Dekimpe (2002), "The Market Valuation of Internet Channel Additions," *Journal of Marketing*, 66 (2), 102–119.

Gulati, Ranjay and Jason Garino (2000), "Get the Right Mix of Bricks & Clicks," *Harvard Business Review*, May-June 2000, 107-114.

Hitt, Lorin, Mei Xue, and Pei-Yu Chen (2007), "The Determinants and Outcomes of Internet Banking Adoption," *MSI Reports*, [07-122].

Hoch, Stephen J., Eric T. Bradlow, and Brian Wansink (1999), "The Variety of an Assortment," *Marketing Science*, 18 (4), 527-546.

IBM (2008), "Customer Centricity Drives Retail's Multichannel Imperative," white paper, IBM Global Business Services, Fall 2008.

InternetRetailer.com (2006), "Retailers Don't Fully Coordinate Marketing across Channels, Study Says," September 21, 2006.

Kilcourse, Brian and Steve Rowen (2008). *Finding the Integrated Multi-Chanel Retailer*. Miami: Retail Systems Research.

Konus, Umut, Peter C. Verhoef, and Scott A. Neslin (2008), "Multichannel Shopper Segments and Their Covariates," *Journal of Retailing*, 84 (4), 398-413.

Kumar, Nanda and Ranran Ruan (2006), "On manufacturers complementing the traditional retail channel with a direct online channel," *Quantitative Marketing & Economics*, 4 (3), 289-323.

Kumar V. and Rajkumar Venkatesan (2005), "Who are the Multichannel Shoppers and How do They Perform? Correlates of Multichannel Shopping Behavior," *Journal of Interactive Marketing*, 19 (2), 44-61.

Levy, Michael and Barton A. Weitz (2009), *Retailing Management*, 7th Edition. New York, N.Y.: The McGraw-Hills/Irwin Companies, Inc.

Moriarty, Rowland T., Gordon S. Swartz, and Charles A. Khuen (1988), "Managing Hybrid Marketing Channels with Automation," *MSI Reports*, [88-113].

Myers, Joseph B., Andrew D. Pickersgill, and Evan S. VanMetre (2004), "Steering Customers to the Right Channels," *McKinsey Quarterly*, 4, 36-48.

Nam, Changi, Chanhoo Song, Euehun Lee, and Chan Ik Park (2006), "Consumers' Privacy Concerns and Willingness to Provide Marketing-Related Personal Information Online,"

Advances in Consumer Research, Volume 33, 213-217.

Neslin, Scott A., Dhruv Grewal, Robert Leghorn, Venkatesh Shankar, Marije L. Teerling, Jacquiline S. Thomas, Peter C. Verhoef (2006), "Challenges and Opportunities in Multichannel Management," *Journal of Service Research*, 9 (2), 95-112.

Neslin, Scott A. and Venkatesh Shankar (2009), "Key Issues in Multichannel Customer Management: Current Knowledge and Future Directions," *Journal of Interactive Marketing*, forthcoming.

OCED (2008), *The Future of the Internet Economy*. Organization for Economic Co-Operation and Development. June 2008.

Pauwels, Koen and Scott A. Neslin (2008), "Building with Bricks and Mortar: The Revenue Impact of Opening Physical Stores in a Multichannel Environment." *MSI Reports*, [08-101].

Payne, Adrian and Pennie Frow (2005), "A Strategic Framework for Customer Relationship Management," *Journal of Marketing*, 69 (October), 167-176.

PEW (2007), *Pew Internet & American Life Project Teen/Parent Survey on Writing*, September -November, 2007.

PEW (2008). *Internet & American Life Project*, April 8 – May 11, 2008 Tracking Survey.

Popkowski Leszczyc, Peter T. L. and Harry J. P. Timmermans (1997), "Store-Switching Behavior," *Marketing Letters*, 8 (2), 193-204.

Shankar, Venkatesh and Tarun Kushwaha (2008), "An Empirical Analysis of Cross-Channel Effects in a Multichannel Environment," working paper, Texas A&M University.

Shop.org and J. C. Williams Group (2008), "Organizing for Cross-Channel Retailing," white paper, Shop.org and J. C. Williams Group, January 2008.

Schuman, Evan (2004), "Aberdeen Report: True Multichannel Sales Desirable but Rare," www.eweek.com, October 22, 2004.

Sultan, Fareena and Andrew J. Rohm (2004), "The Evolving Role of the Internet in Marketing Strategy," *Journal of Interactive Marketing*, 18 (2), 6-19.

Van Baal, Sebastian and Christian Dach (2005), "Free Riding and Customer Retention Across Retailers' Channels," *Journal of Interactive Marketing*, 19 (Spring), 75-85.

Venkatesan, Rajkumar, V. Kumar, and Nalini Ravishanker (2007), "Multichannel Shopping: Causes and Consequences," *Journal of Marketing*, 71 (2), 114-32.

Verhoef, Peter C., Scott A. Neslin, and Björn Vroomen (2007), "Multichannel customer management: Understanding the research-shopper phenomenon," *International Journal of Research in Marketing*, 24 (2), 129-48.

10

SHOULD INDIAN RETAIL MARKET WELCOME FDI? A REVIEW

Jhilam Rudra De & Suddhasanta De

INTRODUCTION

Retail is the final stage of any economic activity. By virtue of this fact, retail occupies an important place in the world economy. It is necessary to understand that in the complex world of trade today, retail would include not only goods but also services, which may be provided to the end consumer. In an age where the customer is the king and marketers are focusing on customer delight, retail may be redefined as the first point of customer contact. In fact, India retail industry is the fastest growing industry in India and it accounts for around 12per cent of the country's GDP and is likely to reach 22 per cent by 2010. In 2009, the retail industry in India amounted to US$ 511billion and out of this the organized retail sector in India amounted to around 5%. India's overall retail sector is expected to rise to US$ 833 billion by 2013 and to US$ 1.3 trillion by 2018, at a compound annual growth rate (CAGR) of 10 per cent(source: IBEF) fuelled by an impressive growth in consumer spending. Over 100 malls of over 30 million sq feet of new shopping centre space are projected to open in India between 2009 and end-2010 (Mall Realities India 2010: Jones Lang LaSalle Meghraj and Cushman & Wakefield India).. Many Indian companies have entered the retail industry in India and this is also a factor in the growth of Indian organized retail sector. Global retail giants are also entering the retail industry in India and this is also one of the factors in the growth of the organized retail sector in India.

The need for larger FDI is because India is at a stage where it needs US investments, technology, and management policies to sustain and enhance its economic growth. In 2006, Foreign Direct Investment (FDI) in India amounted to US$37 billion, out of which only $5 billion was from the US.

This was not a very encouraging figure in view of the goal of increasing the GDP by 34-36%. Therefore, it can be said that there is a need for larger FDIs. The need for larger FDI calls for major issues and areas to be taken into consideration, such as:

- Market potential and accessibility
- Political stability
- Market infrastructure
- Easy currency conversion

The current debate on allowing foreign direct investment (FDI) in India's retail trade primarily focuses on two issues – employment and consumer welfare. Supporters of this move have developed consumer centric arguments while the opponents are more concerned with its adverse impact on employment.

THE EVOLUTION OF RETAIL SECTOR IN INDIA

While barter would be considered to be the oldest form of retail trade, since independence, retail in India has evolved to support the unique needs of our country, given its size and complexity. They still continue to be present in most parts of the country and form an essential part of life and trade in various areas.

In the past decade, the Indian market place has transformed dramatically. However, from the 1950's to the 80's, investments in various industries were limited due to low purchasing power in the hands of the consumer and the government's policies favouring the small scale sector.

With the success of the branded menswear stores, the new age Departmental store arrived in India in the early nineties. This was actually, the beginning of a new era for

Evolution of Retail in India

Traditional formats

- Itinerant salesman
- Haats
- Melas
- Mandis etc

Established formats

- Kirana shops
- Departmental stores
- Multi brand showrooms
- Fair price shops
- Co-operative stores
- Pan/beedi shops

Emerging formats

- Exclusive retail outlets
- Hypermarkets
- Internal retail
- Malls/speciality malls
- Multiplexes
- Rural oriented formats
- Fast food outlets
- Service galleries

retail in India. The fact that post liberalization economy had opened up and a large middle class with spending power had emerged, helped shape this sector. This has fuelled the growth of departmental stores, supermarkets and other speciality stores. The concept of retail as entertainment came to India with the advent of malls. The development of malls is now visible not only in the major metros but also in other parts of the country.

FACTORS WHICH INFLUENCED INDIAN RETAIL INDUSTRY

Economic Growth- The gradual increase in GDP and the purchase power of Indians provided an excellent opportunity for organized retail industry.

Country	*Private Consumption/* GDP %
US	68.4
China	47.5
India	61.4
Japan	61.2
Germany	51.9
France	54.4
UK	64.6
Italy	62.7

Urbanization- While the total population of India grew by 3.5 times from 1901 to 1991; its urban population increased nine fold, from 25 million to 217 million during same period. Moreover the share of urban population in class I cities in the total urban population has increased from 26% to 65%. It is growing gradually in this decade also.This led to fantastic growth of retailing in metros and mini metros.

Consumerism- The influence of western lifestyle has led to considerable change in living standard and style of Indian consumer. The economic well being of Indian middle class and upper middle class and their growing aspirations for comforts has also been responsible for consumerism slowly gaining momentum in India. Today, Indian urban consumer is more inclined towards buying the goods, irrespective of need.

Holding Inventory- Retailers carry inventory of finished goods and make the products available to consumers at a convenient place and time. Retailers make it possible for consumers to make instant purchases. This action of retailer frees consumers from investing into stocking of goods and uses the money profitably.

Providing Services- Retailers not only sell the goods but also provide a variety of value added services, which make it easier for customers to buy and use the products. These value added services include providing free home delivery, accepting credit cards, accepting payments in installments, arranging consumer finance etc.

Providing information- Retailers play important role in providing product related information to their consumers. Retailers, in collaboration with manufacturers, may plan advertising to make nearby consumers aware about arrival of new product; also it might provide in-store sales persons to provide product information and demonstration, which help the consumer to simplify his purchasing process.

EMERGING TRENDS IN INDIAN ORGANIZED RETAIL SECTOR

The emerging trends in the Indian organized retail sector would help the economic growth in India. The growth factors in Indian organized sector are various but it is mainly due to the fact that India's economy is booming. There is a fantastic rise in the Indian organized retail sector in a very short period of time between 2001 and 2006. Eventually, out of the shadows of the unorganized retail sector, India has a chance of tremendous economic growth, both in India and abroad.

The emerging trends in the Indian organized retail sector are also adding up to the development of the Indian organized retail sector. The relaxation by the government on regulatory controls on foreign direct investments has added to the process of the growth of the Indian organized retail sector.

The infrastructure of the retail sector will evolve radically in the recent future. The emergence of shopping malls are increasing at a steady pace in the metros and there are further plans of expansion which would lead to 100 new ones of over 30 mn sq feet coming up in India by end of 2010. As the count of super markets is going up much faster than rate of growth in retail sector, it is taking the lions share in food trade.

The growth of the Indian organized retail sector is anticipated to be heavier than the growth of the gross domestic product. Alterations in people's lifestyle, growth in income levels, and encouraging conventions of demography are proving favorable for the new emerging trends in the Indian organized retail sector. The success of this retail sector would also lie in the degree of penetration into the lower income strata to tap the possible customers in the lowest levels of society. The demands of the buyers would also be enhanced by more access to credit facilities.

With the arrival of the Transnational Companies (TNC), the Indian retail sector will undergo a transformation. At present the Foreign Direct Investments (FDI) is not encouraged in the Indian organized retail sector but once the TNC'S get in they inevitably try to oust their Indian counterparts. This would be challenging to the retail sector in India.

The trends to follow in the future:

- The Indian Organized retail sector will grow up to 10% of total retailing by 2010.
- No one single format can be assumed as there is a huge difference in cultures regionally.
- The most encouraging format now would be the hypermarts.
- The hypermart format would be further encouraged with the entry of the TNCs.

GROWTH FACTORS IN INDIAN ORGANIZED RETAIL SECTOR

The rise in the working population which is young, pay- packets which are hefty, more nuclear families in urban areas, rise in the number of women working, more disposable income and customer aspiration, western influences and growth in expenditure for luxury items. All these are the factors for the growth in Indian organized retail sector.

In fact, India retail industry is the fastest growing industry in India and it accounts for 12% of the country's GDP. In 2009, the retail industry in India amounted to US$ 511 billion and out of this, the organized retail sector in India amounted to around 5%. By 2011, the Indian organized retail sector is expected to rise to US$ 50 billion according to a research report by RNCOS titled 'Booming Retail Sector in India'.

Many Indian companies have entered the retail industry in India and this is also a factor in the growth of Indian organized retail sector. Reliance Industries Limited is planning to invest US$ 6 billion in the organized retail sector in India by opening 1500

Leading Retail Markets of India

Retail marketer	No. of retail outlets	Retail space(sq. Ft)	Format	Product port folio	Expansion plans	Sales per sq. FtRs./ft
Bata	1500	10,00,000	Brand chain	Own & mnc footwear, shoe and accessories	Wants to expand the sales to 100 million pairs	80,000
Liberty	360	2,00,000	Brand chain	Foot wear, shoe and accessories	Planning 10 more retail outlets per annum	25,000
Kodak	890	2,00,000	Imaging chain	Photography, processing and peripherals	Plans 200 stores every year	1,40,000
Food world/ music world/super store etc	110	4,93,000	Super market, speciality stores, hyper markets	Food, music, health and beauty products, grocery	Plans for Rs. 60 cr.	23,834
TitanIndustries	314	2,30,000	Brand chain	Watches, clocks and jewelery	Investment everyyear to add 30 outlets	19,391
Raymond	263	4,00,000	Speciality stores	Fabric, apparels and accessories	Wants to open 10 new retail outlets every year	10,000
Shoppers stop	13	4,09,000	Departmental stores	Clothing, accessories, books etc	Plans 100 more outlets in next 5 years	6968
Pantaloon retail with big bazar	50	3,38,999	Clothing, utilities & groceries	Departmental stores/ hyper market	6 more stores are planned Expansion in investment can increase upto rs. 500 cr.	5178

Source: Image India Retail Report 2002

supermarkets and 1000 hypermarkets. Bharti Telecoms is planning a joint venture worth £ 750 million with Tesco a global retail giant. Pantaloons are planning to invest US$ 1 billion in order to increase its retail space to 30 million square feet. Such huge investment is also a factor in the growth of the organized retail sector in India.

Global retail giants are also entering the retail industry in India and this is also one of the factors in the growth of the organized retail sector in India. The global retail giants who are eager to enter the organized retail sector in India are:

— Wal- Mart

— Tesco

— Carrefour SA

— Metro AG etc.

The factors for growth in Indian organized retail sector are many and that is the reason behind its massive growth. But for this to continue both the Indian retailers and the government will have to work together.

FDI IN INDIAN ORGANIZED RETAIL SECTOR

Given this backdrop, the recent clamour about opening up the retail sector to Foreign Direct Investment (FDI) becomes a very sensitive issue, with arguments to support both sides of the debate. It is widely acknowledged that FDI can have some positive results on the economy, triggering a series of reactions that in the long run can lead to greater efficiency and improvement of living standards, apart from greater integration into the global economy. Supporters of FDI in retail trade talk of how ultimately the consumer is benefited by both price reductions and improved selection, brought about by the technology and know-how of foreign players in the market. This in turn can lead to greater output and domestic consumption.

But the most important factor against FDI driven "modern retailing" is that it is labour displacing to the extent that it can only expand by destroying the traditional retail sector. Till such time we are in a position to create jobs on a large scale in manufacturing, it would make eminent sense that any policy that results in the elimination of jobs in the unorganised retail sector should be kept on hold.

Though most of the high decibel arguments in favour of FDI in the retail sector are not without some merit, it is not fully applicable to the retailing sector in India, or at least, not yet. This is because the primary task of government in India is still to provide livelihoods and not create so called efficiencies of scale by creating redundancies. As per present regulations, no FDI is permitted in retail trade in India.

The (irrational) fear created in the minds is perhaps based on the following myths:

- FDI will bring in global retailers who will wipe out the local retail industry.
- FDI will bring in global retailers who will swamp India with imported merchandise.
- FDI will bring in global retailers who will end up creating massive job losses in India.

The current debate on allowing foreign direct investment (FDI) in India's retail trade primarily focuses on two issues – employment and consumer welfare. Supporters of this move have developed consumer centric arguments while the opponents are more concerned with its adverse impact on employment.

Though FDI in retailing is not allowed, the Government of India has a more liberal policy towards wholesale trade; franchising and commission agents' services. Foreign retailers have already started their operations in India through (i) joint venture where the Indian firm was an export house (ii) franchising (KFC, Nike) (iii) sourcing from small-scale sector; (iv) cash and carry operation (Giant in Hyderabad) (v) Non-store formats-direct marketing (Amway). Large international retailers of home furnishing and apparels like Pottery Barn, Gap and Ralph Lauren have made India as one of their major sourcing hubs.

To analyze the likely impact of FDI on major stakeholders of the Indian retail sector, analysis of few important issues is required.

Uniqueness of Indian retail market - Products and services normally reach the end consumers from the manufacturer/producers through two different channels:

(a) Producers sell via independent retailers (vertical separation),

(b) Directly from producer to consumer (vertical integration) .

In India however, the above two modes of operations are not very common. At present, less than 3% of the retail transactions in India are done in the organized sector (vertical separation), which is likely to be increased to 15%- 20% by 2010 (Fitch Ratings, 2003). Till date, it is restricted to metro cities only. The second type (vertical integration) is common to few national and subsidiaries of global firms. Moreover, Indian wholesale trade is not properly organized. The wholesale trade in India is also characterized with the presence of thousands of small commission agents, stockiest and distributors who operate strictly at a local level. Apart from these, in many cases the small producers - mostly artisans and farmers, sell their goods directly to the end consumers through their participation in the market as sellers. Existence of thousands of such individual producer cum sellers is examples of "vertical integration" of the Indian retail sector.

Another note worthy feature of the Indian retail sector is the absence of any barrier to entry or exit. Anyone can enter or leave the Indian retail sector at any point of time. Retail sector immensely contributes to the political system by acting as a shock absorber and maintaining social stability. Thus when a factory shuts down rendering people jobless; the farmers remain idle during off seasons or get evicted from the land; the stagnant manufacturing sector fails to provide jobs to the thousand of unemployed youths; the retail sector absorb them all. Again when the factory reopens (in exceptional cases); harvesting time arrives; some of these new entrants leave the retail trade and return back to their respective jobs.

After agriculture, probably, the incidence of disguised unemployment (and under employment) is highest in the Indian retail sector. Small retailers most of whom operate in the unorganized sector, dominate the trade.

Identification of major beneficiaries of FDI -There could be the following possible reasons for inviting FDI in retail trade:

(i) Organized domestic retailers want to collaborate with the world leaders to expand their existing business.

(ii) Proprietary expertise in retail trade exists with few global players only. The latter would not transfer their expertise to local firms unless they are allowed to operate in the domestic market.

(iii) Only the global retailers can satisfy the rising and varied demands of Indian consumers.

(iv) Foreign firms are interested in the growing Indian domestic market.

(v) India is an emerging procurement hub for global retailers especially for handicraft products (including textiles) and semi-processed local food items.

(vi) Share of FDI in the trading service is declining in the developed countries. Capital is looking for a better pasture. Major players are loosing their popularity.

(vii) New rules in international trade encourage movement of FDI across nations to maximize return on investment.

Possible impact on marginal producers and work force- The third important issue is the possible impact of such action on numerous small and marginal producers especially in the agrarian and handicraft/ handloom sectors. India still predominantly houses the traditional formats of retailing, that is, the local kirana shop, *paan/beedi* shop, hardware stores, weekly haats, convenience stores, and bazaars, which together form the bulk. The Indian retail industry was, and continues to be, highly fragmented.

According to the global consultancy firms AC Neilsen and KSA Technopak, India has the highest shop density in the world. In 2001 they estimated there were 11 outlets for every 1,000 people. Further, a report prepared by McKinsey & Company and the Confederation of Indian Industry (CII) predicted that global retail giants such as Tesco, Kingfisher, Carrefour and Ahold were waiting in the wings to enter the retail arena. This report also states that the Indian retail market holds the potential of becoming a $300 billion per year market by 2010, provided the sector is opened up significantly. It does not talk about creating additional jobs however, which should be the prime concern of the policy maker. One of the principal reasons behind the explosion of retail and its fragmented nature in the country is the fact that retailing is probably the primary form of disguised unemployment/underemployment in the country. Given the already over-crowded agriculture sector, and the stagnating manufacturing sector, and the hard nature and relatively low wages of jobs in both, many million Indians are virtually forced into the services sector.

Here, given the lack of opportunities, it is almost a natural decision for an individual to set up a small shop or store, depending on his or her means and capital.

And thus, a retailer is born, seemingly out of circumstance rather than choice. This phenomenon quite aptly explains the millions of kirana shops and small stores. The explosion of retail outlets in the more busy streets of Indian villages and towns is a visible testimony of this.

The presence of more than one retailer for every hundred persons is indicative of the lack of economic opportunities that is forcing people into this form of self-employment, even though much of it is marginal. Because of this fragmentation, the Indian retail sector typically suffers from limited access to capital, labour and real estate options. The typical traditional retailer follows the low-cost-and-size format, functioning at a small-scale level, rarely eligible for tax and following a cheap model of operations.

FDI IN DEVELOPING COUNTRIES

FDI has attracted increasing attention in developing countries due to the perceived benefits in terms of injection of capital, technology and knowledge. Specifically, a number of factors have led to increased efforts by developing countries to attract FDI inflows:

- Increased recognition by policy makers that the bundle of assets and capabilities encompassed in FDI could contribute directly to growth and development of the national economy;
- Declining trend of other forms of assistance increased reliance on FDI, and various financial crises may have led to a preference for longer term, relatively stable and often tangible flows of direct investment; and
- Governments in developing countries have gained confidence in their ability to maximize the benefits and minimize the liabilities of transnational corporations.

INDIA'S FDI POTENTIAL

The Indian economy is now well recognized as an attractive destination for investment and a large and growing market for business. India is emerging as a global player in information technology and is in the forefront of the unfolding new area of knowledge economy, with its large pool of scientific and creative human resources and R&D facilities.

While FDI inflows to India has increased in recent years as compared to other select Asian countries, the stock of FDI inflows for India at US$ 38.7 bn in 2004, are lower than that for other Asian countries such as Malaysia (US$ 46.3 bn) and Thailand (US$ 48.6 bn). Further, FDI in India is yet to play its desired and significant role in overall economic activity in India is evidenced by the fact that the share of inward FDI stock to the country's GDP has been much lower as compared to those in other Asian countries. Although India has made progress in some areas for improving the business climate, the most striking feature for India is that it ranks lower than its Asian peers in most of the categories.

Trends in FDI Inflows and Selected Asian Countries (US$mn)

	2002	2003	2004	2005	2006	2007
INDIA	3449	4269	5335	7606	19662	22950
INDONESIA	145	-597	1023	8337	4914	6928
MALAYSIA	3203	2473	4624	3967	6048	8403
PHILIPPINES	1792	347	469	1854	2921	2928
THAILAND	947	1952	1064	8048	9010	9575
VIETNAM	1200	1450	1610	2021	2360	6739

South, East and South-East Asia: top 10 recipients of FDI inflows,a 2006–2007 (Billions of dollars)
Source: World Investment Report 2005 and 2008UNCTAD

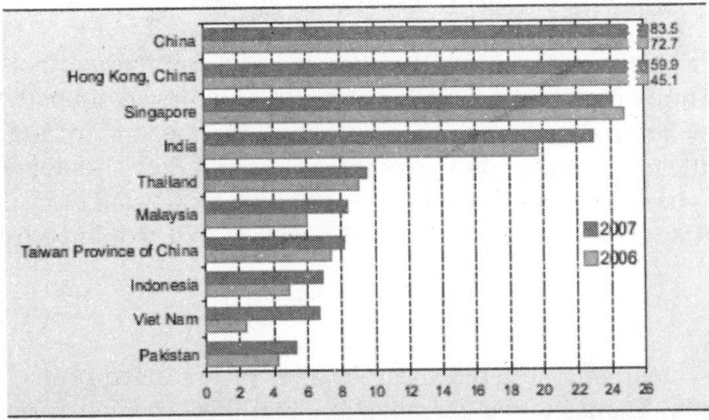

Source: World Investment Report 2005 and 2008UNCTAD

In India, while trade and finance services continue to be major sector, other services sectors such as electricity, telecommunications, water supply and business services (which encompass a diverse group, ranging from real estate to professional services to IT-enabled services) have also emerged as leading FDI recipients in recent years. Health services and education services have also witnessed sharp rise in inward FDI stock. Rapid growth in demand for these services, and privatization and liberalization in many countries have facilitated the surge in services FDI.

IMPACT OF FDI IN RETAIL IN INDIA

It is by now common knowledge that the country's organised retail sector comprising malls, speciality stores and supermarkets is in a state of disarray following the global economic crisis that started in mid-2008. Investors who flocked to this nascent sector as if there was no tomorrow have, in the past several months, been scurrying to cover their risks. Many outlets have shut down. Sales are plummeting, rentals are being renegotiated and employee layoff has become common.

With a fairly stable government in place, investors are beginning to see a ray of hope. Indeed, that hope does not relate to return of customers to malls and high-end luxury goods shops. Hope springs from the belief that the new government will be ready to undertake economic reforms. The opening up of retail trade for foreign direct investment (FDI) promises to usher in revolutionary changes to the Indian consumer market in the days to come.

Recently, in a significant step towards liberalizing India's retail trade, the government has allowed to partially open the retail sector by announcing 51 percent FDI in single brand retailing – a move that has paved way for big names like Nike, Versace, Adidas, Marks & Spencer to set up their own stores in India.

This means that foreign companies willing to enter the Indian market will now be able to invest up to 51 percent in setting up production facilities, distribution network and retail shops and the rest will come from Indian investors.

However, experts are still divided on the problems and prospects of this move. Some say it will shrink employment opportunities, completely alter the retail distributional structure and deal a death blow to the corner shop structure.

The optimists, on the other hand, see a whole range of opportunities — from improved collection, processing and better distribution of farm products to generation of more opportunities for the rural and urban unemployed.

Practically no country in the world has banned FDI in retailing. Some do impose conditions such as number of stores, location of stores and ownership pattern but by and large, these are few and contingent on specific conditional factors. In case of China, the FDI in retail has little or no impact on the local retailers and they still dominate the retail sector. There is no global instance of total wipe out of the local retail industry. The risk of the local grocer is the same from a Giant or a Big Bazaar as it would be from a Tesco or Sainsbury etc.

CONCLUSION

Indian Consumers have long suffered from decades of excessive protectionism of the manufacturing sector. Thanks to the liberalization, that they are now at least able to buy world class products at somehow reasonable prices. Retailing in India is most inefficient and least productive. FDI helped organized retail to grow in Thailand, Malaysia and Brazil to around 40-50% and in Poland and China to around 20%.

Globally the retail sector is one of the largest employers. Employment is not limited to metro cities but all cities, small and large. In India also, it is probably the largest industry employing the largest workforce after agriculture.

FDI in retail is forbidden today for fear of large unemployment that it might create. But large retail formats would come up only in large cities, which constitute not more than 10-15% of the total population. Hence, the majority of retailers in small/ medium cities and rural areas shall remain unaffected. The 'kirana shop' round the corner will remain. Clearly, the benefits of large retail formats and FDI far outweigh the disruptions of any. Opening up FDI in retail will not open the flood gates overnight. In China, it took around 15 years to reach 20% penetration- time enough for Indian industries to adapt and grow within the competition.

REFERENCES

Acharya, B. Retail: Hope on FDI? (May 2009), The Hindu Business Line

A Report on Economic Slowdown Hampers Global FDI Flows (September, 2009), The Hindu Business Line

Chandrasekhar,G. FDI in Retail Can Wait (June, 2009), The Hindu Business Line

Cox,R and Brittain, P. Retailing An Introduction (2006), 5th Edition, Pearson Education, New Delhi

Kulkarni, M.V. Retail Marketing Management (2005), 1st Edition, Everest Publishing House, Pune

Pradhan, S. Retailing Management Text and Cases (2008), 2nd Edition,Tata McGrawhill Publishing Company Ltd, New Delhi

Storai, - The Voice of the Retailers Association of India, Vol 3, Issue 6, January- February, 2008

Part–II

Innovations in Human Resource Management

11

INFLUENCE OF GOAL ORIENTATION OF SALESPEOPLE ON THEIR PERFORMANCE–AN EMPIRICAL STUDY

Binu Markose

INTRODUCTION

Individual goal orientation is defined as "a mental framework for how individuals interpret and respond to achievement situations" (Brett & VandeWalle, 1999). Goal orientation theory suggests that individuals can possess one of two types of superordinate goals during task performance: a goal focused on improving competencies and acquiring new skills (*learning goal*) and a goal focused on demonstrating competence and comparing one's own abilities to those of others (*performance goal*). Recent studies in sales research (Kohli, Shervani, and Challagala 1998; Sujan, Weitz, and Kumar 1994; VandeWalle et al. 1999; Paparoidamis 2005; Silver, Dwyer, and Alford 2006), such as those in the psychology disciplines (Dweck and Legget 1988; Elliot and Dweck 1988; Ames and Archer 1988; Meece, Blumenfeld, and Hoyle 1988), have focused on these two distinct goal orientations of salespeople – Learning and Performance. Learning and performance goal orientations are associated with different personal beliefs about ability and effort. A learning goal orientation is associated with an incremental theory, which is the belief that ability can be developed and that effort is an efficacious strategy for developing the wherewithal needed for successful task performance. In contrast, a performance goal orientation is associated with an entity theory, which is the belief that ability is difficult to develop and that successful task performance is primarily based on possessing the requisite innate ability.

Learning and Performance Orientation: One, Two or Three Dimensions?

Theory and research in the field of education has implied that learning and performance goals are opposite ends of the same continuum, as indicated by studies that assign individuals to one of these orientations or the other (e.g., Ames & Archer, 1988) and then manipulate participants' orientations. This would imply that the traits associated with learning orientations are exactly the opposite of those associated with performance orientations and that one person could not possess both types of goal orientation in the same situation. Some researchers, however, suggest another idea: that learning orientation and performance orientation are actually two separate constructs (Nicholls, Cheung, Lauer, & Patashnick, 1989). Nicholls and Dweck (1979) argue that learning and performance orientations are not the opposite ends of a continuum, rather these represent two distinct dimensions and a person can have both high learning and performance orientations. According to Sujan, Weitz and Kumar (1994), in a selling contest, learning and performance orientations of salespeople are not opposites rather the managerial interventions to increase the learning orientation are unlikely to hurt their performance orientation.

Recently, the suggestion has been made that goal orientation could be conceptualized as a three-dimensional construct. Middleton and Midgley (1997) argue that both learning orientation and performance orientation in its traditional sense can be considered "approach" tendencies. They note, however, that motivation theorists generally speak in terms of approach tendencies and avoid tendencies. Consistent with this reasoning, VandeWalle (1997) argues that the desire to gain positive evaluations and the desire to avoid unfavorable judgments are actually two separate constructs, rather than one performance orientation construct. Middleton and Midgley (1997) and VandeWalle (1997) therefore advocate breaking goal orientation into three dimensions: learning, performance-prove, and performance-avoid. Research conducted after Nicholls and his colleagues (1989) has indicated that the three-dimensional conceptualization of goal orientation may be preferable to the two dimensional conceptualization. For example, Attenweiler and Moore (2006) conducted a series of factor analyses, and concluded that a three-factor model was superior to a two factor model. Elliot and Harackiewicz (1996) found that prove and avoid orientations were associated with different levels of motivation for a problem-solving activity. Very recently few studies in the sales research also talk in favour of a three factor conceptualization of goal orientation. McFarland and Kidwell (2006) propose and empirically test a theoretical model that identifies salesperson learning, prove, and avoid goal orientations as mediators of Instrumental and expressive (I/E) traits and performance. The study by Silver, Dwyer, and Alford (2006) revisits the conceptualization and operationalization of salesperson goal orientation and proposes that performance goal orientation is comprised of two distinct components: a performance-prove goal orientation (called "performance-approach" in their study) and a performance-avoidance goal orientation.

Although research comparing the two-dimensional versus three-dimensional nature of goal orientation is still in its early stages, preliminary studies indicate that the three dimensional conceptualization is more informative. Therefore, in the current study, we have conceptualized goal orientation in the three-dimensional manner, focusing on learning orientation, performance-prove orientation and performance-avoid orientation.

RESEARCH OBJECTIVES

Several scholars reported that goal orientation leads to enhanced performance of the individuals. Kohli, Shervani, and Challagalla (1998) reported that performance orientation significantly enhances performance of the salespeople. In a longitudinal field study, Vandewalle et al. (1999) found that learning goal orientation had a positive relationship with sales performance. In a conceptual paper by Paparoidamis (2005), the author highlighted that both learning orientation and performance orientation of salespeople will be positively related to sales performance. Silver, Dwyer, and Alford (2006) also reported that salesperson's goal orientation has effects on sales performance. But no studies have been undertaken taking into consideration another important dimension of salesperson's performance viz. behavioural performance. The two important dimensions of salespersons' performance which received considerable attention in the literature are output performance and behavioural performance. Output performance related to outcome of selling (attainment of quotas) whereas behavioural performance related to process of selling (activities that are related directly to generating sales like sales presentations or price negotiations called selling behavioural performance and activities that are not directly related to generating sales like providing information or controlling expenses called nonselling behavioral performance). Jaworski and Kohli (1991) while analyzing the effect of supervisory feedback on salesperson performance, two dimensions were considered viz. output performance and behavioural performance. They reported that supervisory feedback has strong effect on both dimensions of performance. Cravens et al (1993) used three dimensions of performance in examining salesforce control systems viz. output performance, selling behavioural performance and nonselling behavioural performance. The authors support the need to differentiate between salesforce outcome performance and salesforce behavioral performance. Kohli and Jaworski (1994) reported that both output performance and behavioural performance are important in the analysis of coworker feedback on salesperson performance. Jackson, Schlacter and Wolfe (1995) examined various dimensions of both quantitative and qualitative performances in evaluating salesperson performance. They suggested that behavioural performance is relevant in the evaluation of salesperson performance. Oliver and Anderson (1995) highlighted the importance of both output performance and behavioural performance in examining salesforce control systems. Grant and Cravens (1996) used output performance and behavioural performance in examining salesforce performance and found that behavioural aspect is as much important as output aspect of performance. Baldauf and Cravens (1999) while analyzing contribution of salesforce performance to sales organization effectiveness found very much relevance of behavioural performance in contributing to organization effectiveness.

Also very few studies incorporated the three factor conceptualization of goal orientation while analyzing the effect of goal orientation on salesperson performance. Silver, Dwyer, and Alford (2006) used these three aspects in analyzing salesperson performance but the study lacks the dimension, salesperson behavioural performance.

Based on the above discussion, the research objective is formulated as follows.

- To study the effect of learning orientation, performance-prove orientation, and performance-avoid orientation of salespeople on their behavioural performance and output performance.

CONCEPTUAL MODEL AND RESEARCH HYPOTHESES

First we will discuss about the hypotheses linking learning orientation and performance. Then, the hypotheses linking performance-prove orientation and performance will be discussed and finally, the hypotheses linking performance-avoid orientation and performance will be discussed. Figure 1 depicts the relationships examined here.

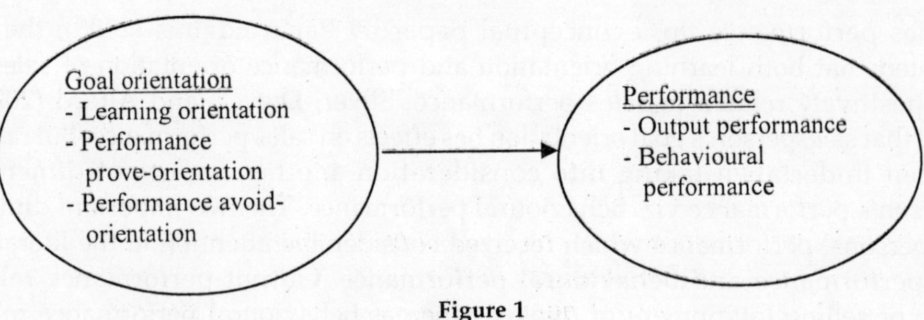

Figure 1

LEARNING ORIENTATION AND PERFORMANCE

People with a learning orientation have a strong desire to improve and master their selling skills and abilities continually and view achievement situations as opportunities to improve their competence (Dweck and Leggett 1988; Elliott and Dweck 1988). Dweck and Leggett (1988) suggest that persons with a learning orientation are not concerned unduly with making mistakes and persist in their efforts even if they fail. Under a learning orientation, also referred to as a mastery orientation (Ames and Archer 1988), salespeople enjoy the process of discovering how to sell effectively. They are attracted by challenging sales situations and not unduly bothered by mistakes. They value the feelings of personal growth and mastery they derive from their job. There is empirical evidence that learning orientation encourages salespeople to work hard, presumably because they enjoy work, which leads to higher performance (Sujan, Weitz and Kumar 1994). In addition, sales people with a learning orientation tend to adapt their responses to selling situations and therefore perform at a higher level and a learning goal orientation adds significantly to a performance goal orientation in causing salespeople to be effective (Sujan, Weitz and Kumar 1994). In contrast, according to the research by Kohli, Shervani, and Challagalla (1998), learning orientation appears to be unrelated to output performance. Therefore to reassess the relation between learning orientation and output performance in our context, the following hypothesis is introduced.

H1a: Learning orientation is positively related to output performance of salespeople:

Learning orientation is supposed to have a significant influence on behavioural performance of salespeople for several reasons. Behavioural performance relates to the application of selling strategies, customer presentations, and technical knowledge and so on for which learning behaviour is very helpful. Moreover, learning oriented salespeople are expected to use self-regulation strategies (e.g., solution oriented self-instruction, self-checks) that help develop the salesperson's selling skills and knowledge which there by leads to superior performance (Vande Walle and Cummings, 1997). A learning goal orientation stems from an intrinsic interest in one's work- a preference for challenging work, a view of oneself as being curious, and a search for opportunities that permit independent attempts to master material. Hence it may be expected that salesperson having learning orientation leads to better behavioural performance and hence propose the following hypothesis.

H1b: Learning orientation is positively related to behavioural performance of salespeople

Performance-prove orientation and performance: The prove goal orientation can be defined as the desire to prove one's competence and to gain favorable judgments about it (VandeWalle 1997). Elliot and Harackiewicz (1996) found, in two experiments involving college students, that performance-approach (prove) goal orientation resulted in higher levels of intrinsic motivation leading to higher performance. In a study by Elliot and Church (1997) which measured achievement goal orientation of undergraduates, showed that performance prove orientation enhanced graded performance. Because performance prove oriented individuals desire the extrinsic rewards associated with higher demonstrated performance, are likely to exert effort, which is viewed to have a positive impact on performance. Silver et al. (2006) found that performance approach orientation has a significant influence on output performance of salespeople in their selling context of life insurance agents. To confirm this relationship in our selling context, we put forward the following hypothesis.

H2a: Performance-prove orientation is positively related to output performance of salespeople

The study by Grant and Cravens (1996) renders substantial support for the fact that the behaviour based control system followed by the sales managers produced both high behavioural performance and high outcome performance of salespersons. It also provides strong support for the fact that salespersons having high behavioural performance produced high outcome performance. The processes that result out of performance prove orientation, similar to those of a learning goal orientation, are excitement, concentration, task absorption, and sensitivity to success-relevant information, all mastery patterns of achievement outcomes (Elliot 1999; Elliot and Church 1997; Elliot and Harackiewicz 1996). This implies salespersons who are performance prove oriented will try to achieve mastery in the process of selling to prove their competence. Hence the following hypothesis is suggested.

H2b: Performance-prove orientation is related positively to behavioural performance of salespeople.

Performance-avoid orientation and performance: People with a performance-avoidance goal orientation act to avoid negative evaluations and will not have a desire to compete others (Elliot and Church 1997; Elliot and Harackiewicz 1996; Middleton and Midgley 1997; Skaalvik 1997; VandeWalle, Cron, and Slocum 2001). The study by Elliot and Church (1997) on college graduates has shown that performance-avoidance goal orientation negatively influenced both intrinsic motivation and graded performance. Silver et al. (2006) found that performance avoid orientation has a significant negative influence on output performance of salespeople in their selling context of life insurance agents. We are trying to reiterate the same effect in our selling context. Hence the following hypothesis is introduced.

H3a: Performance-avoid orientation is negatively related to output performance of salespeople

In a study by Onatsu-Arvilommi and Nurmi (2000), elementary students with performance-avoidance behavior were found to develop a negative self-fulfilling prophecy in math and reading skills. Students who feared failure avoided skill improvement tasks and, subsequently, performed poorly on later tests. The self-fulfilling prophecy arises due to the attributional aspects of the performance-avoidance construct. Students who do poorly in a subject attribute failure to a lack of ability. Since performance-avoidance individuals do not see a relationship between effort and ability, they do not put forth the necessary effort to improve their skills. Instead, they disparage or avoid the subject. Similarly, in a selling arena, salespeople who have avoidance behaviour will try to avoid skill improvement efforts during the process of selling which may results in poor behavioural performance like poor selling strategies, poor time management etc. Hence we propose the following hypothesis.

H3b: Performance-avoid orientation is negatively related to behavioural performance of salespeople

RESEARCH METHODOLOGY

Our sample consists of automobile retail field salespeople and pharmaceutical salespeople. The questionnaire is administered directly to the salespeople by convenience sampling and snowball sampling procedures. We have also utilized the service of sales managers in showrooms and area sales managers of pharmaceutical firms in administering questionnaire. Of the 375 questionnaires administered, 340 were received back. Out of the 340 received, 314 were found to be useful. Of the 314, 171 were from pharmaceutical salespeople and 143 from automobile retail salespeople.

Measures

Goal orientation: Learning orientation was measured by a 9 item scale drawn from Sujan et al. (1994) study. The scale includes items such as "It is important for me to learn from each selling experience I have"; "It is worth spending a great deal of time learning new approaches for dealing with customers". Performance-prove orientation and performance-avoid orientation were measured using scales drawn from Silver et al. (2006) study having 6 items each. Performance-prove orientation scale includes items such as "It is important to me to do better than other salespeople in my firm" and performance-avoid orientation scale includes items such as "I just want to avoid doing poorly in my job". All items were scored on a 7-point format ranging from "strongly disagree" (1) to "strongly agree" (7).

Performance: An important issue in the measurement of performance is whether the use of supervisory evaluations or company records (e.g., Bagozzi 1980; Behrman, Bigoness, and Perreault 1981; Weitz 1978) is more desirable than the use of salespersons' self-reports (e.g., Behrman and Perreault 1984; Tyagi 1985). Behrman and Perreault (1982) argue that individual salespersons have more complete knowledge of their behavioral performance than supervisors and hence are in a better position to provide more accurate information. Additionally, on the basis of a very comprehensive meta-analysis, Churchill et al. (1985, p. 117) conclude that traditional concerns of an upward bias in findings due to the use of self-reports are without foundation. In support of these arguments, Sujan et al. (1994) and Kohli et al. (1998) used self reported measures for measuring output performance of salespeople. These considerations led to the employment of self-ratings by salespeople. Output performance of the salespeople is measured by a 7 item scale adapted from Sujan, Weitz, and Kumar (1994). The scale includes items such as "Quickly generating sales of company's new products"; "Exceeding sales targets". A 5 item scale adapted from Jaworski and Kohli (1998) was used to measure the behavioural performance. The scale includes items like "Accuracy of paper work"; "Time management". The scale items for both output performance and behavioural performance were scored on a 7-point format ranging from "strongly disagree" (1) to "strongly agree" (7).

Table 1

Learning orientation	0.891
Performance prove orientation	0.842
Performance avoid orientation	0.783
Behavioural performance	0.812
Output performance	0.869

Pretesting of questionnaire

The pretesting of the questionnaire was done in two stages. In the first stage, feedback was obtained from three academic experts in this area. All constructs were clearly identified so that the academic experts could evaluate scale items and the order of questions critically. In the second stage, scale items were pretested with 5 auto salespeople and 5 pharmaceutical salespeople. The salespeople were asked to fill out the questionnaire, point out items that were not applicable, unclear, or ambiguous, and indicate any other difficulties with the questionnaire. On the basis of their comments, we revised the scale items successively until they were clear and easy to respond to.

ANALYSIS AND FINDINGS

We tested our hypotheses using multiple linear regression analysis. The reliability of the scales used for measuring the constructs (cronbach's alpha) is given in table 1. The reliability of each scale exceeds the 0.70 threshold for acceptable reliability, which suggests that the measures are internally consistent.

The test results which show the significant paths and nonsignificant paths are given in Table-2.

Table 2
Significant and Nonsignificant Paths

Hypothesized paths		*Sign*	*Standardised regression coefficients and (t values)/*	*Significant (s) Not significant (ns)*
Learning orientation	Output performance	+	0.34 (2.40)	s*
Learning orientation	Behavioural performance	+	0.49 (4.82)	s***
Performance-prove orientation	Output performance	+	0.52 (5.13)	s***
Performance-prove orientation	Behavioural performance	+	0.46 (4.1)	s**
Performance-avoid orientation	Output performance	-	-0.42 (3.31)	s**
Performance-avoid orientation	Behavioural performance	-	0.03 (1.40)	ns

* $p < 0.1$ ** $p < 0.05$ *** $p < 0.01$

As expected, learning orientation of salespeople significantly elevates their output performance and behavioural performance (Hypotheses H1a and H1b are supported).

Output performance and behavioural performance of salespeople are found significantly influenced by performance-prove orientation (Hypotheses H2a and H2b are supported). Performance-avoid orientation negatively influences output performance of salespeople (H3a supported) whereas the negative effect of performance-avoid orientation on behavioural performance is not significant (H3b not supported).

DISCUSSIONS

By analyzing the influence of learning orientation, performance-prove orientation, and performance-avoid orientation of salespeople on their output performance and behavioural performance, several findings are notable. As predicted, high learning oriented salespeople produced high behavioural performance as well as output performance. It is reasonable to argue that salespeople having more knowledge and selling skills (acquired through practice) will produce better results. Especially the sectors, pharmaceutical and automobile which we considered for our study requires both knowledge and selling skills. It is understandable that highly learning oriented salespeople will definitely have these two characteristics which will enable them to produce high performance. The analysis shows that performance-prove oriented salespeople produce high behavioral performance and high output performance. In the two sectors of our study (pharmaceutical and automobile), rigorous monitoring is done in the selling phase also, apart from output phase. Hence, those salespeople who are performance-prove oriented will try to show their talent in these two phases of evaluation by producing higher performance. As per the results, highly performance-avoid oriented salespeople have shown a lower level output performance. This finding is in tune with the nature of performance-avoid oriented salespeople who will try to exhibit only the minimum requirement in their performance. The negative impact of performance-avoid orientation on behavioural performance is not significant. This may be due to the fact that the supervisors are more keen on the final evaluation rather than on process evaluation.

MANAGERIAL IMPLICATIONS

Supervisors should select salespeople having learning orientation and performance-prove orientation since these two orientations enhances both output performance and behavioural performance of the salespeople. Supervisors should not select salespeople having performance-avoid orientation since it lowers the output performance. Supervisors should try to enhance learning orientation and performance-prove orientation of salespeople during their process and output stages (say, by providing proper feedback or by providing sufficient recognition to the task achievers). Supervisors also should try to reduce performance-avoid orientation of salespeople (say, by rigorous monitoring and giving proper feedback or even adopting punishment measures).

LIMITATIONS AND SCOPE FOR FUTURE WORK

Even though our study throws light into the interrelationships between the three dimensions of goal orientation of salespeople and the two performance dimensions, we acknowledge the limitations of the study and prescribe directions for future research. The study has been confined to two sectors viz. pharmaceutical and automobile. Other sectors such as insurance, encyclopedia, and home appliances can be considered for future study. We have considered two dimensions of performance viz. behavioural performance and output performance. Qualitative performance indicators like appearance, dress sense, and neatness in reports can be considered for further analysis. Whether these indicators have an impact on the behavioural performance and output performance can also be verified.

REFERENCES

Ames, C. and Archer, J. (1988), Achievement Goals in the Classroom: Students' Learning Strategies and Motivation Processes, Journal of educational psychology, Vol. 80, No. 3, pp 260-267.

Attenweiler, W. J. and Moore, D. (2006), Goal Orientations: Two, Three, or More Factors?, Educational and Psychological Measurement, Vol. 66, No. 2, pp 342-352.

Bagozzi, R.P. (1980), Causal Models in Marketing, New York: John Wiley & Sons.

Baldauf, A. and Cravens, D.W. (1999), Improving the Effectiveness of Field Sales Organizations, Industrial Marketing Management, Vol. 28, No. 1, pp 63-72.

Behrman, D.N., Bigoness, W.J., and Perreauit, Jr., W.D. (1981), Sources of Job Related Ambiguity and Their Consequences upon Salespersons' Job Satisfaction and Performance, Management Science, Vol. 27, No. 11, pp 1246-1260.

Behrman, D.N. and Perreault, Jr., W.D. (1982), Measuring the Performance of Industrial Salespersons, Journal of Business Research, Vol. 10, No. 3, pp 355-370.

Behrman, D.N. and Perreault, Jr., W.D. (1984), A Role Stress Model of the Performance and Satisfaction of Industrial Salespeople, Journal of Marketing, Vol. 48, No. 4, pp 9-21.

Brett, J.F. and VandeWalle, D. (1999), Goal Orientation and Goal Content as Predictors of Performance in a Training Program, Journal of Applied Psychology, Vol. 84, No. 6, pp 863-873.

Churchill, G.A., Jr., Ford, N.M., Hartley, S.W., and Walker, Jr., O.C. (1985), The Determinants of Salesperson Performance: A Meta-Analysis, Journal of Marketing Research, Vol. 22, No. 2, pp 103-118.

Cravens, D.W., Ingram, T.N., LaForge, R.W., and Young, C.E. (1993), Behavior Based and Outcome-Based Salesforce Control Systems, Journal of Marketing, Vol. 57, No. 4, pp 47-59.

Dweck, C.S. and Leggett, E.L. (1988), A Social Cognitive Approach to Motivation and Personality, Psychological review, Vol. 95, No. 10, pp 256-273.

Elliot, A.J. (1999), Approach and Avoidance Motivation and Achievement Goals, Educational Psychologist, Vol. 34, No. 3, pp 149–169.

Elliot, A.J. and Church, M.A. (1997), A Hierarchical Model of Approach and Avoidance Achievement Motivation, Journal of Personality and Social Psychology, Vol. 72, No. 1, pp 281–292.

Elliott, E.S. and Dweck, C.S. (1988), Goals: An Approach to Motivation and Achievement, Journal of Personality and Social Psychology, Vol. 54, No. 1, pp 5-12.

Elliot, A.J. and Harackiewicz, J.M. (1996), Approach and avoidance achievement goals and intrinsic motivation: A mediational analysis, Journal of Personality and Social Psychology, Vol. 70, No. 3, pp 461-475.

Grant, K. and Cravens, D.W. (1996), Examining Sales Force Performance in Organizations That Use Behavior-Based Sales Management Processes, Industrial Marketing Management, Vol. 25, No. 5, pp 361-371.

Jackson Jr, D.W., Schlacter, J.L., and Wolfe, W.G. (1995), Examining the Bases Utilized for Evaluating Salespeople's Performance, Journal of Personal Selling and Sales Management, Vol. 15, No. 4, pp 57-65.

Jaworski, B.J. and Kohli, A.K. (1991), Supervisory Feedback: Alternative Types and their Impact on Salespeople's Performance and Satisfaction, Journal of Marketing Research, Vol. 28, No. 2, pp 190-201.

Kohli, A.K. and Jaworski, B.J. (1994), The Influence of Coworker Feedback on Salespeople, Journal of Marketing, Vol. 58, No. 2, pp 82-94.

Kohli, A.K., Shervani, T.A. and Challagalla, G.N. (1998), Learning and Performance Orientation of Salespeople: The Role of Supervisors, Journal of Marketing Research, Vol. 35, No. 2, pp 263-274.

Meece, J.L., Blumenfeld, P.C., and Hoyle, R.H. (1988), Students' Goal Orientations and Cognitive Engagement in Classroom Activities, Journal of educational psychology, Vol. 80, No. 4, pp 514-523.

McFarland, R.G. and Kidwell, B. (2006), An Examination of Instrumental and Expressive Traits on Performance: The Mediating Role of Learning, Prove, And Avoid Goal Orientations, Journal of personal selling and sales management, Vol. 26, No. 2, pp 143-159.

Middleton, M.J. and Midgley, C. (1997), Avoiding the Demonstration of Lack of Ability: An Underexplored Aspect of Goal Theory, Journal of Educational Psychology, Vol. 89, No. 4, pp 710-718.

Nicholls, J.G. and Dweck, C.S. (1979), A Definition of Achievement Motivation, University of Illinois at Champaign-Urbana.

Nicholls, J.G., Patashnick, M., Cheung, P., Thorkildsen, T.A., and Lauer, J.M. (1989), Can Achievement Motivation Theory Succeed with only One Conception of Success?, In F. Halisch & J. Van den Beroken (Eds.), International perspective on achievement motivation, pp 187-208.

Oliver, R.L. and Anderson, E. (1995), Behavior-and Outcome-Based Sales Control Systems: Evidence and Consequences of Pure-Form and Hybrid Governance, Journal of Personal Selling & Sales Management, Vol. 15, No. 4, pp 1-14.

Onatsu-Arvilommi, T. and Nurmi, J. (2000), The Role of Task-Avoidant and Task-Focused Behaviors in the Development of Reading and Mathematical Skills During the First School Year: A Cross-Lagged Longitudinal Study, *Journal of Educational Psychology*, Vol. 92, No. 3, pp 478–491.

Paparoidamis, N.G. (2005), Learning Orientation and Leadership Quality- Their Impact on Salespersons' performance, Emerald Management Decision, Vol. 43, No. 7, pp 1054-1063.

Silver, L.S., Dwyer, S., and Alford, B. (2006), Learning and Performance Goal Orientation of Salespeople Revisited: The Role of Performance-Approach and Performance-Avoidance Orientations, Journal of Personal Selling & Sales Management, Vol. 26, No. 1, pp 27-38.

Skaalvik, E.M. (1997), Self-Enhancing and Self-Defeating Ego Orientation: Relations with Task and Avoidance Orientation, Achievement, Self-Perceptions, and Anxiety, Journal of Educational Psychology, Vol. 89, No.1, pp 71–81.

Sujan, H., Weitz, B.A., and Kumar, N. (1994), Learning Orientation, Working Smart and Effective Selling, Journal of Marketing, Vol. 58, No. 3, pp 39-52.

VandeWalle, D. and Cummings, L.L. (1997), A Test of the Influence of Goal Orientation on the Feedback-Seeking Process, Journal of Applied Psychology, Vol. 82, No. 3, pp 390-400.

VandeWalle, D., Brown, S.P., Cron, W.L., and Slocum, Jr., J.W. (1999), The Influence of Goal Orientation and Self-Regulation Tactics on Sales Performance: A Longitudinal Field Test, Journal of Applied Psychology, Vol. 84, No. 2, pp 249-259.

VandeWalle, D., Cron, W.L., and Slocum, Jr., J.W. (2001), The Role of Goal Orientation Following Performance Feedback, Journal of Applied Psychology, Vol. 86, No. 4, pp 629-640.

Weitz, B.A. (1978), Relationship between Salesperson Performance and Understanding of Customer Decision Making, Journal of Marketing Research, Vol. 15, No. 4, pp 501-516.

12

INNOVATIONS IN WORK MOTIVATION: A STUDY OF EMPLOYEES IN SOFTWARE DEVELOPMENT

Amirul Hasan Ansari & Vimal Babu

INTRODUCTION

Proactive behaviour is defined as 'taking initiative in improving current circumstances; it involves challenging the status quo rather than passively adapting to present conditions' (Crant, 2000). Instead of 'carrying out narrowly defined tasks' (job performance), employees are expected to engage in broad work-roles (Parker, 2000). However, despite its importance in today's work context, the antecedents of proactive behaviour are not well understood (Parker, Williams, & Turner, 2006).

Previous research has examined the motivation to engage in proactive behaviour (Axtell, Holman, Unsworth, Wall, & Waterson, 2000; Morrison & Phelps, 1999; Parker et al., 2006; Sonnentag, 2003; Speier & Frese, 1997), mostly using self-ratings of proactive behaviour. The aim of the present study is to examine multiple motivational predictors of proactive behaviour to replicate and extend previous studies using a different rating source (co-workers). It has been argued that specific motivation is needed for proactive behaviour (Parker, 2000). However, other forms of motivation such as job self-efficacy and intrinsic motivation have a long tradition in predicting job performance. To examine their relevance to proactive behaviour, we include intrinsic motivation and job self-efficacy (traditional forms of motivation) as well as role breadth self-efficacy and role orientation (proactive motivation) in this study.

Job self-efficacy (JSE) is the belief 'in one's capabilities to organize and execute the courses of action required to produce given attainments' (Bandura, 1997, p. 3) at work. Job self-efficacy has been found to be related to proactive behaviour (Morrison & Phelps, 1999; Speier & Frese, 1997). Since proactive behaviour may involve overcoming barriers and difficult actions, and high self-efficacy increases effort and persistence on difficult tasks (Bandura, 1997), we expect that:

Hypothesis 1: Job self-efficacy will be positively related to proactive behaviour

Role breadth self-efficacy (RBSE), which is 'the extent to which people feel confident that they are able to carry out a broader and more proactive role' (Parker, 1998, p. 835), is expected to be related to proactive behaviour because employees high in RBSE expect to be successful when they show proactive behaviour, thereby making this behaviour more likely (Parker et al., 2006). This view was supported in previous studies (Axtell et al., 2000; Parker et al., 2006). Thus, we hypothesize that:

Hypothesis 2: Role breadth self-efficacy will be positively related to proactive behaviour

Another form of motivation which is potentially relevant for predicting proactive behaviour is intrinsic work motivation. It is defined as the 'motivation to engage in work primarily for its own sake because work itself is interesting, engaging or in some way satisfying' (Amabile, Hill, Hennessey, & Tighe, 1994, p. 950). When work is interesting, engaging or satisfying, an employee will be more likely to show proactive behaviour because such behaviour helps to further improve the work situation. In addition, intrinsic work motivation shields against the temptation to detach oneself from work when difficulties arise (cf. Sonnentag, 2003), making proactive behaviour more probable. While the specific relationship between intrinsic motivation and proactivity has not been empirically examined, research indicates that work engagement, a concept similar to intrinsic work motivation, was positively related to daily proactive behaviour (Sonnentag, 2003). Thus, we hypothesize that:

Hypothesis 3: Intrinsic work motivation will be positively related to proactive behaviour

Role orientation targets the degree to which individuals incorporate certain responsibilities into their work-role (cf. Parker, Wall, & Jackson, 1997), for example, feeling responsible for the improvement of one's work. Research indicates that role orientation is related to proactive behaviour (Morrison & Phelps, 1999; Unsworth, Wall, & Carter, 2005). Feeling responsible for improvements at work and having a broad role orientation make it more likely that employees engage in tasks that are not part of their work-role. Thus, we hypothesize that:

Hypothesis 4: Role orientation will be positively related to proactive behaviour

RESEARCH METHODOLOGY

Sampling Procedure

Participants in this study were employees from multiple Indian software development companies in Delhi National Capital Region (NCR). Primary data were collected between summer 2004 and summer 2007. Software development companies were contacted and informed about the study, which was labelled as 'Behaviours at work'. Organizations received feedback about study results. Sources of secondary data were taken from journals, bulletins, annual reports etc.

Surveys were sent to a contact person in the participating organizations and distributed to employees. Each participant was instructed to give a 'co-worker survey' to a co-worker with whom they worked together closely. Out of the 342 questionnaires distributed, 135 were returned (response rate 39.5%), of which 98 had matching coworker data. Out of the 98 respondents, 86 were male (87.8%) and 52 had the equivalent to a master's degree (53.1%). Mean age was 36.2 years (SD ¼ 9:7) and mean job experience in the current job was 12.46 years (SD ¼ 9:3). First comparisons indicate that respondents in the final sample reported lower levels of intrinsic motivation and RBSE than individuals without matching co-worker ratings.

Measures

Cronbach's alpha for all scales are given in Table 1. Intrinsic work motivation was measured with 10 items from the enjoyment subscale of the Work Preference Inventory (WPI; Amabile et al., 1994) on a four-point scale. In addition, we measured intrinsic work motivation with six items from the Job Diagnostic Survey (JDS, Hackman & Oldham, 1975) on a seven-point scale to test if results were consistent across measures of intrinsic work motivation.

Role breadth self-efficacy was measured with 10 items from Parker (1998). Ratings were given on a seven-point scale. Job self-efficacy was measured using 12 items following recommendations by Lee and Bobko (1994). Items referred to the employee's confidence in being able to do core job tasks. To ensure that job self-efficacy was specific for the core job tasks, participants were asked to first list three common work tasks (A, B and C), and then to rate their confidence to be able to fulfil each of these tasks. Tasks listed by participants included, for example, 'programming', 'network administration' or 'support'. Item wording was 'How confident are you to be able to accomplish at least 50% [70%, 90%, 100%] of the tasks in work area A [B, C]?' Ratings were given on a 10-point scale.

Role orientation was measured with three items developed for this study. They target the extent to which employees see developing and implementing new ideas at work as their responsibility (cf. Unsworth et al., 2005). Items were 'It is my job to develop new ideas and to test them.' 'It is my task to be innovative'. and 'My job requires the development and implementation of new ideas.' Ratings were made on a five-point scale ranging from 1 ¼ 'not true at all' to 5 ¼ 'totally true'.

Proactive behaviour was rated by a co-worker using the seven-item personal initiative scale (Frese, Fay, Hilburger, Leng, & Tag, 1997). Items were answered on a seven-point scale. Demographic variables (age, gender and education) were measured with one item each. Education was operationalized as the highest degree reached (1 ¼ none, 2 ¼ apprenticeship completed, 3 ¼ master craftsman, 4 ¼ vocational school or 5 ¼ master's degree).

RESULTS

Means, standard deviations and intercorrelations of the measures can be seen in Table-1. The data indicate that role breadth self-efficacy and role orientation are positively related to co-worker rated proactive behaviour, while job self-efficacy and intrinsic work.

Motivation is unrelated to co-worker rated proactive behaviour. To examine which motivational variable is most relevant for proactive behaviour, we regressed co-worker rated proactive behaviour on all four motivational variables. Since none of the

Table 1

Means Standard Deviations, Intercorrelations and Internal Consistencies of Study Variables

	M	*SD*	*1*	2	3	4	5	6	7	8	9
Age	36.19	9.69	-								
Gender	1.88	.33	.06	-							
Education	3.38	2.33	.05	.10	-						
Job Self-efficacy	7.15	1.18	.13	-.18	.01	.88					
Role Breadth Self-efficacy	4.97	1.00	.18	.09	-.07	.34	.93				
Intrinsic Work Motivation WPI	2.88	.42	.12	-.06	-.22	.14	.11	.74			
Intrinsic Work Motivation JDS	4.81	.59	-.04	-.23	-.19	-.04	.11	.37	.64		
Role orientation	3.75	.82	.22	.33	.05	.04	.29	.13	.17	.87	
Co-worker rated proactive behaviour	5.13	1.04	.08	.06	.07	.07	.27	.06	.10	.24	.89

Note. N=98.

Gender is coded as I= lfemalem2=malemWPI, Work Preference Inventory; JDS, Job Diagnostic Survey.

$r > .22, p < .05; r > .27, p < .01; r > .37, p < .001$

demographic variables were related to proactive behaviour (Table-1), they were not entered into the regression equation (Including age, gender and education into the regression equation did not change the pattern of results.) Results (using the WPI measure of intrinsic work motivation) can be seen in Table-2. Results using the JDS measure of intrinsic work motivation are virtually identical and are thus not shown here.

Table 2
Co-Worker Rated Proactive Behaviour Regressed on Motivational Variables

	Proactive behaviour	
	β	t
Job Self-efficacy	-0.04	-0.35
Role Breadth self-efficacy	0.27	2.35*
Intrinsic Work Motivation WPI	0.08	0.75
Role Orientation	0.14	1.32

Source: Calculated value, Note- N = 98. WPI, Work Preference Inventory ***p<.05.**

Result revealed that only RBSE is significantly related to proactive behaviour when examining all motivational variables simultaneously. Thus, H1, H3 and H4 are not supported, while H2 receives full support. Based on results from previous research (Parker et al., 2006), we tested for interactive effects of role orientation and RBSE. However, the interaction was not significant.

DISCUSSIONS

We examined four types of work motivation that may enhance proactive behaviour: job self-efficacy, role breadth self-efficacy, intrinsic work motivation and role orientation. Results provide evidence for the importance of role breadth self-efficacy, and to a lesser extent of role orientation, but not for the more traditional forms of work motivation. For example, we found no evidence for the hypothesized relationship between job self-efficacy and proactive behaviour. Although this result is in contrast to previous findings (Morrison & Phelps, 1999; Speier & Frese, 1997), the different operationalizations of job self-efficacy may explain the difference in results. Whereas previous studies used measures of general job self-efficacy, we assessed the confidence in doing specific core job tasks. The results for RBSE, the confidence to execute a broader range of tasks, suggest that it is valuable to distinguish between these two forms of self-efficacy. Although JSE and RBSE were moderately correlated (Table-1), only RBSE was related to proactive behaviour.

Based on our study and previous results, it seems that both general job self-efficacy and RBSE are related to proactive behaviour (Morrison & Phelps, 1999; Speier & Frese, 1997). Since RBSE specifically targets behaviour that goes beyond what is formally required in a given job (Parker, 2000), we recommend its use in future research. Intrinsic work motivation (measured with the JDS or WPI) was not related to proactive behaviour. Having work that is interesting, engaging or satisfying is apparently not enough for an employee to engage in proactive behaviour. This result suggests that proactive behaviour, operationalized here as personal initiative, is not the same as intrinsic work motivation, despite claims to the contrary (Gagne & Deci, 2005).

Research indicates that a suboptimal work environment characterized by high time pressure or situational constraints demands proactive behaviours at work (Sonnentag, 2003). Thus, the work environment that elicits intrinsic motivation probably differs from the one that enhances proactive behaviour. This argument is in line with research showing that under some circumstances, negative mood or attitudes, rather than intrinsic motivation, fosters creativity (George & Zhou, 2002). Future research should test this argument, examining job dissatisfaction or negative mood. However, before dismissing intrinsic motivation as predictor of proactive behaviour, the different levels of autonomous motivation as discussed by Gagne and Deci may be examined. Our results also revealed that our measure of role orientation was related to proactive behaviour, but only when RBSE was not taken into account. Different result might be obtained when using other measures of role orientation (Parker et al., 1997). The divergent findings with regard to zero-order correlations and the regression analysis suggest that role orientation is partly overlapping with role breadth self-efficacy.

Indeed, both were moderately correlated (Table-1), indicating that feeling responsible for a broader range of tasks might foster the confidence to do them. Alternatively, one might feel more confident for tasks that one has done before because one sees them as part of one's work-role. Owing to the cross-sectional nature of our study, we do not know which one of these explanations is true. The nature of our study also prohibits any causal inferences regarding the relationship between RBSE and proactive behaviour. However, since we used co-worker ratings of proactive behaviour, some alternative explanation for our results can be ruled out (common-source bias, consistency, and self enhancement).

CONCLUSION

Given that some forms of motivation were not significantly related to co-worker ratings, it seems unlikely that co-worker ratings were inflated by the rater liking a person who is highly motivated. Taken together, the present study suggests that proactive motivation (RBSE and, to a lesser extent, role orientation) is predictive of proactive behaviour. Since previous research has shown that RBSE can be enhanced through training, involvement in extra-role tasks (improvement groups), and by granting job control (Axtell & Parker, 2003; Parker et al., 2006), we suggest that through the same means, proactive behaviour can be promoted.

REFERENCES

Amabile, T.M., Hill, K.G., Hennessey, B.A., & Tighe, E.M. (1994), The Work Preference Inventory: Assessing Intrinsic and Extrinsic Motivational Orientations. Journal of Personality and Social Psychology, 66, 950–967.

Axtell, C.M., Holman, D.J., Unsworth, K.L., Wall, T.D., & Waterson, P.E. (2000), Shopfloor innovation: Facilitating the Suggestion and Implementation of Ideas. Journal of Occupational and Organizational Psychology, 73, 265–285.

Axtell, C.M., & Parker, S.K. (2003), Promoting Role Breadth self-efficacy through Involvement, work Redesign and Training. Human Relations, 56, 112–131.

Bandura, A. (1997), Self-efficacy: The Exercise of Control. New York: Freeman.

Crant, J.M. (2000), Proactive Behavior in Organizations. Journal of Management, 26, 435–462.

Frese, M., Fay, D., Hilburger, T., Leng, K., & Tag, A. (1997), The Concept of Personal Initiative: Operationalization, Reliability and Validity in Two German Samples. Journal of Occupational and Organizational Psychology, 70, 139–161.

Gagne, M., & Deci, E.L. (2005), Self-determination Theory and Work Motivation. Journal of Organizational Behavior, 26, 331–362.

George, J.M., & Zhou, J. (2002), Understanding when Bad Moods Foster Creativity and Good Ones Don't: The Role of Context and Clarity of Feelings. Journal of Applied Psychology, 87, 687–697.

Hackman, J.R., & Oldham, G.R. (1975), Development of the Job diagnostic Survey. Journal of Applied Psychology, 60, 159–170.

Lee, C., & Bobko, P. (1994), Self-efficacy Beliefs: Comparison of Five Measures. Journal of Applied Psychology, 79, 364–369.

Morrison, E. W., & Phelps, C.C. (1999), Taking Charge at Work: Extrarole Efforts to Initiate workplace Change. Academy of Management Journal, 42, 403–419.

Parker, S.K. (1998), Enhancing Role Breadth Self-efficacy: The Roles of Job Enrichment and Other Organizational Interventions. Journal of Applied Psychology, 83, 835–852.

Parker, S.K. (2000), From Passive to Proactive Motivation: The Importance of Flexible Role orientation and Role Breadth Self-efficacy. Applied Psychology: An International Review, 49, 447–469.

Parker, S.K., Wall, T.D., & Jackson, P.R. (1997), That's Not my Job: Developing Flexible Employee Work Orientations. Academy of Management Journal, 40, 899–929.

Parker, S.K., Williams, E.S., & Turner, N. (2006), Modeling the Antecedents of Proactive behavior at Work. Journal of Applied Psychology, 91, 636–652.

Sonnentag, S. (2003), Recovery, Work Engagement, and Proactive Behavior: A New Look at the Interface between Nonwork and Work. Journal of Applied Psychology, 88, 518–528.

Speier, C., & Frese, M. (1997), Generalized Self-efficacy as a Mediator and Moderator between Control and Complexity at Work and Personal Initiative: A Longitudinal Field Study in East Germany. Human Performance, 10, 171–192.

Unsworth, K.L., Wall, T.D., & Carter, A. (2005), Creative Requirement: A Neglected Construct in the Study of Employee Creativity? Group and Organization Manangement, 30, 541–560.

13

CHANGING HR ROLES IN ACHIEVING GLOBAL TALENT MANAGEMENT IN CURRENT BUSINESS SCENARIO

Vinita Sinha

INTRODUCTION

Recruiting and retaining talents have always been a struggle for global companies, and today the challenges are larger than ever. As more companies develop global aspirations, the demand for talent increases at the same time. With demand rising and supply dwindling, companies are finding that the talent issue, especially in rapidly developing economies is one of their most critical challenges. It is a key obstacle to developing and executing their best strategies and attaining their most important objectives. Achieving a global talent advantage requires companies to change their mindset and processes. Talent management must be managed rigorously and globally-across languages, cultures, and time zones. Given how long it takes to build an organization, companies should be making plans that look out at least three to five years. At the same time the systems and processes involved in managing talent must be sufficiently flexible to permit customization to local conditions and markets. On the basis of recent experience with global companies and of a research project in which according to a recent study (Friedman et.al, 2008) 100 executives were surveyed or interviewed and five key actions have been identified for overall organizational excellence:

1. *Create a new global model:* Global companies need to reorient their organizations, operations and processes to reflect the new order of talent management.
2. *Elevate global talent planning to an item on the CEO's agenda:* Talent management is too important to be just another item on the HR agenda.

3. *Expand the hiring horizon:* Many global companies rely largely on poaching talent from their competitors when they enter new markets.
4. *Accelerate careers and create global leaders:* To capture rapid growth economies global companies need to build high-performing management and leadership teams in a fraction of the time it takes to put them together in developed economies.
5. *Ensure that all leaders embrace the new global mindset:* If companies are to grow quickly in local markets, they need strong local leaders with an entrepreneurial bent and the beliefs in the global values of the organization.

For too long, companies have treated talent and strategy as separate spheres. Top executives have taken care of strategy delegated talent to HR or to junior staffs. That approach no longer works. Talent and strategy need to fit together like a hand in glove, requiring senior executives to work closely with their HR Staffs and local business-unit executives. HR challenges are getting respect. The term "Talent Management" is now part of the corporate lexicon and has become a board level concern. Yet the HR profession, which evolved from "personnel" in the 80's and 90's, seems unable to make a definitive move up the corporate ladder – in prestige or influence. In some ways, it's almost as if corporate leaders have made a collective, unconscious decision that talent management is too important to be left to HR. Progressive and credible HR executives agree – at least in part. Across the board, leaders say that talent management is the most difficult, least

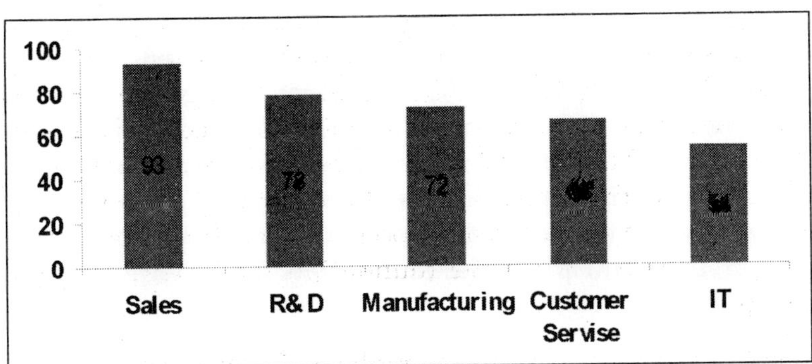

Percentage of companies that plan to increase sales and operations in RDE in the next five years

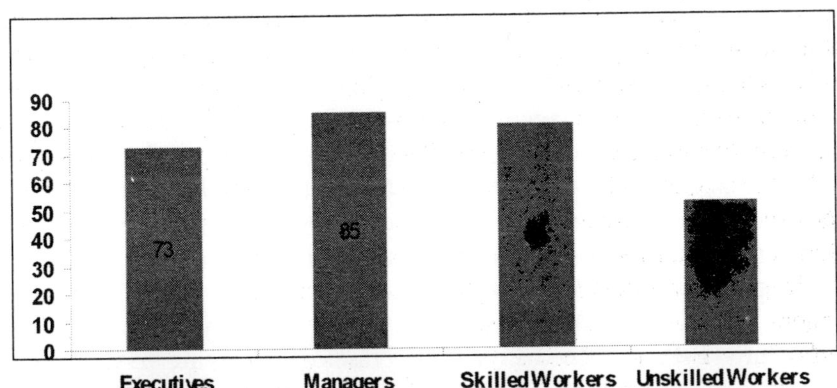

(Source: BCG 2007Aligning Talent for Global Advantage Survey of Global Companies).

Percentage of companies that plan to increase resource deployment in RDE in the next five years

understood and most important thing for organizations to master. Accordingly, the most successful organizations make talent management a priority for every leader, manager and supervisor while leveraging the expertise of a reinvented (and often bifurcated) HR group. This, and the points below, represents the central findings from a study (Schweyer, 2008). Other key findings include the following:

- HR is making progress. 66% of respondents state that HR is either respected or highly respected and occasionally or frequently consulted on corporate strategy.
- Across multiple measures of business proficiency and knowledge, there is an alarming lack of expertise among senior HR leadership.
- Despite the impact and importance of globalization, HR is on the sidelines. It is regularly involved and consulted on global strategy less than one-third of the time, even where it directly affects the workforce.
- Respondents top current challenges are attracting and engaging talent, succession planning, and leadership identification & development. Over the next three years, respondents expect specific skills shortages, finding leaders and successors, and retaining & engaging top talent to be their main challenges.

CHANGING ROLE OF HR TECHNOLOGY

Talent Management Software

This option gives organizations an opportunity to try before they buy. Yet, despite its value, many companies don't take advantage of the offer or, when they do, they don't involve those who will be directly impacted by the talent management technology. May be it seems like too much work upfront. Today, organizations need to look at the upfront work done to review a new HR technology system at their company as a smart investment. For many companies today, the investment in HR technology review by a variety of employees doesn't seem worthwhile. Yet, the process can improve employee engagement in the software over time and place the foundation for a widely adopted talent management strategy.

Talent Management Technology Can Boost Employee Engagement

One aspect of a talent management strategy is employee engagement–which includes both the managers who manage your talent and the employees being managed. Including employees at all levels in the process of trying out new HR technology can improve the likelihood that this technology is used and integrated into the team's routine. For example, improving your performance management strategy through software is an effort where employee engagement can make a difference. Performance management ensures that your employee goals stay aligned with your overall business strategy? Engaging the managers and employees during a software trial could be as simple as assigning goals that are directly related to the trial itself. It should be easy enough to create an organizational goal such as, "Implement a performance management solution." Then, assign that goal to your managers who then cascade those goals to their employees on the project team. Employees who have been involved in a HR technology software trial are going to be much more likely to take ownership for its success. Identify enthusiastic team leads and involve them in deployment and training-make them champions for new talent management solution. Consider the concept of Employee Ambassadors who are going to help to build a strong sense of community and positively impact user adoption.

Give Straightforward Education and Training

During trial periods, it's no surprise that the question most often asked by companies is, "How will we train all of our employees on this new HR technology? Out of the gate, we need to figure out how much training employees will need to get started. This will depend heavily on how we have configured the solution. We should have specific objectives for the trial period and avoid being distracted by all the bells and whistles a solution has to offer. May be that means removing sections or fields from an employee talent profile, or limiting the trial to requesting the employees to update their goals as a starting point. A system that makes this self configuration easy is good for any organization.

Involve Employee Ambassadors

Next, engage with Employee Ambassadors to help provide training and education sessions to other end users. Don't be afraid to embrace social media, wikis and blogs to facilitate these peer-to-peer interactions, further deepening your sense of community. It's also important to understand what HR technology vendors have to offer. A vendor focused on user adoption will not only provide training tools and documentation that can be distributed to your employees during deployment, but also make resources readily accessible on an ongoing basis. According to a study done by the Sand Hill Group and Neochange, the most critical factor (70 percent listed it as number 1) for software success and return-on-investment is effective user adoption.

Create More Community

The word "community" makes us think of two things - communication and unity. Any HR software we invest in must address the needs of everyone in our workplace to create a greater sense of community. When employees feel valued and are involved in business decisions there is a strong sense of unity within the organization. This unity then leads to strong internal communication. Evaluating talent management technology software as a work community provides organizations additional insight into how all the pieces - recruiting, on boarding, performance management, goals and compensation - work together. It makes sense to find vendors that have this "unity" inherent in their design, commonly referred to as a "Unified Platform."

Motivating Top Talent

February 10 2009 - Two recent reports offer guidance on motivating and developing talented employees in the current global economic downturn.

Motivating and Retaining Top Talent

A report from On Point Consulting identifies strategies for motivating and retaining top talent in the current economic climate when the emphasis on bonus payments is no longer possible or appropriate. Previous research has found that earnings and benefits have a 2 per cent impact on job satisfaction and engagement compared to 70 per cent provided by job quality and workplace support.

The report suggests the following survival strategies:

- *Create a sense of purpose-* Engagement and retention improves when people understand how they connect to the "Big Picture" and how they make a difference.
- *Provide meaningful work-* Allowing people to do what they do best and make a significant contribution is key to engagement and retention.
- *Solicit ideas-* Involvement in decisions gives people a sense of control in uncertain times, shows them their opinions matter, and improves decision acceptance.
- *Let people know where they stand-* Setting tough but realistic goals is motivating even in a tough environment.
- *Enhance trust and communication-* Trust is built when leaders improve credibility by being candid, demonstrate reliability by ensuring their actions are consistent with business objectives and values, and are accessible.

Rick Lepsinger, president of On Point Consulting commented: "Feeling connected to the people you work with also helps create a sense of purpose.... Providing opportunities to learn and grow is icing on the cake.... Clear goals are only part of the equation. People need regular feedback so they know when they are on track and recognition when they achieve key milestones....The more people feels you are focused on them, rather than on yourself, the more they trust you."

Employee Goals and Talent Development

A report from Sum Total Systems Inc., a global provider of talent development solutions, argues that implementing effective, universally-accepted goal setting for employees, coupled with a system for managing and tracking these processes can enable HR managers to make a significant contribution to improved organizational performance.

Richard Oyen, director of HR and talent development said: "With the current economic forecast, it is now more important than ever to make sure employees' goals reflect the organization's overall goals to ensure everyone is working toward the same mission. By helping to set organizational alignment, HR departments have the ability to impact their company like never before and create significant productivity improvements."

The report offers the following guidelines for the involvement of HR in employee goal setting:

1. *Know the goals* - HR should be involved when senior managers plan annual goals to be aware of underlying issues and challenges.
2. *Get buy-in* - The executive team should support HR's efforts to align goals and help communicate the importance of the program.
3. *Cascade goals* - Once goals are set at the top of the organization, they should work their way down to all employees.
4. *Ensure consistency* - As goals are established further down the organization, HR can assist by creating standards and monitoring consistency.
5. *Hold everyone accountable* - Managers should ensure goals are measurable with specific deadlines and then hold employees accountable.
6. *Reinforce through development* - Ensure that employees have skills and tools to achieve established goals using development plans monitored by HR.

7. *Work the gaps* - Managers can work with employees individually. HR should identify gaps in organizational provision and address issues proactively with the Learning team.
8. *Encourage year-long communication* - Initial goals may be agreed but paid no further attention. Sending reminders to update goals is one way for HR to encourage a culture of frequent manager/employee communication.
9. *Monitor compliance* - Managers should monitor progress and completion of employee goals HR should review overall process and report to executives and department heads.
10. *Measure twice, cut once* - Goals should be a major component of a company's annual performance appraisal where employees are measured and held accountable.

HRM TRENDS 2009

Human resource management (HRM) will be a key area of focus in 2009 as companies and government organizations put in place strategies to cope with the economic crisis and recovery. The so called "war for talent" is on the backburner as the focus shifts to hiring freezes, benefits and compensation cost management, and workforce reductions in the hardest-hit segments. HRM technology solutions can help savvy human resources (HR) professionals strategically manage through the crisis and prepare as the climate shifts to the upside. Trends that we will follow in 2009 include managing and developing talent, embracing HRM analytics, Web 2.0 adoption, and HR technology strategy.

Human Resources Costs come under scrutiny as the economy falters

As companies look to constrain spending to cope with the reeling global economy, it's no surprise that personnel-related costs are in the crosshairs of any cost-cutting program, since these costs represent more than 35% of annual operating expenses.1 Yet actions such as hiring freezes, delayed salary increases, reduced benefits, and dreaded layoffs have significant hidden costs. These measures dampen employee morale, slow new product rollouts, hasten departures of higher-performing talent, and potentially reduce customer service levels. The following key drivers will affect trends in HRM processes and technology for 2009:

Recruitment activity will decrease while layoffs increase

During 2008, the economic downturn evolved from sector-based (e.g., financial services, automobiles) to broad-based. The economic conditions have brought on increasing layoffs and limited hiring, conditions that may persist through the first half of 2009. Certain geographies (e.g., China, India, Middle East), industries (e.g., healthcare), companies, and job categories may continue to grow as the overall global economy slows to a crawl.

Employee performance and development will drive business performance

Employee Performance objectives will become more aligned with business goals. Firms will attempt to get a grasp on and drive employee skills and competencies through performance management and development to support strategic decisions. For example, this information is needed to fast-track high performers and weed out low performers. Performance information will also drive variable compensation programs, providing some cushion for bottom-line results when targets are missed.

The workforce is becoming younger and more global

Despite the presidential campaign rhetoric to the contrary, off shoring and labor arbitrage will continue as companies invest in globalization.

2009 Trends to Watch in Human Resource Management:

The following technology and business process-driven trends will be evident in HRM in 2009:

Web 2.0 will become institutionalized

Social technologies are critical to reaching and connecting with the younger workforce, infusing and retaining knowledge, and turbo-charging programs such as alumni relations and mentoring. Fifty-five percent of HR decision-makers agree that this innovation is very important, but 51% believe that their current tools and process capabilities are below average.2 this means that HR pros will start to augment their transactional process-based apps by institutionalizing today's rogue social technologies

Core HR systems strategies will focus on master data

The notion of a single source of truth for who works for the company today is still an elusive goal. Based on pioneering work done with customer data hubs, we will start to see strategies evolve for master data management related to the employee life cycle. This will enable the employee data to be kept in sync across multiple HR, payroll, benefits, and talent management systems, as well as third-party business partners and operational applications that use employee data.

The definition of the workforce will continue to evolve

Whereas the workforce has traditionally meant employees who are actually on the payroll, business needs encompass tracking and provisioning a variety of "nonemployees" as well. "Nonemployees include contractors, consultants, temporary workers, volunteers, and others who represent part of the productive workforce. Nonemployees will be managed within the human resource management system (HRMS) to allow for headcount and productivity analysis, project staffing, security provisioning, training programs, and other HR-related processes.

Talent management initiatives and solutions will become more integrated

For years, best of-breed application vendors and enterprise resource planning vendors who offer strategic HR capabilities have been touting and educating buyers about the importance of integrated HR technologies. The real benefit of integration is the ability to leverage employee data across historically soloed processes such as recruiting, performance management, succession planning, compensation management, and learning management. Having fewer HR systems and vendors to manage lowers IT support and integration costs and provides a more consistent user experience for business stakeholders.

Analytics will help HR become more strategic

Traditional metrics that answer "what was" or "what is" will remain to prove operational return on investment, but they'll pale in priority compared to forward-looking analytics. Why? They will arm HR with the ability to predict the future results of process and technology changes made today.

HR outsourcing initiatives will become more focused and selective:

The notion of outsourcing a broad set of HR processes and systems has less and less support. Many of these attempted initiatives have failed to deliver the expected cost savings and service-level goals, and vendors aren't making any money. Outsourcing selective HR processes of a compliance intensive or repetitive nature, like payroll, will remain viable. Cost savings is becoming less of a driver of HR outsourcing, with expertise and reliability being higher priorities.

HRM will continue to lead in software-as-a-service (SaaS) adoption

We continue to find the SaaS model to be more accepted in HRM than other application areas (with the possible exception of customer relationship management). Expect to see continued growth of this deployment model in 2009. Advancements in software technology related to configurability and integration help to make the SaaS model more palatable to bigger companies, especially those that are weary of upgrading on-premise HRM solutions.

HR will be more business-focused and less dependent on internal IT

The traditional HR shop has been heavily focused on managing records in monolithic systems, processing routine transactions, and dealing with compliance and legal issues. This type of HR function has been viewed by top management as a candidate for outsourcing, along with other back-office tasks. The more enlightened HR organization is focused on talent as a strategic resource to make the overall business successful. HR professionals are acquiring more business acumen as HR processes and talent initiatives are becoming more integrated with the day-to-day operations of the lines of business. On the technology front, HR is becoming less technophobic, more self-sufficient, and less dependent on corporate IT. HRM applications are being designed to be owned and managed by the business stakeholders while also being deployed via a vendor managed, SaaS model. These parallel developments signal the ascendancy of the HR function as a more prominent player in strategic business growth.

REFERENCES

The Role of HR in the Age of Talent: A Report from the Human Capital Institute & Vurv Technology. Human Capital Institute. www.vurv.com

Friedman, Danie; Jim, Hemriling; Chapman, Jacquelin (2008), The Boston Consulting Groups. www.bcg.com.

Paul D. Hamerman; Thomas, Zach (2008), Trends 2009: Human Resource Management.

Talent Strategies Adjust to the Business Climate. Forrester Research, Inc.

14

SUPPORT SYSTEM TO WOMEN ENTREPRENEURSHIP IN INDIA-AN OVERVIEW

K.S. Sarala

INTRODUCTION

Half of the world population consists of women but for centuries women are treated as home makers and to take care of children. In comparison to men, women's unemployment level is higher both in educated and less educated categories. But there is a change gradually taking place is the change in socio-cultural values where women go outside and abroad on official tours. Many Indian women entrepreneurs have made name all round the world. Women entrepreneurship has gained momentum in India particularly in the nineties. But, Indian women entrepreneurship cannot be compared to the developed countries.. There has been a phenomenal increase in the women entrepreneurs after the world war II. The percentage of women entrepreneurship is 45% in USA, 43% in UK, 40% in Indonesia, 35% each in Brazil and Sri Lanka and in India it comes to 32%.

The safest and the only way to lift India out of poverty is through education and increasing the status of country's women. Late Prime Minister Jawaharlal Nehru and Mahatma Gandhi supported this view. According to Smt Indira Gandhi, women have trailed behind men in almost all sectors and their status could be raised by providing with opportunities for their independent means of employment (Entrepreneurship) In India, rights of women of public employment recognised under articles 16(1) and 16(2) of the constitution, grant the right of equal opportunities in regard to employment to men and women without any distinction. According to Nehru "when women move forward, the family moves, the village moves and nation moves".

CONCEPT OF WOMEN ENTREPRENEUR

The woman or a group of women who initiate, organize and operate a business enterprise is known as women entrepreneur. A woman entrepreneur has to perform all the activities involved in establishing an enterprise. These include idea generating and screening, determination of objectives, project preparations, product analysis etc.

DEFINITIONS

Following are some of the definitions of woman entrepreneurship given by different authorities:

- Any woman or group of women which innovates, imitates or adapts an economic activity may be called woman entrepreneurship

–Frederick Harbison

- Woman who innovates, imitates or adopts a business activity is called woman entrepreneur"

–J. Schumpeter

- A woman entrepreneur is defined as an enterprise owned and controlled by a woman and having a minimum financial interest of 51 per cent of the capital and giving at least 51 percent of the employment generated in the enterprise to women"

-Government of India

CHARACTERISTICS OF WOMAN ENTREPRENEURS

Woman management and control, Employment for women, Good organizer, Self confidence, Risk taking, Decision maker, Visionary, Hard worker, Achievement oriented, Optimistic, Technically competent, Bold and brave mentally, Sound Leadership.

PROBLEMS OF WOMEN ENTREPRENEURS

The women entrepreneurs face a variety of problems in their efforts to develop their enterprise. The major problems cover the shortage of finance, Marketing problems, shortage of raw materials. Stiff competition, limited managerial ability, high cost of production, lack of entrepreneurial attitude, family responsibilities, low risk taking ability, social attitudes, lack of formal education etc. Of all the problems, the problems of financing their venture, marketing their products and the necessary training as well as lack of awareness of various initiatives of government and non governmental organizations are considered to be major hurdles.

SUPPORT TO WOMEN ENTREPRENEURSHIP

Kofi Annan, Secretary General of the United Nations, rightly put it: "When the poorest, especially woman receive credit, the become economic actors with power. Power to improve not only their own lives, but in a widening circle, to impact the lives of their families, their communities, and their nations".

In the words of Ex president of India, **APJ Abdul Kalam**, " empowering women is a pre requisite for creating a good nation, when women are empowered, society with stability is assured. Empowerment of women is essential as their thoughts and their value systems lead to the development of a good family, good society and ultimately a good nation".

It is only from fifth five year plan (1974-78) and onwards that the role of women entrepreneurs has been explicitly recognised with a marked shift from welfare to development and empowerment of women. The Industrial Policy of Government of India of 1991 stressed the need for conducting special entrepreneurship programmes for women. It also suggested for conducting product and process oriented courses for women to enable them to start small scale business industrial enterprises. The seventh five year plan (1985-90) provided a special chapter on Integration of women in development. In this chapter several suggestions were made for the development of a woman like to treat woman as specific target group in all developmental programmes, to properly diversify vocational training facilities for women to suit their varied needs and skills, to provide marketing assistance etc.

During the eighth five year plan (1992-97) some special programmes were introduced to increase employment and income generating activities for women. Some of them were a programme for formation of women co-operatives was launched for helping women engaged in agro based industries. Khadi and Village Industries Commission (KVIC) took measures to provide more and more employment opportunities for women. Several developmental programmes were launched like Entrepreneurship Development Programmes, Development of Women and Children in Rural Areas, Prime Minister's Rozgar Yojana.To facilitate export by women entrepreneurs, the National Small Industries Corporation Ltd. (NSIC) will assist them to participate in 25 exhibitions over the period co-terminus with the XI plan period (2007-12)

The Khadi and Village Industries Commission (KVIC)

Khadi and Village Industries Commission is a statutory body created by an Act of Parliament. Established in April 1957, it took over the work of the former All India Khadi and Village Industries Board. The broad objectives that that the KVIC has set before it are : the social objective of providing employment, the economic objective of producing saleable articles, and the wider object of creating self reliance amongst the poor and the building up of a strong rural community spirit. The KVIC is charged with the planning, promotion, organisation and implementation of programmes for the development of Khadi and other Village industries in rural areas in co-ordination with other agencies engaged in rural development wherever necessary.

National Small Industries Corporation (NSIC)

The National Small Industries Corporation Limited an ISO 9001:2000 company, was established in 1955 by the Government of India with a view to promote, aid and foster the growth of small industries in the country. NSIC continues to remain at the forefront of industrial development throughout the country with its various programmes and projects, to assist the small scale sector in the country. The corporation provides integrated technology, marketing and financial support to small scale sector.

Small Industries Development Board of India (SIDBI) Schemes

Mahila Udyam Nidhi (MUN): The purpose of this scheme is to meet gap in equity in setting up new industrial projects in SSI sector. Women entrepreneurs for setting up new projects in tiny/small scale sector and rehabilitation of viable sick SSI units are the Eligible

Borrowers for this scheme. Existing tiny and small scale industrial units & service enterprises undertaking expansion, modernization technology upgradation and diversification can also be considered.

The Scheme is operated through SFCs / twin function SIDCs / Scheduled Commercial Banks/Select Urban Co-operative Banks. Assistance is provided in the form of seed capital as a soft loan to meet the gap is equity after taking into account the promoter"s contribution to the project. Project eligible for assistance under this scheme would also be eligible for term loan assistance with interest rates and repayment period in congruence with the women entrepreneurial scheme. No security or collateral needs to be provided by the borrowers for soft seed capital.

Mahila Vikas Nidhi (MUV): A trained and skilled woman can earn her livelihood and effectively contribute to the national income. SIDBI operationalises this concept under its Mahila Vikas Nidhi (MVN) programme by assisting accredited NGOs to create training and marketing infrastructure especially for rural women it was introduced during 1990. The main Objectives of MUV is to bring about economic empowerment of women, especially rural poor, by providing them avenues for training and employment opportunities by facilitating creation of infrastructural and training facilities for the purpose .

MVN is SIDBI's specially designed fund for economic development of women, especially the rural poor, by providing them avenues for training and employment opportunities. In addition, activities like vocational training, strengthening of marketing set up for the products of the beneficiary group, arrangements for supply of improved inputs, production and technology improvement are also covered under the MVN scheme.

State Fund for Micro Credit (SFMC): The launch of SFMC by SIDBI has been with a clear focus and strategy to make it as the main purveyor of micro finance in the country. Operations of SFMC in the coming years are not only expected to contribute significantly towards development of a more formal, extensive and effective micro finance sector serving the poor in India, but also ensure sustainability at all levels viz., at the apex level, (SFMC) at the MFI level and at the client level to ensure continuance of such arrangement. SFMC has strived to create a mechanism in which there should be no barriers to growth. Under the dispensation, there is focus on innovation and action research.

Entrepreneurship Development Programmes (EDP): Entrepreneurship can be developed by training. Towards this end and also to make the Entrepreneurship Development Programmes (EDPs) result-oriented, SIDBI has been supporting suitable agencies to train and guide potential entrepreneurs to set up enterprises. EDPs aim at training various target groups in entrepreneurial traits so that they obtain adequate information, motivation and guidance in setting up their own enterprises. In order to maintain a homogeneous nature of participating groups, EDPs focus on rural entrepreneurs, women, SC/ST, etc.

Consortia: Organisations/Associations/Women Groups/Marketing Consortia that have an exclusive marketing mandate and have, as their vendor base, a wide range of small and tiny units owned and managed by women entrepreneurs. While the terms and conditions for sanction of assistance would be flexible, they would essentially depend upon the soundness of the management, track record of performance and viability of future operations.

Development Assistance: Besides providing financial assistance, SIDBI could also consider, on a selective basis, developmental assistance by way of soft loans/grants for organising group activities and programmes such as trade fairs, exhibitions, buyer-seller meets, seminars, workshops, training programmes etc. to promote marketing of products manufactured by women entrepreneurs.

Marketing Fund for Women (MFW): The assistance under the Fund is available to women entrepreneurs and organizations involved in marketing of products manufactured by women entrepreneurs to increase their reach, both in domestic and international markets. Finance from the Fund is given to marketing related service providers either organizations or units in the corporate/co-operative/NGO sectors which are providing support services like internet, trade related information, advertising, marketing research, warehousing, common testing centres, etc. to enterprises owned and managed by women.

National Bank for Agriculture and Rural Development (NABARD) Programmes

Women Development Assistance for Marketing of Non Farm Product of Rural Women (MAHIMA): The main Objective of this programme is the promotion of marketing of products produced by women entrepreneurs. NGOs Women Development Corporations. KVIC/KVIB. Cooperative Societies, Trusts etc. can get the assistance under this programme. NABARD provides 100% refinance to banks on the credit component. The quantum of promotional assistance to development agencies, is to the tune of 25% of the project outlay of Rs.10 lakh or 25% minimum sales turnover, whichever is lower.

Assistance to Rural Women in Non-Farm Development (ARWIND): This is a single window scheme containing' _credit as well as promotional com ponents of assistance for conducting skill or EDP type of training for women, establishment of production units at the sponsoring agencies level or to set up household units with loan assistance from banks. NGOs, Women Development Corporations, KVIS, KVIB, Cooperative Societies, Trusts etc. are eligible for this scheme. The amount of assistance is upto Rs. 10000/ per women. NABARD extends 100% refinance assistance to banks in respect of credit extended to women entrepreneurs under the scheme agency's stake is 15% of the project outlay.

Vikas Voluntary Vahini (VVV): NABARD has raised a cadre or volunteers under its programme of Vikas Volunteer Vahini (VVV) to spread the message of "Development through Credit" to tanners and non-farm rural entrepreneurs. NABARD has encouraged banks to launch Farmers Clubs VVV in 1983 to overcome the problem of over dues of loans advanced in the agricultural sector. Farmers' club is an informal forum of a group of 15 to 20 progressive farmers and artisans chosen from among good borrowers in a village. The club serves as a nerve centre promoting all development activities, creating borrower awareness and for ushering the process of speedy rural development by enabling the banks in extending adequate and timely credit, ensuring proper utilisation of credit leading to higher productivity and paving the way.

Mahila Samridhi Yojana (MSY)

For empowerment of minorities, maximum emphasis is required to be given on empowerment of women because they are the weakest link among the minorities scheme of Mahila Samridhi Yojana which links micro-credit to the women after training. During the training, the group is formed into a Self Help Group. The scheme has been made broad-based to cover all the trades and activities practiced by women.

After the training, the group is provided credit, jointly or individually, for pursuing the activity of training.

Swarna Jayanthi Shahari Rozgar Yojana (SJSRY)

The programme will devote special attention to women, persons belonging to Scheduled Castes (SC)/ Scheduled Tribes (ST), disabled persons and other such categories as may be indicated by the Government from time to time. The percentage of women beneficiaries under this programme shall not be less than 30%. Central Allocation under SJSRY has been enhanced to Rs 515 Crores in 2009-10.

(SJSRY) in implementation from 01.12.1997, has been comprehensively revamped by the Union Housing and Urban Poverty Alleviation ministry. The new scheme has commenced from 2009-2010. SJSRY will have five major components. namely- Urban Self Employment Program (USEP) ,Urban Women Self-help Program (UWSP) , Skill Training for Employment Promotion amongst Urban Poor (STEP-UP) ,Urban Wage Employment Program (UWEP) and Urban Community Development Network (UCDN)

The following major changes have been effected in the scheme:

- For the beneficiary under the Urban Self Employment Program (USEP now no minimum or maximum educational qualification level has been prescribed for the purpose of eligibility of assistance.
- For the self-employment (individual category), the project cost ceiling has been enhanced to Rs. 2.00 Lakhs from the existing Rs. 50000/- and the subsidy has also been enhanced to 25% of the project cost (subject to a maximum of Rs. 50000/-).
- For the group enterprises set up by urban poor women, the subsidy has been made as 35% of the project cost or Rs. 300,000 or Rs. 60000/- per member of the group, whichever is less.
- The Skill Training of the urban poor component has been restructured and quality skill training will be provided to the urban poor linking it with certification, imparted preferably on Public-Private Partnership (PPP) mode with the involvement of reputed institutions like IITs, NITs, Poly-techniques. ITIs, other reputed agencies etc,

Trade Related Entrepreneurship Assistance and Development Scheme for Women (TREAD)

In order to alleviate problems of poor and rural women, Government of India launched a scheme entitled "Trade Related Entrepreneurship Assistance and Development" (TREAD) during the 9th plan period. The scheme envisaged economic empowerment of such women through trade related training information and counseling extension activities related to trades, products. Services etc. This Assistance was to be provided for self employment ventures by women for pursuing any kind of non-farm activity. The Scheme is fully women specific.

SALIENT FEATURES OF THE REVISED TREAD SCHEME

Government Grant up to 30% of the total project cost as appraised by lending institutions which would finance the remaining 70% as loan assistance to applicant women, who have no easy access to credit from banks due to cumbersome procedures and the inability -of poor and usual illiterate/semi-literate women to provide adequate security demanded by banks in the form of collaterals. Government Of India Grant and the loan portion from the lending agencies to assist such women shall be routed through NGOs engaged in assisting poor women through income generating activities. Only those NGOs, who are having considerable experience (minimum 3 years) in taking and managing funds, taken either as loan or grant, shall be eligible under the Scheme.

Integrated Rural Development Programme (IRDP)

The Integrated Rural Development Programme was launched on 20th October 1980, as a major credit linked self-employment programme for povcerty alleviation. The objective of the programme is to identify rural poor families, to augment their income and to enable them to cross the poverty line through acquisition of employment on a sustainable basis. Assistance is given in the form of subsidy by the government and credit advances by financial institutions for income generating activities in the rural areas. To ensure better participation of women in the development process, it has been specified that atleast 40% of those assisted should be women.

Development of Women and Children in Rural Areas (DWCRA)

The scheme - DWCRA was aimed to improve the socio-economic status of the poor women in the rural areas through creation of groups of women for income- generating activities on a self-sustaining basis. The main strategy adopted under the programme was to facilitate access for poor women to employment, skill upgradation, training credit and other support services so that the DWCRA women as a group could take up income-generating activities for supplementing their incomes. It encouraged the habit of thrift and credit among poor rural women to make them self-reliant.

The Scheme had been merged into Swarnajayanti Gram Swarojgar Yojana (SGSY) with IRDP, TRYSEM etc. from April, 1999. In the early 1980s, the Government of India launched the Development of Women and Children in Rural Areas (DWCRA) program under the Integrated Rural Development Program.

Rural Employment Generation Programme (REGP)

Rural Employment Generation Programme (REGP) is a flagship scheme of the government for employment generation programmes in the unorganized sector. Though there are no specific reservation for women entrepreneurs under this scheme, still there has been substantial participation (around 30 per cent) of women as a result of the promotional efforts undertaken in this regard. Under this programme, 3,656 projects of women entrepreneurs involving margin money of Rs. 6397.99 lakh have been assisted as government grant during 2007-08 up to December 2007.

Rashtriya Mahila Kosh (RMK)

The vast gap between demand for and supply of credit to women particularly in the rural and unorganized sector established the need for a National Credit Fund for Women. The National Credit Fund for Women or the Rashtriya Mahila Kosh (RMK) was set up in March 1993 as an independent registered society by the Department of Women & Child Development in Government of India's Ministry of Human Resource Development. The Kosh has three main roles: Wholesaling Role, Market Development Role and Advocacy Role. The main features of the micro-finance services being provided by RMK are :

— It is a tool for empowerment of the poorest

— Delivery is normally through Self Help Groups (SHGs).
— It is essentially for promoting self-employment
— It is not just a financing system, but a tool for social change, specially for women.
— Because micro credit is aimed at the poorest, micro-finance lending technology needs to mimic the informal lenders rather than the formal sector lending.

Prime Minister's Rozgar Yojana (PMRY)

The Government of India is implementing a subsidy-linked self-employment scheme for providing employment to educated unemployed in the rural and urban areas in the age group of 18 to 35 years through setting up micro enterprises under the scheme. This scheme was launched on 2nd October 1993.There is no separate target for women but preference is to be given to women beneficiaries regarding the age relaxation upto 45 years and other weaker sections. It is observed that about 80000 women borrowers have been sanctioned loans b banks to avail of self- employment during the last three years under the scheme. The minimum educational Qualification fixed is to pass Std. VIII. During 2006-07, the participation of women in terms of employment generation under PMRY was 16.5 per cent. Under the scheme, preference is given to women beneficiaries and several relaxations to women to facilitate the participation of women.

Mahila Coir Yojana (MCY)

Mahila Coir Yojana is a woman-oriented self-employment scheme in the coir industry, which provides self-employment opportunities to the rural women artisans in regions producing coir fibre. The scheme envisages distribution of motorized ratts for spinning coir yarns to women artisans after giving training. Women spinners are trained for two months in spinning coir yarn on motorized ratt at the Coir Board's training centers. A stipend of Rs.500 per month is also paid to the trainees. The Coir Board provides motorized ratts / motorized traditional ratts at 75 per cent cost subsidy During 2007-08, 1,042 ratts have been distributed.

Rajiv Gandhi Udyami Mitra Yojana (RGUMY)

The new scheme was launched on February 7, 2008. The main objective of the scheme is to promote and support establishment of micro and small enterprises through handholding of potential first generation entrepreneurs, who have already successfully completed Entrepreneurship Development Programme (EDP), Skill Development Programme (SDP) etc.

Training of Women Entrepreneurs

The industrial policies of the government announced from time to time, have laid considerable emphasis on promotion of women entrepreneurship, particularly among first generation women entrepreneurs, through various training and support services. Special attention is being given by organizing exclusive Entrepreneurship Development Programmes (EDPs) for women. During 2007-08 upto December 2007, approximately 15,000 women participated in these training programmes. In addition to programmes and schemes of MSME, NSIC, KVIC and Coir Board relating to conduct of EDPs and SDPs for benefit of potential women entrepreneurs, three national level entrepreneurship development institutes set up by the Ministry, particularly Indian Institute of

Entrepreneurship (IIE), Guwahati, are also undertaking training programmes for skills and entrepreneurship development for women. The National Institute for Entrepreneurship and Small Business Development (NIESBUD), Noida, has conducted seven training programmes exclusively for 227 women participants during 2007-08.

Training of Rural Youth for Self-Employment (TRYSEM)

The Scheme of TRYSEM, a facilitating component of IRDP, aims at providing basic technical and entrepreneurial skills to the rural poor in the age group of 18 to 35 years to enable them to take up income generating activities. The Eighth Plan had emphasized the importance of a proper assessment of the training needs of tile rural youth in relation to self and wage-employment opportunities, quality of training and group training.

Rural Development and Self Employment Training (RUDSET)

"Instead of writing someone else's account through wage employment after three to five years of collegiate education, it is more meaningful to write one's own account by embarking upon some self-employment". Dr. D. Veerendra Heggade, President, RUDSET Institutes

An innovative initiative was taken in the year 1982 jointly by Sri Dharmasthala Manjunatheshwara Educational Trust, Syndicate Bank and Canara Bank to motivate unemployed youth to take up self-employment as an alternative career. The model has proved very successful for the past 22 years in building the morale of the youth and empowering them to acquire a productive identity by taking up self-employment ventures in their own places.

The success rate of 66 per cent and impact of RUDSET Institute training in enabling the youth to establish and sustain in the ventures was recognised and appreciated by Government of India, State Governments, SIDBI, NABARD etc.. RUDSET Institute has established 20 units across 12 States in India.

Enhanced Credit Flow To Medium and Small Enterprises (MSE) Sector

For strengthening the delivery of credit to the MSEs, the Government announced a 'Policy Package for Stepping up Credit to Small and Medium Enterprises (SME)' in August 2005 for doubling the credit flow to this sector within a period of five years. This has resulted in a significant increase in the credit flow from Public Sector Banks (PSBs) to the micro and small enterprises (MSE) sector — with the outstanding credit of public sector banks increasing from Rs.58, 278 crore at the end of March 2004 to Rs.1,48, 651 crore at the end of March 2008.

Skill Development

The Government has taken up skill development as a high priority area through various measures like enhancing the training capabilities of the Tool Rooms, MSME Development Institutes and other organization under the Ministry of MSME. The agencies under the Ministry of MSME conducted programmes for skill development for nearly 1.8 lakh trainees during 2007-08 and the targets set for 2008-09 is 3 lakh persons. The Ministry of MSME provides all such trainings for SCs/STs, free of cost. Similar programmes are also being organized for women and other weaker sections of the society free of cost, besides providing a monthly stipend of Rs.500/- per month during the entire period of training.

Cluster Development Programme

For the last few years, the Government has been focusing on the strategy of Cluster Development for development of the MSEs - through which different 'clusters' and concentrations of enterprises are given the benefit of a whole variety of interventions ranging from exposure to skill development, from credit to marketing and from technological improvements to better designs and products. About 412 clusters have been approved for interventions under the scheme (including 50 clusters for hard interventions, 152 clusters for soft interventions and 210 clusters for diagnostic studies).

National Fund For Unorganised Sector

The National Commission for Enterprises in the Unorganised Sector (NCEUS) in one of its reports has recommended creation of a National Fund for the unorganized sector. A token provision in the Budget 2009-10 has been proposed. MSME has continued to contribute significantly in the gross domestic product, industrial production, employment generation and exports and has acquired a prominent place in the economy of the country.

Self Employment Training Programme (STEP)

The Self Employment Training Programme had evolved in 1986 after the National Commission for Self Employed Women and Women in the Informal Sector has made a situational review of women in the informal sector and had suggested introduction of protective measures which would ensure guarantee of employment and income generation, minimum wages, welfare and support services, training and upgradation of skills.

The programme of STEP advocates the objective of extending training for upgradation of skills and sustainable employment for women through a variety of action oriented projects, which employ women in large numbers. The Scheme covers 8 traditional sectors of employment, viz., Agriculture, Small Animal Husbandry, Dairying, Fisheries, Handlooms, Handicrafts, Khadi and Village Industries and Sericulture. Two more sectors, namely, Social Forestry and Waste Land Development have been added later. The target group to be covered under the STEP programme includes marginalized, assetless, rural women and urban poor with special focus on SC/ST households, women' headed households and families below the poverty line.

Promotional Package

In March 2007, the Government has announced a comprehensive Package for the Promotion of Micro and Small Enterprises, which comprises several proposals and schemes having direct impact on the promotion and development of the micro and small enterprises. These, inter alias, include credit and fiscal support, cluster-based development, infrastructure, technology and marketing support. Capacity building of MSME Associations and support to women entrepreneurs are the other important features of this Package.

Industrial Estates for Women Entrepreneurs

There has been an insistent demand for setting up industrial estates particularly for women entrepreneurs. The Andhra Pradesh, Karnataka, Kerala, Gujarat, Maharashtra, Goa and TamilNadu governments have supported the establishment of industrial estates for women.

District Industries Centres (DICs)

District Industries which are established in each district headquarters are making continuous efforts to promote and support women entrepreneurship. They are arranging special training programmes, special lectures and seminars as well as workshops with the collaboration of various training institutions exclusively for women and girls in colleges to inculcate the culture of entrepreneurship

ASSOCIATIONS AND ORGANISATIONS SUPPORTING WOMEN ENTREPRENEURSHIP

The Association of Women Entrepreneurs of Karnataka (AWAKE)

AWAKE– The Association of Women Entrepreneurs of Karnataka was founded in December 1983 and is one of India's premier institutions for women entrepreneurs totally devoted to the development of entrepreneurship among women and is a registered society. AWAKE is a not-for profit, Non-Governmental Organization. AWAKE is an ISO 9001-200 accredited organization. Women entrepreneurs are members who volunteer their time to contribute to the functioning of the organization. AWAKE's members facilitate and guide women who want to start or improve their businesses. Entirely run by entrepreneur–volunteers, the members counsel, train, share experience & expertise, provide peer group support & hand hold when needed.

AWAKE promotes entrepreneurship through Business Incubators along with Entrepreneurship training and skill training so as to enable a successful nurturing of entrepreneurs for emulation world- wide.

The Target Group: All women from urban, rural, national and international areas aspiring to be socially & economically self-reliant, irrespective of their academic, social & economic background. All women entrepreneurs seeking guidance to grow. NGOs engaged in Income Generation Activities & Entrepreneurship Development.

Consortium of Women Entrepreneurs of India (CWEI))

CWEI - Consortium of Women Entrepreneurs of India is a registered civil society, a voluntary organization that works for the economic empowerment of women in the country and world over Cwei acts as a springboard for Entrepreneurship, facilitates technology transfer, improves access to natural resources, product and design development, explore marketing linkages within and outside the country through various Haats, Buyer Seller Meets, Exhibitions and Fairs in India and abroad. This is an important step towards enhancing their entrepreneurial skills, integrating their force into economic power and transforming them into new generation entrepreneurs. Cwei acts as a catalyst providing all escort services leading to higher productivity, competitive prices and stringent quality control for export.

CWEI having the power of using digital information to understand the needs and preferences of consumers and partners, institutions, voluntary organisation and self enterprises and to thereby customizes products and services to suit the requirement of the consumers through E-commerce buying and selling of products and services can be done quickly, through the internet. CWEI's Mission is To motivate the New Generation & Women to opt for Entrepreneurship as a challenging career-the only answer to unemployment. Recognized as the nodal agency by Ministry of Human Resource

Development, Government. of India to organize various Economic Activities in the country. International Women Entrepreneurs Meet and Conference was declared as one of the CWEI's annual events to highlight issues pertaining to marketing finance, training, product design and development and a host of other critical problems in order to bring the issues to the notice of policy makers, implementing agencies and women entrepreneurs themselves.

Federation of Ladies Organization (FLO)

The FICCI Ladies Organization (FLO) is a wing of the Federation of Indian Chambers of Commerce and Industry (FICCI), the apex body of Industry and Chambers of Commerce in India. It was established in 1983 with the basic objective of "women empowerment", to encourage women to exploit to the maximum their own human potential as entrepreneurs, business women and professionals and serve the community and nation at large through activities of social welfare on the cultural and social fronts. As an all India organization for women, FLO has around 1000 members comprising entrepreneurs, professionals and executives. It currently has five chapters – in Chennai, Hyderabad, Kolkata, Mumbai and Coimbatore.

The primary objective of FLO is to promote entrepreneurship and professional excellence in women and society at large. FLO works on three levels. At the basic level, it holds entrepreneurship development programmes for women, working with them in advising on how to start a business and following it through with some help in vocational training. At the middle level, it holds seminars and workshops for women who run small-scale businesses, such as computerization and financial management. At the senior level, FLO has sophisticated programmes for women at the helm in areas such as marketing and finance.

Besides undertaking several business oriented activities for women through entrepreneurship development programmes, workshops and panel discussions, FLO has an active Business Consultancy Cell where free professional guidance is offered and which serves as a single window stop for all information on diversified statutory compliances, procedures and obligations in its Hyderabad chapter. It advises women entrepreneurs on subjects such as company incorporation, registration, preliminary documentation, taxation and policies of Governments. FLO has recently launched Young FLO (YFLO), a forum/community of career women between 20 and 39. In discharge of its functions, FLO has also started giving awards to recognize outstanding women in various walks of life. It presents the "Outstanding Woman Entrepreneur" award for establishing and successfully running a business unit, bringing product innovations and providing employment.

Women's India Trust (WIT)

Women's India Trust (WIT) is a charitable organization established in the year 1968 by Ms. Kamila Tyabji. WIT started by training less privileged and unskilled women in Mumbai to stitch sari petticoats. Since then WIT has helped many women to develop skills and earn a regular income; this has changed their lives and the lives of their families.

In 1983 The Kamila Tyabji WIT Centre and a girls' hostel was built in Panvel, on the outskirts of Mumbai. Here, educational programs and income generating skills are taught. It also houses the production units. WIT has created a sound platform to provide training and employment opportunities for the young girls and women in need. Various employment opportunities are also offered at the two Mumbai centres and at Panvel. The products made by women are then marketed through WIT's retail showrooms at Tardeo, Mahim and Panvel as well as regular sales organized in different parts of the country. The nature of activities at WIT has evolved with the changing needs of society, but as an organization, WIT has remained women-centered and continues to help less fortunate women secure a better future. WIT remains dedicated to the original aims of its founder, Kamila Tyabji: to help women to help themselves; to encourage women from less privileged backgrounds to acquire new skills; to give them the self-confidence and self esteem required to earn by their own industry and initiative; to enable them to carry this newly discovered skill and confidence into the wider world as well as within the framework of WIT. WIT's mission is to help women to help themselves by providing a platform for advancement and empowerment to unskilled and disadvantaged women. WIT provides easy access to education, income generating skills and employment.

The Federation of Indian Women Entrepreneurs (FIWE)

The Federation of Indian Women Entrepreneurs (FIWE) which is a National-level Organization brings the businesswomen on a common platform and ensures that their opinions, ideas and visions are collectively and effectively taken up with policy makers and various other agencies respectively for the development of Enterprise in Women.

Collectively FIWE endeavors to: Create public awareness towards women's contribution to the National Economy, Establish pressure groups advocating the cause of women, and Educate & Train young women entrepreneurs for their right initiation into business. FIWE is working towards National and International Co-operation amongst Women Entrepreneurs with a singular motive: Together Towards a Glorious Future!

Federation of Indian Women Entrepreneurs (FIWE is a National-level organization, founded in 1993, is today one of India's Premier Institution for Women thoroughly devoted towards Entrepreneurship Development, having a large membership base of 15,000 individual members/professionals and 28 member associations spread throughout the country. The objective of the organization is to foster the Economic Empowerment of Women, particularly the SME segment, by helping them to become successful entrepreneurs and become a part of the mainstream industry. FIWE endeavors to provide: Networking platform for women, Technical know-how, Industry research & expertise, Skill development & training and brings the businesswomen on a Common Forum; and ensures that their opinions, ideas and visions are collectively and effectively taken up with policy makers and various other agencies respectively for the development of Enterprise in Women. The organization is a formation of an umbrella group of local organizations around India with a growing member base of 15,000 including those from 28 local affiliated associations in India. Small-Scale entrepreneurs account for approximately 60 percent of FIWE combined membership, with large firms representing 15 percent and micro-enterprises the remainder.

SEWA

SEWA is a trade union registered in 1972. It is an organisation of poor, self-employed women workers. These are women who earn a living through their own labour or small businesses. They do not obtain regular salaried employment with welfare benefits like workers in the organized sector. r. Of the female labour force in India, more than 94% are in the unorganized sector

SEWA's main goals are to organize women workers for full employment. Full employment means employment whereby workers obtain work security, income security, food security and social security (at least health care, child care and shelter). SEWA organizes women to ensure that every family obtains full employment. SEWA has been supporting its members in capacity-building and in developing their own economic organisations.

HOW TO MAKE WOMEN ENTREPRENEURIAL DEVELOPMENTAL PROGRAMMES SUCCESSFUL?

No doubt, a lot of initiatives are being taken by both the government and non-governmental organizations. More and more programmes are launched and new schemes are added to the existing ones. A number of associations are working hard for networking of women both domestically and globally. It is really a good signal to indicate that at last all the concerned- whether it be the government or non governmental organisations have realised that women entrepreneurs should be provided with some special type of support in addition to the regular support available to male entrepreneurs. But, the introduction of more number of schemes and launching programmes will not be sufficient. In this dire ction, following points are worth considering:

— Regular Training programmes for skill building have to be organized.. Training women in getting management skills is the need of the hour.

— Publicity of the existing support available for women entrepreneurs should be made on a mass scale as many women do not have the knowledge of the support system available.

— Better educational facilities should be extended to women especially for rural areas both by the government and private bodies.

— Entrepreneurship as a subject should be introduced at the high school level and attempts should be made to develop entrepreneurial skills through well designed courses.

— More involvement of non governmental organizations should be focused.

— Continuous monitoring of the existing schemes at each level of implementation will help a lot in further improvement and successful implementation.

— Some more programmes should be added or the existing programmes should be modified from time to time based on requirements.

— Programmes for encouraging women to take up entrepreneurship should be organized at the local level and the successful women entrepreneurs from that region should be invited to motivate them.

— Women Entrepreneurship Development Cells should be set up at the local levels.

— Support from the male entrepreneurs and encouragement will go a long way in facing the competitive situation successfully.

— Counselling by NGOs, Psychiatrists and the leading entrepreneurs will definitely help in overcoming their emotional problems and building self confidence building.

- District Industries Centres should take more initiative in guiding and training women entrepreneurs in addition to their existing role.
- Banks and other financial lending institutions should liberalise the terms of credit for women entrepreneurs and support them. They can also have their own guidance cells to guide the prospective women entrepreneurs and address their grievances.
- Above all, realization on the part of women to realize her potential is essentially needed to make use of the existing support system.

CONCLUSION

The number of women entrepreneurs has grown over a period of time especially in the nineties. The number of women willing to take risk and starting their own business is growing. Women entrepreneurs have demonstrated their potential and are capable of contributing much more what they have already had. Many programmes and policies are formulated to support to support women entrepreneurs and may continue to contribute a lot in the coming days. In spite of government and non government support it is evident that the real development activities begin at home. In the formative years of grooming, girls should be given equal treatment and education as boys so that they are groomed to take up future challenges. They should be trained for economic independence and decision making rather than treating them with protection measures. The overall environment should be matured enough to treat women and men equal in trade and industry. It is necessary to formulate appropriate strategies for stimulating, supporting and sustaining their efforts in this direction.

REFERENCES

Badi R.V. and Badi N.V. (2007), (reprint) Vrinda Publications (P) Limited

Baligar G.B. (2008), Entrepreneurial Development and Small Enterprise Management, Ashok Prakashan

Basava K.D. (2008), Entrepreneurial Development and Small Enterprise Management, Vidyavahini Prakashan

Gordon E. and Natarajan K. (2009), Entrepreneurship Development, Himalaya Publishing House

Khanka S.S. (2008), (reprint), Entrepreneurial Development, S. Chand and Co. Ltd

Madhurima Lal and Shikha Sahai (2006), Entrepreneurship, Excel Books

Murthy C.S.V. (2004), (reprint) Small Scale Industries and Entrepreneurial Development, Himalaya Publishing House

Rajesh Marwaha and Jagroop Singh, Entrepreneurship and Small Business (2009), (reprint), Kalyani Publishers

Renu Arora and Sood S.K. (2009), Fundamentals of Entrepreneurship and Small Business, Kalyani Publishers

Vasanth Desai (2006), Small Scale Industries and Entrepreurship, Himalaya Publishing House

On line Sources

Dr. Deepali Pant Joshi "Feminization of Credit ", viewed on 20th December 2009, http://www.change.godrej.com/may june/womens_emp.htm

Development Commissioner (MSME), Ministry of Micro, Small and Medium Enterprises, "Schemes and Incentives", viewed on 20th December 2009, http://.www.smallindustryindia.com/schemes/treadwomen.htm

Development of Women and Children in Rural Areas viewed on on 20th December 2009, http://planning commission.gov.in/reports/sereport/ser/maker/mak_cht2c.pdf

NABARD: Promotinal Programmes, viewed on on 20th December 2009, http://www.nabard.org/nonfarm_sector/pp.wd_arwind.asp

Sundaram Pillai P. and Saraswathi amma K.P., "Women Small Business Owners in India", viewed on 20th December 2009,http://books.google.co.in/books

NABARD in Birhum, viewed on 20th December 2009, http://birhum.gov.in/nabard.htm

Malik D.P., Chandra G.C and Dhanda S.K., Vikas Voluntary Vahini Farmer's clubs- a pivot of rural development abstract, viewed on 20th December 2009, http://www.highbeam.com/doc/1p3-102117572.htmlInstitutional support-Institutions-II-http://class summary.blogspot.com/2009/04/clas-37-institutional-support.html, viewed on 20th December 2009,

Jayalakshmi, "Women Empowerment and their role in SMEs, viewed on 20th December 2009, http://www.theindiapost.com/2009/03/01/

Khadi and Village Industries Commission, viewed on 18th December 2009, http://en.wikepedia.org/wiki/khadi_and_village_industries_commission

Part–III

Innovations in Banking and Finance

15

REGRESSION MODEL FOR THE IMPROVEMENT OF ECONOMIC STATUS OF SELF HELP GROUPS

R. Ganapathi, J. Murugesan, T. Ramasamy

INTORDUCTION

Self Help Groups are about people coming together with others who are affected by a particular issue (experience, disadvantage, discrimination and the like) to support each other and to work together to change the disadvantages affecting them. It is a self-governed, peer-controlled small and informal association of the poor, usually from socio-economically homogeneous families who are organized around savings and credit activities. Funds for credit activities are coming through regular savings deposited by all of its members on a weekly or fortnightly basis. In the meetings they discuss common problems and plan for solution, share information, and make efforts to improve their health and literacy skills. Self Help Groups are not charity or simply community based groups. They are made of and controlled by the people affected. Group members are not volunteers. Although the work is usually unpaid, members work to change their own situation and the support is mutual. The knowledge base of self-help mutual support groups is experiential, indigenous, and rooted in the wisdom that comes from struggling with problems in concrete, shared ways. Self-help groups build on the strengths of their members.

EVOLUTION OF MICRO FINANCE IN INDIA

The irrepressible desire and inherent capacity of poor to improve their living for themselves is considered as the foundation for concept of Micro Finance propelled by the demonstrative success of Bangladesh Grameen Experiment. Micro Finance is acknowledged as an effective channel to take the poor into a new domain of economic empowerment. Micro Finance movement assumed global advocacy through Micro Credit

Summit held in February 1997 at Washington. The summit representing 1500 institutions and 137 countries is a landmark in the collective crusade against poverty undertaken by the developed and developing countries together. The Micro Credit Summit launched a campaign to reach 100 million of the worlds poorest families. Micro Finance is referred as providing credit for self employment, financial and other business services including savings and technical assistance.

In India self-help groups (SHGs) are an integral part of the National Bank for Agriculture and Rural Development (NABARD) program for linking banks and SHGs. Nevertheless, they are generally not registered. Under Indian law, SHGs are only required to be registered (as a society, trust or cooperative) if they have more than 20 members. For this reason, many SHGs restrict their membership to 20 persons or less. It is also found in Gujarat and some other parts of the country that some larger SHGs operate informally and are not registered.

STATEMENT OF THE PROBLEM

Nowadays women are flourishing in all fields. Recently rural poor women are also motivated and associated for mutual help. They have started to improve their status, standard of living and personality. No more women are dependent. They are finding their own way of generating income. They not only improve themselves but they associate other poor women with them and jointly work to improve their status. Self Help Groups have such an association started among the poorest women for mutual help. In order to create awareness among the women and to give a detailed analytical performance of micro finance, the researchers have attempted to analyze the impact of micro finance in Coimbatore District. This district has a large agricultural community and the women folk are involved in various SHGs. This study has been undertaken to study the impact of micro finance and the role of SHGs in the development of women empowerment.

OBJECTIVES OF THE STUDY

The main objective of the study is to analyze the impact of micro finance on women members in SHGs in Coimbatore District. The specific objectives of the study are:

- To study the relationship between demographic factors and socio-economic conditions of members of Self Help Groups.
- To identify the inter relationship among demographic of Self Help Group members and
- To offer valuable suggestions on the basis of findings of this study for the successful implementation of micro finance activities through SHGs.

SCOPE OF THE STUDY

The current study, which is basically a research, study, provided an opportunity to bring awareness among women about their situation, discrimination of rights and opportunities as a step towards gender equality. Collective awareness building provides a sense of group identity and the power of working as a group. This research study will help the women to strengthen their economic activities, to create positive linkages and to support for access to raw materials, skill training, marketing opportunities and credit needs. The present study is aimed at analyzing the impact of micro finance in terms of economic status of the SHGs members and the role of SHGs in the development of women empowerment from the point of view of SHGs and its members. The findings and suggestions will throw light on certain broad features of the micro finance and as such the study may be a practical guide in formulating better plans.

METHODOLOGY

The present study is based on primary data. The main source of the primary data has been collected from SHGs members. The schedule has been used for collecting information relating to the socio economic conditions and the impact of micro finance on SHGs members. The fieldwork for the study was conducted during the period between June 2009 and November 2009. The data thus collected were categorized and posted in the master table for further processing. The collected data are analyzed through simple descriptive statistics to 'F' test. The extent and variation of economic status achieved by the members were measured through scale and analysis on the basis of the scores of components. The factor wise analysis was made. In order to find out the significance of the difference between the average, analysis of variance, 'F' test, co-efficient of correlation analysis and partial regression analysis have been applied.

SAMPLING

The present study proposes to cover the SHGs in Coimbatore District. As census method is not feasible, the researchers have proposed to follow sampling. The sample respondents are selected by following Cluster Sampling Method. The district is divided into three revenue divisions namely Coimbotore, Pollachi and Tirupur. Each division is considered a cluster. The 60 SHGs have been selected by simple random sampling method, using the lottery method from each revenue division at the rate of 20. As the study follows Cluster Sampling Method, proper attention was made to include the 3 models of SHGs of Direct linkage with banks, NGO as facilitator and NGO as intermediary from each cluster in the sample. The present study selected 240 SHGs members from the selected 60 SHGs. In each selected SHGs, four members have been selected as sample respondents from the nominal rolls of the respective SHGs by using the Tippets Random Numbers. Thus, on the whole 240 sample respondents were selected for the study and this number is inclusive of animators and representatives as well as members of the SHGs.

MULTIPLE REGRESSION ANALYSIS

In this foregoing analysis, the relationship of each factor with the SHGs members' economic status has been studied. The analysis has been carried forward into a regression analysis in this section. The simple correlation analysis made in the previous section is given in Table-1 it shows that there is a significant relationship between six factors with economic status.

Table 1
Simple Correlation of Selected Factors with Economic Status

Factors	*Correlation Co-efficient*	*Table value"r"*	*Significance*
Age Group	0.076	0.125	Not Significant
Gender	-0.216	0.125	Significant
Marital status	0.073	0.125	Not Significant

Contd.

Factors	Correlation Co-efficient	Table value"r"	Significance
Social status	-0.128	0.125	Significant
Education	0.139	0.125	Significant
Type of family	-0.024	0.125	Not Significant
Size of the family	0.161	0.125	Significant
Role in SHGs	0.037	0.125	Not Significant
Occupation	0.007	0.125	Not Significant
Monthly Income	0.018	0.125	Not Significant
Awareness	0.199	0.125	Significant
Participation	0.397	0.125	Significant

INTER-CORRELATION

Table-2 shows the inter-correlation among the twelve selected factors. The relationship of economic status (Y) with the factors age group (X_1), marital status (X_3), type of family (X_6), role in SHGs (X_8), occupation (X_9) and income (X_{10}) is not significant. The relationship of age group (X_1) with residence (X_2), marital status (X_3), social status (X_4), size of family (X_7) and income (X_{10}) is not significant. The relationship of gender (X_2) with social status (X_4), size of family (X_7), occupation (X_9) and income (X_{10}) is not significant. The relationship of marital status (X_3) with social status (X_4), type of family (X_6), and occupation (X_9) is significant. The relationship of social status (X_4) with income (X_{10}) is not significant. The relationship of education (X_5) with role in SHGs (X_8), occupation (X_9) and awareness (X_{11}) is not significant. The relationship of type of family (X_6) with occupation (X_9), income (X_{10}) and awareness (X_{11}) is not significant. The relationship of size of the family (X_7) with income (X_{10}) and participation in SHGs (X_{12}) is not significant. The relationship of role in SHGs (X_8) with income (X_{10}) is significant. The relationship of occupation (X_9) with income (X_{10}), awareness (X_{11}) and participation in SHGs (X_{12}) is significant. The relationship of income (X_{10}) with awareness (X_{11}) is not significant. The relationship of awareness (X_{11}) with participation in SHGs (X_{12}) is significant.

STEP-WISE MULTIPLE REGRESSION ANALYSIS

The step-wise multiple regression analysis of economic status (Y) was performed with the variables age group (X_1), gender (X_2), marital status (X_3), social status (X_4), education (X_5), type of family (X_6), size of family (X_7), role in SHGs (X_8), occupation (X_9), income (X_{10}), awareness (X_{11}) and participation in SHGs (X_{12}) and the following regression model is fitted for performance :

$Y = b_0 + b_1x_1 + b_2x_2 + b_3x_3 + \ldots\ldots + b_nx_n$ *where n is the number of observation.* The results are presented in Table-3.

Regression Fitted: $Y = 58.465 - 9.938\ X_{12} + 4.498\ X_1 + 3.613\ X_{11} + 2.910\ X_3 + 0.899\ X_{10}$

The final step-wise multiple regression model indicated that of the 12 variables, five variables namely participation (X_{12}), age group (X_1), awareness (X_{11}), marital status (X_3) and income (X_{10}) have made significant contribution to the economic status. The analysis of variance of multiple regression models for economic status is presented in Table-4.

The Analysis of Variance of multiple regression models for economic status indicates the over-all significance of the model fitted. The co-efficient of determination R^2 value shows that these variables put together explain the variations of economic status to the extent of 25.10%.

Table 2
Inter Correlation Among Independent Variables

Y	X_1	X_2	X_3	X_4	X_5	X_6	X_7	X_8	X_9	X_{10}	X_{11}	X_{12}	
Y	1												
X_1	0.076	1											
X_2	-0.216	0.117	1										
X_3	0.073	-0.108	0.164	1									
X_4	-0.128	0.067	0.010	-0.251	1								
X_5	0.139	0.259	0.216	-0.065	0.151	1							
X_6	-0.024	-0.473	-0.265	0.180	-0.444	-0.288	1						
X_7	0.161	-0.026	0.023	-0.047	-0.166	-0.285	0.151	1					
X_8	0.037	0.150	0.127	-0.040	0.347	0.049	-0.269	-0.491	1				
X_9	0.007	-0.134	0.085	-0.176	0.172	0.072	0.075	-0.160	0.063	1			
X_{10}	0.018	-0.074	0.032	0.057	0.069	-0.252	-0.001	-0.087	0.286	-0.338	1		
X_{11}	0.199	-0.262	-0.283	-0.039	0.222	-0.102	0.088	-0.428	0.092	0.228	-0.022	1	
X_{12}	0.397	0.257	0.366	0.089	-0.259	0.152	-0.345	0.048	0.003	-.0204	0.238	-0.243	1

Note: lr lvalue for 5 % = 0 .125

Table 3
Regression Model for Economic Status

Factors	*Regression Co-efficient*	*Standard Error*	*t - value (DF = 234)*
Constant	58.465	4.958	11.793
Participation (X_{12})	-9.938	1.311	-7.578**
Age Group (X_1)	4.498	1.042	4.315**
Awareness (X_{11})	3.613	1.393	2.594*
Marital status (X_3)	2.910	1.181	2.464*
Income (X_{10})	0.899	0.384	2.342*

* = Significant at 5 % ** = Significant at 1% level $R^2 = 0.2510$

Table 4
Analysis of Variance for Regression

Source	*Degrees of Freedom*	*SS*	*MS*	*F*
Regression	5	6555.23	1311.046	15.665**
Residual	234	19584.16	83.693	
Total	239	26139.39		

** = Significant at 1 % level

SUGGESTIONS

In the light of the findings made in this study, the following suggestions are offered to improve the function of the micro credit at the grass-root level.

1. The government should come forward to provide minimum entrepreneurship program through District Industries Center. This may pave the way for practical and technical training in new areas. Natural talents, aptitudes, capabilities can be multiplied through training programmes to develop self-confidence, self-esteem, assertiveness, courage and risk.
2. Training programmes should be designed in such manners that members can benefit out of their strengths and overcome their weakness; and should provide special assistance for selection of procedure / service so that members can be in a position to perceive and respond to various profitable opportunities.
3. Income generating activity should be based on available local resources and reasonably assured market with profits. Goods to be produced should be either for local needs or to facilitate traditional manufacture.
4. The process of SHGs formation has to be systematic, whether it is formed by a bank or an NGO. Due to their closeness to the people and flexibility of operations, the NGOs seem to be better equipped to undertake SHGs formation.
5. Every group should frame a policy on how to manage the savings of members who leave the group voluntarily or are asked to leave for some unavoidable reason.
6. Micro credit should be used to meet the current demands of the poor women, whether these are for health, education or consumption purposes. This will lead to a gradual improvement in the quality of their life and will enable them to identify activities for economic betterment. In this process they will learn fiscal discipline and be ready to take on market oriented economic activities.
7. Strong members of old groups can be motivated to take up promotional and conflict resolution responsibilities in the new SHGs. They can visit problematic/

sick groups to explain and resolve various issues for smooth functioning of new SHGs.

8. Training in book-keeping, accounts, fund management and other financial matters related to SHGs are essential to make the members competent enough to deal with the increasing volume of transaction.
9. Annual Plans for SHGs activities should be done by the group in consultation with the NGOs. The group leaders from different villages can meet once in a month and present the progress of their groups. Such review by all the groups will promote mutual learning.
10. Exposure visits to relatively successful group ventures of other SHGs can be organized to share the knowledge, experience and expertise.
11. The vertical structure and their management require capacity building and promotion of leadership from the grass-roots upwards within the SHGs structure. But they should not be imposed from above.
12. The involvement of politicians in the selection of the eligible beneficiaries may be avoided. The Panchayat Raj Institution or the Grama Sabha under the New Panchayat Raj System in Tamil Nadu may be involved in selection of the beneficiaries and the nature of assistance under the micro finance to the people living below the poverty line.
13. Voluntary organization operating in the rural areas should be encouraged to participate in the effective implementation of the programme. The programme may provide separately funds for the projects to be taken by such organization.
14. Government should organize micro credit camps and credit cum-recovery camps to facilitate early completion of the formalities required for sanction of loans and to avoid hardship to the beneficiaries.
15. A proper infrastructure facility should be given to the micro credit beneficiaries for effective implementation of schemes like sheep, goat, small dairy farming and other processing etc.
16. The Government, NGO and Financial agencies should help the SHGs in selecting the project or the venture. Depending upon the local condition, availability of raw materials and other factors they can advice SHGs to select the feasible and profitable venture. Ideas of SHGs should be scrutinized with the help of management experts before the venture is finalized. Error in selecting the project may make for closure, as a result the time and money put into the project could become wasteful. Hence, right direction may enable the SHGs to select the right venture.
17. Most of the SHGs procure their raw materials locally for the production. When there is shortage or non-availability of raw materials agencies like SHGs Resource Bank may be established and help the SHGs. This agencies may create a link with SHGs and they may try to solve the problems of SHGs.
18. The commercial banks should give wider publicity on the availability of credit facilities that can be offered to the SHGs. Government should also play an important role in that and it can give information to the public through the District Development Authorities and lead bank. The bank officials can give more

information on the procedures in getting the loan, utilization of loan amount repayment and other related information in securing the credit. Simple procedures and the right encouragement from these bank officials may enable women to form more SHGs in their locality.

19. Government should make the rural people to realize that SHGs are the main medium for rural employment generation, Encouragement and support by the Government will solve the problem of rural unemployment. The entrepreneurial abilities are realized by everyone and India needs rural entrepreneurs to solve the employment problems. This paves a way for women empowerment in India.

CONCLUSION

The researchers present this study with the fervent hope that this will draw the attention of the authorities, departments and organizations concerned with micro finance and SHGs on various issues in respect of the development of women empowerment. The researchers humbly state that this study is not a fascinating one to strengthen the academic value. If the study helps the women towards their empowerment in any way, the researchers will feel happy that they are amply rewarded.

REFERENCES

Aparna Basu (2004), *"Women's Empowerment and Self Help Groups"*, SHELTER, Human Settlement Management Institute, New Delhi, Vol. VII, No. 1, January, pp. 13 – 15.

Chittaranjan Mishra (2005), *"SHGs in the Unorganized Garment Sector A Case Study of Madurai"*, Kurukshetra, New Delhi, July, Vol. 53, No. 8, p. 12.

Desai, Bhupat M. and Namboodiri N.V. (1996), *"Whither Rural Financial Institutions"*, Economic and Political Weekly, Mumbai, August 3, Vol. 31, No.31, pp. 2341-2342.

Kaladhar, K. (2007), *"Micro Finance in India: Design, Structure and Governance"*, Economic and Political Weekly, Mumbai, Vol. 32, No. 42, October, pp. 3512-3513.

Karmakar (2000), *"Rural Credit and Self-Help Groups"*, Journal of Social and Management Science, New Delhi, Vol. XXIX No.1, April – June, p. 15.

Naila Kabeer (2006), *"Is Microfinance a 'Magic Bullet' for Women's Empowerment? Analysis of Findings from South Asia"*, Economic and Political Weekly, Mumbai, October, p. 2642.

National Bank for Agriculture and Rural Development (NABARD), (2000), *"Report on Impact of Micro Finance on the Living Standards of SHG Members"*, 1999-2000, Mumbai, pp.17 - 20.

Panda S. K. (2003), *"Micro Finance in Economic Empowerment of Weaker Sections"*, Yojana, New Delhi, March, Vol. 47, No.3, p. 19.

Revathi K. (2007), *"Micro Finance: A Tool for Poverty Alleviation"*, Facts For You, New Delhi, June, p.16.

Sabyasachi Das (2003), *"Self Help Groups & Micro Credit Synergic Integration"*, Kurukshetra, New Delhi, August, Vol.51, No. 10, p. 13.

Sathish P. (2001), *"Some Issues in the Formation of Self Help Groups"*, Working Paper Published in India Journal of Agriculture Economics, New Delhi, Vol. 56, No.3, p. 15.

Selvaraj R & Vasanthi G. (1999), *"Role of Self-Help Groups in Entrepreneurial Development"*, The Tamil Nadu Journal of Co-operation, Chennai, June, p.23.

Srinivasa Rao K. (2007), *"Microfinance: A Tool for Poverty Alleviation and Women Empowerment"*, Facts For You, New Delhi, January, p.32.

16

A LIQUIDITY-PROFITABILITY TRADE-OFF MODEL FOR WORKING CAPITAL MANAGEMENT

Mihir Dash, Rani Hanuman

INTRODUCTION

Proper planning is necessary for the efficient working of any organization. This can be in terms of marketing, production/operations, human resource, and financial plans. There should be proper flow of funds for running any business. This fund is called working capital. If at any point of time the organization does not have sufficient funds to meet its short-term debts such as creditors and salaries as well as day-to-day expenses it may become technically insolvent. On the other hand, if it is very conservative it will have a surplus of working capital, which will adversely affect profits. The trade-off between profitability and risk is the key to working capital management. Too little working capital increases profit but reduces liquidity, as current assets are more expensive than fixed assets. For instance if a management feels that worker training is a cost they will apportion less funds for it. If on the other hand a management sees it as an investment in manpower, the funds allocated would increase substantially. It is applicable in any case either for procurement, inventory, storage, processing, distribution and human capital and other investment decisions[1].

Businesses must continuously innovate and transform themselves to stay ahead of competition in this fast growing world. An efficient working capital management system has to be designed to run the business and make profits in the long run. As costs are ever-increasing, companies have to make efficient use of funds in managing the procurement, inventory, processing and distribution of finished product to the existing customers, and it is common in many business decision-making situations that certain goals or objectives of the firm can only be met at the expense of other goals. If it is not possible to quantify the exact cost-benefit trade-offs among these goals, it may be necessary for decision makers to rank order the various goals so that the less important goals are pursued only after the more mportant goals are achieved or when no further progress toward goal achievement is possible.

This paper formulates the working capital decision as a goal programming model, balancing the conflicting objectives of liquidity and profitability. The model determines, for given working capital turnover and fixed assets turnover ratios, how funds should be maintained between working capital/current assets and fixed assets to achieve targeted levels of liquidity and profitability, whilst minimizing the opportunity cost/loss of excess liquidity.

REVIEW OF LITERATURE

Goal programming techniques have been widely used in many diverse fields, including operations, marketing, human resources, and finance. Aksoy (1990) presented a bibliography of multiple objective decision-making models applied in various disciplines. He proposed that there was a trend towards utilizing interactive techniques for solving the multiple objective decision making problem, allowing the involvement of the decision-maker throughout the decision process.

A variety of goal programming models have been applied in the operations contexts, usually interlinking operations, marketing, human resource, and financial decisions. Rees et al (1984) analyzed the multi-period, multi-commodity network flow problem. They contended that cost minimization is not the sole or even the most important objective of the firm; other objectives often exist related to preferred customer demand, inventory conditions, and shipping arrangements end contracts, necessitating a goal programming approach. Several commodities are distributed through a network of distribution points (i.e., stores, outlets, terminals, etc.) in order to meet supply end demand constraints at these distribution points at the minimum shipping cost, and the model is further complicated by the fact that shipments occur over several periods.

Tabucanon and Estraza (1989) developed a goal programming model based on several conflicting objectives of companies, including minimization of lead time/delay, maximization of revenue, minimization of production cost, and minimization of overtime. Their model was applied to real data from a company, and sensitivity analysis was performed to give insights to the decision-makers regarding trade-offs between the conflicting objectives.

Kim and Schniederjans (1993) formulated a linear goal programming model for JIT production systems. They showed how the post-optimality analysis of the goal programming model enables a decision maker to examine the effects of production scheduling in a JIT "mixed-model" production environment.

Khorram et al (1994) proposed a unique solution to resource allocation problems by combining goal programming with a qualitative forecasting model (e.g. the Delphi method) and a quantitative forecasting technique (e.g. the Poisson gravity model). In their model, the Delphi method is used initially to elicit the experts' talents to derive the objectives to be considered in resource allocation, and subsequently a quantitative forecasting technique is used to predict the future values for these objectives. This information is then was used to construct a goal programming model.

Rifai (1996) discussed the limitations of linear programming in decision-making, and suggested the use of goal to handle problems with multiple objectives. He advocated caution in using the goal programming, since an improper structure of a goal programming model can induce misleading results.

Schniederjans and Hoffman (1999) proposed a goal programming model for downsizing in order to cut operation costs, based on a thorough analysis of the firm's prioritized opportunities and their limited economic resources to achieve them. They provided a new methodological approach that can be used to determine previously hidden goals in a manufacturing linear programming model of the downsizing problem. Their model illustrated how an optimal allocation of production resources can be achieved while providing useful information in which to ensure other prioritized goals and their economic tradeoffs.

Coskun et al (2008) studied integrative methods for improving business processes. Their approach involved determining and analyzing the weak points and reducing the weakness degrees. They suggested a four-phase business process improvement framework: start-up, self analysis, defining improvement strategy for making changes, feedback, and continuous improvement. They found that decision problems in process improvement could be structured to provide input data suitable for multi-criteria decision making techniques.

Lee and Kang (2008) developed a model for inventory management for multiple periods, considering not only the usual parameters, but also price/ quantity discounts, and storage and batch size constraints. The model is formulated as a mixed binary integer programming problem minimizing the total cost of materials in the system, and the optimal solution determines an appropriate inventory level for each period and the optimal purchase amount in each period.

Several studies have addressed the problem of working capital, and have developed a variety of models to assess the efficiency of working capital management.

Jafar and Sur (2006) studied the efficiency of the working capital management in the National Thermal Power Corporation (NTPC), and showed that the company achieved a higher level of efficiency in managing its working capital during the post-liberalization era by adapting itself to the new environment which had emanated from liberalization, globalization and competitiveness. They pointed out that, while many of the public enterprises are learning to survive and grow by adapting themselves to the new situation, a large group of public sector undertakings, significant both in number and investment, have been beset with serious problems like slow growth, low productivity, inadequate emphasis on research and development, inefficient working capital management, and so on.

Rafuse (1996) argued that attempts to improve working capital by delaying payment to creditors are counter-productive, and that altering debtor and creditor levels for individual tiers within a value system will rarely produce any net benefit. He proposed that stock reduction generates system-wide financial improvements and other important benefits, and suggested that, to achieve this, companies should focus on stock management strategies based on "lean supply-chain" techniques.

Cote et al (1999) explored the limitations of the traditional measures of working capital management and presented alternative measures based on earlier work in the finance literature. They also proposed a new ratio, the "merchandising ratio," which measured the net effect of a firm's working capital management strategy.

Garcia-Teruel and Martinez-Solano (2007) studied the effects of working capital management on the profitability of a sample of small and medium-sized Spanish firms. They found that managers can create value by reducing their inventories and the number of days for which their accounts are outstanding. Moreover, shortening the cash conversion cycle also improves the firm's profitability.

Filbeck and Krueger (2005) suggested that firms should be able to reduce financing costs and/or increase the funds available for expansion by minimizing the amount of funds tied up in current assets. They found significant differences in working capital measures between industries across time, and significant changes in these working capital measures within industries across time.

Chakraborty (2008) evaluated the relationship between working capital and profitability of Indian pharmaceutical companies. He pointed out that there were two distinct schools of thought on this issue: according to one school of thought, working capital is not a factor of improving profitability and there may be a negative relationship between them, while according to the other school of thought, investment in working capital plays a vital role to improve corporate profitability, and unless there is a minimum level of investment of working capital, output and sales cannot be maintained - in fact, the inadequacy of working capital would keep fixed asset inoperative.

Chakraborty and Bandopadhyay (2007) studied strategic working capital management, and its role in corporate strategy development, ultimately ensuring the survival of the firm. They also highlighted how strategic current asset decisions and strategic current liabilities decisions had multi-dimensional impact on the performance of a company.

Singh (2008) found that the size of inventory directly affects working capital and its management. He suggested that inventory was the major component of working capital, and needed to be carefully controlled.

Singh and Pandey (2008) suggested that, for the successful working of any business organization, fixed and current assets play a vital role, and that the management of working capital is essential as it has a direct impact on profitability and liquidity. They studied the working capital components and found a significant impact of working capital management on profitability for Hindalco Industries Limited.

Agarwal (1988) formulated the working capital decision as a goal programming problem, giving primary importance to liquidity, by targeting the current ratio and quick ratio. The model included three liquidity goals/constraints, two profitability goals/constraints, and, at a lower priority level, four current asset sub-goals and a current liability sub-goal (for each component of working capital). In particular, the profitability constraints were designed to capture the opportunity cost of excess liquidity (in terms of reduced profitability).

The literature of goal programming in operational/financial decisions is quite extensive, though only a few studies have directly focused on working capital decisions. Agarwal's (1988) study was a step forward, but no further refinements to his model have been proposed. This paper proposes certain modifications in Agarwal's (1988) model.

LIQUIDITY-PROFITABILITY TRADE-OFF MODEL

The goal programming model proposed in this paper examines the trade-off between liquidity and profitability. Goal programming is appropriate because liquidity and profitability represent conflicting objectives of a firm.

The decision variables for the model are the usual components of working capital, viz. cash, marketable securities, accounts receivable, inventory, current liabilities, fixed assets, sales, and profit. Each of these variables is assumed to have well-defined target levels. Additionally, the current ratio, profit margin, working capital turnover ratio, and fixed assets turnover ratio are assumed to have stable target levels. These variables and targets are represented in Table-1.

Table 1
Variables and Target Parameters

	Variable	*Target*
Cash	x_1	C
Marketable securities	x_2	MS
Accounts receivable	x_3	AR
Inventory	x_4	I
Current liabilities	x_5	CL
Fixed assets	x_f	FA
Sales	π	S
Profit		P
Current ratio		θ
Profit margin		m
Working capital turnover ratio		ω
Fixed assets turnover ratio		ϕ

Highest priority is given to maintaining liquidity, turnover, and profitability, built into the model via the current ratio, the working capital and fixed assets turnover ratios, and the profit margin, followed by the targeted levels of each of the variables. The different priority coefficients (P_i) assigned to each of the different goals is represented in Table-2.

Table 2
Priority Levels Assigned to Constraints

Constraints	*Priority*	*Deviation Variables*
Liquidity	P_1	d_1^- , d_1^+
Working capital turnover	P_2	d_2^- , d_2^+
Fixed assets turnover	P_3	d_3^- , d_3^+
Profit margin	P_4	d_4^- , d_4^+
Oppurtunity cost	P_5	d_5^- , d_5^+
Cash	P_6	d_6^- , d_6^+
Marketable securities	P_7	d_7^- , d_7^+
Accounts receivable	P_8	d_{13}^- , d_{13}^+
Inventory	P_9	d_9^- , d_9^+

Contd.

Constraints	*Priority*	*Deviation Variables*
Current liabilities	P_{10}	d_{10}^-, d_{10}^+
Fixed assets	P_{11}	d_{11}^-, d_{11}^+
Sales	P_{12}	d_{12}^-, d_{12}^+
Profit	P_{13}	d_{13}^-, d_{13}^+

The goal programming formulation for the problem is given below:

$$\min w = \sum_{j=1}^{13} P_j(d_j^+ + d_j^-)$$

subject to the constraints:

- Total assets: $x_1 + x_2 + x_3 + x_4 - x_5 + x_f = C + MS + AR + I - CL + FA$
- Liquidity: $x_1 + x_2 + x_3 + x_4 + d_1^- - d_1^+ = \theta.CL$
- Working Capital Turnover: $y - w(x_1 + x_2 + x_3 + x_4 - x_5) + d_2^- - d_2^+ = 0$
- Fixed Assets Turnover: $y - \phi x_f + d_3^- - d_3^+ = 0$
- Profit margin: $\pi - my + d_4^- - d_4^+ = 0$
- Opportunity cost: $\pi - m\phi[x_1 + x_2 + x_3 + x_4 - x_5 - y/w] + d_5^- - d_5^+ = P$
- Cash: $x_1 + d_6^- - d_6^+ = C$
- Marketable securities: $x_2 + d_7^- - d_7^+ = MS$
- Accounts receivable: $x_3 + d_8^- - d_8^+ = AR$
- Inventories: $x_4 + d_9^- - d_9^+ = I$
- Current liabilities: $x_5 + d_{10}^- - d_{10}^+ = CL$
- Fixed assets: $x_f + d_{11}^- - d_{11}^+ = FA$
- Sales: $y + d_{12}^- - d_{12}^+ = S$
- Profit: $\pi + d_{13}^- - d_{13}^+ = P$
- Non-negativity: $x_1, \ldots x_5, x_f, y, ð, d_1^{\pm}, \ldots d_{13}^{\pm}$ e" 0

The model formulated above addresses a few limitations of Agarwal's (1988) model. Agarwal's model has an inbuilt over-emphasis on liquidity, through its liquidity goals and once again through its current assets and current liabilities sub-goals; in fact, the profitability goals also have an inbuilt liquidity target. Also, the profitability goals in Agarwal's model are somewhat ambiguous: profit as a variable seems to be unrelated to the other (working capital) variables, and the cost of capital term in the profitability goals is not very clear.

The proposed model tries to address some of the limitations of Agarwal's model. In order to relate the profit variable with working capital variables, the model introduces variables for fixed assets and sales, and interlinks the variables via the working capital turnover ratio, the fixed assets turnover ratio, and the profit margin goals. Liquidity remains as a major goal, and Agarwal's profitability goal is replaced by a profitability goal which functions to balance funds between working capital and fixed assets, in accordance with the targeted turnover ratios. The resulting opportunity cost is the profit forgone by excess/deficiency of liquidity (as determined by the turnover ratios).

APPLICATION OF THE MODEL

The goal programming model presented in preceding section was applied to the input data of the firm Vijaya Krishna Spice Farms Pvt. Ltd., a food-processing company mainly involved in the storage of different varieties of chilly and the processing of the same into chilly paste. The financial data required for analysis was obtained from the company, for the five year span from 2004-2009. The target values of the current ratio, working capital turnover ratio, fixed assets turnover ratio, and net profit margin were set approximately at their five-year averages, to eliminate chance fluctuations for a particular period. The optimal working capital position (assuming equal priorities of all goals and sub-goals) of the firm for the year 2008-09 is detailed in Table-3:

Table 3
Results of the Two Models

	Targets	*Data*	*Agarwal's Solution*	*Proposed Model Solution*
Cash		3,721,056.00	3,721,056.00	3,721,056.00
Marketable securities		33,098,161.00	33,098,161.00	33,098,161.00
Accounts receivable		89,186,217.00	89,186,217.00	89,186,217.00
Inventory		51,884,584.00	51,884,584.00	48,911,465.21
Current liabilities		33,433,346.00	33,433,346.00	33,433,346.00
Fixed assets		20,265,723.00	-	23,238,841.79
Sales		322,370,524.00	-	348,582,626.88
Profit		31,782,509.00	34,809,474.76	34,858,262.69
(Opportunity cost)			3,026,965.76	3,075,753.69
Current ratio	2.00	5.32	5.32	5.23
Working capital turnover ratio	2.50	2.23	-	2.46
Fixed assets turnover ratio	15.00	15.91	-	15.00
Profit margin	0.10	0.10	-	0.10

Source: Primary data

The results from Agarwal's model indicate a Rs. 3,026,965.76 opportunity loss due to excess liquidity, while the results the proposed model indicate a Rs. 3,075,753.69 opportunity loss. The results of the proposed model suggest that excess liquidity (in the form of Rs. 2,973,118.79 of inventory) be converted to fixed assets in order to improve profitability. It is observed that, in the solution, while the working capital turnover ratio, the fixed assets turnover ratio, and the profit margin are close to their targeted values, the current ratio is not.

The deviation variables in the optimal solution are presented in Table-4 (for simplicity, only non-zero values are displayed).

Table 4
Deviational Variables in the Optimal Solution

Constraints	*Deviation Variables*
Liquidity	$d_1^+ = 108{,}050{,}207.21$
Working capital turnover	$d_2^- = 5{,}126{,}256.15$
Fixed assets turnover	
Profit margin	
Oppurtunity cost	
Cash	
Marketable securities	
Accounts receivable	
Inventory	$d_9^- = 2{,}973{,}118.79$
Current liabilities	
Fixed assets	$d_{11}^+ = 2{,}973{,}118.79$
Sales	$d_{12}^+ = 26{,}212{,}102.88$
Profit	$d_{13}^+ = 3{,}075{,}753.69$

Source: Primary data

The deviation variables indicate over-achievement of liquidity far in excess of the targeted level, under-achievement of working capital turnover, and over-achievement of sales. Further, the deviation variables and indicate excess liquidity (inventory) that is to be converted to fixed assets.

The sensitivity analysis of the model to different parameters is presented in Table-5.

Table 5
Sensitivity Analysis of the Optimal Solution

	Opportunity Cost	*% Change*	*Elasticity*
CASH			
+5%	3,110,638.59	1.13%	0.2268
+2.50%	3,093,196.14	0.57%	
0%	3,075,753.69	0.00%	
-2.50%	3,058,311.24	-0.57%	
-5%	3,040,868.79	-1.13%	
MARKETABLE SECURITIES			
+5%	3,386,048.95	10.09%	2.0177
+2.50%	3,230,901.32	5.04%	
0%	3,075,753.69	0.00%	
-2.50%	3,230,901.32	-5.04%	
-5%	2,765,458.43	-10.09%	

ACCOUNTS RECEIVABLE			
+5%	3,911,874.47	27.18%	5.4369
+2.50%	3,493,814.08	13.59%	
0%	3,075,753.69	0.00%	
-2.50%	2,657,693.30	-13.59%	
-5%	2,239,632.90	-27.18%	
INVENTORY			
+5%	3,562,171.66	15.81%	3.1629
+2.50%	3,319,045.81	7.91%	
0%	3,075,753.69	0.00%	
-2.50%	2,832,544.70	-7.91%	
-5%	2,589,335.71	-15.81%	
CURRENT LIABILITIES			
+5%	2,762,334.39	-10.19%	
+2.50%	2,919,034.88	-5.10%	-2.0381
0%	3,075,753.69	0.00%	
-2.50%	3,232,472.50	5.10%	
-5%	3,389,191.31	10.19%	
FIXED ASSETS			
+5%	3,265,744.84	6.18%	1.2354
+2.50%	3,170,749.26	3.09%	
0%	3,075,753.69	0.00%	
-2.50%	2,980,758.11	-3.09%	
-5%	2,885,672.11	-6.18%	

Source: Primary data

It is observed that the results of the proposed model are highly sensitive to changes in accounts receivable (with elasticity +5.4369), followed by inventory (with elasticity +3.1629), current liabilities (with elasticity -2.0381), marketable securities (with elasticity +2.0177), fixed assets (with elasticity +1.2354), and, least of all, cash (with elasticity 0.2268).

DISCUSSIONS

Several studies have stressed the importance of effective working capital management. Agarwal (1988) had formulated a goal programming model for working capital decisions, but it had some serious limitations, especially its over-emphasis on liquidity. The model proposed in this paper extends the scope of Agarwal's model, whilst retaining the concept of a liquidity-profitability trade-off.

The results of the model suggest that working capital, and inventory in particular, should be streamlined to profitability. This approach is thus in conformance with the studies of Rafuse (1996), Cote et al (1999), Garcia-Teruel and Martinez-Solano (2007), Filbeck and Krueger (2005), Singh (2008), and Singh and Pandey (2008). In particular, the relationship between different components of working capital, fixed assets, sales, and profits needs to be examined in greater depth and modeled accordingly. Further, the role of inventory and of inventory turnover needs to be made explicit in the model.

The scope of the proposed model is also a question that has to be examined more carefully. In particular, the nature of the industry may determine the scope of applicability of the model. This would be the case, as the working capital problems of manufacturing companies are quite different from those of, for example, trading companies. Also, the model does not take into account such aspects as seasonality, which would play a role in some industries, especially agro-industries. These could perhaps be addressed by considering an industry-specific priority structure in the model. Another important determinant would be that of operations strategies. For example, it would be interesting to apply the model for companies that operate on "negative working capital," with no investment at all in inventory and receivables, thereby reducing costs and enhancing profitability.

There is vast scope for extending the model proposed in this paper. The proposed model is a static, aggregate-level model; a dynamic/multi-stage micro-model, with appropriate inter-linkages between the different variables, incorporating the working capital cycle concept and time value of money, would give more detailed results. Also, the proposed model has some limitations: it considers a specific form of liquidity and profitability goals/constraints, which may not have taken some other relevant parameters into consideration; and it assumes stable turnover ratios, which may limit its applicability in practice. Further, the proposed model is a linear programming model, and thus deals only with the linear behavior of working capital; non-linearities are not taken into consideration.

REFERENCES

Agarwal, J.D. (1988), "A Goal Programming Model for Working Capital Management," *Finance India*, Vol. 2, Issue 2.

Aksoy, Y. (1990), "Interactive Multiple Objective Decision Making: A Bibliography (1965–1988)," *Management Research News*, Vol. 13, Issue 2.

Chakraborty, K. (2008), "Working Capital and Profitability: An Empirical Analysis of Their Relationship with Reference to Selected Companies in the Indian Pharmaceutical Industry," *The Icfai Journal of Management Research*

Chakraborty, P.K. and Bandopadhyay, K. (2007), "Strategic Working Capital Management: Case of a Turnaround Company," *ICFAI Reader*

Coskun, S., Basligil, H. and Baracli, H. (2008), "A Weakness Determination and Analysis Model for Business Process Improvement," *Business Process Management Journal*, Vol. 14, Issue 2.

Cote, J.M. and Latham, C.K. (1999), "The Merchandising Ratio: A Comprehensive Measure of Working Capital Strategy," *Issues in Accounting Education*; Vol. 14, Issue 2

Filbeck, G., Krueger, G. and Krueger, T.M. (2005), "An Analysis of Working Capital Management Results Across Industries," *Mid-American Journal of Business*, Vol. 20, Issue 2.

Garcia-Teruel, P.J. and Martinez-Solano, P. (2007), "Effects of Working Capital Management on SME Profitability," *International Journal of Managerial Finance*, Vol.3, Issue 2.

Jafar, A. and Sur, D. (2006), "Efficiency of Working Capital Management in Indian Public Enterprises during the Post-liberalization Era: A Case Study of NTPC," *The Icfai Journal of Management Research*

Khorram Shahgol, R. and Okoruwa, A. (1994), "A Goal Programming Approach to Investment Decisions: A Case Study of Fund Allocation Among Different Shopping Malls in Atlanta," *Operational Research*, Vol. 73, Issue 1.

Kim, G.C. and Schniederjans, M.J. (1993), "A Multiple Objective Model for a Just-in-Time Manufacturing System Environment," *International Journal of Operations & Production Management*, Vol.13, Issue 12.

Lee, A.H.I. and Kang, H.-Y. (2008), "A Mixed 0-1 Integer Programming for Inventory Model: A Case Study of TFT-LCD Manufacturing Company in Taiwan," *Kybernetes*, Vol. 37, Issue 1.

Rafuse, M.E. (1996), "Working Capital Management: An Urgent Need to Refocus," *Management Decision*, Vol. 34, Issue 2.

Rees Loren., P.; Clayton, Edward R.; Taylor, III, Bernard W. (1987), "A Linear Goal Programming Model of a Multi-period, Multi-commodity Network Flow Problem," *Business Logistics*, Vol. 8, Issue 1.

Rifai, A.K. (1996), "A Note on the Structure of the Goal-programming Model: Assessment and Evaluation," *International Journal of Operations & Production Management*, Vol.16, Issue 1.

Schniederjans, M.J. and Hoffman, J.J. (1999), "Downsizing Production/Operations with Multi-objective Programming" *International Journal of Operations & Production Management*, Vol.19, Issue 1.

Singh, J.P. and Pandey, S. (2008), "Impact of Working Capital Management in the Profitability of Hindalco Industries Limited," *The Icfai University Journal of Financial Economics*

Singh, P. (2008), "Inventory and Working Capital Management: An Empirical Analysis," *The Icfai University Journal of Accounting Research*

Tabucanon, M.T. and Estraza, M.D.E. (1989), "Multi-objective Production Planning Model for a Garment Factory," *International Journal of Clothing Science and Technology*, Vol.1, Issue 3.

17

GLOBAL RECESSION AND INTERNATIONAL ENTREPRENEURSHIP: AN ASSESSMENT

Durga Madhab Mahapatra, Ashok K. Mohanty

INTRODUCTION

Entrepreneurship is a process of creating something new with value by devoting the necessary time and effort, assuming the accompanying financial, psychic and social risks and satisfaction and independence. International entrepreneurship envisages the undertaking of business activities by entrepreneurs across national boundaries. Ovit and McDougall (2005) define international entrepreneurship as the discovery, enactment, evaluation and exploitation of opportunities across national borders to create future goods and services. Initiatives for dismantling the trade barriers by 144 member countries of the WTO on the one hand and the drive towards opening up the domestic economies through policies of economic liberalisation and globalisation by increasing number of countries in recent times on the other do compel entrepreneurs to move into the world of international business. The period of post-1980s and more particularly 1990s and beyond have given greater fillip to international business. Merchandise trade continues to be a driving force of the world economy. Both in volume and dollar terms, world merchandise trade has grown twice as fast as world output. At the global level, the foreign direct investment (FDI) inflows have reached an estimated $ 1.5 trillion in 2007 surpassing the record level achieved in 2000. The financial and credit crises that began in the later half of 2007 have not noticeably affected FDI inflows. Further, world trade in services nearly tripled in value terms between 1990 and 2005 reaching $ 2.4 trillion. All these developments are indicatives of fast growing international business caused by increasing level of international entrepreneurship. International business focuses on the resources of the globe and objectives of the organisation on global business opportunities and threats. Although, both international and domestic entrepreneurs are having significant concerns for sales, costs and profits, the variations in the relative importance of uncontrollable factors like economics, politics, culture and technology sharply differentiate international entrepreneurship from domestic entrepreneurship. Further-more, the sub-prime crisis of the USA and the accompanying global financial meltdown are impacting and will also continue to affect international business for some years in the future. Against such backdrops, authors in this paper analyse the evolution of international business, strategic issues for conducting business at international level, modes of market entry and managerial response to globalisation and current recessionary trend underway in the world economy for making international entrepreneurship more proactive, efficient and result-oriented.

EVOLUTION OF INTERNATIONAL BUSINESS

The business across the borders of the countries had been carried on since times immemorial. But the business had been limited to international trade until the recent past. The post-World War-II period witnessed an unexpected expansion of national companies into international or multinational companies. Precisely stated, the concept of international business has evolved from international marketing which inturn has evolved from the concept of international trade or export marketing. Originally, the producers in the past used to export their products to nearby countries and gradually extended the exports to far-off countries. From mere exporting, the traders/businessmen put efforts to create market for their products abroad by adopting suitable marketing strategy based on the blending of suitable product, price, promotion and place or physical distribution mixes. This is how export marketing or international trade has given way international marketing. With the passage of time, the multinational companies which were producing products in their home countries and marketing their products in various foreign countries before 1980s, started locating their plants and other manufacturing facilities in foreign/host countries. Later they started producing in one foreign country and marketing in other foreign countries. In this way, international marketing has given birth to international business.

STRATEGIC ISSUES IN INTERNATIONAL ENTREPRENEURSHIP

Entrepreneurial abilities and skills of greater depth are needed when entrepreneurs expand their activities from mere exporting (i.e., international trade) to international marketing and finally to international business. Four strategic issues are of paramount importance to the international entrepreneur or an entrepreneur thinking about going international viz., (1) the allocation of responsibility between the parent company and its subsidiaries; (2) the nature of planning, reporting and control systems to be used throughout the international operations; (3) the appropriate organizational structure for conducting international operations and (4) the degree of standardization possible. The success of international business hinges on these four strategic issues taken up by the entrepreneur in right perspectives. For example, when the entrepreneur makes first move into international business, has to adopt highly centralised decision-making process. With gaining experience in international business over years, the international entrepreneur has to decentralise the international operations and hence decentralised decision-making in the appropriate decision-making strategy for adopting them. Basing on the degree of centralization/decentralization, appropriate planning reporting and controlling systems are to be devised. However, without proper organizational structure, the planning, reporting and control mechanisms can hardly work to enable the international entrepreneur to realise the goals of acquiring foreign markets, earning higher profits and foreign exchanges, reducing risks, etc. Finally, much of tangible results emanate from the strategy of standardization drive adopted by the international entrepreneur. For example, standardization is possible in the product or services offered, planning, reporting, control systems and even organizational structure adopted by the entrepreneurs in the international business.

MODES OF MARKET ENTRY BY INTERNATIONAL ENTREPRENEUR

An entrepreneur can enter into international business broadly in three modes, i.e., exporting, non-equity arrangements and equity arrangements. But the choice of entry method and the mode of operating overseas is dependent on the goals of the entrepreneur and the company's strengths and weaknesses. The three modes of market entry by the international entrepreneur are explained as follows:

Exporting: Exporting is the mode through which an entrepreneur may start doing international business. It is selling goods made in one country to another country. Exporting may be direct exporting or indirect exporting. If the entrepreneur wants involvement without any financial commitment, direct exporting through independent distributors or the company's own overseas sales office is a way to get involved in international business. In other words, direct exporting involves selling of goods to another country by taking care of transactions. In case of indirect exporting, selling of goods to another country takes place through a person in entrepreneur's home country. This method of exporting involves the least amount of knowledge and risk of the entrepreneur as foreign purchaser or an export management firm makes purchase of product in the local market of entrepreneur and sells such product abroad.

Non-Equity Arrangement: Non-equity arrangements of doing international business envisages non-involvement of any investment in the transaction. This kind of international business may be carried out mainly in three ways, viz., licensing, turnkey project and management contract. Licensing involves an entrepreneur who is a manufacturer (licensee), giving a foreign manufacturer (licensor) the right to use a patent, trademark, technology, production process or product in return for a payment of a royalty. The licensing arrangement is the most appropriate when the entrepreneur has no intention of entering a particular market through exporting or direct investment. The second method of doing international business is the commissioning of a turnkey project in a foreign country by a foreign entrepreneur. The third non-equity mode of doing international business is the management contract. Several entrepreneurs have successfully entered international business by contracting their management techniques and managerial skills. It is a method for doing a specific international task and the entrepreneur could easily enter the foreign markets that would otherwise be closed due to the want of large equity investment.

Equity Mode of Entry into International Business: The wholly owned foreign subsidiaries have been the preferred mode of ownership for entrepreneurs using direct foreign investment for doing business in international markets. Joint ventures and minority and majority equity positions are also methods for making direct foreign investment. Under joint ventures, two companies join together to form a third company either for purchasing local knowledge and an already established marketing or manufacturing facility or when a rapid entry into a market is needed. In minority equity mode, an entrepreneur or a company occupies less than 50% ownership positions in the company of a foreign market either to tap the source of raw materials or relatively competitive market for its products. Entrepreneurs have used minority positions to gain a foothold or experience in a market before making a major commitment of investment.

Another equity method for the entrepreneur to enter international market is by purchasing a majority interest in a foreign business i.e., having more than 50 per cent ownership stakes. The majority interest allows the entrepreneur to obtain marginal control while maintaining the acquired firm's local identity. An entrepreneur using 100 per cent ownership to engage international business assumes complete control. Mergers and acquisitions have also emerged as important modes of doing international business. During the time of intense merger activity, entrepreneurs may spend significant times searching for a firm to acquire and finalising the transaction. Mergers may be of several types like horizontal merger, vertical merger, product extension merger, market extension merger, diversified activity merger. Mergers are a sound strategic option for an entrepreneur when synergy is present. Economics of scale; unused tax credits, benefits accruing out of combination of complementary resources, etc. are some of the positive outcomes of mergers in the international arena.

GLOBALISATION AND INTERNATIONAL ENTREPRENEURSHIP

Since 1990s, the business dynamics is undergoing a major transformation in the wake of globalisation. Globalisation essentially means integrating the economy of a country with rest of the world. IMF defines globalisation as the growing interdependence of countries worldwide through increasing volume and varieties of cross border transactions in goods and services and international capital flows and also through the more rapid and widespread diffusion of technology. Globalisation is a new world of mega competition for nations and their enterprises. Peter F. Drucker in his book "Management: Challenges of 21st Century" has viewed globalization as "all institutions have to make global competitiveness a strategic goal. No institution, whether a business, a university or a hospital can hope to survive, let alone succeeds unless it matches up to standards set by leaders in the field at any place in the world". Openness and competition being the hallmarks of globalisation, entrepreneurs both domestic and international have to learn how to live with such competition. Emerging markets and emerging technologies present both challenges and opportunities for business and individual entrepreneurs in focussing on competitive advantages for their firms (Thukral *et al.*, 2008). Variables like firm building capabilities, managerial skills, substantial supply of skilled labour and connection to markets are crucial for the initial development of new economy clusters in technology and innovation driven entrepreneurship activities. Subsequently, increasing social returns and external effects arise after the clusters have been completely formed. The success of Silicon Valley is a direct evidence of these conditions (Brushenan *et al.*, 2001). Further, an examination of the rapid growth of emerging markets like China, India and Vietnam identifies two driving forces for their growth; First economic reforms have changed prevailing laws, regulations and implicit rules that dominate economic activity. Second, all three countries have experienced the emergence of new companies in which entrepreneurship plays a crucial role (Daokui Li, 2006). In case of advanced economies like US, Germany, UK, etc., the spectacular economic performance can be attributed to strong growth of productivity caused by entrepreneurs playing critical role in the sphere of generating new ideas and technologies, developing new products and successfully bringing these products to the market. Evidences also reveal that entrepreneurship boosts economic performance in transitional economies.

WORLD FINANCIAL CRISIS AND INTERNATIONAL ENTREPRENEURSHIP

The current financial crisis the world is passing through, has its origin in the US. This has started with upheaval created by sub-prime crisis in 2007 in the world's largest and most significant US financial markets. Later in 2008, the whole of the investment and banking sector were plagued with losses and now this has impacted the economy of the whole world. According to ILO estimates, 20 million people will be rendered jobless and the world unemployment level will be raised to 210 million people by the end of 2009. Apart from real estate and construction sectors, the other sectors include service in general and finance, IT, BPOs, etc. in the particular. The automotive sector and even manufacturing sectors are likely to be affected adversely. Going by the latest forecast of IMF, the economies of the US and Europe would virtually stop growing and Japan would experience only 0.5 growth rate. The ongoing recessionary trend in the world economy would impact individuals by way of job-loss and enterprise and entrepreneurial activities to go slow till the crisis is over.

As the economies of most of the countries of the world have been integrated due to economic liberalization and globalization, international entrepreneurship will be hurt and would take a back seat. At global level, entrepreneurships have to adjust till the slump is over.

CONCLUSION

International business is becoming increasingly important to more and more entrepreneurs and to their country's economy. Entrepreneurship is key to the transition both in small start ups and in restructuring large enterprises. In international entrepreneurship, the entrepreneurs who takes business activities across national boundaries, confronts complex decision-making process due to the prevalence of variable economic, social, legal, political and cultural environments in various countries. The foregoing analysis reveal that an entrepreneur will enter international business arena broadly through three modes viz., exporting, non-equity and equity mode. Selection of a particular mode will depend on the objectives of the firm on the one hand and the skill and expertise of the entrepreneur to make capital out of the prevailing socio-economic, political and legal environment in the host country. Further, the analysis reveals that the on-going global economic recession would decelerate the growth of international entrepreneurship till the phase of economic slowdown is reversed.

REFERENCES

Daokui Li, David, *et al.* (2006), "Institutional Entrepreneurs", *American Economic Review*, Vol. 96, Issue 2, May, pp. 358-362.

Ellerman, D. (1996), "Entrepreneurship Development in Transitional Economies", *World Bank*, June.

——(1999), Entrepreneurship Development Colombo Plan Staff College for Technician Education, Manila and Centre for Research and Industrial Staff Performance (An Indo-German Technical Cooperation Project), Tata McGraw Hill Publishing Company Limited, New Delhi.

Hoenig, T. (2005), "Entrepreneurship and Growth", *Entrepreneurs Experience: A Town Hall Meeting*, Entrepreneurs Exchange, Kansas City, Missouri, April 28.

Khanna, T. (2008), *Billions of Entrepreneurs: How China and India are Reshaping Their Future and Yours*, Harvard Business School Press.

Oviat, B & McDougal, P. (2005), "Toward a Theory of International New Ventures", *Journal of International Business Studies*, Vol. 36, No. 1, pp. 29-41.

Peters, H. (2000), "International Entrepreneurship Opportunities", *Entrepreneurship*, Tata McGraw Hill Publishing Co., 4th Edition, New Delhi, pp. 88-168.

Thurkal, I.S., James V.R., *et al.* (2008), "Entrepreneurship, Emerging Technologies, Emerging Markets", *International Small Business Journal*, Vol. 26, Issue 1, February, pp. 101-116.

Venkataramany, S., "Globalisation of Entrepreneurship: Overwhelming Institutional Response in Favour of SMEs in India" 2008 EABR & TIC Conference Proceedings, Rothenberg, Germany.

Zahra, S.A. & Gerry, G. (2002), "International Entrepreneurship: The Current Status of the Field and Future Research Agenda" in Hitt, M.A., Ireland, S.M. *et al.*, *Strategic Entrepreneurship Creating New Mindset*, Oxford, Blackwell Publishers.

18

CHOICE OF FINANCIAL INSTRUMENTS FOR INDIAN CORPORATE IN FINANCIAL MARKET

Ankur Srivastava, Shashank Dublish

INTRODUCTION

Financial instruments are an important component of financial system in an economy. Various constituents of financial system viz. financial institutions, financial services, practices and procedures, financial markets and financial instruments, are closely inter – mixed and operate in conjunction with one another. Financial Instruments refers to financial claims, financial assets and securities. As per AS-31, a financial instrument is any contract that gives rise to a financial asset of one entity and a financial liability or equity instrument of another entity. A financial asset is any asset that is (a) Cash; (b) An equity instrument of another entity; (c) A contractual right: (i) To receive cash or another financial asset from another entity; or (ii) To exchange financial assets or financial liabilities with another entity under conditions that are potentially favourable to the entity; or (d) A contract that will or may be settled in the entity's own equity instruments and is: (i) A non-derivative for which the entity is or may be obliged to receive a variable number of the entity's own equity instruments; or (ii) A derivative that will or may be settled other than by the exchange of a fixed amount of cash or another financial asset for a fixed number of the entity's own equity instruments. For this purpose the entity's own equity instruments do not include instruments that are themselves contracts for the future receipt or delivery of the entity's own equity instruments. A financial liability is any liability that is (a) A contractual obligation: (i) To deliver cash or another financial asset to another entity; or (ii) To exchange financial assets or financial liabilities with another entity under conditions that are potentially unfavourable to the entity; or (b) A contract that will or may be settled in the entity's own equity instruments and is (i) A non-derivative for which the entity is or may be obliged to deliver a variable number of the entity's own equity instruments; or (ii) A derivative that will or may be settled other than by the exchange of a fixed amount of cash or another financial asset for a fixed number of the entity 's own equity instruments. For this purpose the entity's own equity instruments do not include instruments that are themselves contracts for the future receipt or delivery of the entity's own equity instruments.An equity instrument is any contract that evidences a residual interest in the assets of an entity after deducting all of its liabilities.

Financial instruments can be categorized by form depending on whether they are cash instruments or derivative instruments: Cash instruments are financial instruments whose value is determined directly by markets. They can be divided into securities, which are readily transferable, and other cash instruments such as loans and deposits, where both borrower and lender have to agree on a transfer. Derivative instruments are financial instruments which derive their value from the value and characteristics of one or more underlying assets. They can be divided into exchange-traded derivatives and over-the-counter (OTC) derivatives. Alternatively, financial instruments can be categorized by "asset class" depending on whether they are equity based (reflecting ownership of the issuing entity) or debt based (reflecting a loan the investor has made to the issuing entity). If it is debt, it can be further categorized into short term (less than one year) or long term. Foreign Exchange instruments and transactions are neither debt nor equity based and belong in their own category.

EQUITY & PREFERENCE INSTRUMENTS

According to the section 2(46) of the Company's Act 1956, share means a part in the share capital of the company and it also includes stock except where a distinction between stock and share capital is made expressed or implied.As per the provision of section 85 of the Companies Act, 1956, the share capital of a company consists of two classes of shares, namely: Preference Shares & Equity Shares. Preference Shares: According to Sec 85(1), of the Companies Act, 1956, a preference share is one, which carries the following two preferential rights: a) The payment of dividend at fixed rate before paying dividend to equity shareholders; b) The return of capital at the time of winding up of the company, before the payment to the equity shareholder.

Both the rights must exist to make any share a preference share and should be clearly mentioned in the Articles of Association. Preference shareholders do not have any voting rights, but in the following conditions they can enjoy the voting rights: in case of cumulative preference shares, if dividend is outstanding for more than two years, in case of non-cumulative preference shares, if dividend is outstanding for more than three years, on any resolution of winding up, on any resolution of capital reduction. Equity shares: According to section 85 (2), of Companies Act, 1956, Equity share can be defined as the share, which is not preference shares. In other words equity shares are those shares, which do not have the following preferential rights: Preference of dividend over others, & Preference for repayment of capital over others at the time of winding up of the company. These shares are also known as 'Risk Capital', because they get dividend on the balance of profit if any, left after payment of dividend on preference shares and also at the time of winding up of the company, they are paid from the balance asset left after payment of other liabilities and preference share capital. Apart from this they have to claim dividend only, if the company in its A. G. M. declares the dividend. The rate of dividend on such shares is not pre-determined, but it depends on the profit earned by the company. The equity shareholders have the right to vote on each and every resolution placed before the company and the holders of these shares are the real owners of the company.

Private placement of shares: According to Section 81 (1A) of the Companies Act, 1956 private placement of shares implies issue and allotment of shares to a selected group of persons such U.T.I., L.I.C. etc. in other words; an issue which is not a public issue but offered to a select group of persons is called Private Placement of shares.

Preferential allotment: A preferential allotment is one that is made at a pre-determined price to the pre-identified people who wish to take a strategic stake in the company such as promoters, venture capitalists, financial institutions, buyers of companies products ore its suppliers. In other such a case, the allottees will not sell their securities in the open market for a minimum period of three years from the date of allotment. This period is known as the lock-in-period.

The preferential allotment can take place only if three-fourths of the shareholders agree to the issue on preferential basis. S.E.B.I. has prescribed that the minimum price of such an issue has to be an average of highs and lows of the 26 week preceding the date on which the board resolves to make the preferential allotment.

Employee stock option plan: In order to retain high caliber employees or to give them a sense of belonging, companies may offer their equity shares to be purchased at their will. Such scheme is called Employee stock option plan (ESOP). Following are the characteristics of this scheme: ESOP implies the right, but not an obligation, the employee has a right to exercise the option of purchase of shares within the vesting period, i.e., the time period during which the scheme remains in operation, any share issued under the scheme of ESOP shall be locked-in for a minimum period of one year from the date of allotment.

Buy-back of shares: The term buy-back of share implies the act of purchasing its own shares by a company either from free reserves, securities premium or proceeds of any shares or securities. According to Section 77A of the Companies Act 1956, a company can buy its own shares either from the: existing equity shareholders on a proportionate basis, Open market, Odd lot shareholders, employees of the company pursuant to a scheme of stock option or sweat equity.

Right shares: Under Section 81 of the Companies Act, the existing shareholders have a right to subscribe, in their existing proportion, to the fresh issue of capital or to reject the offer, or sell their rights. The existing shareholders can authorize the company by passing a special resolution to offer such shares to the public.

DEBT INSTRUMENTS

A tradable form of a loan is normally termed as Debt Instruments. They are usually obligations of issuer with regards to certain future cash flows representing interest and principal, which the issuer would pay to the legal owner of the instrument. There are various types of fixed income instruments, which cater to the needs of both investors and issuers. These instruments can be classified on the basis of interest, time duration, etc. Further, there are also derived fixed income instruments. Certain hedge instruments are also available that reduce risk. The classification of fixed instruments is given below: 1. Fixed Income Products; Deposit & Fixed Deposit 2. Interest Based Bonds: Coupon Bonds & Zero Coupon Bonds. 3. Derived Instruments: These instruments are not direct debt instruments. Instead they derive their value from other debt instruments: Mortgage Bonds, Pass through Certificates (PTCs), Participation Certificates (PCs). 4. Benchmarked

Instruments: There are certain debt instruments; wherein the fixed income earned is based on some bench mark rate. For instance, the Floating Interest rate Bonds are benchmarked to either the LIBOR, MIBOR etc: Floating Interest Rate & Inflation linked Bonds (Inflation Index Bonds)

Money Market Instruments includes Call/Notice Money, Treasury Bills, Inter-Bank Term Money, Certificate of Deposits, Inter Corporate Deposits, Commercial Papers & Commercial Bills.

Hedging Instruments are certain hedge instruments that help to reduce the risk of investing in Fixed income instruments: Interest Rate Swaps, Interest Rate Options & Swaptions

Corporate Debentures A Debenture is a debt security issued by a company (called the Issuer), which offers to pay interest in lieu of the money borrowed for a certain period. In essence it represents a loan taken by the issuer who pays an agreed rate of interest during the lifetime of the instrument and repays the principal normally, unless otherwise agreed, on maturity. These are long-term debt instruments issued by private sector companies. These are issued in denomination as low as Rs. 1000 and have maturity ranging between one and ten years. Long maturity debentures are rarely issued, as investors are not comfortable with such maturities. Debentures enable investors to reap the dual benefits of adequate security and good returns. Unlike Fixed and Bank Deposit they can be transferred from one party to another by using transfer form. Debentures are normally issued in physical form. However, corporates/PSUs have started issuing debentures in Demat form. Generally, debentures are less liquid as compared to PSU bonds and their liquidity is inversely proportional to the residual maturity. Debentures can be secured or unsecured. Debentures are divided into different categories on the basis of: Convertibility of the instrument & Security.

FIXED INCOME INSTRUMENTS

Deposits serve as medium of saving and as a means of payment and are a very important variable in the national economy. A bank basically has three types of deposits: 1. Time deposits are those funds that are deposited by savers on the basis of obtaining the same on the maturity of certain period of time, 2. Saving deposits are deposits that are maintained on a continuous basis on which the bank offers a certain interest. There is certain limit on the number of withdrawals from the account by means of a cheque on this account. Interest is allowed on minimum monthly balances and not on daily basis, 3.Current Account - A current account is a running account. This account does not provide any interest and hence the account provides no limit on the number of withdrawals from this account. 4. Fixed Deposits are sums accepted by most of the NBFCs, corporates and banks. The amount of deposits that may be raised by NBFCs and corporates is linked to its net worth and rating. *However, the* interest rate that may be offered by a NBFC & corporate is regulated. The maximum interest rate that may be offered by these companies is 15%, provided the company has submitted its application for registration and has two years of good track record after its incorporation. The deposits offered by NBFCs are not insured whereas the deposits accepted by most banks are insured upto a maximum of Rs.1,00,000.

Interest-based Instruments

Coupon Bonds : Bonds typically pay interest periodically at the pre specified rate of interest. The annual rate at which the interest is paid is known as the coupon rate or simply the coupon. Interest is usually paid every half-year though some bonds pay interest monthly, quarterly, annually or at some other frequency. The dates on which the interest payments are made are known as the coupon due dates. *Zero Coupon Bonds:* A plain bond is offered at its face value, earns a stream of interest till redemption and is redeemed with or without a premium on maturity. A zero coupon bond is issued at a discount to its face value with no periodic interest and is redeemed at face value on maturity.

Derived Instruments are not direct debt instruments. Instead they derive value from other debt instruments. Mortgage bonds, Pass Through Certificates etc fall under this category. *Mortgage Bonds:* Mortgage backed bond is a collateralized term-debt offering. Pledged collateral backs every issue of such bonds. Eligible collateral will be a property that can be pledged as a security. The bonds are secured by a first charge on the pledged collateral and delivered to the trustee of the issue. This ensures that a smooth liquidation takes place in the event of default on the part of the issuer of bonds. The terms of these bonds are like any other bonds in the market with semi-annual or quarterly payments of interest and final bullet payment of principal.

Pass Through Certificates (PTCs)

When mortgages are pooled together and undivided interest in the pool is sold, pass-through securities are created. The term 'undivided' in this context means that each holder of the security has a proportionate interest in each cash flow generated in the pool. The pass-through securities promise that the cash flow from the underlying mortgages would be passed through to the holders of the securities in the form of monthly payments of interest and principal.

Participation Certificates (PCs)

These are strictly inter-bank instruments confined to the Scheduled Commercial Banks. There are 2 types: 1) PCs with Risk Sharing - This instrument provide flexibility in the Credit portfolio of banks. These PCs are issued for 91-180 days in respect of certain types of Loan Advances. Interest is to be determined between the issuing and the participating bank freely. 2) PCs without Risk Sharing - This instrument are a money market instrument with tenure not exceeding 90 days. The two contracting banks determine the interests on such PCs.

BENCHMARKED INSTRUMENTS

There are certain debt instruments, wherein the income earned is based on a benchmark. For instance, the Floating Interest rate Bonds are benchmarked to either the LIBOR, MIBOR etc.

Floating Interest Rate : Floating rate of interest simply means that the rate of interest is variable. Periodically, the interest rate payable for the next period is set with reference to a benchmark market rate agreed upon by both the lender and the borrower. The benchmark market rate in India is NSE MIBOR and in the overseas markets its LIBOR or US Treasury Bill Rate. For- e.g., A LIBOR +1% indicates that the interest earned on that bond will be 100 basis points higher than the going LIBOR rate at that particular time.

Inflation linked bonds: A bond is considered indexed for inflation if the payment of coupons is indexed by reference to the change in the value of a general price or wage index over the term of the instrument. The options are that either the interest payments are adjusted for inflation or the principal repayment or both.

MONEY MARKET INSTRUMENTS

Call/Notice Money

Call/Notice money is an amount borrowed or lent on demand for a very short period. If the period is more than one day and upto 14 days it is called 'Notice money' otherwise the amount is known as 'Call money'. Intervening holidays and/or Sundays are excluded for this purpose. No collateral security is required to cover these transactions. The call market enables the banks and institutions to even out their day-to-day deficits and surpluses of money. Commercial banks, Co-operative Banks and primary dealers are allowed to borrow and lend in this market for adjusting their cash reserve requirements with the RBI. Specified All-India Financial Institutions, Mutual Funds and certain specified entities are allowed to access Call/Notice money only as lenders. It is a completely inter-bank market hence non-bank entities are not allowed access to this market. Interest rates in the call and notice money market is market determined. In view of the short tenure of such transactions, both the borrowers and the lenders are required to have current accounts with the Reserve Bank of India. It serves as an outlet for deploying funds on short-term basis to the lenders having steady inflow of funds.

Treasury Bills

In the short term, the lowest risk category instruments are the Treasury Bills (TBs) issued by Central government. RBI on behalf of central government issues them at a prefixed day and for a fixed amount. The TBs are issued with varying maturity usually not exceeding more than one year. 1. 91 - day T-bill – (Tenor is of 91 days) Its auction is on every Wednesday of the week and issued on following Friday. The notified amount for this auction is *Rs. 500 crore.* 2. 182 - day T-bill – (Tenor is of 182 days) Its auction is on every alternate Wednesday (which is not a reporting week) and issued on Friday. The notified amount for this auction is *Rs. 500 crore.* 3. 364 - Day T-bill – (Tenor is of 364 days) Its auction is on every alternate Wednesday (which is a reporting week) and issued on Friday. The notified amount for this auction is *Rs. 1000 crore.* A considerable part of the central government's borrowing happens through Treasury Bills of various maturities. Based on the bids received at the auctions, RBI decides the cut off yield and accepts all bids below this yield. Banks are the major investors in these instruments as they can park their short-term surpluses and also since it forms part of their SLR investments. Besides banks other investors in TBs are insurance companies, primary dealers, mutual funds, FIs and FIIs. These TBs, which are issued at a discount, can be traded in the market. Most of the time, unless the investor requests specifically, they are issued not as securities but as entries in the Subsidiary General Ledger (SGL), which is maintained by RBI. The transactions cost on TBs are non-existent and trading is considerably high in each bill, immediately after its issue and immediately before its redemption. The yield on TBs is mainly dependent on the rates prevalent in Call/Notice market. Low yield on TBs, generally a result of high liquidity in banking system as indicated by low call rates, would divert the funds from this market to other markets. This would be particularly so, if banks already hold the minimum stipulated amount (SLR) in government paper.

Inter-bank Term Money: Inter bank market for deposits of maturity beyond 14 days and upto three months is *referred to as the term money market. The specified entities are not allowed to lend beyond 14 days.*

Certificate of Deposits: After treasury bills, the next lowest risk category investment option is the certificate of deposit (CD) issued by banks and FIs. Allowed in 1989, CDs were one of RBI's measures to deregulate the cost of funds for banks and FIs. A CD is a negotiable promissory note, secure and short term (up to a year) in nature. A CD is issued at a discount to the face value, the discount rate being negotiated between the issuer and the investor. Though RBI allows CDs upto one-year maturity, the maturity most quoted in the market is for 90 days. The secondary market for this instrument does not have much depth but the instrument itself is highly secure. CDs are issued by banks and FIs mainly to augment funds by attracting deposits from corporates, high net worth individuals, trusts, etc. the issue of *CDs reached a high in the last two years as banks faced with a reducing deposit base secured fund by these means.* Banks, which do not have large branch networks with lower deposit base, use this instrument to raise funds. The rates on these deposits are determined by various factors. Low call rates would mean higher liquidity in the market. Also the interest rate on one-year bank deposits acts as a lower barrier for the rates in the market.

Inter-corporate Deposits

Apart from CPs, corporates also have access to another market called the Inter Corporate Deposits (ICD) market. An ICD is an unsecured loan extended by one corporate to another. Existing mainly as a refuge for low rated corporates, this market allows funds surplus corporates to lend to other corporates. Also the better-rated corporates can borrow from the banking system and lend in this market. As the cost of funds for a corporate in much higher than a bank, the rates in this market are higher than those in the other markets. ICDs are unsecured, and hence the risk inherent in high. The ICD market is not well organised with very little information available publicly about transaction details.

Commercial Papers

CPs are negotiable short-term unsecured promissory notes with fixed maturities, issued by well rated companies generally sold at a discount basis. Companies can issue CPs either directly to the investors or through banks / merchant banks (called dealers). These are basically instruments evidencing the liability of the issuer to pay the holder in due course a fixed amount (face value of the instrument) on the specified due date. These instruments are normally issued in the multiples of five crore for 30/45/60/90/120/180/270/364 days maturity.

Commercial Bills

Bills of exchange are negotiable instruments drawn by the seller (drawer) of the goods on the buyer (drawee) of the goods for the value of the goods delivered. These bills are called trade bills. These trade bills are called commercial bills when they are accepted by commercial banks. The RBI introduced the Bills Market scheme (BMS) in 1952 and the scheme was later modified into New Bills Market scheme (NBMS) in 1970. Under the scheme, commercial banks can rediscount the bills, which were originally discounted by them, with approved institutions (viz., Commercial Banks, Development Financial Institutions, Mutual Funds, Primary Dealer, etc.). With the intention of reducing paper movements and facilitate multiple rediscounting, the RBI introduced an instrument called Derivative Usance Promissory Notes (DUPN). So the need for physical transfer of bills has been waived and the bank that originally discounts the bills only draws DUPN. These DUPNs are sold to investors in convenient lots of maturities (from 15 days upto 90 days) on the basis of genuine trade bills, discounted by the discounting bank.

HEDGING INSTRUMENTS

There are certain hedge instruments that help to reduce the risk of investing in Fixed income instruments.

Interest Rate Swaps

A standard fixed to floating interest rate swap is an agreement between two parties in which each contracts to make payments to the other on particular dates in the future till a specified termination date. One party, known as the fixed rate payer, makes fixed payments all of which are determined at the outset. The other party known as the floating rate payer will make payments the size of which depends upon the future evolution of a specified interest rate index.

Interest Rate Options

Interest rate options are of two types, call option and put option. A call option on interest rate gives the holder the right to borrow funds for a specified duration at a specified interest rate without an obligation to do so. A put option on interest rate gives the holder the right to invest funds for a specified duration at a specified return without an obligation to do so. In both cases, the buyer of the option must pay the seller an up-front premium stated as a fraction of the face value of the contract.

Swaptions

Swaptions are options to enter into a swap at a specified future date, the terms of the swap being fixed at the time the swaption is transacted.

Ready Forward Contracts / Repos

It is a transaction in which two parties agree to sell and repurchase the same security. Under such an agreement the seller sells specified securities with an agreement to repurchase the same at a mutually decided future date and a price. Similarly, the buyer purchases the securities with an agreement to resell the same to the seller on an agreed date in future at a predetermined price. Such a transaction is called a Repo when viewed from the prospective of the seller of securities (the party acquiring fund) and Reverse Repo when described from the point of view of the supplier of funds. Thus, whether a given agreement is termed as Repo or a Reverse Repo depends on which party initiated the transaction. The lender or buyer in a Repo is entitled to receive compensation for use of funds provided to the counter party. Effectively the seller of the security borrows money for a period of time (Repo period) at a particular rate of interest mutually agreed with the buyer of the security who has lent the funds to the seller. The rate of interest agreed upon is called the Repo rate. The Repo rate is negotiated by the counter parties independently of the coupon rate or rates of the underlying securities and is influenced by overall money market conditions. The Repo/Reverse Repo transaction can only be done at Mumbai between parties approved by RBI and in securities as approved by RBI (Treasury Bills, Central/State Govt securities).

DERIVATIVE INSTRUMENTS

A derivative is an instrument whose value depends on the values of one or more basic underlying variables. SCRA act 1956 defines 'derivatives ' as, A security derived from a debt instrument, share, loan whether secured or unsecured, risk instrument or contract for differences or any other form of security. A contract which derives its value from the prices or index of prices of underlying securities. : Each derivative product has an "underlying" associated with it, the value of the derivative depends on, among other things, the value of the underlying. The underlying can be Physical commodities: Coffee, Crude oil, Wheat etc. or Financial assets: Currencies, Stocks, Bonds, etc. or Financial Prices: Interest rates, stock indices & Other Derivatives, Recently: Weather derivatives, emission derivatives etc.

Derivative products initially emerge as a hedging device against fluctuation against commodity prices, commodity-linked solemnly remained the sole form of such products for almost three hundred years. Financial derivatives came into spotlight in the post-1970 period due to growing instability in the financial markets. However, since their emergence these products have become very popular by 1990's, they accounted for about two-third of the total transactions in derivative products. In recent years, the market for financial derivatives has grown tremendously in terms of variety of instruments available, their complexity and also turnover. In the class of equity derivatives the world over, futures and options on stock indices have gained popularity than on individual stocks, especially among Institutional investors, who are major users of index-linked derivatives. Even small investors find these useful due to high correlation of the popular indexes with various portfolios and ease of use.

Various Types of Derivative Products: Forward contracts: A forward contract is an agreement to buy or sell an asset at a certain time in the future for a certain price (the delivery or contract price).

Futures: A futures contract, like a forward contract is an agreement between two parties to exchange one asset for another, at a specified date in the future.

Swaps: Swaps exploit some capital market imperfection or special tax legislation or differences in financial norms to provide savings in borrowing costs or enhanced return on assets.

Options: An option is a contract in which the *buyer* of the option has the right to buy or sell a specified quantity of an asset, at a pre-specified price, on or upto a specified date if he chooses to do so; however, *there is no obligation for him to do so.*

Option on Swaps (Swaption): Swaptions, as the name indicates are options to enter into a swap at a specified future date, the terms of the swap being fixed at the time the swaption is transacted. *Exchange Traded Derivatives:* Derivatives which are traded on an exchange are called 'exchange-traded derivatives'. Trades on an exchange generally take place with anonymity. Generally go through the clearing corporation. *OTC Derivatives:* A derivative contract which is privately negotiated is called the OTC derivative. OTC trades have no anonymity and they generally do not go through a clearing corporation. Every derivative product can either trade OTC or an exchange. OTC future contracts are called 'forwards' (or exchange-traded forwards are called futures). Features of OTC compared to exchange–traded: Counter party risk is decentralized and located within individual institutions, No formal centralized limits on individual positions, No formal rules for risk and burden sharing, No formal rules or mechanisms for ensuring market stability, & No regulation from the authorities of exchanges.

Index Derivatives: It is a type of derivative contract which have the Index as the underlying asset. The popular Index derivative products are Index futures and Index options. The very first derivative instrument in the NSE's market was Index futures contract with NIFTY as the underlying, and then followed by Index options and sectoral indexes like CNX IT and Bank Nifty contracts.

NSE 's Derivative Market: Derivative trading on NSE started with the instrument S&P CNX Nifty Index futures. It started on June 12th ,2000. Trade in Index options commenced on June 4, 2001. Single stock futures were launched on November 9, 2001. NSE is the largest derivatives exchange in India. Three contracts like 1month, 2month & 3month contracts are available. New contract is introduced on the next trading day following the expiry of the contract..

CURRENCY FUTURES

Financial futures contracts were first introduced by the International Monetary Markets Division of Chicago Mercantile Exchange, in order to meet the needs for managing currency risks, and promoted by a galloping growth in international business. London International Financial Futures and Options Exchange (LIFFE), set up in 1982 had been dealing in currency futures, but have restricted their activity to interest-rate futures.A currency futures contract is a derivative financial instrument that acts as a conduit to transfer risks attributable to volatility in prices of currencies. It is a contractual agreement between a buyer and a seller for the purchase and sale of a particular currency at a specific future date., at a predetermined price.

Exotics Options

Barrier Options: Options die or become alive when the underlying touches a trigger level. Other Exotic options are

1. Preference Options– Decide call or put later.
2. Asian Options.
3. Look-back Options– Payoff based on most favourable rate during option life
4. Average Rate Option– Payoff based on average value of the underlying exchange rate during option life.
5. Bermudan Options– exercise at discrete points of time during option life. Sort of compromise between American and European options.
6. Compound Options– Option to buy an option.
7. Other innovative combinations.

FINANCIAL SWAPS

It represents an asset-liability management technique which permits a borrower (investor) to access one market and then exchange the liability (asset) for another type of liability (asset) Swaps by themselves are *not* a funding instrument; they are a device to obtain the desired form of financing indirectly which otherwise might be inaccessible or too expensive. Swaps exploit some capital market imperfection or special tax legislation or differences in financial norms to provide savings in borrowing costs or enhanced return on assets. Swaps may also be used purely for hedging purposes. All swaps involve exchange of a series of periodic payments between two parties, usually through an intermediary which is normally a large international financial institution which runs a "swap book". The two major types are *interest rate swaps (also known as coupon swaps)* and *currency swaps*. The two are combined to give a *cross-currency interest rate swap*. Other less common structures are equity swaps, commodity swaps : *Liability swaps* exchange one kind of liability for another *Asset swaps* exchange incomes from two different types of assets. *Interest Rate Swaps*: A standard fixed-to-floating interest rate swap, known in the market jargon as a *plain vanilla coupon swap* (also referred to as "exchange of borrowings") is an agreement between two parties in which each contracts to make payments to the other on particular dates in the future till a specified *termination date* . One party, known as the *fixed rate payer*, makes fixed payments all of which are determined at the outset. The other party known as the *floating rate payer* will make payments the size of which depends upon the future evolution of a specified interest rate index. A number of variants of the standard structure are found in practice a *zero-coupon swap* has only one fixed payment at maturity, a *basis swap* involves an exchange of two floating payments, each tied to a different market index, in a *callable swap* the fixed rate payer has the option to terminate the agreement prior to scheduled maturity while in a *puttable swap* the fixed rate receiver has such an option, In an *extendable swap*, one of the parties has the option to extend the swap beyond the scheduled termination date, In a *forward start swap*, the effective date is several months even years after the trade date so that a borrower with a future funding need can take advantage of prevailing favourable swap rates to lock in the terms of a swap to be entered into at a later date, An *indexed principal swap* is a variant in which the principal is not fixed for the life of the swap but tied to the level of interest rates - as rates decline, the notional principal rises according to some formula.

Currency Swaps

In a currency swap, the two payment streams being exchanged are denominated in two different currencies: *Fixed-to-fixed currency swap &a fixed-to-floating currency swap* also known as cross-currency coupon swap will have one payment calculated at a floating interest rate while the other is at a fixed interest rate. *Cross-Currency Interest Rate Swaps* involves the swap of floating-rate debt denominated in one currency for fixed-rate debt denominated in another currency.

AMERICAN DEPOSITORY RECEIPTS (ADRS)

An American Depository Receipt (ADR) is a negotiable receipt which represents one or more depository shares held by a US custodian bank, which in turn represent underlying shares of non-issuer held by a custodian in the home country. ADR is an attractive investment to US investors willing to invest in securities of non US issuers for following reasons: ADRs provide a means to US investors to trade the non-US company's shares in US dollars ADR is a negotiable receipt (which represents the non US share) issued in US capital market and is traded in dollars. The trading in ADR effectively means trading in underlying shares. ADRs facilitate share transfers. ADRs are negotiable and can be easily transferred among the investors like any other negotiable instrument. The transfer of ADRs automatically transfers the underlying share.The transfer of ADRs does not involve any stamp duty and hence the transfer of underlying share does not require any stamp duty, The dividends are paid to the holders of ADRs in U.S. dollars.

GLOBAL DEPOSITORY RECEIPTS (GDRS)

Global Depository Receipts are negotiable certificates with publicly traded equity of the issuer as underlying security. An issue of depository receipts would involve the issuer, issuing agent to a foreign depository. The depository, in turn, issues GDRs to investors evidencing their rights as shareholders. Depository receipts are denominated in foreign currency and are listed on an international exchange such as London or Luxembourg. GDRs enable investors to trade a dollar denominated instrument on an international stock exchange and yet have rights in foreign shares.

The principal purpose of the GDR is to provide international investors with local settlement. The issuer issuing the shares has to pay dividends to the depository in the domestic currency. The depository has to then convert the domestic currency into dollars for onward payment to receipt holders. GDRs bear no risk of capital repayment. GDRs are also issued with warrants attached to them. Warrants give the investors an option to get it converted into equity at a later date. Warrants help the issuer to charge some premium on the GDRs sold and it also helps to increase the demand of the GDR issue. The other advantage to the issuer is that it will not have to pay dividends on the warrants till the conversion option is exercised. The disadvantage to the issuer lies in delayed receipt of full proceeds from the issue and in case the conversion option is not exercised the expected proceeds will not be realized.

FOREIGN CURRENCY CONVERTIBLE BONDS (FCCBS)

A type of convertible bond issued in a currency different than the issuer's domestic currency. In other words, the money being raised by the issuing company is in the form of a foreign currency. A convertible bond is a mix between a debt and equity instrument. It acts like a bond by making regular coupon and principal payments, but these bonds also give the bondholder the option to convert the bond into stock. These types of bonds are attractive to both investors and issuers. The investors receive the safety of guaranteed payments on the bond and are also able to take advantage of any large price appreciation in the company's stock. (Bondholders take advantage of this appreciation by means of warrants attached to the bonds, which are activated when the price of the stock reaches a certain point.) Due to the equity side of the bond, which adds value, the coupon payments on the bond are lower for the company, thereby reducing its debt-financing costs. FCCBs is a bond issued in accordance with the guidelines, dated 12th November, 1993 as amended from time to time and subscribed for by non-residents in foreign Currency and Convertible into ordinary / equity shares of the issuer company in any manner whether in whole or in part or on the basis of any equity related warrants attached to debt instruments.

EURO-CONVERTIBLE BONDS

A convertible bond is a debt instrument which gives the holders of the bond an option to convert the bond into a predetermined number of equity shares of the company. Usually, the price of the equity shares at the time of conversion will have a premium element. The bonds carry a fixed rate of interest. If the issuer company desires, the issue of such bonds may carry two options viz. - Call Options: (Issuer's option) - where the terms of issue of the bonds contain a provision for call option, the issuer company has the option of calling (buying) the bonds for redemption before the date of maturity of the bonds. Where the issuer's share price has appreciated substantially, i.e. far in excess of the redemption value of the bonds, the issuer company can exercise the option. This call option forces the investors to convert the bonds into equity. Usually, such a case arises when the share prices reach a stage near 130% to 150% of the conversion price, (ii) Put options – A provision of put option gives the holder of the bonds a right to put (sell) his bonds back to the issuer company at a pre-determined price and date. In case of Euro-convertible bonds, the payment of interest on and the redemption of the bonds will be made by the issuer company in US dollars.

CONCLUSION

There were limited financial instruments available to the financial sector. However, with economic liberalization and financial sector reforms in India, the financial instruments have significantly increased. Thus the Innovation of Financial Instrument focuses on the Design, analysis and construction of financial contracts to meet the needs of Financial Sector i.e., the corporate as well as investors. This is a process that seeks to adopt existing financial instruments and development of new instruments to enable financial market participants to cope more effectively with changing scenario.

REFERENCES

Berry, Leonard L., Venkatesh Shankar, Janet T. Parish, Susan Cadwallader, and Thomas Dotzel (2006), "Creating New Markets through Service Innovation," *Sloan Management Review*, 47 (2), 56-63.

Avlonitis, George J., Paulina G. Papastathopoulou, and Spiros P. Gounaris (2001), "An Empirically-Based Typology of Product Innovativeness for New Financial Services: Success and Failure Scenarios," *Journal of Product Innovation Management*, 18 (5), 324-342.

Blazevic, Vera and Annouk Lievens (2004), "Learning during the New Financial Service Innovation Process: Antecedents and Performance Effects," *Journal of Business Research*, 57 (4), 374-391.

R.M.Srivastava & Divya Nigam (2009), "Management of Indian Financial Institutions",Himalaya Publishing House (Eight Edition).

Ravi M. Kishore (2008), "Financial Management", Taxmann (Sixth Edition)

M.Y.Khan (2008), "Financial Services", The McGraw Hill Companies (Fourth Edition).

L.M.Bhole (2008), "Financial Institutions and Markets – Structure, Growth and Innovations", TMH (Ninth Edition).

Madhu Vij (2006), International Financial Management, Excel Books (Second Edition).

P.N.Varsney & D.K. Mittal (1991), "Indian Financial System", Sultan Chand & Sons (First Edition).

Study material issued by Board of Studies of Institute of Chartered Accountants of India.

Study material issued by Board of Studies of Institute of Cost & Works Accountants of India

Study material issued by Board of Studies of Institute of Companies Secretaries of India

Accounting Standards 30 "Financial Instruments: Recognition and Measurement" issued by Institute of Chartered Accountants of India.

Accounting Standards 31 "Financial Instruments: Presentation" issued by Institute of Chartered Accountants of India.

Accounting Standards 32 "Financial Instruments: Disclosure" issued by Institute of Chartered Accountants of India.

19

THROUGHPUT ACCOUNTING – INVENTORY, COST MANAGEMENT AND CONTROL ANALYSIS

Atul Shiva, Monica Sethi

INTRODUCTION

Ever since the development of Cost Accounting in 1890, Labour cost has been the most volatile, significant and vulnerable cost in the product cost. The labour cost depends primarily on how efficiently managers used labour in an organization. Eliyahu M Goldratt argues that under current conditions labour efficiencies leads to decisions that harm rather than help organizations. Throughput accounting, therefore, removes standard cost accountings reliance on efficiencies in general and labour efficiency in particular from management practice. Many cost and financial accountants agree with Goldratt's critique, but they have not agreed on a replacement of their own and there is enormous inertia in the installed base of people trained to work with existing practices.

The Concept of Throughput Accounting: Throughput Accounting is an alternative to cost accounting proposed by Eliyahu M Goldratt. It is not based on standard costing or Activity Based Costing. Throughput Accounting is not costing and it does not allocate costs to product or services. It can be viewed as business intelligence for profit maximization. Throughput Accounting is the management accounting system based on the theory of constraints, which was popularized by Goldratt's business novel – 'The Goal'. According to him the concept of allocating costs to products is wrong and leads to erroneous decisions. Many, especially by ABC advocates, have criticized Goldratt's viewpoint. It seems that ABC advocates are now partially agreeing with Goldratt, as it is better for sort term decision, however, for long tern cost must still be allocated to products.

Measures of Throughput Accounting: Goldratt's alternative begins with the idea that each organization has a goal and that better decisions increase its value. Throughput Accounting uses three measures of Income and expense:

(a) Throughput (T) is the rate at which the system produces 'goal units'. When the goal units are money, throughput is sales revenue less the cost of raw materials (T = S-RM). Throughput can arise only when there is a sale. Idle stock does not count. Throughput is similar to contribution of Marginal Costing i.e. Sales–Variable Costs.

(b) Investment (I) is the money tied up in the system. This is money associated with Inventory, machinery, buildings and other assets and liabilities. Theory of constraints given by Goldratt recommends inventory be valued strictly on totally variable cost associated with creating the inventory, not with additional cost allocations from overhead.

(c) Operating expense (OE) is the money the system spends in generating 'goal units'. For physical products, OE is all expenses except the cost of the raw materials. OE includes maintenance, utilities, rent, taxes etc.

All the organizations where Throughput Accounting is utilized must try to understand these above mentioned facts as how to increase their throughput by reducing investment and operating expenses. Throughput Accounting is an important development in modern accounting that allows managers to understand the contribution of constrained resources to the overall profitability of the enterprise.

Inventory Cost Management Via Throughput Accounting

Besides managing capacity levels, managers in companies and industries with high fixed costs care about decisions that affect their operating income numbers i.e

- Top management uses operating income numbers to evaluate the performance of managers. Operating income also affects a company's stock price. Therefore, any stock based compensation such as stock options that managers receive would also be affected.
- Planning decisions typically include analysis of how the alternatives under considerations would affect future reported income.
- Planning decisions typically include analysis of how h alternatives under considerations would affect reported income.
- Reported income is often used to evaluate the performance of managers.

Inventory costing choices relate to which manufacturing costs are treated as inventoriable costs. There are three types of Inventory-Costing:

- *Absorption Costing:* It is a method of inventory costing in which all variable manufacturing costs and all fixed manufacturing costs are included as inventoriable costs. In other words, inventory absorbs all manufacturing costs.
- *Variable Costing:* It is a method of inventory costing in which all-variable manufacturing costs are included as inventoriable costs. All fixed manufacturing costs are excluded from inventoriable costs. The fixed manufacturing costs are treated as costs of the period in which they are incurred.
- *Throughput Costing:* It is also called as super-variable costing which matches only for direct materials focusing on throughput contribution. The concept of Throughput Costing can effectively utilized to manage the Inventory cost Management system. The advocates of throughput costing maintain that, in the

short run, manufacturing costs other than direct materials are relatively fixed. Some managers maintain that even variable costing promotes an excessive amount of costs being inventoried since it is only the Direct Material Cost that is truly variable. All the other costs are costs of the period in which they are incurred. In particular, variable direct manufacturing labour costs and variable indirect manufacturing costs are regarded as period costs and deducted as expenses of the period.

RESEARCH OBSERVATIONS

The concept of Throughput costing can be explained with the help of an example mentioned as below viz a viz absorption costing and variable costing.

	2006	2007	2008
Beginning Inventory	0	200	50
Production	800	500	1000
Sales	600	650	750
Ending Inventory	200	50	300
Selling Price			1000
The variable manufacturing cost per unit:			
Direct material cost			110
Direct manufacturing labour cost			40
Indirect manufacturing cost			50
Total variable manufacturing cost per unit			200
Variable marketing cost per unit sold (all indirect)			190
Fixed manufacturing costs (all indirect)			120000
Fixed marketing costs (all indirect)			108000

SITUATION–I: ABSORPTION COSTING

		2006	2007	2008
Revenues: Rs 1000*600; 650; 750 units		600000	650000	750000
Less: Cost of Goods Sold				
Opening Stock		NIL	70000	17500
Variable Manufacturing Cost		160000	100000	200000
Fixed Manufacturing Costs		120000	75000	150000
Less: Closing Stock		(70000)	(17500)	(105000)
Adjustment for Manufacturing Variances		NIL	45000	(30000)
Gross Margin		210000	272500	232500
Less: Operating Costsa		390000	377500	517500
Variable marketing costs		114000		
Fixed marketing costs	108000	222000	231500	250500
Operating Income		168000	146000	267000

SITUATION–II: VARIABLE COSTING

	2006	2007	2008
Revenues:	600000	650000	750000
Rs 1000*600; 650; 750 units			
Less: Variable Costs			

Opening Stock	NIL	40000	10000
Variable manufacturing costs 160000	100000	200000	
Less: Closing Stock	(40000)	(10000)	(60000)
Variable COGS	120000	130000	150000
Variable Marketing Costs	114000	123500	142500
Total Variable Costs	234000	253500	292500
Contribution Margin	366000	396500	457500
Less: Fixed Costs			
Fixed Manufacturing Costs	120000	120000	120000
Fixed Marketing Costs	108000	108000	108000
Total Fixed Costs	228000	228000	228000
Operating Income	138000	168500	229500

SITUATION–III: THROUGHPUT COSTING

	2006	*2007*	*2008*
Revenues:	600000	650000	750000
Rs 1000*600; 650; 750 units			
Less: Direct Material COGS			
Opening Stock	NIL	22000	5500
Direct Material	88000	55000	110000
Less: Closing Stock	(22000)	(5500)	(33000)
Total Direct Material COGS	66000	71500	82500
Throughput Contribution	534000	578500	667500
Less: Other Costs			
Manufacturing Costs	192000	165000	210000
(Fixed Cost + Variable Cost * Units Produced)			
(120000 + 90*800; 500; 1000 units)			
Marketing Costs	222000	231500	250500
(Fixed Cost + Variable Cost * Units Produced)			
(108000 + 190*600; 650; 750 units)			
Total Other Costs	414000	396500	460500
Operating Income	120000	182000	207000

The summary of the operating income differences during 2006-2008 is as below:

	2006	*2007*	*2008*
Absorption Costing Operating Income	168000	146000	267000
Variable Costing Operating Income	138000	168500	229500
Throughput Costing Operating Income	120000	182000	207000

The calculations clearly illustrate why managers whose performance is measured by reported income and the choice of method between absorption costing, variable costing and throughput costing. If the unit level of inventory increases during an accounting period, less operating income will be reported under variable costing and throughput costing than absorption costing. Conversely, if the inventory level decreases, more operating income will be reported under variable costing and throughput costing than absorption costing.

THE RESULTS OF RESEARCH OBSERVATION

The overall evaluation of Comparative Income effects of Absorption costing, Variable costing and Throughput costing is as below:

Major Findings	*Absorption Costing*	*Variable Costing*	*Throughput Costing*
1. Are fixed manufacturing costs inventoried?	Yes	No	No
2. Is there a production – volume variance?	Yes	No	No
3. Are classifications between variable and fixed costs routinely done?	Infrequently	Yes	Yes
4. How do changes in unit inventory levels affect operating income?			
Production = Sales	Equal	Equal	Equal
Production > Sales	Higher	Lower	Lower
Production < Sales	Lower	Higher	Higher
5. What are the effects on Cost-Volume-Profit-Analysis?	Driven by (a) unit level of sales (b) unit level of production (c) chosen denominator level	Driven by unit level of sales	Driven by unit level of spending for direct materials costs as product costs.
6. Application of GAAP	Yes	No	No
7. External Reporting Purposes	Applied	Not utilized	Not utilized

After evaluating Throughput Accounting in comparison of traditional cost accounting, the following observations can be derived on the basis of decision-making criteria of finance managers

1. Throughput Accounting focuses only on overall cost reduction of the company while cost accounting takes into account the decision relating to cost reduction per unit of the company.
2. Throughput Accounting tries to maximize only throughput of the concern while cost accounting does not tackle into account the impact on throughput.
3. In Cost Accounting any increase inefficiency is acceptable whereas in Throughput Accounting only increased in efficiencies that increase throughput or that reduces overall cost are acceptable.

CRITICISM TO THROUGHPUT ACCOUNTING

1. The major limitation of Throughput Accounting is that it is primarily oriented towards the achievement of short-term objectives of the organization. Throughput accounting focuses only on fixed supply of resources and maximize throughput. The theory ignores all other aspects relating to the product mix in future except materials. It concentrates on maximizing throughput, inventory management and the impact on operating expenses only.
2. Another shortcoming of Throughput Accounting is that the operating expenses of the company are unrelated to decisions made about the product sold and customers served. The approach of Throughput Accounting is that only throughput can be traced to the products. There must not be any attempt made to trace operating expenses to the products, whereas operating expenses represents how much the company is paying to have its resources available to generate throughput. Therefore the company must track its capacity levels, constraints and idleness so as to generate enough flexibility to increase the production volume and product variety to increase its throughput without increasing operating expenses.

The application of Throughput Accounting is limited for internal reporting systems of the company only. Since Absorption costing is utilized for external reporting systems and is famous among practicing corporate finance professionals supported by GAAP and for tax considerations, thereby making very less scope for Throughput Accounting in use.

CONCLUSIONS

The Theory of constraints as described by Throughput Accounting is based on its basic assumption that whatever period is being analyzed; the company will always have at least one constraint. The basic difference between Activity Based Costing and Theory of Constraint is that in short term a company will have few constraints, however in long term it will not. Activity Based Costing assumes that in long run all of company's resources are equally important. Activity Based Costing has cost drivers and tries to increase local efficiencies everywhere. In ABC a chains long-term resistance can be accomplished by strengthening any link. However, the view of Theory of Constraints is that chain's resistance is determined by its weakest link. Therefore Theory of Constraints is recommended for short-term decisions and activity based costing for long-term decisions. If corporate finance professionals agree with a view that a company is a system, and that a system will have very few constraints, theory should use only throughput accounting. f they do not think that the company will have few constraints in the long run if they believe high level efficiencies everywhere will lead to good overall performance, Activity based costing should be used for long term decisions.

REFERENCES

Bih-Ru-Lea, Fredendall Lawrence D., "The Performance of ABC Costing, Throughput Accounting and Traditional Costing in A theory of Constraints Environment".

Horngren Charles T, Datar Srikant M, Foster .G. (2009), "Cost Accounting – A Managerial Emphasis, Inventory Costing and Capacity Analysis", Chapter 9, Pearson Prentice Hall, 2009, p.no.350.

Goldratt E. (1990), "The Theory of Constraints" (New York: North River Press, 1990).

Noreen E., Smith D. and Mackey J.T (1995), 'The Theory of Constraints and Its Implications for Management Accounting' (Great Barrington, MA; north river Press, 1995) 144.

Corbett T (2000), "Throughput Accounting and Activity-Based Accounting: The Driving factors behind each methodology", Journal of Cost Management (January-February 2000), 37-45.

20

WHAT IS IFRS AND WHY ARE GLOBAL ECONOMICS LOOKING AT ONE ACCOUNTING STANDARD?

Atul Bansal

WHAT IS IFRS?

International Financial Reporting Standards (IFRS) is a set of accounting standards, developed by the International Accounting Standards Board (IASB) that is becoming the global standard for the preparation of public company financial statements. IFRS are accounting rules ("standards") issued by the International Accounting Standards Board (IASB), an independent organization based in London, UK. They purport to be a set of rules that ideally would apply equally to financial reporting by public companies worldwide. Between 1973 and 2000, international standards issued by the IASB's predecessor organization, the International Accounting Standards Committee (IASC), a body established in 1973 by the professional accountancy bodies in Australia, Canada, France, Germany, Japan, Mexico, Netherlands, United Kingdom and Ireland, and the United States. During that period, the IASC's rules were described as "International Accounting Standards" (IAS). The IASB describes its rules under the new label "International Financial Reporting Standards" (IFRS), though it continues to recognize the prior rules (IAS) issued by the old standard-setter (IASC).

STANDARDIZING INTERNATIONAL FINANCIAL REPORTING

Primarily, financial reporting is aimed at providing information to the existing and the potential partners of an enterprise as well as to the public. Well founded decisions are supported by the information resulting from the management's stewardship. The framework of financial reporting standards mentions the concept of useful decision making. These kinds of frameworks are used in countries where there is non-codified law on financial reporting. With this, the standard setters are provided with important guidelines.

Paragraph 12 of the International Financial Reporting standards state that "The objective of a financial statement is to provide information about the financial position, performance and changes in financial position of an enterprise that is useful to a wide range of users in making economic decisions." Moreover, the Statement of Financial Accounting Concepts says that financial reporting function primarily to provide useful information to those who make economic decisions regarding business enterprise and investments to these enterprises (2004).

The International Financial Reporting Standards (IFRS) refers to a set of standards in the area of accounting. This body of financial reporting standards is developed by the International Accounting Standards Board (IASB). To date, major nations are adopting these standards to a certain extent.

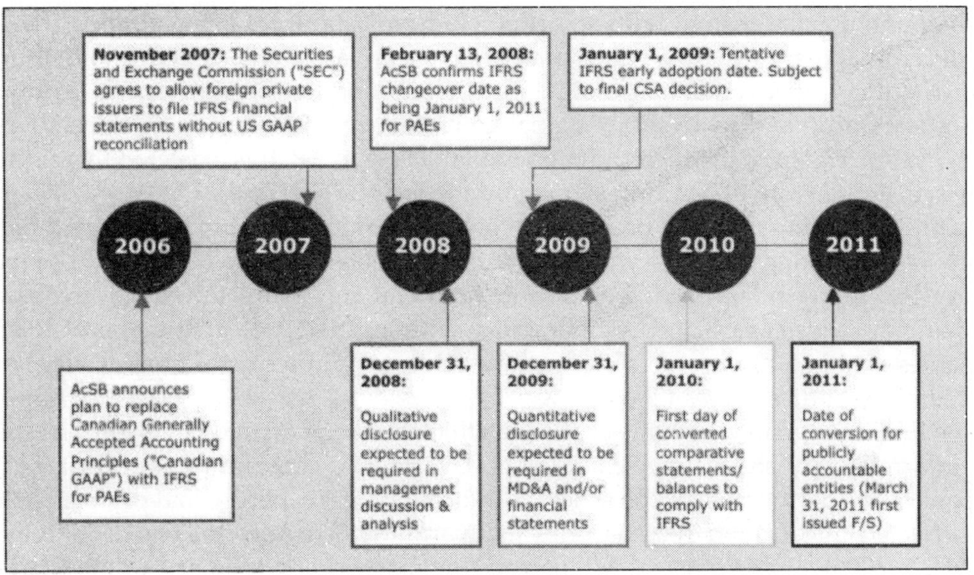

A trend towards the use of the International Financial Reporting Standards (IFRS) is emerging in the global financial markets. Historically, such standards are used on voluntary basis. Today, there have been a growing number of jurisdictions requiring the use of IFRS among companies for local reporting as well as listing purposes. In Europe alone, public listed companies are required by the European Commission quartered within the European Union to prepare financial statements that are in accordance with the IFRS. Such requirement affects about 7,000 enterprises. The evolution has affected the nature and the scope of national standard-setters which include that of the U.S Financial Accounting Standards Board (FASB) (2005)

The primary focus of the International Accounting Standard Board is the convergence of accounting standards worldwide. In order to achieve this, the IASB will designate official liaisons to national standard-setters. As such they are responsible for close contact with their respective national standard setters. Agenda coordination and the assurance that IASB and national bodies are working for convergence are part of their responsibility.

Among the countries with formal liaison are Australia (including New Zealand), Canada, France, Germany, Japan, the United Kingdom and the United States (, 2005) Impact on the U.S GAAP

IMPLEMENTATION

Significant consistency in accounting recognition and measurement and the greater disclosure of information regarding financial statements are among the benefits of the IFRS implementation. However, there is still a long way before reasonable consistency can be achieved under the IFRS. Primarily, this is caused by the fact that there remains to be no substantial body of custom and practice or an accepted way by which IFRS shall be applied. A number of years of implementation by representatives of cross section businesses in different countries and industries are needed to attain a consensus on how IFRS can be applied. Until that is achieved, divergent practices and the limited comparability remain unavoidable

Undoubtedly, the current IFRS reporting platform is far from being perfect. The IASB announced that there will be no new international standards to be effective until the year 2009. Ongoing improvements are aimed at the elimination of deficiencies within the current standards and to facilitate global convergence and ultimately, to remove the onerous requirement of the reconciliation with the US GAAP. It is expected that five new or revised standards will be implemented by the year 2009(2006).

Continued discussions are being made in the UK with regard to the future direction of corporate reporting and as to what type of convergence with the IFRS should be made. Among the many benefits of a common financial reporting language are greater transparency, consistency and comparability with entities. The adaptation of IFRS by companies is aimed to provide a competitive advantage in terms of quality, clarity and the credibility of disclosures (2006).

The IFRS conversion is a huge challenge which has been dictated by the International Law in a relatively short time scale. In the UK finance community, almost all of the companies are able to achieve it on schedule indicating their expertise and professionalism. It is projected that around 100 countries will permit and require the use of IFRS by the year 2007(, 2006). In this sense, it will become the most widely used accounting standard in the world. The challenge remains on the part of the investors to engage in the debate and to influence future developments.

Implementing IFRS requires the companies to an extensive change as well as risk management process. The conversion process would entail time, cost, effort and expertise to be able to be able to meet deadlines. Larger listed groups found it vital to use effective and timely communication with investors and analysts. The conversion to IFRS is not just changing a set of accounting principles with another. It involves a number of different financial accounting and disclosure requirements that may result to differences in the financial report. With it, the company executives are provided with the opportunity to challenge the way the company is evaluated by investors, stakeholders and competitors. Since the IFRS will affect every decision of the company, it is necessary that the management is able to foresee changes in terms of market perception.

One of the key issues that need to be addressed by companies is to educate the employees who are responsible for the preparation and use of financial statements. It is only in 2004 that international standards are introduced onto the syllabi by the professional bodies. Professional training firms need to be considered by the companies to provide training. Since the use of IFRS is expected to impact the transactions processes and the way they are given value, businesses should ensure the understanding of the impacts by the analyst and investors. Lastly, an accounting system that is capable of collecting, processing and reporting the information under the IFRS format is required of for the transition (2004)

SALIENT FEATURES OF IFRS

International Financial Reporting Standards are standards adopted by the International Accounting Standards Board (IASB), a body earlier known as IASC (C for Committee). The London-based Board started its operations in 2001 for developing global accounting standards. IFRS came into limelight when the European Union decided to adopt it for all its member countries starting 2005. Since then, IFRS has spread swiftly all over the world. IFRS standards are principle-based whereas US GAAP standards are rule-based. Indian standards are basically modeled on the basis of IFRS.

Convergence

Convergence means a coming together from different directions, especially a merging of groups that were originally opposed or very different. In the accounting standards parlance, convergence means alignment of national requirements with the international norms.

Applicability

As of now, 102 countries have either adopted or are converging to IFRS, including Australia, Akash New Zealand, Pakistan, Singapore, China, West Asia, Japan, Africa and countries in the European Union (EU). Now, the ICAI, India's premier accounting body, has decided to adopt IFRS with effect from April 1, 2011, for public limited companies and will be extended to other entities in a phased manner. The numerous unstated to IFRS came about after the EU made IFRS mandatory for all its listed companies starting 2005. Consequently, more than 8,000 EU-listed companies adopted IFRS in one go. In the USA, the Securities and Exchange Commission (SEC, akin to our SEBI) is proposing to eliminate, for IFRS foreign filers, the reconciliation requirement to US GAAP. In April 2007, SEC lined up proposals to allow companies listed in the US to choose between IFRS or US GAAP for reporting purposes to make a choice from 2009.

BENEFITS OF IFRS

Immediate benefits of convergence are comparability of financial statements, portability of professional skills across countries, ease of Mergers & Acquisitions process, and doing away with the need to translate to different accounting norms. There are several more benefits with the convergence of the IAS with the IFRS. They are:

- This will greatly bolster the ability of Indian companies to raise and attract foreign capital at low cost
- Once Indian companies adopt IFRS, the global acceptability of them will be enhanced
- The adoption of IFRS is expected to increase transparency of financial statements
- Indian companies will be able to save on costs concomitant with reconciliation procedures

- The risk of being exposed to errors in reporting under different accounting frameworks for Indian multi-national companies will be eliminated
- Indian professionals trained under IFRS could be benefited immensely as they can scout for new clients around the globe

With the ongoing integration of Indian economy with the global economy, several Indian companies are becoming truly multi-national. Tata Steel has recently acquired Corus, UK, creating the fifth biggest steel producer in the world. Hindalco Industries has taken over Novelis Inc. Companies, like, Dr.Reddy's, Aban Offshore, Sun Pharma, and Bharat Forge have acquired foreign firms thus globalising the world.

WORLDWIDE ADOPTION OF IFRS

From the past few years many changes have been seen by many in finance and accounting sectors. Today it is observed that many major economies in the world are under way to adopt IFRS. Nearly 100 countries have adapted their local accounting standards to conform to *IFRS.* It is under practice that many nations developed their own local Generally Accepted Accounting Principles (GAAP). The advent of *IFRS* has brought with it the choice of adopting a globally accepted set of standards instead of using local GAAP.

CHALLENGES FACED IN ADOPTING IFRS

Conversion to IFRS will often challenge fundamentally a company's existing business model. It will affect the way the company presents itself to investors and other users of its financial statements.

It is vital that company managements recognize the far-reaching impact that IFRS will have on their businesses. Failure to do so could place their companies at a competitive disadvantage. IFRS conversion presents management with an opportunity to reconsider the business reporting model.

For many companies, the impact of IFRS on investor relations will be considerable.

Although entities are frequently required to adopt new accounting standards under their national Generally Accepted Accounting Principles ('GAAP'), adopting IFRS, an entirely different basis of accounting, poses a distinct set of problems:

- Information may need to be collected that was not required under the previous GAAP.
- Practical experience of applying a principles-based system of financial reporting standards such as IFRS does not exist in many entities.
- the requirements of individual standards will often differ significantly from those under an entity's previous GAAP;
- Indian accounting standards will converge fully with the International Financial Reporting Standards (IFRS) by 2011, The National Advisory Committee on Accounting Standards (NACAS) is reviewing AS-30, AS-31 and AS-32. Following this, AS-32 will become mandatory from April 2011. It would be difficult for banks to follow IFRS.

But why IFRS is so important and why is convergence of accounting standards so advantageous or even necessary?

International Financial Reporting Standards remove some of the subjectivity from financial reporting and provide a consistent basis for recognition, measurement, presentation and disclosure of transactions and events in financial statements. In recent Past, there have been cases where companies reporting under IFRS in Europe record a loss but when these same companies re-state their accounts according to US GAAP they record a profit!

Financial statements are prepared based on a number of accounting principles and assumptions. Accountants use their judgment to apply these principles and produce financial statements for use by management, shareholders, analysts, finance providers, governmental agencies, the general public and other stakeholders.

WHY IS THE WORLD LOOKING AT IFRS?

Convergence of accounting standards will have the effect of attracting investment through greater transparency and a lower cost of capital for potential investors. In recent times Companies are finding it increasingly difficult to raise money and get them listed on stock exchanges as they were not following the standard in accordance with IFRS. Differences in accounting practice make it difficult for investors, whether individual or institutional, to compare the financial results of different companies and make investment decisions.

TO WHOM IT BENEFITS

Multinational companies will find it easier to comply with reporting requirements of overseas stock exchanges since they would no longer have to re-state their accounts. Governments will be in a better position to assess the tax liabilities of multinational companies receiving income from overseas as well as for foreign multinationals setting up shop in their own country.

In 2005 the European Union formally adopted IFRS as the single accounting standard throughout their member countries. Australia, Russia, China, South Africa and the GCC nations have already converged or are in the process of converging with IFRS. Canada has committed to adopting IFRS by 2011. Japan, India, Brazil and Mexico are also pursuing convergence or adoption of IFRS.

In 2007 the US Securities & Exchange Commission made the landmark decision to allow non-US companies to file their financial statements based on IFRS without reconciling back to US GAAP. This is widely regarded as the most significant step by the SEC towards full adoption of IFRS in the not too distant future. This change by the SEC is an effort to reduce the barriers to capital flows between countries using IFRS and US GAAP.

The IASC expects that by 2011 more than 150 countries will have adopted IFRS including the US which is expected to at least have converged with IFRS to a great extent either by changing US GAAP or adopting IFRS outright.

WHO GETS AFFECTED BY THE CHANGE?

A country's intention to adopt IFRS or converge with IFRS is highly admirable and to be applauded. However, the accounting profession, governments, regulators, national accounting standard setters, and other constituents must continue to work together to eliminate differences between national and international standards. The principal actions needed to support convergence are outlined below.

- The Accounting Profession needs to assist governments and standard setters in formulating and enacting convergence plans, provide IFRS training and education and support the preparation of national language translations of IFRS.

- Governments must establish formal convergence plans that include target dates for implementation and address impediments to convergence, for example the link between financial accounting and lax legislation.
- Regulators should set up efficient and effective enforcement mechanisms to increase the consistency and quality of application of IFRS as well as support the International Financial Reporting Interpretations Committee (IFRIC) and the IASB as the sole clearing house for interpretation of IFRS.
- National Standard Setters must decide on a strategy and timetable for achieving convergence and develop an active standard setting agenda aimed at eliminating existing differences with IFRS.
- The IASB is required to address concerns about the complexity and operational practicality of IFRS, prioritize the SME project as an agenda item and oversee and authorize translations of IFRS in various languages.
- The Preparers of financial statements must actively participate in the standard setting process, in particular to identify practical application concerns, as well as providing IFRS training for staff and managers, including those in non-financial roles.
- Universities need to include IFRS in the core accounting curriculum.
- Analysts and Investors are required to promote convergence of national accounting standards with IFRS. They should also actively participate in the IASB's standard setting process, in particular to identify users' needs, and educate their staff regarding the IFRS reporting model.

SEC OFFERS ROADMAP TO GLOBAL ACCOUNTING STANDARDS

The Securities and Exchange Commission has proposed roadmap that could lead to the use of international financial reporting standards (IFRS) by U.S. issuers beginning in 2014. Currently US Companies are using US GAAP. In 2011 SEC would make a final decision whether to adopt IFRS.

"An international language of disclosure and transparency is a goal worth pursuing on behalf of investors who seek comparable financial information to make well-informed investment decisions," said SEC Chairman Christopher Cox. "The increasing worldwide acceptance of financial reporting using IFRS, and U.S. investors' increasing ownership of securities issued by foreign companies that report financial information using IFRS, have led the SEC to propose this cautious and careful plan. Clearly setting out the SEC's direction well in advance, as well as the conditions that must be met, will help fulfill our mission of protecting investors and facilitating capital formation."

CONCLUSION

The objective of having a single accounting standard worldwide is clearly manifested by the IFRS efforts. Indeed, such standards will foster benefits to the global financial market as it introduces a new trend in the area of financial reporting. However, it is also important not to disregard the possible implications of such standardization. Companies who are converting to IFRS are faced with the challenge of changing not only their accounting procedures but the understanding of the real impact of IFRS on their accounting system. Moreover, companies are confronted with the lack of general accepted ways of applying these standards. The IFRS implementation is at its early years and only through continued implementation can a consensus be laid on how to effectively apply it. And as far as adoption is concerned, international standards must be appropriate to the economic problems of the countries worldwide to be truly beneficial.

The transition from GAAP to IFRS is not only inevitable, but a positive development that would help make capital markets more competitive. Transitioning to IFRS would allow companies to compete for capital in other countries, while reducing cost and complexity for companies operating internationally; we also think that embracing a single set of global accounting standards would contribute to a higher degree of investor understanding and confidence. Also IFRS is very important for US Investors as they own 2/3 rd of securities issued by foreign companies. Because of IFRS there will be greater comparability and greater confidence in the transparency of financial reporting for the US investors. In conclusion, there are many positive and negative aspects of IFRS. More than one hundred countries currently follow those standards, creating a global standard. It seems as though slowly but surely, the U.S. will make the transition from GAAP to IFRS.

REFERENCES

Rao P.M. (2006), Accounting Theory and Standards, New Delhi: Deep&Deep Publication P. Ltd.

The Institution of Chartered Accountant of India (2007), "Concept paper on convergence with IFRS in India".

The Economic Times, 17th Sept (2008), "IFRS, Slow on Transition" Debojyoti Ghosh

International Financial Reporting Standard (2005), Taxman India Publications (P) Ltd., p-23.

"IFRS and Indian GAAP – A Comparison"- A Report by Delloite.

S. Saudagaran,' International Accounting – A User Perspective' Taxmann, India Ltd, New Delhi.

"International Financial Reporting Standard (IFRS) US-GAAP, UK-GAAP and INDIAN – GAAP" Snow White Publication.

"IFRS Convergence (2008), Challenges and Implementation Approaches for Banks in India" KPMG Report.

Part–IV

Innovations in Production and Operations Management

21

INNOVATION AS A TOOL FOR IMPROVING SUPPLY CHAIN COORDINATION AND DEMAND MANAGEMENT- A CASE STUDY ON CPFR MODEL

Anil Kumar Chojar

INTRODUCTION

Innovation is about knowledge for creating new possibilities through combining different knowledge sets. These can be in the form of knowledge about what is technically possible or what particular configuration of this would meet a latent need. Successful innovation management requires that we get hold of and use knowledge about components but also about how to put those together, which is termed as an architecture of an innovation.(Tidd, Bessant and Pavitt, 2005). Most of the time innovation takes place within a set of rules which are clearly understood by all players who are involved in innovating the product, or its processes to make it a better or improved one by doing generally the incremental or marginal innovations. These can be in the form of variations around the central innovation. But sometimes rules of the game change, and a completely new innovation comes through which dislocates the established rules of the game. This happens with the experimentations by either the new players or existing players who are trying to face up to the new market conditions for survival and growth. Such experimentations are usually accompanied by failures till a dominant design, or organizational format is accepted and begins to set up the new rules of game. Such a process is referred to as a Discontinuous innovation when the existing rules of game are replaced by new rules of game to establish new technology, product or process design.

In this paper, an attempt has been made to understand as to how the concept of supply chain management has undergone a change through a series of innovations, which has its roots in the 1960s concept of logistics management – a planning tool that seeks to develop a system-wide, integrated view of the firm. Subsequently, supply chain management extends the concept of logistics management to external integration of the firm. The supply chain is conceived as "a series of linked suppliers and customers" (Handfield and Nichols Jr., 1999). It encompasses all activities associated with the flow and transportation of goods from the raw materials stage through the end user plus the concomitant information and financial flows. Supply chain management refers to the coordination and alignment of materials, financial, and information flows for all activities and processes involved in a supply chain (Simchi-Levi et al., 2003).

Companies are facing difficult business environment and as result they are not able to make forecasts in medium to long-term Consumer constraints are becoming more obvious as they require and purchase smaller quantities, exhibit higher variation in their buying practices, go for increased customization, and prefer higher quality, shorter delivery and product life cycles. It is therefore important for companies to be able to adapt quickly to achieve an overall efficiency. Overall efficiency is the purpose of integration and co-ordination among supply chain partners. A change in coordination has been observed among companies from an earlier version of supply chain where each partner-company operated independently in its self-interest by using only locally available information, to a supply chain with a fully coordinated decision-making approach, in which all information and decisions are aligned to accomplish the system-wide objectives. However, even in such networks, the supply chain partners remain autonomous entities and are governed by their individual objectives and constraints. On the other hand, a well coordinated supply chain management can be a tremendous asset for companies as it can reduce inventories and costs, improve the profit margin, and offer a better return on investments. However, companies may still require to overcome problems related to data, technology, and or vendors. Obtaining and using quality data requires a few considerations. In order to do proper forecasting, the predictions must be based on data from a large sample. If few orders are used as the basis for the predictions, the results are likely to be quite unreliable. Additionally, managers generally do not realize that data can change or show variations in short period of time. For these reasons, SCM data must be continuously re-evaluated in order to make it realistic. Also, a proper training can go a long way to improve the data collection and processing to improve the overall effectiveness of SCM. While vendors, suppliers, and other processors are the necessary elements of the supply chain, companies need to meet with the decision-makers in those companies and outline clearly what benefits supply chain coordination will bring for them(Affonso, et. al., 2006).

SUPPLY CHAIN MANAGEMENT: A COMPLEX COORDINATION PROBLEM

Supply chains consist of networks of organizations which are involved, through upstream and downstream linkages, in the different processes and activities that produce value for the ultimate customer in the form of products and services. SCM is also a coordination and integration of entire range of activities associated with moving of raw materials, components or goods from the basic stage through to the end-user. This includes activities like procurement, in-bound and out-bound transportation, production scheduling, order processing and fulfillment, inventory management, warehousing, and customer service. When it comes to decision making, the understanding of the co-ordination mechanisms helps in selecting the best available alternative. The supply chain partners when forming a collaborative supply chain bring with them new resources and constraints. Collaboration can also contribute to the reduction in local shortcomings if tasks and responsibilities are well managed by supply chain partners(Affonso et. al., 2006).

DEMAND MANAGEMENT

Demand management is generally related to estimation and management of customer's demand with a view to use this information to streamline and enhance operational effectiveness. The traditional supply chains usually start at the point of manufacture or assembly point and end-up with the sale of product to individual consumers or business buyers. In spite of understanding of the supply chain performance enhancement metrics such as use of technology, information sharing, inventory turnover, delivery efficiency, the manufacturers continue to play a major role in determining what product-mix will be available for sale, at what point, in how much quantity and at for what duration of time. However, in reality there might be a mismatch between manufacturing and demand at the point of consumption-regardless whether it is at retailers, retail customers or business consumers' level. If the members of the supply chain pay any attention to the demand management, the efforts are likely to bring-in results for the entire supply chain.

The key point here is that there should be collaboration between supply chain members-right from the manufacturing through the customer. They must collaborate on activities related to product flows, services, information and capital. The desired result should be to create additional value for the end-user or consumer for whom all supply chain operations have been constituted.

In order to develop an effective demand management, a manager must identify the problems and needs of the consumers; this information must be shared with other supply chain members. They should be in position to develop products and services which have the capacity to solve customers' problems. The supply chain members should also make use of reliable and efficient transportation facilities, logistics and employ distribution methods and strategies to deliver products to the consumers in the desired format.

KEY SUPPLY CHAIN MANAGEMENT ISSUES

These mainly relate to :

Distribution Network Configuration: This refers to the number, location and network of suppliers, production facilities, distribution centers, warehouses, cross-docks and customers.

Distribution Strategy which includes:

Decision-making with respect to operating control –whether it should be centralized, decentralized or shared;

Delivery Systems- whether direct shipment, cross-docking, or direct store delivery system would be appropriate;

Mode of Transportation- how the supplies/consignments should be dispatched-whether by land –rail or road route, or by sea or air carriers. Besides, managers have to work on trade-offs between freight, delivery time and customer satisfaction.

Replenishment Strategy is used to decide whether pull, push or combination of both to replenish inventory.

Logistics Control- This refers to the transportation ownership whether a firm should have owner-operated, contract carrier or use 3 PL logistics.

In order to achieve the lowest net logistics cost, the above activities must be coordinated well. Trade-offs exist that increase the total cost if only one of the activities is optimized. For example, full truckload (FTL) freight rates are more economical on a per unit cost basis rather than paying more for less than truckload (LTL) shipments, which turn out to be expensive in terms of freight costs and effective or net price of the consignment. On the other hand, FTL consignment may result in increase in inventory holding costs. It is therefore important to take a systems approach when planning logistical activities. These trade-offs are key to developing the efficient and effective Logistics and SCM strategy.

Other important supply chain management issues are:

- *Information:* It refers to the Integration of processes through the supply chain to share information, including customer demand, forecasts, inventory, transportation, and possibility of collaboration as well.
- *Inventory Management:* This mainly relates to Quantity and location of inventory- be it raw materials, work-in-process (WIP) or finished goods inventory.
- *Cash-Flow:* It aims at finalizing the payment terms and the methodologies for exchanging funds between trading partners across the supply chain.

Since supply chain execution is managing and coordinating the movement of materials, information and funds across the supply chain, the flow of information and planning activity takes place in both upstream and downstream directions.

ROLE OF FORECASTING

A major component of demand management is **forecasting** – the quantity of product that will be purchased by consumers or end-users. The main focus of the forecasting is to determine the primary demand. One of the key objectives is to anticipate and respond to the primary demand across the supply chain. There are short term forecasts and they extend to medium term to long-term forecasts. One of the objectives of integrated supply chain management is to anticipate and respond to primary demand as it unfolds itself in the market.

Collaboration

Collaboration between different members of supply chain is now recognized as a joint activity to plan, forecast and replenish the stocks/inventories ranging from raw materials/ goods, components, sub-assemblies, assemblies to finished products across the supply chain.

Firms may pursue collaboration because it creates strategic advantages resulting in revenue and profit growth through increased market share, access to strategic knowledge or operational effectiveness through risk-sharing risk and by achieving economies of scale. One of the initiatives which is aimed at achieving realistic supply chain integration is *Collaborative Planning, Forecasting and Replenishment (CPFR).* It is a business model that takes a collective approach to supply chain management and information exchange among trading partners. It uses common metrics, standard language, and firm agreements to improve supply chain efficiencies for all participants. The driving force of CPFR is a synchronized forecast of supply chain members. Every member or the trading partner in a CPFR process — supplier, manufacturer, distributor, retailer — can view and amend forecast data to optimize the process from end to end. Essentially, CPFR puts a break to guesstimates in forecasting. It means that manufacturers and retailers share their plans, with detailed knowledge of each others' assumptions and constraints.

AN OVERVIEW OF THE MODEL

Collaborative Planning, Forecasting and Replenishment (CPFR) is a business practice that aims at planning and fulfillment of customer demand by combining the inputs of multiple trading partners. This practice started in 1995 as a pilot program between Wal-Mart and Warner Lambert called CFAR, for "Collaborative Forecasting and replenishment." In 1997, the *Voluntary inter-industry Commerce Solutions Association (VICS)* developed the CPFR model and in 1998 published the first CPFR guidelines. A joint committee of *Voluntary inter-industry Commerce Solutions Association* (VICS) and the *Efficient Consumer Response (ECR)* organization revised the guidelines in 2001 to incorporate global requirements, sanctioned by the Global Commerce Initiative (GCI).

Since then, according to the VICS, more than 300 companies have implemented the CPFR process in the USA. As these companies worked with CPFR, shortcomings were identified and innovations were developed, which were included in a 2004 major model revision by the VICS CPFR committee. By linking sales and marketing to supply chain planning and execution processes, CPFR increases products' availability while reducing inventory, transportation and logistics costs. The experience gained from pilot projects and production planning as CPFR guidelines has provided many insights.

Over time, the VICS initiative reported benefits of CPFR in terms of inventory reductions of 10 to 40 percent across supply chains. However, several barriers to adoption CPFR have been noticed, which include difficulties in information exchange, investments in human resources as CPFR is process-intensive.

Salient Features of Collaborative Planning, Forecasting and Replenishment (CPFR)

CPFR is a business practice that combines the intelligence of multiple trading partners in the planning and fulfillment of customer demand.

- Links sales and marketing best practices to supply chain planning and execution processes
- Objective is to increase availability to the customer while reducing inventory, transportation and logistics costs
- The consumer is the ultimate focus of all efforts
- Buyers" (retailers) and "sellers" (manufacturers) collaborate at every level
- Joint forecasting and order planning reduces fluctuations in the supply chain
- The timing and quantity of physical flows is synchronized across all parties
- Exception management is made systematic

CPFR is an initiative that facilitates the reengineering of the relationships between trading partners and thus transactions. This initiative is based on an industry-recognized set of standards.

CPFR model provides platform for supply chain partner collaboration

COLLABORATIVE PLANNING, FULFILMENT & REPLENISHMENT(CPFR) MODEL IN PRACTICE

A Case Study of Motorola Company Background with regard to its Products and Customers

Like most leading makers of mobile phone handsets, Motorola, Inc. understands customer segmentation very well. Managers in Motorola's Mobile Devices business know that the technology-sensitive consumer will not buy the same handset as the everyday communication instrument. It is for this reason, Motorola offers over 120 models globally. The difficulty comes in determining as to how many of which models to make and sell. Accurate replenishment to retailers' shelves is critical factor. If a retailer is out of stock of a particular handset that a consumer has his mind-on, he is likely to buy a competitor's product rather than Motorola's standard model. In such circumstances, there is a possibility that Motorola loses that customer permanently.

Accurate forecasting is further complicated because one phone model can have multiple Stock-keeping units(SKUs)- such as GSM, color, dual mode, etc. Further, rapid new product introduction adds complexity. Life cycles of Cell phones average a little more than a year, with some models having a life cycle as low as six months. Industry statistics indicate that 50 percent of stock-outs in the consumer goods industry are due to poor retail ordering and replenishment/forecasting processes, 25 percent are caused by overall demand planning and upstream shortages, and 25 percent by inadequacies of in-store processes such as shelving and replenishment. While these statistics are similar for the mobile handset industry, the out-of-stock rate for mobile handsets can be many times larger than for typical consumer packaged goods. Accurate forecasting is critical in this industry because the cost of stock-outs can have a significant negative business impact.

Prior to its move to collaborative planning, forecasting and replenishment (CPFR), the Mobile Device division's sales were highly variable and were not synchronized with customer demand. Motorola had visibility only to shipments into retailers' distribution centers, but not shipments from the retailers' distribution centers to the stores. Forecast error was very high, resulting in excessive stock-outs. Motorola recognized that it needed to improve its collaboration with customers and forecast ability in order to compete effectively in its highly price-sensitive market.

In 2001, the handset division turned to CPFR to improve sell-through performance with its retailers. After demonstrating the potential of CPFR, under the collaborative pilot project with one of the division's retail phone customers, Motorola launched a major CPFR program in mid-2002, accompanied by an organization- wide shift to customer-focused operations teams. These teams were organized around *major customers such as cellular operators and consumer electronics retailers.* The goals were to reduce forecast error by 50 percent, achieve a 30 percent drop in its inventory, cut channel inventory by 50 percent, and improve on-time delivery by 30 percent. To meet its goals, the division's managers knew they had to share with their retailers their real-time data and plans including forecasts, inventory, sell-through – i.e. sales to retailers' shelves, not to end consumers, promotions, product plans, and exceptions.

ANALYSIS AND DISCUSSION

Requirements for Successful CPFR Implementation

It is vital that the participants are strategically aligned. An interesting reflection of Motorola's commitment to that concept: A core business operations team and its customer-focused operations teams employed both Motorola and customer metrics such as inventory and sell-through in its goals and performance plans. Besides, all the customer team members had the division's retail customers' names with them. It is also crucial to have strategic alignment within Motorola and the customer organization—alignment of process, organizational and technology strategies with collaborative business strategies.

This implies that the business that is advocating CPFR implementation-in this case Motorola-must refine its business strategy to focus on collaboration. It should also decide what information will be shared with its customers and then get into agreement with customers in order to share the business strategy with them. There must also be an internal alignment of the process, organizational and technology factors, all of which support and are in synchronization with the core business strategy. Specifically, organizational and process changes must be made concurrently with the acquisition and implementation of technology tools that will support more effective information-sharing. The customer must also see to changes in process, organization and technology factors with support from its own executive team.

Realigning the Business Strategy

Fundamentally, CPFR requires a change in business strategy from the typical "arm's length" transactional relationship with a customer to one that emphasizes collaboration. Common goals must be established and the supplier and customer must reach agreement on what information they will share. Motorola's handset division had always produced phones that customers really wanted, and its attitude to collaboration reflected that fact. Changing the culture would take many months for each customer. Using the "Roadmap to CPFR Implementation" that it had developed quite early, Motorola selected North American retailer to agree upon appropriate service levels, metrics and a plan for continuous improvement. To properly qualify the retailer, Motorola considered the retailer's culture as well as its relationship with Motorola. For properly implementing CPFR, the Motorola focused on overcoming the then existing delivery problems by holding daily meetings to review every purchase order, demonstrating improved on-time delivery in order to gain trust. As replenishment improved in the short term, the relationship improved, and Motorola convinced the retailer that it could collaborate and find improvised ways to work together without simply building up inventory.

Target lead times and inventory levels were established. The retailer's executive management team bought into the necessary changes to its processes, organization, and technology. Motorola and the retailer jointly created a master agreement and joint business plan that they continually reviewed and adjusted as the environment changed. Motorola and the retailer jointly reviewed cross-linked metrics. This included the retailer measures of forecasts and Motorola measures of delivery; the retailer measures of inventory and Motorola focuses on order changes. They also used the VICS CPFR handbook to determine what should be measured. Collaboratively, they used a Six Sigma approach to review the root causes of stock-outs. They jointly agreed to monitor product availability, order confirmation, on time delivery performance, flexibility of order quantity, sell through, inventory, order changes, and order accuracy.

REWORKING KEY PROCESSES

To help rationalize business processes for planning, forecasting, and replenishment, Motorola set up formal communication processes at multiple points along the supply chain. The processes included weekly reviews. Every week during a collaborative planning meeting, Motorola and the retailer reviewed replenishment, prior/current week sell-through, inventory position, and open orders. Additionally, the participants set up a new process for continual dialog between marketing and finance. While regular telephone conferences kept the collaboration moving, the participant teams met face to face at least once every six weeks.

RETHINKING THE ORGANIZATIONAL STRUCTURE

The purpose was to redefine the organizational structure in order to put the spotlight on collaborative relationships. One key move was to set up account-based operations teams. The separate functions that had previously provided input to the sales team, including customer advocacy, business operations management, finance and credit, regional marketing, product operations, pricing programs, and customer development were pulled together into a dedicated customer account team headed by the strategic account manager for that retailer. This team could directly discuss with the retailer the lead times, time fences, operational calendars, product roadmaps, promotion plans, and key triggers. Individual roles also changed–collaborative customer skills were now required. Previously, the handset division's call-center personnel had essentially been order-takers, each handling two to three customers at a time. With CPFR as a core framework, they were retrained to become replenishment analysts focused on managing customer inventory. After completion of the six month pilot project, the division made its major customer-centric move. Two new roles were added: a director of customer operations and a customer alliance manager. Order management and demand and supply planning roles were reduced and personnel were distributed into customer teams. Business planning and business analysts became part of the customer-focused teams. A single view of demand began to crystallize where once there had been multiple views in different groups within Motorola. For its part, the retailer combined separate functions that had previously provided input to its supplier management team, including purchasing, logistics and inventory management, finance, product marketing, product operations, and sales operations. The retailer's new group became a supplier- focused demand planning team. Collaborative relationships were strengthened because there was direct communication on all issues between Motorola's new account sales team and the customer's new supplier management team.

Benefits for Motorola and its Retailer

Motorola's CPFR initiative made a big difference to forecast accuracy almost immediately. MAPE (mean absolute percent error) is now a fraction of its previous levels. CPFR allowed quick reductions in inventory at the retailer's distribution center because there was less need for buffer stock. Stock-out rates are now less than a third of what they were previously. However, Motorola sales revenue did not immediately increase since it was necessary to clear out the sales channels. Motorola reduced shipments initially while recalibrating inventory levels. It took a few months to get the inventory aligned with channel consumption. Once that happened, shipments began to pick up as out-of-stocks began to drop. The retailer soon responded with increased sales as it saw Motorola looking out for its inventory levels. The increase in shipments more than made up for the initial reduction in shipments; and established a new run-rate in sales, higher than the pre CPFR run-rate. After the CPFR initiative had been established, the inventory that Motorola reserved for the retailer decreased by 30 percent compared to the general inventory for its other non-CPFR retailers. Collaborative forecasting and replenishment also produced a secondary benefit. Transportation costs were cut in half because Motorola was no longer shipping multiple pallets daily, many of which had been in less-than-truckload (LTL) shipments. Using its CPFR systems, Motorola could plan longer production runs, ship full containers and thus improve utilization of production capacity because supply chain set-up could be reduced-and because it was less variable. At the same time, the results of cell phone promotions improved because the participants' marketing teams were more involved with each other and because they had greater visibility of supply chain milestones.

CONCLUSIONS

CPFR creates a win--win scenario, by bringing the buyer and seller together so that their goals are compatible. By competing in the market as one, the buyer and seller form a value chain that comes out ahead of other buyers and sellers who are still negotiating prices.

CPFR has evolved from a previously tried Supply Chain Solutions. CPFR is considered to be the next stage in the evolution of supply chain initiatives. Older supply chain operations had gaps in their practices, including financial plans taking precedence over forecasts and non-integrated supply chain planning. This resulted in higher inventory levels, and lower order execution rates. Companies were not realizing the benefits that they had expected. For successful CPFR adoption and implementation, the following points are summarized:

(1) *Collaboration is the Foundation-* The real key to a successful implementation of CPFR is the forging of cultural alliances rather than traditional supplier-customer relationship. Such alliances involve peer-to-peer relationships, common goals and measures, and governance through formal communication points. Collaborative efforts should begin by first developing internal cross-functional teams and measures and then linking them to the participant's comparable teams and measures. Linked performance measures should focus on common goals.

(2) Both Participants must be Ready- Both participants must be focused on deeper supply chain visibility such as data on sales to the end consumer. Participant readiness must be assessed to determine the appropriate business model. A standardized model might not work with every customer. No single business process fits all customers; thus, collaborative processes must be customized. Assessments of customer readiness should gauge management stability, high-level ownership of distribution and the current or potential share of the manufacturer's sales going to each customer.

(3) *Customer Service Focus is Critical to Success*- Customer intimacy is a real strength to sales team. Motorola learnt to adapt to how the customer wants to conduct business—regionally or locally. Motorola's philosophy was: Never say no to an important customer. The firm always tries to find a way to say "yes" to something that's beneficial for both Motorola and the customer."

(4) *Time-based Decision-making is Key*- Both participants must adopt a common calendar for planning. In addition, Motorola standardized the decision-making dates, ensuring that both participants had appropriate information and plans ready for concurrent decision-making.

(5) *Collaboration is Focused on Building Relationships*- The strength of these relationships determines how long collaboration will continue and how successful it will be. One of the most significant determinants will be the development of peer-to-peer relationships.

(6) *Organizational Roles must Change*- The organization must change to become customer-focused rather than product-focused. Customer- and supplier-focused teams help develop the strong peer-to-peer relationships that form the basis of all interactions.

RECOMMENDATIONS

For initiatives as complex and long-term as CPFR, it is recommended that there should be a strong and educated executive support from the top management. Implementation of a CPFR process takes time, and if it is to be done right, it requires that executives have the capacity to absorb significant changes in organizational roles and relationships. The initiative has to be driven by committed professionals who understand the process and the long-term value of CPFR, and they have to stick with the initiative for at least eighteen months to make it work. The case of Motorola's CPFR initiative serves as a compelling example of a supplier's commitment to the industry and its customers.

LIMITATIONS

The weakness of CPFR efforts has been due to its over-emphasis on replenishment. While streamlined replenishment is main objective, effort directed towards planning and forecasting is an important input. Many CPFR projects fail due to lack of executive support, lack of collaboration effort or because of unclear objectives at the outset, or they cannot work consistently with many of the company's key trading participants. It is especially true when they involve many items and locations, high degrees of required automated processing and lots of exception management. *Exception management* is the practice of investigating, resolving and handling such occurrences either by using skilled staff or through the application of software tools. Good exception management can contribute to efficiency of business processes.

An analysis of this multi-year project reveals significant learning among the managers at Motorola. Motorola's CPFR initiative turned out to be a time-consuming, painstaking endeavor. CPFR requires fundamental changes not only in the nature of the relationship with the retailers, but also in the way each participant conducts business. This collaboration required Motorola to develop new business processes, redesign its organization and adopt systems to support real-time information. Instead of retailer driven CPFR, it was Motorola that initiated the adoption of CPFR with its downstream retail customers. Past experiences of supplier-retailer information linkages have reported varying benefits when suppliers have made the first moves.

Supplier-driven initiatives often require the suppliers to make substantial investments to set up linkages such as Electronic Data Interchange (EDI). In Motorola's case, an EDI infrastructure already was in place. Such initiatives also favor suppliers that are motivated to initiate major internal cultural change. For example, it takes true collaboration to push back on a customer that is ordering too much. When this first happened at the handset division, the customer asked whether the manager who suggested these order reductions really worked for Motorola! Traditionally, suppliers and buyers in most supply chains prepare independent demand forecasts.

Suppliers have a limited view of the buyer's markets, while buyers lack a broad view of category or market insights as well as of production and capacity planning. This often leads to excess inventory and sometimes adversarial relationships.

Reasons for Slower Rate of CPFR Adoption and Its Implementation

CPFR pilot projects undertaken between companies, such as Nabisco and Wegman's, Kimberly-Clark and Kmart, and Wal-Mart and Sara Lee, have resulted in significant improvements in product availability, increased sales and reduced inventory (VICS, 1999), the adoption rate has been slower than expected. Most implementations involve only two or a few parties, and only a limited number of products. Large-scale implementations were not observed, especially in Europe. Several reasons have been presented to explain the difficulties in implementing CPFR. There have been problems related to trust and information sharing by adversaries, change management and the difficulty in reaching critical mass. The single most important obstacle in Europe may, might be due to the retailer's lack of forecasting processes and resources.

The CPFR model was developed based on work done by Wal-Mart, a retailer with exceptional logistics processes, in the area of demand planning and forecasting(Smaros, 2002).

REFERENCES

Affonso, R., Marcotte, and Grabot, B. (2006), "Coordination Model in Supply Chain" In Intelligent Production Machine Systems, conference. http://conference.iproms.org accessed Dec 27, 2009

Aqua Management Consulting Group" Five Essential Elements of Integrated Supply Chain Management-How Best in Class Manage their Supply Chains", a White paper, www.aquamcg.com, accessed, Nov 18, 2009

Bowersox, D., Closs, D., and Cooper, M.B. (2008), "Customer Accommodation", In *Supply Chain Logistics Management*, 2nd ed., TMH, N. Delhi

Businessweek (2009), "Supply Chain Collaboration-CPFR means Process and Practice", http://*www.businessweek/adsections/chain/2 , accessed June 16, and September 21, 2009*

Cederlund J., Kohli, R., Sherer, S., and Yao, Yuliang ((2007), "How Motorola put CPFR into action", *Supply Chain Management Review*, October 2007

Coyle *et al.* (2009), "Demand Management and Customer Service", In *A Logistics approach to Supply Chain Management*, Cengage Learning, New Delhi

Handfield, R. and Nicholas, E., Jr.(1999), "Introduction to Supply Chain Management" Prentice-Hall, New York

J.D. Edward and Company (2003), "CPFR-Collaborative, Planning, Forecasting and Replenishment, Delivering results for Manufacturers-Serving the Retail, A white paper", Denver, CO, USA. *http://wwwjdedwards.com, accessed June 16, 2009*

Power, D. (2008), "Capability and Practice in Procurement Collaboration: A Vendor's Perspective of Benefits", *Operations and Supply Chain Management* ,Vol.1, No 2, pp 72-84

Simchi-Levi, D., Kaminsky, P., Simchi-Levi, E. (2003), " Designing and Managing the Supply Chain-Concepts, Strategies and Case Studies", Tata-McGraw-Hill, New Delhi

Smaros, J. (2002), "Collaborative Forecasting in Practice", a paper presented at the *Logistics Research Network Conference*, Birmingham, U.K.

Tidd, J., Bessant, J., and Pavitt (2005), "Managing Innovation-Integrating Technological, Market and Organizational Change", 3rd ed. Wiley India, New Delhi

22

NEED OF PROMOTING STREET VENDORS FOR INCLUSIVE GROWTH: A CASE STUDY IN ASSAM

Kumud Chandra Goswami

INTRODUCTION

The growth and development of the informal sector has become a pertinent issue to ensure inclusive growth of a country. The urban people are becoming very much dependent on the services provided by the street vendors. But it is very unfortunate to mention here that the service takers not to talk about the other people are now and then criticized the existence of this vital sector of the economy. The street vendors are the energetic and essential sellers but most neglected by the regulators and by the various formal people's forums. But it is very much interesting to note that as an individual more or less all people are dependent on their services or products they are dealing with. Some people even from the allied class also take fast food from some reputed street shops for various reasons like quality, price, taste etc. But when those people stand in a platforms they generally try to say against such vendors very rarely they stand in favour of this very vital segment of the economy. Therefore, it is very pertinent to take this sector into confidence before talking about inclusive growth.

Liberalization of the economy all over the globe creates lots of opportunities to the informal sector including the street vendors. The formal sector of the economy has outsourced their activities to the tiny and small enterprises to avail economies of scale and to reduce their burden of work load by capitalizing their brand image in the market. It is seen that the small and medium enterprises are not very much capable to compete with the well established sector. As a result, the big houses have come forward to develop understanding with the small players. This new approach has helped both the big bosses and the small players. The small players need not bother about the marketing part; as the big houses take over the marketing part. The small manufacturers also feel comfortable to produce more as they get a ready market through the big houses. As a consequence, the informal sector is becoming high in demand for the betterment of the economy. One such most important informal sector is the street vendors that are actively taking part in the distribution system. The Street Vendors are self employed person who runs their businesses mainly from the public places. Since these vendors are doing their businesses from the streets in most cases they are term as street vendors. Their work is full of insecurity and uncertainty. Even if some Street Vendors do very well in their trade, but a single raid from the municipality or other local govt. can turn them into paupers. Street Vendors are one of the most neglected sections in the society. Street Vendors have been defined as – a person who offers goods or services for sale to the public at large without having a permanent built up structure from which they sell. Street Vendors may be stationary in the sense that they occupy space on the pavement or other public or private spaces or they may be mobile in the sense that they remain moving from one place to another by carrying their wares on push carts, in baskets or on their heads.

OBJECTIVES OF THE STUDY

The study is a humble attempt to investigate into the problems being faced by the Street Vendors in running their business in Sibsagar Town and to find out an amicable solution to minimize the magnitude of such problems so that they also can contribute to the growth of the economy.

LIMITATIONS OF THE STUDY

The researchers faced certain problems in conducting the study about the street vendors of Sibsagar Town. There is no system of keeping any records about the street vendors by the local authority of the study area. It is not possible to find out the actual number of street vendors working in Sibsagar Town. As such, we have met some of the street vendors at random to know about their problems. No such extensive literature is available in this area of study that has further make the study more critical.

METHODOLOGY OF THE STUDY

The study is primarily based on primary data collected by interviewing 50 sample street vendors selected at random operating in Sibsagar Town area. The researcher took interview of the vendors on two days i.e. on 15th and 16th November, 2009. Data and information have been collected from the vendors with the help of a questionnaire and face to face interview method was followed. Data so collected have been analysed and inference has been made. Secondary data about the street vendors of Sibsagar Town are not available with the local authority. So question of using secondary source does not arise.

OVERVIEW OF THE SIBSAGAR TOWN

Sibsagar Town is the head quarter of Sibsagar District. It is one of the historically important towns of Assam. As per the 2001 census, Sibsagar had a population of 54,482. Males constitute 56% of the population and females 44%. Sibsagar has an average literacy rate of 81%, higher than the national average of 59.5%: male literacy is 83%, and female literacy is 79%. In Sibsagar, 10% of the population is under 6 years of age. The road to the town is flanked by tea gardens on either side which stretch like carpets of green bushes.

Sibsagar, earlier known as Rangpur, was once the capital of the Ahom rulers who dominated Assam for more than 600 years until their kingdom fell to the British, in 1826.Sibsagar Town is a place of tourist attraction for its heritage sites. There are three temples(*"Dol"s in Assamese*) on the bank of Sibsagar man-made lake. The most prominent is the *Sivadol*, standing tall at 104 feet (32 m), drawing large crowds on *Shiv Ratri*. The other temples are the Vishnudol and Devidol. The temples were built by Queen Ambika, wife of *Swargadeo Siba Singha*, in the year 1734.Other attractions include the *Rang Ghar*, the double-storied, oval shaped amphitheatre with a roof which is shaped like an inverted boat, the seven-storied, *Talatol Ghar* which is a palace with two secret tunnels and three underground floors. *Joysagar*, said to be the biggest man-made lake in the country, is spread over 318 acres (1.29 km) of water on the edge of the town in an area called *Rangpur*. This lake was built by *Swargadeo Rudra Singha* in honor of his mother *Joymoti*.

A new addition for tourist attraction is the Ahom Museum on the bank of the Sibsagar. It stores artistic works of the rulers, including swords, clothes, manuscripts, goblets and platters. The ancient capital of the Ahoms is *Gargaon* about 13 km east from Sibsagar, where the major draw is the *Kareng Ghar*, a seven-storied palace built by 18th century architects. *Charideo* situated nearby, is another old capital which was built by *Sukapha*, the founder of the *Ahom* dynasty. There are *maidams* or vaults for the king and members of royal families here. Travellers cross the *Namdang* stone bridge, carved out of a single boulder hundreds of years ago, over which a busy highway still runs today.

For convenience of the tourists local entrepreneurs have started giving tourism related services to the domestic and the foreign tourists. The nearest railway station is *Simaluguri*, 16 km from Sibsagar town. Buses ply regularly from *Simaluguri* towards Sibsagar. Taxis are available for hire from the railway station. It is approximately a half-hour bus ride from Simaluguri town. The nearest airports are *Jorhat* (55 km), Dibrugarh (80 km) and Guwahati (369 km). Buses ply regularly from Jorhat, Dibrugarh and Guwahati.

AN OVERVIEW OF THE STREET VENDORS IN SIBSAGAR TOWN

The actual number of street vendors functioning in the Sibsagar Town is not exactly known as there is no data base on the street vendors. But from an informal estimation made by the street vendors themselves, there are about 700 to 900 vendors working in the Sibsagar Town on regular basis and around 200 to 300 street vendors are working as casual sellers of services or products. They are mainly centralized at Central Market, Station Chariali, K.P. Chariali of Sibsagar Town areas. They are also seen at various bus terminus, bus stops and other areas where there is rush of people like near schools, colleges etc. The street vendors are working to serve the people either selling goods or services where gathering of people is always expected. It is obvious that the income of the Street Vendors depends upon their sell. On an average, they are earning 10% to 30% on their sale value depending upon the nature of the product, and varieties of products. Their daily sale as reported by some of the vendors ranges from Rs.150 to Rs.1500. This indicates their inconsistency in earning revenue from this business. The vendors said that they are required to pay Rs.10 to the municipality only for sitting on the road side but they are not provided with any licenses for doing business from the street. These are the common characteristics of the street vendors functioning in our country irrespective of their place of business.

In the Sibsagar Town almost all the Street vendors are male and a very negligible number from the female also. The researcher has classified the Street vendors functioning in the town area into two main categories –

— The Stationary (fixed) Street Vendors and

— The Mobile Street Vendors.

Stationary Street Vendors

The Stationary Street Vendors sell goods at different parts of a locality. Most important feature of such vendors is that they remain sitting at one place constantly. Although the place from where the vendor is working is a public place meant for other use but the vendors occupy that place to run his/her business. Those who are doing business from their carts also more or less place their carts at a fixed place daily. As a sole user of that particular place by the vendor for sometime it becomes almost equivalent to his/her own plot of land and usually he/she does not allow others to sit at the same place in his presence even in some cases during his/her period of absence also..

Mobile Street Vendors

Mobile Street Vendors are the vendors those who sell goods or services by wandering from one place to another taking their goods in *thelas* (push carts) or moblile ghumtis or in some case on their heads also. They can give coverage to a big area of the same locality as they remain moving from one place to another with varieties of their products. The number of these vendors are many in our country such as vegetable cart puller, fruit cart puller etc.

The Street Vendors can also be classified on the basis of varieties of their product in which they deal. In this regard, an attempt has been made to classify the street vendors in the following ways. All these varieties of the street vendors are available everywhere in our country.

Food Vendors: Food Vendors are those who deal in edible items. These Vendors are mostly found in town areas. They remain stationary at one place and permanently running their business. These vendors are mainly found in the main market area where there has been regular gathering of people. They are the *Chatwallas, Chanawallas, Phuchkawallas, Ice-creamwallas* etc. Some of these vendors keep on moving from one place to another from the morning to evening. They are the *Chanawallas,* (seller of processed mixture) etc. These vendors are mostly found near schools, colleges of the town area; in rural area also these vendors are operating. Some of the *Phuchkawalla, Ice-creamwallas* suppliers of food items are not very successful in providing quality food. Some of them supply food items to the customers not in proper hygienic condition. As a result, there is every possibility of doing harm to the consumers of this food item. One of the most pertinent problems created by them is that the vendors and the customers throw the waste product (i.e. paper, polythine etc.) on the road or in the drain which makes the environment dirty.

Vegetable Vendors: Vegetable Vendors are those who sell vegetables either in *Thela* (hand Push/pull Cart) or at roadside of the Town area. The Vegetable Vendors are generally localized at a particular location of the town where there is gathering of people for some other purposes. At certain point of time only one or two vendors also sit together for selling their items from the same place. The vegetable vendors are found selling their products throughout the day from same locality and they are also seen operating only in the morning and/or evening hours. They generally buy vegetables from the wholesalers and sometime they also buy goods from the village people who are involved in the process of cultivation. They are supplying comparatively fresh product as such their products are sold almost like hot cakes. There are some mobile vegetable vendors who carry their goods mostly in pull cart and keep on moving from door to door. The mobile vegetable vendors usually charge nominally higher price but because of the convenience of marketing some customers used to purchase from them only. As a result these vendors are selling their products to their permanent customers although they have some casual customers too. Some permanent customers said that now and then they face problem of short supply when the mobile vegetable vendors do not visit their place of residence. It seems that these vendors create such a situation that without their support some people suffer. Here lies the importance of the street vendors to the society. The presence of the mobile street vendors saves time and energy of their customers.

Pan Vendors or Panwallas: They are people who sell pan either at a *Gumti* or in *Thela*. Pan is one of the most popular items among the people of this region. So the services of this type of vendors is considered to be very much essential. all over the state. These vendors sell pan as well as cigarettes etc. at their shop (Gumti). In most cases the *Pan Vendors* are operating from road side in some cases they do business from over the drainage system. The panwalas make their product available to their customers at their place so that they need not spent much time in search of a pan. These vendors made the life easier to the consumers of the pan and some other product which are mostly consumed as mouth fresheners.

Juice Vendors: The juice vendors are those who sell juice of different fruits. They do their business in *Thelas*. They buy the fruits and take out the juice of the fruits and sell them after mixing with some spices to make it tasty. These vendors are found more in number during the summer season and a very few in the winter season. Since fruits are more seasonal all such vendors are not found throughout the year. They deal mainly of the Juices of Sugarcane, Orange, Lemon etc. As because of the changing weather, the people like to have a drink and take up the fruit juice to feel themselves comfortable. After talking with some of them we have come to know that they are not very much aware about how to maintain quality of their products so it is venerable to food poisoning.

Pheriwallas: Pheriwallas are those who sell clothes and other goods such as *Churies, Sandles,* Ornaments etc. They are mostly mobile vendors doing business on bicycles or in Thelas. These *Pheriwallas* used to visit different areas in a town and they also visit village areas to sell their goods. They mainly deal in cheaper goods that encourage the poor people to buy these ornamental items from them. The Pheriwallas are mainly belonging to the poor section of the society.

Head loader: The Headloaders are those people who sell goods in bamboo containers *(Kharahi)* specially designed for them. These vendors cannot afford a *Thela* to be used for carrying goods because of their very poor economic background. They mainly deal in single variety of product that too in lesser quantity. They are dealing mainly in fruits like Bananas, Orange, and Mangoes etc. They do their business by selling seasonal fruits. They purchase the goods daily and sell them and earn their livings during normal season.

Fruit Vendors: The Fruit Vendors are those who sell fruits of different varieties either in *thelas* or at roadside. They make their purchase from the local market daily and sell the fruit daily and thereby generating income to live their livelihood. The constraints of capital compelled the fruit vendors to buy a meager quantity of fruits generally on daily basis. Since they can not purchase variety of fruits in bulk their margin on sale is also less. Circumstances compel them to enter into this venture as a means of generating income. The fruit vendors are supplying fruits from road side and in some cases they also work as mobile vendors. These vendors deal mainly in seasonal fruits. They personally go to the wholesale market and select fresh fruits and purchase them in order to resale it. These vendors are mainly found in town areas but their services are also available in rural areas.

THE PROBLEMS OF THE STREET VENDORS IN SIBSAGAR TOWN

The street vendors are facing a plethora of problems at the time of entering into this business and also to remain in it. Some of such problems they face while they remain in their business and on the contrary problems created by them to the society are highlighted in the following paragraphs. Looking into these problems, the researcher has categorised the problems as follows:

— Problems faced by the Street Vendors and

— Problems created by the Street Vendors

Problems faced by the Street Vendors:

The main problems faced by the Street Vendors can be summarized as follows:

Problems of Space- Most of the Street Vendors are lacking space to run their business. About 60% (30) of the sample vendors said that space is their main problem now and then facing by them. The vendors started their business sitting at a certain place and sale their products. But if he/she remain absent for one or two days than the place is occupied by some the other vendors. This situation put a big question mark regarding the survival of the first vendor who used to sit in that particular place for a long time. This is happening because of no system of allotting space to the vendors by the local authority.

Problems of Finance- Finance is the life blood of all the business concern. Without finance a business can't run and grow. The street vendors are running shortage of finance at the time of purchasing their goods from their suppliers. In some cases, they have resorted to purchase on credit for very short time even for a day. The suppliers charge very high price from the vendors in the name of blockage of their capital and for the risk factor when they sale on credit. The street vendors used to repay to the suppliers generally on daily basis but still the suppliers charge some hidden interest. Sometime the vendors have to go for informal market credit at very high rate of interest and as a result their expense increases reducing their level of margin. The Banks are not interested to provide loan to them because of their nature of business. The vendors are apparently less permanent; they do not have any kind of business assets other than certain amount of stock, lack of surety, guarantee and collaterals etc prevent the bankers to come forward to release loan to the street vendors. Micro finance institutions may give some solution to the vendors by giving loan on daily basis or by issuing card to them to meet their financial requirement at the time of resource problem. 70% of the sample respondents are of the view that finance is their major problem and then it is storage facility and space problem is in the third rank.

Problems created by the Law of the Nature- The street vendors are doing their businesses under the sky. As such, they are facing problem created by weather condition like heavy rainfall, very hot weather etc. They are also facing problem from natural calamities like flood, storm etc. For 20% of the respondent who are very poor and not very regular, weather condition is more significant then any other problems. As they do not have any kind of permanent structure to protect themselves from the nature these problems become unmanageable for them. The local authority can extend help by providing some permanent sheds so that they can operate from that particular place on payment basis.

Table 1
Nature Magnitude of Problem faced by the Sample Street Vendors

Nature of Problem	*Number of Vendors & p.c.*	*Rank*
Problems of Space	30 (60)	I
Problems of Finance	35 (70)	I
Problems created by the Law of the Nature	10 (20)	I
Lack of storage facilities	28 (56)	I
Other problems	15 (30)	I

Source: Field survey

Lack of Storage Facilities- The street vendors are in need of storage facilities to store daily unsold goods. The vendors who are dealing in perishable goods they are in need of cold storage facilities. For the vegetable and fruit vendors this is a big problem. 56% of the sample vendors ranked this as their major problem then others. As the street vendors are running with financial shortage they can not afford hire charge to use the cold storage facility provided by some private parties. As a result, they get major set back when they could not sell adequate quantity of their product on a particular day. In this situation, they sell some of their product only just at their cost price to get rid of the possible wastage of goods.

Other Problems- In addition to the above the street vendors are also suffering from the ill treatment from the local authority, problems from the law and order machinery and in some cases from their customers and the public. 30% of the respondents are facing some other problems like eviction drive. This problem is facing by those vendors who are doing their business at very rush places.

In Assam, the position of fruit vendors is not so much praiseworthy same is the case with Sivasagar Town vendors. The street vendors can earn during his/her actual days of work and during their absence from duty they can not earn. They cannot afford to employ worker to help at the time of their absence. In this regard they are the worst sufferer for the frequent 'Bandh' called by different organizations. These 'Bandhs' create more problem to the vendors.

We have talked with some street vendors and collected some information from them. The vendors revealed that they are unorganized to fight for their common interest. Most of the street vendors are school dropouts. They are in this business only to earn their livelihood as there is no scope for them to get employment. As they are daily earner they spent more when they could earn more. Their savings habit is not very much satisfactory. Most of the vendors are not very much aware about the mode of savings. The vendors expressed their resentment over some members of the society that they neglect them and try to penalize them.

Problems created by the Street Vendors

The Street Vendors are helping the public by supplying their necessary goods or services comparatively at cheaper price but their negative contribution to the society also to be taken care of. The Street Vendors provides a lot many services over and above supplying goods to their customers at their residence. On the other hand, the street vendors create some problems to the society at large and they also create problems to a particular area of the town. Some of such problems are stated in the following

Traffic Problem- In Assam, there is no such system of issuing licenses to the vendors. As a result any number of people can enter into this business. This situation has made a negative contribution to the society at large. Because of increase in the number of such vendors the roads are becoming more and more congested creating traffic problem in the urban areas. The street vendors generally try to sit at those places where there is more scope to sell their product where there is more gathering of people. This particular attitude of the vendors increases the magnitude of the problem.

Problems for the Paddlers- The vendors occupy a considerable portion of the road side to display their goods for the customers that is otherwise to be used by the paddlers. As a consequence, the paddlers face difficulties at the time of walking comfortably. It is really a very severe problem created by the street vendors.

Making the Environment Dirty- At the time of daily closing of their stalls the vendors left the place filled with the garbage or other waste materials. This kind of behaviour of the vendors makes the environment dirty. The town inhabitants are supposed to bear with this dirty environment created by the street vendors. The local administration is not taking more interest to clean that area immediately the vendors left the place.

The street vendors are the real entrepreneurs who are running their business in a very much complicated situation facing a lot of problems. This is one of the most important sectors of the economy facilitating self employment. It has been observed that the street vendors are operating with both the positive and negative contribution. In Sibsagar Town we have seen that the Street Vendors are creating many problems. Considering the problems created by the Street Vendors and benefits derived from them we have to survive with the presence of the vendors. If we can minimize the problem created by them then we shall be able to increase its benefits.

MODEL TO UPLIFT THE SERVICES OF THE STREET VENDORS

The researcher has made an attempt to develop a model covering all aspects relating to the street vendors so the problem created by them and the problems faced by them can be minimized to a considerable extent. The model shown above will work with its eight components (few more can be added) in a coordinated way. At the first instance, the model will work as a sub system of the formal sector so they will also have to cooperate with the street vendors. Secondly, the customers on their part should think good for the SVs not only blaming the SVs but by offering helping hands by dealing with them at par with the formal sector. In the third, the local authority must extend their help by issuing work permit to them to do business at the places meant for them so that the public nuisance can be minimized. In the fourth, the FIs including the Micro Finance Institutions (MFIs) must extend financial support at easy terms and conditions at the time of their recourse crisis so that they can solve their financial problem at comparatively low cost.

Here the insurance institutions must come forward to cover their personal and business risks by offering micro insurance schemes for the SVs. The fifth component of this model is the need for separate set of regulations for the benefit of the SVs to protect their rights and to get protection from haphazard eviction drive from the local administration and police.

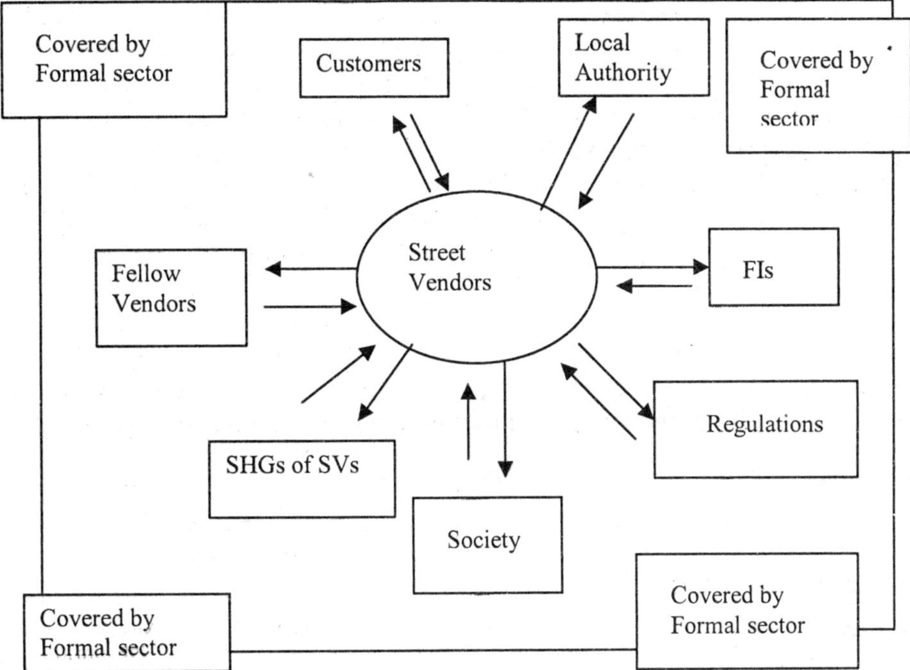

Diagram-1: Model to Uplift the Services of the Street Vendors

The sixth place is occupied by the society as a whole. All the members of the society must give a second thought before taking any drastic action on the SVs because without the services of the SVs the society will also suffer a lot. The seventh component of this model is creation of small group of SVs. These small groups on the line of SHGs or forming SVs Clubs can make them responsible for fellow SVs. This type of platform can be used to get financial benefits and other support at the time stringent business situation. Last but not the list, the SVs must extend helping hands to their fellow SVs. The competition among themselves should be friendly not rivalry. They must help each other when any member face any problem may be personal or may be business related problem.

SUMMARY AND CONCLUSION

The street vendors are the real entrepreneurs who are running their business in a very much complicated situation facing a lot of problems. This is one of the most important sector of the economy facilitating self employment. It has been observed that the street vendors are operating with both the positive and negative contribution. In Sivasagar Town also we have seen that the Street Vendors are creating many problems. Considering the problems created by the Street Vendors and benefits derived from them we have to survive with the presence of the vendors. If we can minimize the problem created by them then we shall be able to increase its benefits.

Street vendors in our country are playing a very significant role. In most of the cities and towns (including metropolitan cities viz. Mumbai, Kolkata, Delhi and Chennai) a considerable number of fruit vendors running their mobile shops to earn their bread and butters. Most of them are hailed from backward areas where majority of the people are living below poverty line.

One of the important features of our country is that a good number of people are still jobless. Many of them are educated unemployed. There is example where many such educated youth are engaged them in this type business. They are compelled by the poverty to adopt such a way to earn for their livelihood. It is also seen that these people can very well apply salesmanship skills in selling their product they deal in. Many of them know many languages and can speak these languages very fluently. It is true that the street vendors of our country have contributed a lot in solving the present unemployment problem. Very recently one post graduate in management from IIM is in news because he started selling vegetable on push cart. He has started his agricultural firm with cooperation from the villagers and selling at his own brand. He is trying to create a brand of his products. He is using all modern storage facilities for displaying his goods (vegetables) on the road side. So the street vendoring no longer remain as a business of the down trodden and uneducated people. It is attracting the modern educated youth.

REFERENCES

Goswami, K & Borgohain, K (2008), A Study of Street Vendors (Entrepreneurs) With Special Reference to Dibrugarh Town, Dibrugarh. Paper presented in a national seminar organized by Gauhati Commerce College on 19th March.

Mali, D.D. (2000), Entrepreneurship Development in North East, Indian Institute of Entrepreneurship, Guwahati.

www.nasvi.org.in searched on 22th Dec. 2009 at 12.15 PM

http://onlinesivasagar.com . searched on 22th Dec. 2009 at 12.15 PM

http://sivasagar.nic.in searched on 22th Dec. 2009 at 12.45 PM

23

SUPPLY CHAIN MANAGEMENT: A GLOBAL PERSPECTIVE

N. Venkateswaran

INTRODUCTION

Today companies are often not considered independent entities, but parts of multi-company, multi-echelon networks, i.e. supply chains, delivering goods and services to the final customer. Supply chain management (SCM) literature proposes that integrated control of these multi-company networks can provide significant benefits; the utilization of information technology (IT), in turn, is considered an imperative requirement for managing these networks, and has been associated with significant supply chain efficiency improvements.

One of the ways by which companies and production chains construct differential characteristics for competition is by adopting information technology. It has been suggested that information technologies contribute to improving coordination among the various links in a production chain by increasing the ability of their agents to transmit information, stimuli and controls along the sequential stages which comprise the operations needed to address the market. These stages, taken jointly, have conventionally been known as the Production Chain, but more recently have been called the Supply Chain.

Inter Organizational Systems (IOS), a name coined in the 1970s, constituted one of the forms which enabled information interchange among companies. These systems were developed and owned by the large companies themselves. Due to their nature, such systems faced resistance from these companies' potential partners, fearful of losing their autonomy. Based on work carried out by certain associations, the problem was resolved by developing structured standards to govern inter-company information exchange by electronic means, defined as Electronic Data Interchange (EDI). Once these standards were adopted, the companies could electronically transact with no special need to adapt to one another. The adaptations which do occur are in the sphere of negotiations/ commercial agreements, and have little to do with the technology used for exchanging the information.

The rapid development within the information technology and software engineering gives unprecedented opportunities for integration and coordination. The modern computer networks have the ability to rapidly distribute information to all concerned entities of an enterprise. The networks also present an infrastructure for coordination of planning and operational processes, not only within organizations, but also among them.

Although the importance of IT for efficient SCM is widely acknowledged, empirical research assessing how IT is in practice used for the purposes of SCM is narrow. More specifically, majority of the prior research has focused either on modeling the benefits of inter-organizational information technologies and information sharing, or on assessing the impact of specific technologies on supply chain efficiency. Consequently, the actual uses of IT in supply chain management as well as the reasons for using IT in a specific way still remain unclear. Due to these identified limitations in the previous literature we address the following research problem: "How and for what purposes do companies use information technology in supply chain management?"

SUPPLY CHAIN AND I T: THEORETICAL CONSIDERATIONS

According to Bowersox and Closs (1996), the basic notion of Supply-Chain Management is based on the premise that efficiency along distribution channels can be improved when the various agents involved share information and carry out joint planning. In the opinion of Cooper, Lambert and Pagh (1997), one basic condition for implementing supply-chain management is that there be some level of intra- and inter-organizational coordination. Farina and Zylbersztajn (1994) state that coordination involves a process of transmission of information, stimuli and controls along the chain for this latter to respond to changes in the competition environment.

In terms of relationships between manufacturers and distributors (retailers - wholesalers-distributors), in order to implement coordinating mechanisms and thus attain greater efficiency in supply management, the partners must share information, for a number of reasons, including the following:

- These mechanisms allow the manufacturers to understand each customer's specific aspects and address them in a distinct manner, adding value (through services, for example) to the line of products;
- Characteristics such as segmentation of the points-of-sales and types of customers along the supply chain should be taken into account, especially in decisions to launch new products and in dealing with each store's mix.

EDI IN THE SUPPLY CHAIN

Colla (1997) suggests that a change takes place in the division of tasks among the different links in the chain when new information technologies, such as EDI, are adopted. This change is reflected in the reorganization of functions among the various agents involved. One example of this, cited by Colla, is the fact that the companies must include bar codes when conceiving their packaging. In a review of the literature on the adoption of EDI, various obstacles were mentioned regarding its implementation, such as:

— incompatibility with the internal systems already in operation
— few short-term benefits
— resistance to change inside the companies, especially in supplier companies ;
— the need for changes and cooperation among the companies;
— few gains of scale;
— lack of direct financial benefits;
— large number of persons involved.

Among the advantages of employing EDI are:

— An image of being on the technological vanguard;
— Gains in more efficient supplying and reduction of uncertainties;
— Higher quality of information and consequent increase in the ability to react to changes in the market, as well as more coordination;
— Increase in workers' skills;
— More interaction with partners;
— Better management of stocks and consequent cost reductions;
— Improved customer services, faster communication and greater customer loyalty;
— Fewer errors.

LITERATURE REVIEW

Our literature review on SCM as well as on the IT solutions developed for SCM showed that the definitions for these two concepts are ambiguous. In this article, SCM refers to the practices and processes aiming for effective and efficient flow of materials and information between a company and its immediate suppliers and customers. This definition has a twofold justification. First, recent empirical studies have shown that management and integration of supply chains only rarely extends beyond the first tier suppliers and customers (e.g. Frohlich and Westbrook, 2001). Second, this definition corresponds to the perception our case companies have on SCM

As for IT systems, when discussing the use of IT in SCM, we refer to the use of inter-organizational systems that are used for information sharing and/or processing across organizational boundaries. Thus, besides internal IT systems such as Enterprise Resource Planning systems, the article also excludes identification technologies such as RFID from the scope of this study.

While integration, information technology and retail power may be key catalysts in the surge of interest surrounding supply chains, eBusiness is fueling even stronger excitement. eBusiness facilitates the virtual supply chain, and as companies manage these virtual networks, the importance of integration is magnified. Firms like Amazon.com are superb at managing the flow of information and funds, via the Internet and electronic funds transfer. Now, the challenge is to efficiently manage the flow of products.

PRIOR RESEARCH

An abundance of literature deals with the use of IT in SCM. Gunasekaran and Ngai (2004), for example, have included over a hundred journal articles in their recent literature survey addressing the use of information systems in supply chain integration and management.

In this literature review, the aim is to discuss the main contributions and shortcomings of three research approaches–analytical research, empirical studies, and classification frameworks–in relation to the topic of this paper.

EMPIRICAL STUDIES

Two streams of empirical studies on the use of IT in SCM can be identified. The first stream focuses on a specific technology or application area, and the second stream studies the application and benefits of IT in general.

As compared to the research focusing on specific technologies or application areas, research on the use and benefits of IT in SCM without the focus on specific technology is fewer in number. The research on the benefits of the use of IT in SCM includes a number of surveys investigating the impact of IT on supply chain integration, customer integration and service (Closs and Savitskie, 2003), supply chain time performance (Jayaram et al., 2000), financial performance, or a combination of these (Vickery et al., 2003). Meanwhile, Auramo et al. (2005) performed an exploratory multiple case study on the benefits of IT in SCM, and McLaren et al. (2004) conducted a multiple case study on how different SCM IS capabilities support different operations environments. However, common to these studies is that while helping to assess and understand the value of IT use and integration for SCM, they do not help in determining how companies actually use IT in SCM.

Some recent innovations, such as increased communication about consumer demand, via electronic data interchange (EDI) and the Internet, and everyday low pricing5 (EDLP) (to eliminate forward buying of bulk orders), can mitigate the bullwhip effect.6 In fact, the number of firms ordering, and receiving orders, via EDI and the Internet is exploding. The information available to supply chain partners, and the speed with which it is available, has the potential to radically reduce inventories and increase customer service. Other initiatives can also mitigate the bullwhip effect.

TYPES OF IT USE IN SCM

The first construct, types of IT use in SCM, refers to the ways in which companies employ IT for the purposes of SCM. Based on prior research discussed above, three different types of IT use in SCM – transaction processing, supply chain planning and collaboration, and order tracking and delivery coordination – were identified and chosen to represent the first construct.

The first type of IT use, transaction processing stands for the use of IT for increasing the efficiency of repetitive information exchanges between supply chain partners. In this type of IT use the exchanged information is typically related to such tasks as order processing, billing, delivery verification, generating and sending dispatch advices, and producing order quotes. The second type of IT use, *supply chain planning and collaboration*, represents the use of IT for sharing planning-related information such as demand forecasts and other demand information, inventory information, and production capacity information, with the intention of increasing the effectiveness of the supply chain. Finally, the third type of IT use in SCM, *order tracking and delivery coordination*, refers to the monitoring of individual orders or shipments, which may consist of components or final products, with the aim of coordinating their delivery or conveying timely information of their location.

Transaction Processing

Most of the case companies, 10 out of 16 (A, C, D, G, H, I, J, K, L, N), used IT to process transactions with their suppliers. Eight of the case companies (B, C, E, F, I, K, M, P), in turn, used IT to transaction processing with their customers. Consequently, only three of the companies (C, I, K) used IT for transaction processing towards both up- and downstream of the supply chain. EDI, XML, or Extranet solutions were typically used for the processing of orders and invoices in the companies. In some cases, IT was also used to process delivery verifications and dispatch advices.

Some conclusions can be made regarding the business environment of the companies that utilize IT for transaction processing with their customers. Based on our sample, these companies are located in the upstream part of the supply chain (i.e. they are either equipment or component manufacturers). Further, compared to the non-users, these companies have fewer customers and more concentrated customer base, which is well in line with the identified drivers of transaction volume and business continuity.

Supply Chain Planning and Collaboration

The use of IT for supply chain planning and collaboration was more limited in our sample than the use of IT for transaction processing. This result supports the earlier findings on the sharing of planning information (Kemppainen and Vepsäläinen, 2003; Kauremaa et al., 2004). Less than half of the companies (A, C, D, I, J, K) used IT for supply chain planning and collaboration with their suppliers, and three of these companies (A, C, I) applied IT for this purpose also with their customers. Furthermore, unlike assumed, unpredictable and logistically demanding environment did not stand out as a driver for this type of IT use among the case companies. Instead, an important commonality among most of the companies using IT for supply chain planning and collaboration was that they used the information shared through the IT system for running a specific cross-organizational process.

Order Tracking and Delivery Coordination

As to business environment characteristics, the use of IT for order tracking and delivery coordination seemed to be associated with a customized nature of the offered products. Aside this, no further commonalities between the companies were found regarding the characteristics of their business environments.

To summarize, based on our sample of companies, project-orientation of business and in transit consolidation seem to drive the use of IT for order tracking and delivery coordination.

Furthermore, this role of IT is especially emphasized when other deliveries or human activities (such as installation tasks) are controlled based on the progress of specific tracked deliveries.

Some of the key success factors for global supply chain management strategy include:

- Need for an advanced planning system APS or, at least, a set of transactional-based solutions such as enterprise resource planning (ERP), logistics execution system (LES), etc.
- Need for smooth installation and coordination of the IT system(s) across the supply chain.

— Need for training (and continuous upgrade with regards to technology changes) for the personnel along the value chain.
— Ensure that product design is conducive to a postponement process. Otherwise, change the design process.
— Communicate the vision to ensure it is shared with all stakeholders.
— Obtain leadership commitment to the postponement process. Otherwise, there will be no spokesperson to help share the risk of the endeavor.
— Gain employee involvement in the design, of the postponement process. Otherwise, there is no ownership and thus doom for failure will probably result.
— Incorporate the appropriate organizational changes with the new postponement process. Otherwise there is no integration within the organization.
— Change the performance measures looking at order-to delivery cycle time as the driving metric, but balance that with the appropriate overall cost and quality metrics to ensure a balanced scorecard.

CONCLUSIONS

In this article the use of IT for SCM purposes was studied by dividing the use of IT into three categories, 1) transaction processing, 2) supply chain planning and collaboration, and 3) order tracking and delivery coordination. Further, the drivers behind these different IT use types were examined. Based on the empirical data collected for this study, the three IT use categories proposed represent well the roles that IT plays in SCM. In addition to clarifying this widely discussed topic, the categorization provides a basis for further research on the use of IT in SCM.

The central aim of supply chain management, to have the right products in the right quantities (at the right place) at the right moment at minimal cost, is translated into the interrelated issues of customer satisfaction, inventory management, and flexibility. Customer satisfaction is to a high degree dependent on the flexibility of the supply chain, i.e. its ability to respond to changes in demand. Flexibility is often imperfect because of long lead times, uncertainties, and unforeseen event. To counterbalance this lack of flexibility companies will keep inventories at various levels of the supply chain. Balancing the costs of imperfect customer satisfaction and holding inventory is a classic issue of logistics and supply chain management

The use of IT in supply chain planning and coordination, in turn, was found to be driven by the implementation of cross-organizational processes, most often the VMI system. Unlike assumed, unpredictable and logistically demanding environment did not stand out as a driver for this use of IT. Finally, project orientation of business and in-transit consolidation were found to drive the use of IT for order tracking and delivery coordination. Moreover, this use of IT was mostly driven by the need to coordinate other activities or deliveries based on the progress of specific tracked deliveries.

Increasing globalization of supply chains causes longer lead times, which worsen flexibility, and creates the need for more inventory. When lead times can no longer be shortened, an important tool for improving the supply chain performance is that of increased coordination.

To conclude, we want to acknowledge that the second category of IT use, supply chain planning and collaboration, was not defined in sufficient detail. Consequently, there is a need for further research on the different ways of using IT for supply chain planning and collaboration. Furthermore, a detailed analysis of the possible explanations for the lack of information sharing for supply chain planning is invited. Finally, in order to better understand the complex phenomenon of supply chain management, the research on the use of IT in SCM should be complemented by research on the other means of supply chain coordination.

The functional areas most affected by the adoption of EDI are Commercial and Logistics. Data-processing plays a major role, especially at the beginning of the process. With evolution, the EDI project eventually becomes corporate both at the manufacturers and retailers, especially when other ECR tools are employed, such as category management and continuous replenishment. This fact was mentioned by most of the respondents as a change needed for successful use of the technology, including appropriation of benefits. A trend can therefore be seen to create the function of EDI or ECR coordinators, who are not directly attached to any area but who work to develop a system between individuals in the areas impacted by the use of EDI. This internal system deals with the implementation and evolution of EDI and other ECR tools.

REFERENCES

Bagchi, P.K. and Skjoett-Larsen, T. (2002), "Integration of Information Technology and Organizations in a Supply Chain", *The International Journal of Logistics Management*, Vol.14, No. 1, pp. 89-108.

Supply Chain Management (2004), Best Practices and Its Potential for Consultants-Consultant Best Practices Feature Article, May.

Cooper, M.C., Douglas M. Lambert, and Janus D. Pagh (1997), "Supply Chain Management: More Than a New Name for Logistics," *International Journal of Logistics Management*, 8 (1), 1–14.

Disney, S., Naim, M.M. and Potter, A. (2004), "Assessing the Impact of E-business on Supply Chain Dynamics", *International Journal of Production Economics*, Vol. 89, No. 2, pp. 109- 118.

Evans, C.N., Naim, M.M. and Towill, D.R. (1993), "Dynamic Supply Chain Performance: Assessing the Impact of Information Systems", *Logistics Information Management*, Vol. 6, No. 4, pp. 15-26.

Frohlich, M.T., Westbrook, R. (2001), "Arcs of Integration: An International Study of Supply Chain Strategies", *Journal of Operations Management*, Vol. 19, No. 2, pp. 185–200.

Gavirneni, S., Kapuscinski, R. and Tayur, S. (1999), "Value of Information in Capacitated Supply Chains", *Management Science*, Vol. 45, No. 1, pp. 16-24.

Cooper, M.C. & Lambert, D.M. & Pagh, J.D. (1997), Supply Chain Management: More than a New Name for Logistics. *The International Journal of Logistics Management.* v.8, n.1, p.1-13.

Part–V

Innovations in Information Technology

24

ELECTRICAL LOAD FORECASTING USING ARTIFICIAL NEURAL NETWORKS AND GENETIC ALGORITHM TECHNIQUES

Pradeepta Kumar Sarangi, Nanhay Singh, R.K. Chauhan, Raghuraj Singh

INTRODUCTION

Artificial Intelligence techniques, such as expert systems and neural networks have shown promising results in many systems. Recent progress in the applications of Artificial Neural Networks (ANN) technology to power systems in the areas of forecasting, security assessment and fault diagnosis among others, have made it possible to use this technology to overcome the limitations of the other methods used for electrical load forecasting. This is due to the fact that instead of relying on explicit rules or mathematical functions between past load and temperature variations, neural networks draw a link between input and output data. Thus the neural networks that deviate from relying on statistical models and large historical databases hold a good promise for the purpose of load forecasting.

Over the years, the application of Artificial Neural Network (ANN) in power industries has been growing in acceptance. This is because ANN is capable of capturing process information in a black box manner. Given sufficient input-output data, ANN is able to approximate any continuous function to arbitrary accuracy. This has been proven in various fields such as pattern recognition, forecasting, system identification, prediction, signal processing, fault detection and others.

On the other hand, GA is a global search algorithm based on the principle of "survival of fittest". It simultaneously searches for solutions in several regions, thus increasing the probability of global convergence. Furthermore, since it is impossible to formulate a priori exact model of the system, a more practical approach is off-line set up a rough model, followed by on-line update of the model using GA. In this way, the merging of GA and

ANN will gain adaptability to dynamic environment and lead to significantly better intelligent systems than relying on ANN or GA alone. In other words, the ANN-GA model developed should be more robust to dynamic nonlinearity of the process involved.

BACKGROUND

The development of a good ANN model depends on several factors. These factors may be: Data being used, Network architecture or model structure, Model size & complexity and network training. Selection of a suitable topology for a specific problem is not well established. The most practical and widely used method for optimum topology selection is trial and error search method. However, here we present some propositions by various researchers regarding selection of number of hidden neurons.

Number of Hidden Neurons

Hidden neurons are required to compute difficult functions. The numbers of input and output neurons are determined by the application at hand. However, there are no standard rules or theories in determining the number of neurons in the hidden layers except some rules of thumb suggested by various ANN researchers. Some important of them are discussed as below:

Shih (1994) suggests that the network topology should have a pyramidal shape; that is to have the greatest number of neurons in the initial layers and have fewer neurons in the later layers. He suggests that the number of neurons in each layer should be a number from mid-way between the previous and succeeding layers to twice the number of the preceding layer. He specifies that a network with 12 neurons in its previous layer and 3 neurons in the succeeding layer should have 6 to 24 neurons in the intermediate layer.

Where as according to Azoff (1994), a rough guideline based on theoretical conditions of what is known as the "Vapnik-Chervonenkis dimension", recommends that the 20 number of training data should be at least ten times the number of weights. He also quoted a theorem that suggests a network with one hidden layer and 2N+1 hidden neurons are sufficient for N inputs.

Lawrence (1994) gives the following formula for determining the number of hidden neurons required in a network:

$$\textit{number of hidden neurons} = \textit{training facts} \times \textit{error tolerance.}$$

Baum and Haussler (1988) suggest that the number of neurons in the hidden layer should be calculated as $j = m\,e\,/(n + z)$, where 'j' is the number of neurons in the hidden layer, 'm' is the number of data points in the training set, 'e' is the error tolerance, 'n' is the number of inputs and 'z' the number of outputs.

Sarle (1996) suggests a method called *"early stopping* or *stopped training"* whereby a larger number of hidden neurons are used with a very slow learning rate and with small random initial weight values. The out-of-sample error rate is computed periodically during training. The training of the network is halted when the error rate in the out-of-sample data starts to increase.

Gowri and Reddy (2008) suggest that for a three layer ANN, the number of hidden neurons can be selected by using any one of the following thumb rules:

1. (i-1) hidden neurons, where 'i' is the number of input neurons
2. (i+1) hidden neurons, where 'i' is the number of input neurons.

3. For every 5 input neurons, 8 hidden neurons can be taken. This is developed seeing the performance of network within 5 inputs, 8 hidden neurons and 1 output.
4. Number of input neurons / number of output neurons
5. Half the sum of input and output neurons.
6. P/i neurons, where 'i' is the input neurons and 'P' represents number of training samples.

From all these discussions above, we can conclude that there is no fixed rule to decide number of hidden neurons, it is only problem specific. Hence we propose to analyze the impact of change in number of hidden neurons for short term load forecasting using artificial neural network technique.

RESEARCH OBJECTIVES

In this research work, an attempt has been made to develop different artificial neural network models with varying number of neurons in hidden layer. It is also proposed to develop a genetic algorithm based back propagation (GA-BPN) model.

The specific objectives of this research are:

(1) Proposition of different neural network models for predicting the future power demand.
   - Training of the models (using back propagation algorithm) so that each input produces a desired output.
   - Testing of the developed models to get the values of future power demands.

(2) Improvement of back propagation method by hybridizing GA and BPN for determination of optimum weight set with different population size.

(3) Comparison of results of BPN and GA-BPN.

RESEARCH METHODOLOGY

The methodologies adopted in this research are explained below:

- Construction of different ANN architectures having (i) three neurons in input layer, two to ten neurons in hidden layer and one neuron in output layer (3-2-1 to 3-10-1) .
- Training of the networks using back propagation algorithm with different learning rates, keeping the momentum factor as constant and under maximum permissible error.
- Finding the best learning rate for test patterns.
- Finding the forecasted values using the best value of learning rate.
- Hybridization of BPN with GA. i.e extraction of weights for BPN by implementing genetic algorithm.
- Training of the GA-BPN network with different values of population size.
- Finding the best value of population size for GA-BPN forecasting.
- Finding the forecasted values for the best value of population size.

The pictorial representation for ANN implementation methodologies is given in the Figure-1.

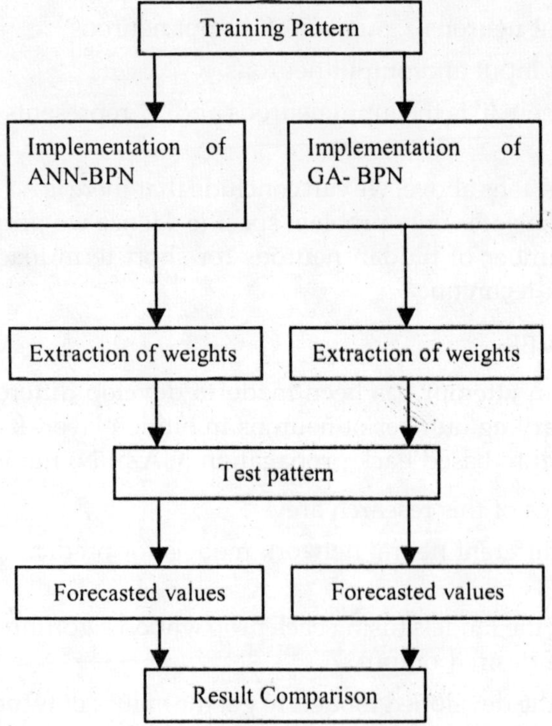

Figure 1: Methodology Diagram

SIMULATION DESIGN

Simulation design includes architecture define, parameter selection, pattern formation and processing of data.

Requirement of Minimum Number of Patterns

Gowri and Reddy (2008) suggest that for a three layered ANN architecture, we need minimum of P/2 number of patterns where, P is the number of input neurons. This study uses a total number of 15 input data divided into two sets, training set consisting of first 9 days data and the second one is the test set consisting of last 6 days data. The data used in this research is the daily load (un restricted demand) data for the state of Delhi. The data (un-normalized) have been collected from "State Load Despatch Centre (SLDC), Delhi" from their website "http://www.delhisldc.org/report/monthly-power-data/July-2008 (block year 2008-09) in the month of February, 2009.

Selection of Input Variables

Papalexopoulos et. al. (1993) state that, there is no general rule for selecting number of input variables. It largely depends on engineering judgment, experience and is carried out almost entirely on trial and error basis. The importance of the factors may vary for different customers. According to Wang. et al. (2004), for most customers historical data (such as weather data, weekend load, and previous load data) is most important for predicting demand in short term load forecasting (STLF). In practice, it is neither necessary nor useful to include all the historical data as input. Autocorrelation helps to identify the most important historical data. Wang describes the importance of recent daily loads in daily load prediction based on correlation analysis is described as below:

Table 1
Selection of Input Variables

Factors	X_1	X_2	X_3	X_4	X_5	X_6	X_7
Importance	1	2	3	5	7	6	4

The first line shows the recent daily load history. X_i represents the load consumed and the subscripts show the time index, i.e., 1 means yesterday (one day ago), 2 means the day before yesterday (two days ago), 7 means the same day of last week (7 days ago). In the second line the importance is described. 1 means the most important and 7 means the least important. These information and results help us to decide what factors should be included in input. According to table-1, when we perform daily load prediction, we should include X_1, X_2, X_3, X_7 as our inputs.

In this work, we have used three input variables i.e recent three previous days load data. Hence the data sets have been grouped into three to form the pattern as described in Table-2 below.

Table 2
Pattern Formation

Training Pattern No.	*Input-1*	*Input-2*	*Input-3*	*Target Value*
1	Day1	Day2	Day3	Day4
2	Day2	Day3	Day4	Day5
3	Day3	Day4	Day5	Day6
4	Day4	Day5	Day6	Day7
5	Day5	Day6	Day7	Day8
6	Day6	Day7	Day8	Day9

The Back Propagation Learning Algorithm

The procedural steps considering 3 layer networks are as follows:

Step 1 : Construction of the three layered architectures (3-2-1 to 3-10-1)

Step 2 : Initializing the parameters and setting all weights to small random values.

Step 3 : Presenting the input patterns and desired outputs (D) to the architectures.

Step 4 : Calculating the output (O) at the output layer

Step 5 : Calculating the Errors. (D-O)

Step 6 : Back propagating the error.

Step 7 : Updating the weights using Error Back propagation rule and repeating the entire process till desired result is obtained.

Implementation Strategy

For training purposes, in this research, we have used batch update method. i.e., each pattern is fed once and the error is calculated for that pattern. Let this error be å. Now, the next pattern is fed and error is calculated and this error is added to the error of previous pattern to form a global error. In this way all patterns are fed and the global error is calculated. Then the global error is compared with the maximum permissible error. If maximum permissible error is greater than the global error then the above procedure is repeated for all patterns till maximum permissible error is less than or equal to the global error. The program flow diagram for implementation strategy of back propagation algorithm is explained in Figure 2.

Selection of Network Parameters

Most of the works on feed forward networks use constant values of learning rate (η) and momentum factor (α). Gwori and Reddy (2008) have reported that learning rate (η)= 0.25

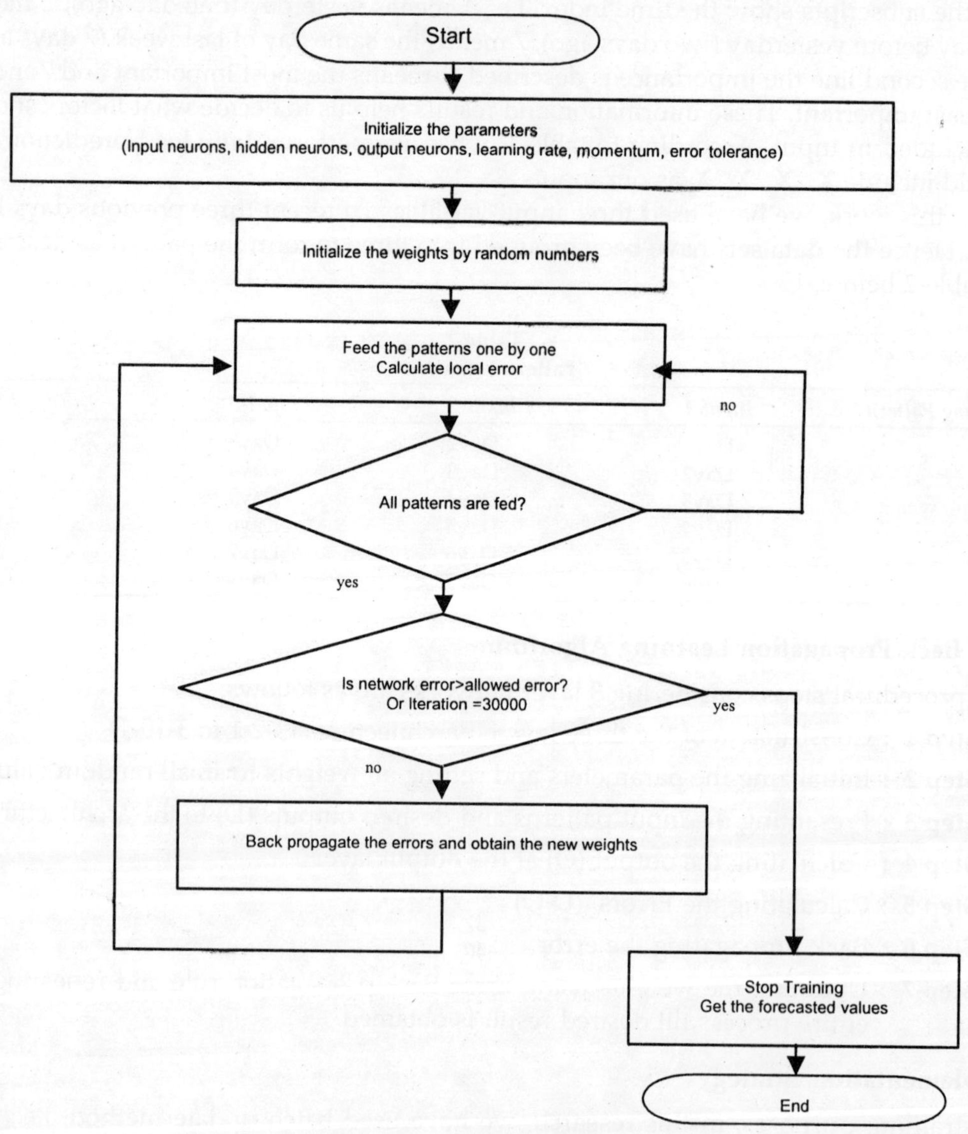

Figure 2: Implementation Strategy for ANN-BPN

and momentum factor (α) = 0.9 yield good results for most of the problems. However, the selection of best value of "η" and "α" is again problem dependant. In this research, we have used fixed value of α (=0.9) and the of best suitable value of "η" is selected from a set of values . The transfer function used is sigmoid logistic function, error tolerance is taken as 0.001 and maximum number of iterations allowed is 30000.

IMPLEMENTATION DETAILS AND RESULTS

The program for back propagation has been executed 45 times for each of the architectures (3-2-1 to 3-10-1) one after another. The momentum factor has been kept constant (0.9) for all executions. First, the 3-2-1 architecture is taken. The learning rate "η" has been taken from 0.2 to 1.0 with an increment of 0.1. For each value of "η" the program has been executed 5 times and the root mean square error (RMSE) value is calculated for each execution and then the average RMSE is calculated for that "η" value. The best result (the case having lowest RMSE value) has been considered for testing purposes. The same procedure has been adopted for all architectures. The forecasted values are given in Table-3 below.

Various parameters used in this research are:

Architecture	:	3-2-1
Number of hidden layers	:	01
Number of input neurons	:	03
Number output neurons		
Transfer function: sigmoid	:	01
Error calculation method	:	RMSE
Momentum	:	0.9
Error tolerance	:	0.001
Maximum iterations	:	30000

Table 3
Result of ANN-BPN-3-2-1 Architecture with Different η Value

Learning Rate (η)	*Run-1 RMSE*	*Run-2 RMSE*	*Run-3 RMSE*	*Run-4 RMSE*	*Run-5 RMSE*	*Average RMSE*
0.2	0.083152	0.083152	0.083772	0.094993	0.095381	0.088090
0.3	0.105557	0.064257	0.082709	0.091428	0.080139	0.084818
0.4	0.086354	0.097523	0.095382	0.088128	0.082283	0.089934
0.5	0.087587	0.086616	0.054740	0.083519	0.089394	0.085807
0.6	0.091182	0.083656	0.093625	0.055129	0.085205	0.081759
0.7	0.087298	0.082263	0.099737	0.106579	0.097383	0.090084
0.8	0.087792	0.085533	0.090640	0.107744	0.081677	0.090677
0.9	0.095300	0.093074	0.095156	0.093162	0.093197	0.093978
1.0	0.083956	0.085056	0.083133	0.082564	0.098655	0.086673

Table-3 is used to find the best value of learning rate 'η' for our research work under fixed value of momentum for the architecture ANN-BPN-3-2-1.

The Root Mean Square Error (RMSE) has been calculated as:

RMSE=Square root of [(Σ (Target Value – Obtained Value)²)/6] (1)

Table-3 contains the RMSE and average RMSE values of BPN 3-2-1 architecture with various learning rates for a fixed momentum value of 0.9. This table is used to find a suitable value of learning rate for experiment of BPN 3-2-1 architecture.

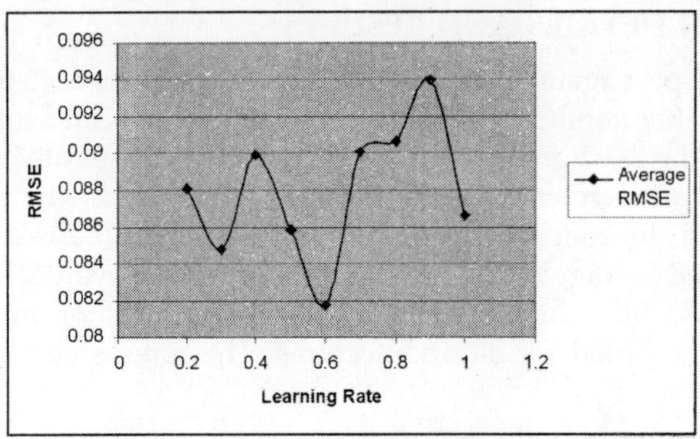

Figure 3: Learning Rate Versus Error Rate (BPN-3-2-1)

The graph in Figure-3 is drawn by taking the learning rate in X-axis and the average RMSE obtained for that learning rate after five time executions. It can be observed from the graph that, the error term has not followed a specific pattern which indicates that the error term in case of BPN training is not biased with the learning rate. A lower value of learning rate may give high error or vice-versa. How ever, our architecture BPN-3-2-1 gives lowest error for the combination of momentum=0.9 and learning rate=0.6 for the daily demand data of SLDC.

Calculation of Training Error

Once a suitable value of learning rate is determined, the network was tested for the training pattern with that learning rate. Here training error is calculated by taking η=0.6 and α=0.9.

Table 4
Training Error, BPN 3-2-1

Pattern No	*Actual Value*	*Trained Value*	*Squared Error*
1	0.7976	0.7665	0.000967
2	0.6924	0.7236	0.000973
3	0.6308	0.6099	0.000437
4	0.5920	0.5755	0.000272
5	0.6060	0.6182	0.000149
6	0.6560	0.6715	0.00024

Table-4 contains the desired values and calculated values for the training patterns. After the network is trained, the training patterns have been feed as testing pattern and the forecasted values and squared error have been calculated.

It can be observed from the Table 4 and graph (Figure-4) that the training error is less than 0.001 which indicates that our BPN-3-2-1 architecture has been trained very accurately with the given data sets and parameters.

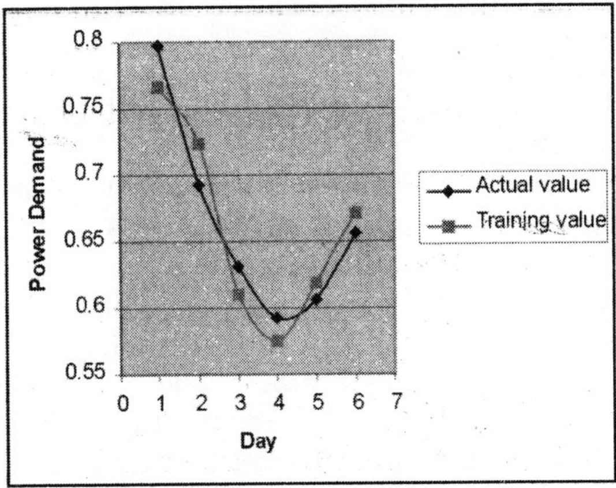

Figure 4: Daily Power Demands, Actual vs Trained Values (BPN 3-2-1)

Forecasted Values (ANN-BPN)

Once the networks are trained and validated, the forecasted values have been calculated. Similar methodologies have been applied for other architectures also. The forecasted values are given in table-5 below.

Table 5
Results Comparison, All ANN-BPN Models

Techniques	*Actual / Target Value*	*Forecasted Value*	*Squared Error*	*Error (RMSE)*
Architecture: 3-2-1	0.5876	0.5587	0.000835	0.081935
α=0.9, η=0.6	0.6672	0.7238	0.003204	
	0.6892	0.8161	0.016104	
Architecture: 3-3-1	0.5876	0.5561	0.000992	0.097711
α=0.9, η=0.8	0.6672	0.7344	0.004516	
	0.6892	0.8413	0.023134	
Architecture: 3-4-1	0.5876	0.5565	0.000967	0.078534
α=0.9, η=0.6	0.6672	0.7194	0.002725	
	0.6892	0.8109	0.014811	
Architecture: 3-5-1	0.5876	0.5358	0.002683	0.057986
α=0.9, η=0.3	0.6672	0.7062	0.001521	
	0.6892	0.7659	0.005883	
Architecture: 3-6-1	0.5876	0.5493	0.001467	0.042536
α=0.9, η=0.4	0.6672	0.6899	0.000515	
	0.6892	0.7479	0.003446	
Architecture: 3-7-1	0.5876	0.5406	0.002209	0.050211
α=0.9, η=0.8	0.6672	0.6932	0.000676	
	0.6892	0.7576	0.004679	
Architecture: 3-8-1	0.5876	0.5643	0.000543	0.057799
α=0.9, η=0.7	0.6672	0.7069	0.001576	
	0.6892	0.7781	0.007903	
Architecture: 3-9-1	0.5876	0.5362	0.002642	0.049602
α=0.9, η=0.4	0.6672	0.6945	0.000745	
	0.6892	0.7524	0.003994	
Architecture: 3-10-1	0.5876	0.5446	0.001849	0.050123
α=0.9, η=0.4	0.6672	0.6936	0.000697	
	0.6892	0.7598	0.004984	

GA BASED WEIGHT DETERMINATION

Genetic algorithm which uses a direct analogy of natural behavior, work with a population of individual strings, each representing a possible solution to the problem considered. Each individual string is assigned a fitness value which is an assessment of how good a solution is, to a problem. The high-fit individuals participate in "reproduction" by cross-breeding with other individuals in the population. This yields new individuals strings as offspring which share some features with each parent. The least-fit individuals are kept out from reproduction and so "die out". A whole new population of possible solutions to the problem is generated by selecting the best (high-fit) individuals from the current generation. This new generation contains characteristics which are better than their ancestors. Processing in this way, after many generations, owing to mixing and exchange of good characteristics, the entire population inherits the best characteristics and therefore turns out to be fit solution to the problem.

The success of any neural network (NN) architecture depends on the search for the optimized weights for given training data set. GA has been shown in practice that it is very effective at function optimization and can perform efficient searching for the approximate global minima. Thus, GA can be effectively utilized for NN weight selection. The mathematical expression for extraction of weights using GA for BPN is as below (Rajasekaran et al., 2007)

$$w_k = +\frac{x_{kd+2}\,10^{d-2} + x_{kd+3}10^{d-3} + \ldots.. + x_{(k+1)d}}{10^{d-2}} \quad if \quad 5 \le x_{kd+1} \le 9 \tag{2}$$

$$w_k = -\frac{x_{kd+2}\,10^{d-2} + x_{kd+3}10^{d-3} + \ldots.. + x_{(k+1)d}}{10^{d-2}} \quad if \quad 0 \le x_{kd+1} \le 5 \tag{3}$$

where w_k is the actual weight extracted from the chromosome, x_1, x_2...represents chromosomes and x_{kd+1}, x_{kd+2}... $x_{(k+1)d}$ represents the kth gene(ke"0) in the chromosome.

Pseudo Code for Implementation of GA-BPN

Rajasekaran et al. (2007) describe an algorithm for implementation of GA-BPN as described below.

Algorithm FITGEN ( )

{

Let (I_i, T_i), i = 1,2,. . . ,N where $I_i = (I_{1i}, I_{2i}, \ldots, I_{li})$

and $T_i = (T_{1I}, T_{2I}, \ldots, T_{ni})$ represent the input–output pairs of the problem to be solved by BPN with a configuration l - m - n. (the architecture and l>0, me"0, n>0)

For each chromosome C_i, i = 1,2,. . ,p belonging to the current population P_i whose size is 'p'

{

Extract weights W_i from C_i using equation (2) and (3) above.

Keeping W_i as a fixed weight setting, train the BPN for the N input instances;
Calculate error E_i for each of the input instances using the formula,

$$E_i = \sum_j (T_{ji} - O_{ji})^2 \tag{4}$$

Where O_{ji} is the output vector calculated by BPN;
Find the mean square E of the errors E_i, i = 1,2,. . . ,N;

$$E = \sqrt{\frac{\sum_i E_i}{N}} \tag{5}$$

Calculate the fitness value F_i for each of the individual string of the population as

$$F_i = \frac{1}{E} \tag{6}$$

}
Output F_i for each C_i, i = 1, 2. . . p
}

END FITGEN

GA based Weight Determination

Algorithm GA-BPN-WEIGHT ()
{
i ← 0;
Generate the initial population P_i of real-coded chromosomes C_{Ji} each representing a weight set for the BPN;

While the current population P_i has not converged

{

Generate fitness values F_I^J for for each $C_I^J \in P^i$ using the Algorithm FITGEN ();
Get the mating pool ready by terminating worst fit individuals and duplicating high fit individuals;
Using the cross over mechanism, reproduce offspring from the parent chromosomes;

i ← i + 1;

Call the current population P_I;

Calculate fitness values F_I^J for each C_I^J ª P^i

}

Extract weights from P_i to be used by the BPN

}

END GA-BPN-WEIGHT

The methodology for computation of fitness value for the (initial) population is given in Figure-5 below.

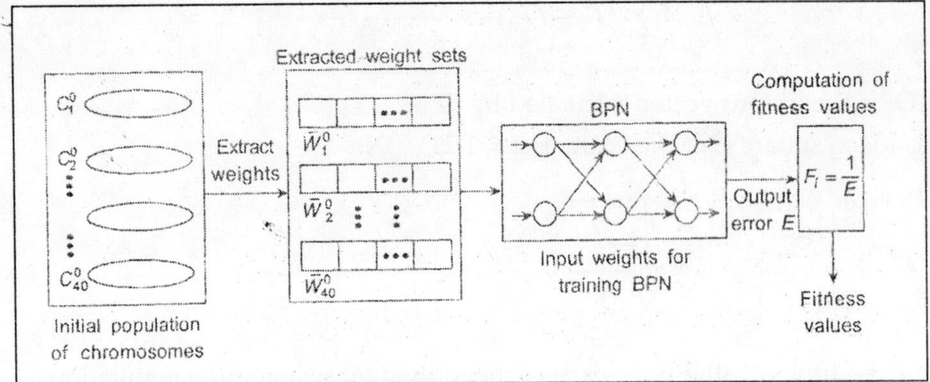

Figure 5: Methodology for Computation of Fitness Value (Rajasekaran et al., 2007)

GA-BPN TRAINING METHODOLOGY

A BPN determines its weights based on a gradient search technique and hence runs the risk of encountering the local minimum problem. GA on the other hand is found to be good at finding "acceptably good" solutions. The idea to hybridize the two networks has been successful to enhance the accuracy of forecasting. In the present work, the initial weights for the BPN have been obtained by using a GA. Genetic algorithm (GA) which uses a direct analogy of natural behavior, work with a population of individual strings, each representing a possible solution to the problem considered.

Each individual string is assigned a fitness value, which is an assessment of how good a solution is to a problem. The high-fit individuals participate in "reproduction" by crossbreeding with other individuals in the population. This yields new individual strings as off-spring, which share some features with each parent. The least-fit individuals are kept out from reproduction and so they "die out". A whole new population of possible solutions to the problem is generated by selecting the high-fit individuals from the current generation. This new generation contains characteristics, which are better than their ancestors. The parameters, which represent a potential solution to the problem, genes, are joined together to form a string of values referred as a chromosome. In this research, a real coding system has been adopted for coding the chromosomes. The network configuration of the BPN for the present work is 3-2-1. Therefore, the numbers of weights (genes) that are to be determined are 3 X 2 + 2 X 1 = 8. With each gene being a real number, and taking the gene length as 5, the string representing the chromosomes of weights will have a length of 8 X 5 = 40. This string represents the weight matrices of the input-hidden-output layers. An initial population of chromosomes is randomly generated. Weights from each chromosome have been extracted. For cross over, we have used a two-point cross over selected at random and the selection is made on the basis of fitness value (1/MSE) . The strategy for implementation of GA-BPN algorithm is explained in Figure-6.

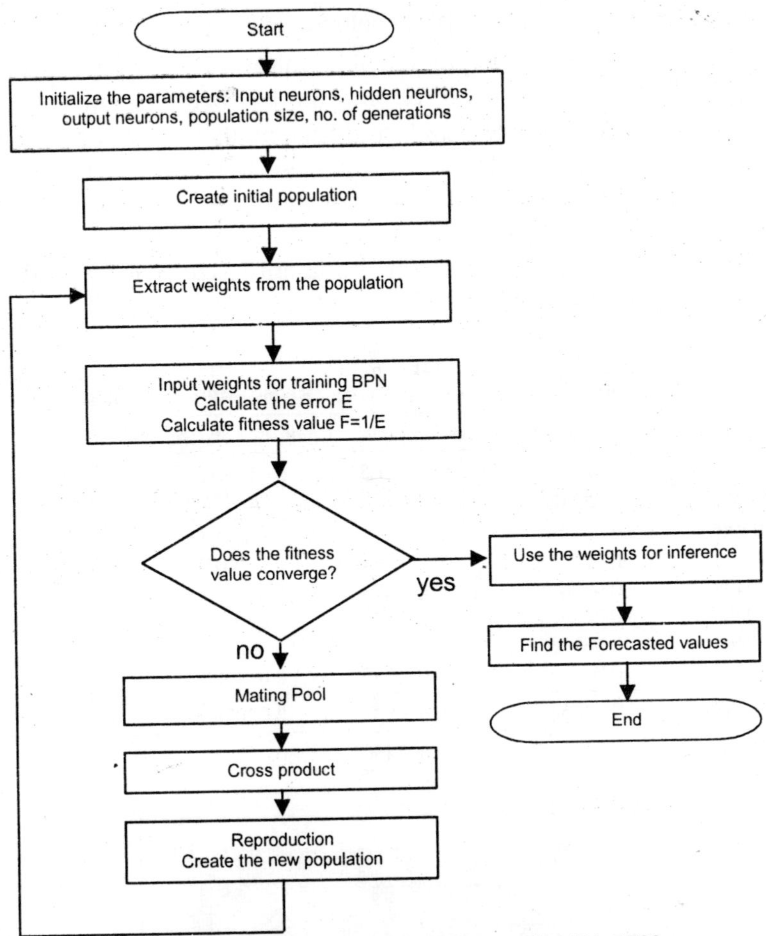

Figure 6: Implementation Strategy for GA-BPN

GA-BPN Training Results

The GA-BPN has been implemented by taking the architecture 3-2-1 , with different population size. For each value of population, the program has been executed 5 times and the RMSE value has been calculated in the same manner as in case of BPN. The best result (the case having lowest RMSE value) among all these cases (indicated as bold italic letters) has been considered for comparison with other methods.

Various parameters used in this research are:

Architecture	:	3-2-1
Number of hidden layers	:	01
Number of input neurons	:	03
Number output neurons	:	01
Selection	:	Based on fitness value
Fitness function	:	1/ (MSE)
Crossover	:	Two point Crossover
Stopping criteria	:	when fitness converged

The training results are shown in Table-6 below.

Table-6 contains the RMSE and average RMSE values of GA-BPN 3-2-1 architecture with various population sizes. The GA-BPN program has been executed five times and the RMSE values are given in Run-1 to Run-5 column. Finally the average RMSE has been calculated by taking the average of the values of these five RMSE values. This table is used to find a suitable value of population size that produces the lowest error for experiment of GA-BPN 3-2-1 architecture. It can be observed from the table that, our architecture GA-BPN-3-2-1 performs better with population size of 90 by producing lowest RMSE for the daily demand data of SLDC.

Table 6
Result of GA-BPN 3-2-1 Architecture with Different Population Size

GA-BPN- Results Under Various Parameters Change (Architecture=3-2-1)						
Population Size	*Run-1 RMSE*	*Run-2 RMSE*	*Run-3 RMSE*	*Run-4 RMSE*	*Run-5 RMSE*	*Average RMSE*
30	0.066981	0.066981	0.066981	0.066981	0.066981	0.066981
40	0.078319	0.078319	0.078319	0.078319	0.078319	0.078319
50	0.079478	0.079478	0.079478	0.079478	0.079478	0.079478
60	0.070381	0.070381	0.070381	0.070381	0.070381	0.070381
70	0.060463	0.060463	0.060463	0.060463	0.060463	0.060463
80	0.071385	0.071385	0.071385	0.071385	0.071385	0.071385
90	0.020585	0.020585	0.020585	0.020585	0.020585	0.020585
100	0.045430	0.045430	0.045430	0.045430	0.045430	0.045430

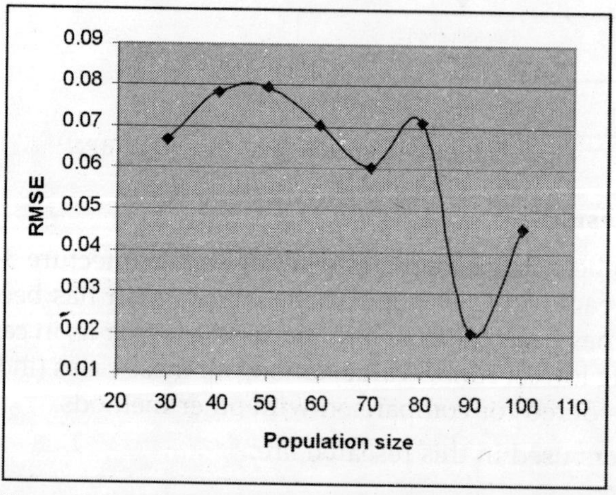

Figure 7: Population Size Versus Error Rate (GA-BPN-3-2-1)

The graph in Figure-7 is the graphical representation of Table-6

GA-BPN Training Error

Once a suitable value of population size is found, the GA-BPN architecture is trained with that population value. It was found that the best value of population size for the architecture 3-2-1 is 90. Hence the GA-BPN architecture is trained with population size of 90. The training error for 3-2-1 architecture is given Table-7 .

Table 7
Training Error, GA BPN 3-2-1

Pattern No	*Desired Value*	*Calculated Value*	*Squared Error*
1	0.7976	0.745094	0.00275688
2	0.6924	0.714433	0.000485453
3	0.6308	0.615623	0.000230341
4	0.5920	0.619830	0.000774509
5	0.6060	0.621423	0.000237869
6	0.6560	0.659507	1.2299E-05

Table-7 is derived on the basis of data obtained after the training of GA-BPN architecture 3-2-1. The objective of this table is to demonstrate that how closely the network is trained. From the table it can be seen that the squared error for training the GA-BPN is less than 0.01 which is quite appreciable. The figure-8 is the graphical representation of the Table-7

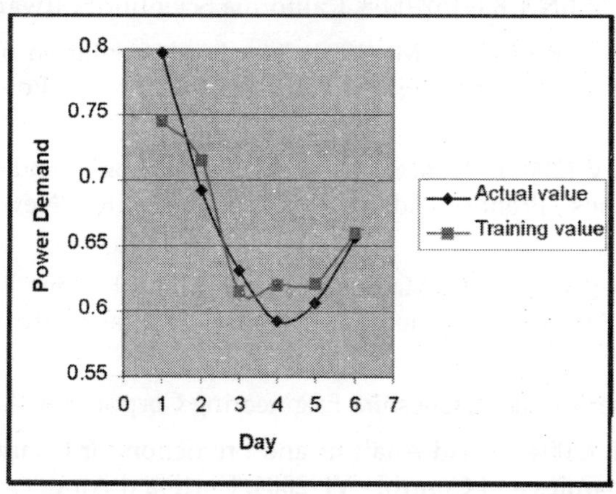

Figure 8: Daily Power demands, Actual Vs Trained Values (GA-BPN 3-2-1)

Forecasted Values (GA-BPN)

Once the training is over, the forecasted values for next days have been calculated. The values are given in Table-8 below.

Table 8
Forecasted Values, GA-BPN 3-2-1 Architecture

Techniques	*Actual / Target Value*	*Forecasted Value*	*Squared Error*	*Error (RMSE)*
Genetic Algorithm based Back Propagation Method	0.5876	0.585405	4.82E-06	
Architecture: 3-2-1,	0.6672	0.687654	0.000418	0.020585
Population size=90	0.6892	0.718321	0.000848	

CONCLUSION

In this research, we have implemented different ANN-BPN architectures for short term load forecasting. It is found that the results using back propagation varies with the parameter change such as learning rate. In this research, we found that our ANN architecture 3-6-1 performs better (with momentum 0.9 and learning rate of 0.4) over other architectures. However, hybridization of GA and ANN produces tremendous improvement in results.

REFERENCES

Azoff, E.M. (1994), 'Neural Network Time Series Forecasting of Financial Markets', John Wiley & Sons, pp. 50-51, England, ISBN: 0-471-94356-8.

Baum E.B. and Haussler D. (1988), 'Neural Computation 1', 151–160.

Gowri T.M. and Reddy V.V.C. (2008), 'Load Forecasting by a Novel Technique Using ANN', ARPN Journal of Engineering and Applied Sciences, Vol.3, No. 2.

Khotanzad A., Rohani R.A., and Maratukulam D.(1998), 'ANNSTLF– Artificial Neural Network Short-Term Load Forecaster–Generation Three', IEEE Transactions on Neural Networks, 13:1413–1422.

Lawrence J. (1994), 'Introduction to Neural Networks: Design, Theory, and Applications 6th edition', edited by Luedeking, S., ISBN 1-883157-00-5, California Scientific Software, California, USA.

Papalexopoulos A.D., Hao S., and Peng T.M. (1994), 'An Implementation of a Neural Network Based Load Forecasting Model for the EMS', IEEE Transactions on Power Systems, 9:1956–1962.

Rajasekaran S. and Pai G.A.V (2007), 'Neural Networks, Fuzzy Logic, and Genetic Algorithms: Synthesis and Applications', Prentice Hall of India Private Limited, New Delhi, ISBN 978-81-203-2186-1.

Sarle W.S. (1996), 'Neural Network FAQ, Maintainer: How Many Hidden Units Should I Use?', Neural Network FAQ Part 1-7,aifaq/neural-nets/part3,Available: ftp://ftp.sas.com/pub/neural/FAQ3.html.

Shih Y.(1994), 'Neuralyst User's Guide', Cheshire Engineering Corporation, USA, pp.74.

Wang X. and Tsoukalas L.H. (2004), 'Load Analysis and Prediction for Unanticipated Situations', Bulk Power System Dynamics and Control - VI, 2004, Cortina d'Ampezzo, Italy.

25

MANAGEMENT OF E-GARBAGE: A CASE STUDY OF SURI AND KARIDHYA

Goutam Chatterjee

INTRODUCTION

Electronic waste is a relatively new type of waste. Ironically, its history is as old as the history of production of electronic goods. Large quantities of electronic equipments are wasted every year. The event that probably marked the inauguration of the electronic age was the invention of the Radio. Gradually, with the invention of electronic watch, TV, Computer, Mobile, MP3, MP4 player, CD, DVD player and the Blue Ray player, the electronic age has taken a big leap forward. That is why we are emboldened to say that 2010 is the age of fourth wave, which has found manifestations in phenomena like e-commerce and m-commerce. In this e-age, the necessity for the use of paper has diminished but the uses of electronic transactions have increased and as a result, there has been a reduction in the rate of felling of trees. This is no doubt better for environment as more trees mean less pollution.

But a new type of pollution i.e. e-garbage has been doing incalculable harm to the environment as unused old electronic goods and their parts continue to form heaps in the houses of public.

Now the moot question is how it to be managed.

Statement of the Problem

E-garbage is one of the consequences of using electronic instruments. It is common knowledge that use of new equipments has concurrent side effects. E-commerce and m-commerce have given us certain benefits such as the reduction of the load of paperwork but these have brought in their trail the problem of e-garbage. The regularly occurring technological progress, giving birth to new electronic equipments, is rendering old equipments obsolete and the latter are put aside as garbage, which ultimately produces e-pollution. The result is persistent headaches and worries mainly on the part of the developed countries. Our problem is how to manage the e-garbage in an eco-friendly manner.

Objectives of this Paper

The main objectives of this paper are as follows-

— To examine and explain the concept of e-garbage, and related terms.

— To review the causes of the accumulation of e-garbage.

— To venture some suggestions on the procedure of disbursement of e-garbage and to explain its implications of reducing pollution.

CONCEPTS AND DEFINITIONS

- *E-garbage:* Electronic waste is a new type of waste. Electronic waste, e-waste, e-scrap, describes loosely discarded, surplus, obsolete, broken, electronic devices.
- *M-Commerce:* It involves direct cooperation of mobile in the transaction of business.
- *E-Commerce:* When the entire business is regulated by electronic media, e.g. the Internet and the Computer, it is called electronic commerce, or e-commerce.
- *E-pollutions:* Electronic waste, e-waste, e-scrap, or Waste Electrical and Electronic Equipment(WEEE) describes loosely discarded, surplus, obsolete, broken, electrical or electronic devices. The processing of electronic waste causes serious health and pollution problems because electronic equipment contains some very serious contaminants such aslead, cadmium, beryllium and brominated flame retardants

CAUSES OF E-GARBAGE

Rapid technological progress in the field of electronics is one of the main causes of increase of e-garbage. Other causes are as follows: -

(i) All multinational companies are spending huge amounts of money on research and development works oriented towards inventions of new electronic goods for expanding and capturing markets, which will supply the oxygen for the survival i.e. continuous accumulation and innovation, of these companies. This ever-expanding process is responsible for the increase in the incidence of obsolescence.

(ii) The demonstration effect that drives one to outdo one's neighbors or colleagues in the purchase of fashionable items of goods and services. It leads to more goods being laid aside as unusable.

(iii) The common human aspiration to covet new goods for easing the life-style.

(iv) The growth of consumerism and dazzling effects of advertisements enhance our appetite for earthly pleasures and luxuries. We know that there is no end of luxury or sensuality in men's life. Human beings, particularly those with better entitlements and capabilities, are running after new luxuries, producing heaps of e-garbage in every household.

PROBLEMS RELATED TO E-GARBAGE

Electronic goods are made from many components in factories. After they are shaped into finished goods, we use them for communication or entertainment. After the use we can either lay them aside, or out them to further use. E-waste can be very valuable because it's the source of materials for new products. About 97% of computer's contents can be recycled, so instead of wasting them in order to fill up our dumping grounds, we could recycle the contents and use them in new computers. This would reduce the amount of e-waste.

(a) E-garbage is not biodegradable so it does not get mixed in the soil. There fore it spreads pollution.

(b) Continuous accumulation of e-garbage reduces the space in the houses, making it increasingly problematic to provide space for the waste itself. .

(c) Much plastic and metallic elements are contained in the e-garbage, which can be put to further uses.

(d) With the development of modern technology new electronic goods are making a better market. The owners of new electronic goods are indirectly being compelled to block their finance in the e–garbage of old electronic goods.

(e) Dumping of such garbage always create a problem to every country by way of spread of toxicities and of consumption of space.

E-GARBAGE IN INDIA

In concurrence with other countries India is thinking about e-garbage. Different laws and rules are being framed, but effective measures on the society are yet to be taken. The applications of these laws have been started for some industries only.

EXPERIENCE FROM SURVEY

Hypothesis

An *a priorie* assumption or statement about the population is a statistical Hypothesis. There are two types of Hypotheses i) Null Hypothesis, denoted by the symbol H_0 (In tests of significance we start with a certain hypothesis about the population characteristics this is called Null hypothesis) ii) Alternative Hypothesis denoted by the symbol H_1 (Any hypothesis which differs from the null hypothesis is called alternative hypothesis)

The following Null hypotheses (Ho) have been formulated for the study

— Ho:- The public is not so aware about e-garbage; rather they are interested with new electronic goods.

— Ho:- Hawkers peddling in e-garbage are environment friendly in the sense that they help in the disposal of this garbage.

May be there is an alternative hypothesis i.e.H_1

— H_1:- The public is aware about e-garbage.

— H1:- Hawkers are valueless in field of e-garbage solutions.

Data and Methodology

The study is based on both types of data i.e. primary and secondary. Primary data were collected with the help of interviews (with questionnaire) with public while for collection of secondary data, the sources tapped were books, journals, Internet and reports having a bearing on the research topic. Primary data were collected using the method of simple random sampling. I have conducted a 'man to man' survey of a large number of hawkers in a district town, namely Suri, of the district of Birbhum, West Bengal. The second part of the survey was conducted with many village hawkers in Karidhya village, adjacent to Suri town. I made a questionnaire with which I conducted an interview on every Sunday and Monday (5th Apr. 2009 to 5th Dec. 2009) from 12 Noon to 5 P.M.

The questionnaire ran as follows:

(a) What is your name, age, address, Phone No?

(b) In which age did you join this profession?

(c) What is your educational level?

(d) Do you have any government support?

(e) What type of problem did you face during door-to-door campaign?

(f) Have you any problem with the police or with any other corner of the society?

(g) How you worked with this e-garbage?

(i) What is you monthly income?

(j) Why you not go to other profession?

FINDINGS OF THE STUDY

The following are the salient findings of the study from survey.

I have conducted the survey in a mofussil town, Suri, and an adjacent village, Karidhya, about e-garbage and have found a new way out to utilize e-garbage. In Karidhya village there are 3 *katai* shops (the local nomenclature for the scrap go-down) whereas the town of Suri has 4 *katai* shops. Main *Katai* shops owners are called *mahajans*. In Suri town and Karidhya village there are some hawkers whose profession is to collect scraps like old plastic, iron, copper, aluminum etc from different houses at low prices. I have taken interviews of 52 hawkers. Most of the hawkers (90%) are members of a particular religious community, i.e. the Muslim community and 10% from Hindu Dalits. They sell these scraps goods to the local scrap go-downs or local *katai* shops at somewhat higher rates. These owners of petty *katai* shops then supply these goods to the main *Katai* shops situated in Suri town. Those main Katai shops owners sell these scrap goods to different small-scale industries at Durgapur or Howrah at much higher rates. These small-scale industries now produce different new goods by recycling process.

A flow chart of the above recycling process is shown below for ready reference:-

Problems in Recycling- E-Waste has a large variety of types of garbage; some are computers and appliances. E-Waste is an important part of our world economy. Just think of the disastrous consequences if we did not follow the rules of the disposal of e-waste. Although e-Waste is very important it is also important to take care of its disposal, but some problems are there regarding the management of e-garbage. These are as follows:

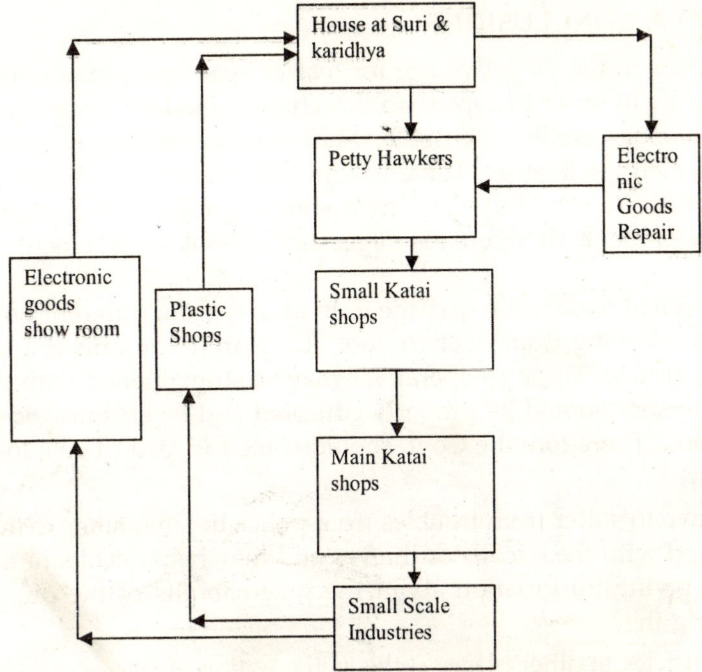

Flow Chart of the Recycling Process of E-garbage

(i) This business is run with the financial support from the main *katai* shop owners (*mahajan*) because the capital of hawkers is very small. Some times they have no capital other than their own human capital, i.e. capacity of exert of their muscles..

(ii) The hawkers are caught in a money-lending nexus. They borrow from the mahajans and purchases those scrap goods and they have to sell those goods to those very Mahajans at low prices according to the previous agreement.

(iii) Hawkers have to face troubles both from the public and the police who are prone consider them as informers of dacoits and thinks that they manage stolen articles..

(iv) They are not capable of standing up to those troubles, as they have no proper education.

(v) Child labourers are found in large numbers in this trade. Majority of the hawkers come to this profession in their childhood because of poverty and lack of opportunities of alternative professions.

(vii) The Survey Report indicates that 90% of the Hawkers are from other districts. This migration highlights some sort of uneven development among various districts as far as economic progress is concerned. This phenomenon can possibly be explained with the help of the notion of 'backwash effect', a la Gunner Myrdal.

(viii) As the incomes of the hawkers are comparatively low, they cannot send enough money to their families after maintaining themselves. Therefore the idea of their links with dacoits for extra income cannot be ruled out. But such links, if any, are produced by social compulsions, not by natural criminal inclinations.

SUGGESTIONS & CONCLUSIONS

We cannot go back to the primitive age for fear of –garbage or pollution. The world is always changeable. In order to cope with this change, modern inventions in the field of science and technology are indispensable.. Man can convert the raw materials into their usable items by their intelligence. There lies the differences between human beings and animals.. According to the Holy Gita, man should go forward and proceed towards sustainable development. Therefore my suggestions about management of e-garbage are as follows:-

- Hawkers had to collect e-garbage individually from different houses and repair shops by moving from door to door. They are to be united and co-operatives may be formed. These co-operatives may be strengthened with proper finances. Other persons should be properly educated and be encouraged to come to this profession. There fore the Govt. should come forward to give loans to these co-operatives.
- They have to suffer from troubles from police because some dishonest Hawkers are linked with the dacoits or thieves and they help dacoits in different respect i.e., by giving information about the whereabouts of the public and also by removing the
- Stolen articles to other places —this is the notion of police and local public.
- The mentalities of the hawkers are to be changed by giving some education. Their names are to be registered at the local police station. There fore the police will have no pretext to harass them.
- Loan should be given by the Govt not only to the hawkers but also to the small katai shops owners and even to the main katai shops owners i.e. to the mahajans.
- Hawkers may be educated through an adult education programme; it is necessary to prevent exploitation. Our findings have brought home another point. There is a law banning child labor. But hunger and destitution constantly generate a never-ending supply of child labor, which constitutes something like a reserve army of labor for the *katai* shops.
- If this problem has to be attacked, raising the level of education of lower strata of Muslims and Hindu dalits is an absolute necessity.

  Govt should give different kinds of relief and exemptions in order to encourage the small-scale industries that make other products by recycling the e-garbage.
- The public should be made aware by proper advertisement that e-garbage is harmful to environment, so it should be handed over to the hawkers for recycling instead of dumping. In a word, the awareness level of the public in this regard should be raised.
- It should be impressed upon the public through proper advertisements that hawkers are not dacoits or thieves or their informers; rather, they may be called e-garbage sweepers. They are also friends of the society like doctors, teachers etc.

REFERENCES

Bajaj, K, K and Nag, D. (2005), "E-Commerce" Tata McGraw-Hill Pub. New Delhi

Bhadra, B., Satpati, A and Mitra C. (2003), "Karbari Ainer Ruparekha" (Business Law Outline). Chaya prakasani. Kolkata.

Chakraborty, S. (2005), "Information Technology & Its Business Applications" Books and Allied (p) Ltd. Kolkata.

Dutta, D.L. (2004), "Business Regulatory Framework" T.D. Publications. Kolkata.

Dhar P. & Dutta S.P. (2003), "Fundamentals of Information Technology &Its application in Business" ABS Publishing House, Kolkata.

Morris Mano M. (2008), "Digital Logic and Computer Design", Dorling kindersly(India) pvt Ltd, Licenses of pearson education in South Asia, Delhi.

Rajanraman, D. and Rajanraman, V. (1996), 'Computer Primer' Prentice-Hall Pvt Ltd, New Delhi.

Sinha, P. and Sinha, P. (2005) "Computer fundamentals" BPB publications, New Delhi,

Websites

E GARBAGE A WEBSITE ABOUT EVERYTHING GARBAGE, 2009: Viewed on 21May, 2009 (http://www.lincoln.bizland.com/trash/id23.htm)

What is E - Garbage?, 2009: In: Miscellaneous [Edit categories](2009) Viewed on 21November, 2009(http://wiki.answers.com/Q/What_is_E_-_Garbage)

Rediff business, 2009: Water, air and noise pollution: The other threats, December 10, 2009 10:32 IST, Viewed on 12 December, 2009